The Memory
of the Modern

THE MEMORY
OF THE MODERN

Matt K Matsuda

New York   Oxford
OXFORD UNIVERSITY PRESS
1996

Oxford University Press

Oxford   New York
Athens   Auckland   Bangkok   Bombay
Calcutta   Cape Town   Dar es Salaam   Delhi
Florence   Hong Kong   Istanbul   Karachi
Kuala Lampur   Madras   Madrid   Melbourne
Mexico City   Nairobi   Paris   Singapore
Taipei   Tokyo   Toronto

and associated companies in
Berlin   Ibadan

Library of Congress Cataloging-in-Publication Data
Matsuda, Matt K
The memory of the modern / Matt K Matsuda.
p.   cm.
Includes bibliographical references and index.
ISBN 0-19-509364-X (cloth).—ISBN 0-19-509365-8 (pbk.)
1. France—Civilization—1830–1900.   2. Memory—History.
3. Technology—Social aspects—France—History—19th century.
4. France—History—Third Republic, 1870–1940—Philosophy.
I. Title.
DC33.6.M34   1996
944.081'2—dc20   95-30287

Portions of this book have previously appeared in the scholarly
journals *Historical Reflections/Réflexions Historiques* and
History and Memory. I am grateful to the editors of these
publications for permission to republish this material here.

1 3 5 7 9 8 6 4 2

Printed in the United States of America
on acid-free paper

Acknowledgments

Unless you have torn away this page, it is followed by a book—one which would have been impossible without the support and collaboration of numerous friends, colleagues, teachers, and institutions. I of course reserve the right to offer it first to my family. Still, I will dedicate it as a work to my teacher David Sabean, who was there before the beginning, and whose critical intellect, superb imagination, and endless generosity have seen it through. His support and enthusiasm were the stuff of legend; he was also the first to call it *haiku*.

I am indebted and immensely grateful to Edward Berenson, Debora Silverman, and M. Norton Wise, whose advice and teachings are—to me—evident on every page; I hope they will be pleased by what they see. My thanks also to others who have shaped my thinking: Sande Cohen, Carlo Ginzburg, Saul Friedlander, Peter Reill, Eugen Weber, Robert Wohl. My great appreciation goes out to the UCLA Department of History and the Chancellor's office for their aid and support over many years.

In Paris, my thanks to Samuel Weber, Jacques Derrida, and the gracious Pierre Nora, who allowed me to share and test my ideas early in the writing, and whose own "memory" work has so greatly marked my own. At Rutgers University, I owe grand debts to Rudolph Bell, Sy Becker, Paul Clemens, and Ginny Yans, John Chambers, Ziva Galili, Jennifer Jones, Omer Bartov, Sam Baily, Belinda Davis, and Don Kelley. Special appreciations to John Gillis for so many "memorable" exchanges, and Bonnie Smith for her splendid, critical readings of the manuscript.

For their time and insight, thanks also to Patrick Hutton and Michael S. Roth, and, naturally, Nancy Lane, Thomas Le Bien, and Oxford University Press.

As befits a work on the treacherous terrain of memory, I will have certainly forgotten some of those who, perhaps, aided me the most. I hope you will accept the book as my monument to your help and friendship, knowing that it could not have been done without you.

Contents

Introduction: Histories: The Philosophy of Today   3

1 Monuments: Idols of the Emperor   19
2 Numbers: The Temple of Time   41
3 Words: The Grammar of History   61
4 Bodies: The Third Convolution   79
5 Testimonies: Deserving of Faith   101
6 Identities: Doctor, Judge, Vagabond   121
7 Distances: In the Revolutionary Garden   143
8 Spectacles: Machineries of Magic   165
9 Desires: Last Tango at the *Académie*   185
Afterword: Memories: The History of the Present   205

Notes   209
Index   243

The Memory
of the Modern

Figure 1 Constructions of memory: transporting Victor Hugo to the Place
Victor Hugo, 1902. (*Source:* L'illustration/Sygma)

Introduction

Histories: The Philosophy
of Today

Memories of the turn of the century: revolutionaries and a bronze colossus at the Place Vendôme; a doctor with Europe's finest collection of brains; a murderer and rapist on the road; a magician and master of illusion; savages on the floor of the stock exchange; a scholar in the world of the ancients; cynical politicians and a woman outraged; in a glittering ballroom, a couple dancing a tango; at the edge of town, a desperate wanderer with a question.

Why call these images "memories," a word so overcharged with meanings and allusions? What follows is after all in some ways a general history of France and Europe between the Franco-Prussian War in 1870 and the beginning of the Great War in 1914, arranged around conventional historical themes. The reader will find, if desired, the familiar markers of that tumultuous era, in chapters dedicated to politics, economics, society, and cultural movements, framed by the violence of two wars. In course I examine political revolt and revolutionary socialism, public monuments and the Paris of Haussmann, the cycles of the French economy and financial system. I also examine literature and teaching, debates on imperialism and colonialism, the rise of the popular press and the mass of public opinion. Equally featured are chapters on the professions, the practices and politics of doctors and lawyers, courts of law and clinics. Women, children, family, and property, the disappearance of the rural world and the relation of church and state are all "questions." No work on this period of French history would be complete without a few words on the Belle Epoque, and so finally I pay respects to the world of popular entertainments, the marvels of industrial technology, and the imperious trend-setting of Paris, the fashion capital.

I have called my subject "memory." What is the form of a memory-history? In his classic study, *L'Identité de la France*, Fernand Braudel followed Michelet in arguing for a "total" history in which "everything stands and falls together," while also maintaining that "it is certainly futile to try to reduce France to one discourse, one equation, one formula, one image or one myth." In his search for a sweeping yet disparately complex story, Braudel organized his inquiries around geography, anthropology, demography, political economy, politics, cultures, sociology, and international relations.[1] Could I take such categories as politics, economics, society, and culture themselves as my "memory objects"? In my own attempt to write a general history, I have retained as subjects what I consider "familiar" historical categories: politics and class struggle, nationalism, imperialism, education and pedagogy, economic development. The fact that these subjects will appear as rites of monument destruction, interpretations of bamboo engravings, discourses on mnemonics, or fevered idols of the marketplace is not the result of my choosing unusual themes or strange objects of study. The themes and subjects, I insist, are the recognizable stuff of "general" history: I have chosen them for their familiarity. Their strangeness results from writing that history in terms of memory.

I have selected two terms to frame my overall project: "memory" and "modern." Why the association of these two? The most general assumption underlying the chapters which follow is that memory has a history, and that this memory history of the late nineteenth century is quite unlike that of any other period.[2] In her classic study of Medieval and Renaissance mnemonic strategies, *The Art of Memory* (1966), Frances Yates explains how mnemonic systems developed in the Ancient, Medieval, and Renaissance periods are based on loci, the placement of allegorical images within constructed mental architectures. Despite the continuity in technique, Yates nonetheless argues that the Renaissance memory systems reveal a different order of intellectual universe when compared with their Medieval predecessors—in her comparison an expanded belief in the power of the imagination. The general point, concisely expressed in the preface to the work, is that memory ought to obey the order of Classical, Gothic, and Renaissance periods customarily used to define artistic and historical epochs.[3]

Formulated another way, "memory" is not merely a theme to search out in literary texts, nor a convenient trope to impose generically upon recollections, rituals, or remembrances: "Classical" memory can be studied as an historical entity, perfectly distinct from "Renaissance" memory. I will argue that this thesis holds equally true for the late nineteenth century, where my reevaluation of historical evidence suggests a memory which I shall call distinctively that of "modernity," and which I shall attempt to characterize below.

September 1870. The French Emperor Napoleon III mounts his horse and rides off onto the battlefield of Sedan, hoping to be shot. His armies have been encircled by the Prussians; the name of his uncle has not insured him a gift for military strategy. He rides for hours, suffering from painful gallstones; no one is willing to oblige his desperate drama of heroism. He is taken prisoner and surrenders.

I have chosen to open up my analysis with the Franco-Prussian War of 1870, for this conflict marks a period of European national reorganization with significant repercussions in France and on the Continent. The defeat of the French armies at Sedan marks the end of the Empire of Louis Napoleon Bonaparte and the accession of the Third Republic in France, yet of perhaps greater significance for Europe over the century to come would be the simultaneous rise of Germany as a state, politically unified and militarily dominant. In matters of international strategy, Otto von Bismarck's politics threatened an uneasy French state, not only diplomatically, but also in the perceived challenges which German economic development, heavy industry and arms manufacture, and possible colonial ambitions would produce to French commercial and strategic interests. The Teutonic power east of the Rhine marked a new era in which Germanic learning and culture matched the influence of German statecraft, establishing the renown of figures like Ernst Haeckel, Wilhelm Wundt, Leopold von Ranke, and Richard Wagner, and inspiring a neo-Kantian revival among Paris intellectuals. French social thinkers were haunted by the "degeneration" of their own culture.

A lost war for France, a newly powerful Germany, and a continuing hostility toward another Great Power, England, shaped the state system into which the Third Republic was born, a system of shifting alliances and fierce national rivalries. The forty-odd years leading up to August 1914 were, for France, a period fueled by a rhythm of urgency and acceleration not originating from technological developments of the time alone. What concerns me here is not so much geopolitics, but the ways in which the new mappings of space and power were also restructuring the *chronopolitics* of the later nineteenth century. Beginning with upheavals of the Paris Commune and ending on the eve of the Great War, I will show how the generation and a half which spans the period between 1870 and 1914 was an age which struggled mightily over the politics of time, and as such was obsessed with the meanings and uses of memory.

How should the material of history—as memory—be presented? This is a question posed by the historian Pierre Nora in the many volumes of his grand project, *Les Lieux de mémoire*: "Comment écrire l'histoire de

France?" How to write the history of France?[4] The question is both an historiographical and practical dilemma. What is the organization which transforms memory into historical writing? What are its paragraphs and chapters? Nora addressed these questions by engaging the talents of one hundred and thirty collaborators to produce seven volumes of diverse and often exhilarating scholarship about memory as a "vast typology of French symbolics," emblems, commemorations, practices and rituals, figures, books, monuments. As a series of "locations," it is a collaboration for which there is no particular author or analytical style, for which no total story could ever be fashioned out of its collected parts. The very "memory" design of the project calls attention to its own logic of inclusion, exclusion, and selective incompleteness.

A similar logic orders my own studies in which "memory" appears first as a broad and disparate series of actors and circumstances. Though I am seeking the paradigm, *épistéme*, or discursive framework of "late nineteenth-century memory," I do not wish to simply reread, for example, political history as political "memory." A truly historical project must be attentive to the ways in which "memory" is not a generic term of analysis, but itself an object appropriated and politicized. Or, equally, nationalized, medicalized, aestheticized, gendered, bought and sold.

My project is thus structured around particulars: distinct literatures, institutions, events, actors which shape and contest different "memories," according to interest and circumstance: many memories, many locations. Where do I search for evidence of such "memories"? My first chapter presents the destruction of a Napoleonic monument by revolutionaries in 1871 and the polemics of commemoration and anti-commemoration. Chapter Two is a journey through the corridors of the Paris stock exchange at the turn of the century, a reading of the unsettling social and political amnesias generated by an institution whose logic is the relentless buying and selling of the future. Chapter Three surveys the popular literature on mnemonics after 1870 and the histories of pedagogy and moral education hidden in the magical number-letter codes of memory. Chapter Four stands at the dissection table and the debates of neurologists over the brain's center of memory and language. Chapter Five is a meditation on legal testimony, medical views of women and children, and the dilemmas of reconstructing a reliable past through the category of "the witness." Chapter Six traces "the memory of the State" through the tracking of vagabonds by the passport and identity card, and frames the hunt for a serial killer by the agents of forensic medicine. Chapter Seven embarks for the Pacific island of New Caledonia and a penal system founded upon redeeming prisoners by abolishing personal memory—a prescription violently resisted not by the prisoners, but by Melanesian islanders threatened by the extinction of their own memory traditions. Chapter Eight studies the early cinema and the first motion-picture cameras, the meaning of "instant history," and the illusions of the "memory" of machines. Chapter Nine details the 1911–14 "tangomania" in Paris, the European vision of South America, and the multiple nostalgias of the dance craze on the eve of the World War.

An odd lot of subjects, at first disconcertingly dissimilar. My aim is to elaborate "memory" as a multiplicity of unique locations whose very range and complexity will demonstrate the common characteristics of the "general history" I wish to describe. Here I would follow Pierre Nora's project. Though engaging dozens of specialists for the different chapters of *Les Lieux de mémoire*, Nora nonetheless insisted that his aim in collaboration was to show how the subjects, "to all appearances diverse, could be brought together under the same category of analysis and interpretation." The studies were bound by the term *lieux de mémoire* as a central figure: "the entire work consists in the elaboration of this idea, its classification, hierarchy, and typology."[5]

What draws together the multiple studies of *Les Lieux* is a vocabulary: patrimony, memory, commemoration. My own "memory" is also linked by words. I pay particular attention to the problematics of absence, distance, witness, testimony, tradition, nostalgia, trace, primitive/modern, and forgetting. Though the chapters stand alone, they are connected by this vocabulary and by the actors who used it.

In a series of essays on *Histoire et mémoire*, Jacques Le Goff quotes Hippolyte Taine to make a point about the "relative unity of style of an epoch" within the seeming randomness of historical selection. "Between a hedgerow at Versailles, a philosophical reasoning of Malebranche, a versification precept of Boileau, one of Colbert's laws on mortgages, a sentence by Bossuet on the kingdom of God the distance might appear infinite. The facts are so dissimilar that at first glance they are judged isolated and separate. But the facts communicate among themselves by the definition of groups which comprise them."[6]

Taine's individual "facts" are bounded by the high culture of the Classical age, and by monarchy, mercantilism, and the Divine. For my designated "modern" period 1870–1914 the most compelling generalities about memory are marked by the use of a language which suggestively expresses the intersection of national politics, scientific discourse, and the acceleration of time in biology and chronology: the language of generation—most notably its root cousins, degeneration and regeneration. Memory in the late nineteenth century is first of all the story of an *organism*.[7]

In 1871 the glorious Grande Armée had failed against the enemy; for the left, the forces of tyranny and reaction triumphed in crushing the revolutionary Paris Commune; for the right, the reign of the mob and its demagogues was narrowly averted, and only by drowning the streets of Paris in blood. In the decades which followed the double specter of an emasculated military machine and the ferocious threat of dictatorial rule, anarchist and proletarian violence only contributed to the era's self-described sense of a world coming apart. "Degeneration," or what Robert Nye has called the "medical concept of national decline," was the biological-political construct of a tense, tired, sick society which framed the sensibility of threat and nervous fragmentation of the fin de siècle.[8]

Despite, or perhaps because of degeneration fears, a Janus image is appropriate to this turn of the century, which seemed to tumble into decadence even while accelerating in a paroxysm of technological and biological energies. New machines and modes of communications helped materialize this quickening of rhythms, yet fierce expressions of aggressive energy also took historical form as "the nationalist revival" in France. Much of this patriotic fervor was anti-German sentiment, aimed especially at the German occupation of the Alsace-Lorraine. Yet much more sprung from deep criticism of France itself as a nation in decline, populated by effete ranks of intellectuals, fractured by feminisms and obsessed with declining birth rates. At the dawning of a new century, Charles Maurras and other poets to the glory of the patrie championed a nation rejuvenated by a strength of will drawn from Greco-Roman traditions, reinforced by the discipline and vitality of sport, hygiene, and physical culture.

Representations of a constantly transformed physical organism were thus an ideal figure to express the understanding of memory in the fin de siècle. For this insight I draw upon inferences not only from French history, but from one of the grand statements of fin-de-siècle memory, Henri Bergson's 1896 *Matière et mémoire*. In this text—part of an *oeuvre* which would make its author the most celebrated philosopher of his time—Bergson defined memory as "the state of our body." For Bergson "memory" was not a series of recalled mental images, but the physical being as incarnation of all the possibilities of acting out the past in the present. Memory was the "virtual state" of the organism, the accumulated past "which acts on us and which makes us act; it is sensory and it is motor."[9]

Strikingly, Bergson conceived a memory charged with an evolutionary scheme of progress and dynamism, a memory of an organism regarding its past and preparing its future. "The truth is that memory does not consist in a progression from the present to the past, but, on the contrary, in a progression from the past to the present." Memory was not a passive or reactive faculty of storage and retrieval—it was that which *acted*. Memory was the instantaneous materialization and adaptation of senses, reflexes, perceptions to the moment at hand; the past was fully realized as memory "where it becomes a present, active state."[10]

Historically, Bergson's articulation of memory as an active quality of organisms was not the product of one peculiar professor in the fin de siècle. Stephen Jay Gould has noted the importance of the "memory

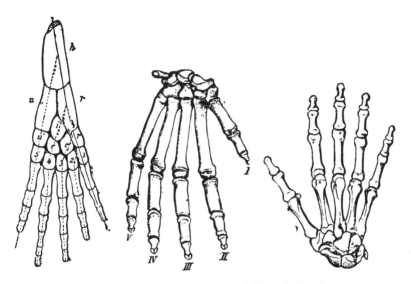

Figure 2 The memory of an organism: amphibian, simian, human. From Ernst Haeckel's *The Evolution of Man, 1910. (Source*: Central Research Division, The New York Public Library, Astor, Lenox and Tilden Foundations)

analogy" for Lamarckian evolutionary theorists in the second half of the nineteenth century (Hering, Butler, Haeckel, Rignano, Hartog, Russell), and the general acceptance among them that active instincts were the unconscious remembrance of things strongly learned, passed on as an "inheritance" to future generations. The morphological unfolding of an individual organism was thus "the organism's memory of its past history."[11]

The intrusion of this hereditary and species memory into the traditional memories of rhetoric and language is a defining characteristic of the late nineteenth-century mnemonic universe, and the biological-evolutionary reading of life histories had ideological dimensions implicated in the degenerative and regenerative anxieties of the period. As memory becomes the inheritance of an organism, questions arise: which memory "inheritance," which characteristics—moral, racial, sexual—would define the most progressive of groups, peoples, or states?

As historical memories were written as phylogenetic inheritances in organisms, so also were ideologies of accelerating time. A body accelerated? This idea was not foreign to scientific discourse of the late nineteenth century. Evolutionary theorists imagined the memory of an organism in terms of its recapitulation of a species inheritance, yet how could an organism not be overwhelmed in reproducing every set of acquired patterns from every generation of the species? The strikingly simple answer was that each generation passed on as memory not only its patterns, but also its lifetime of practice in mastering them. In effect, each generation would adapt its inheritance more quickly than its predecessor, a principle designated as "universal acceleration."[12]

Set within this general framework, Bergson's memory of action only proves that he was an avid student of all the sciences of his time, including newly legitimized researches in anthropology, psychology, and neurophysiology. Clinics, hospitals, and laboratories were staffed and visited by psychologists and neurologists who located memory in the tissues, organs, muscles, and structures of the human form, and used the nervous system to describe both maladies and ideals of civilization—generative or degenerate.

The memory-body became the site of pathological decline as well as strength in the name of science, industry, and progress. Divided thus between regressive and resurgent chronotypes, my texts read the history of 1870–1914 in terms of former historical epochs as much as in terms of the politics and ideologies of the Third Republic. Every occasional citation of parliamentary debates or Jules Ferry's compulsory education and colonial expansionist policies is entangled in mythical Roman republics, anthropoid ancestors, medieval pilgrimages and carnivals, the chill of the ice age or the gardens of tropical islands. Though I have put these pasts into the mouths of psychologists, politicians, and revolutionaries by allowing them to "talk" about other epochs, I consider these epochs neither vanished nor superseded, nor do I believe my actors did. As Bergson would appreciate, memory was a *presence*. A child pronouncing Latin grammar manifested the living soul of the ancients by stirring up the timeless power of their language. An atavistic criminal was a living prehistoric relic, imprinted in his body with the savage traits of his ancestors. A fashionable dance was both glittering entertainment and a pagan rite to the passions of the body in some dim dawn.

The narrative time of my "histoire générale" is thus the imbrication of many selected ages and epochs, many pasts and many presents of the sort described in the late nineteenth century by the anthropologist E. B. Tylor: "When a complete change is produced in a people as a result of the progress of time, one frequently observes a great number of phenomena which conform not to the new conditions, but which come from the former conditions."[13] Through memory, historical time is an aggregate of shifting images, epochs, civilizations, endlessly recomposed. As historian Mona Ozouf has noted, "Memory is largely indifferent to a linear unrolling, the calendar is not its religion." Of far greater importance to memory history is an understanding of why certain moments surface or submerge in historical tides, before, after, or beside each other, cast up, to use Eric Santner's evocative term, as "stranded objects."[14] In my own work such objects remain engimatic as historical memories. Revolution is the falling of a bronze colossus. The economy becomes an inscription of charted lines played out against a grid of numbers. Colonialism is a prisoner and his wife eaten by cannibals. The State is a decomposed portrait of noses, eyes, ears, and fingers. Memory is a machine which conquers death. History is a child who lies.

To be true to my project I must decipher not only "memory" in the late nineteenth century, but memory as defined by my second chosen term: "modern." My use of "modern" will embrace a vast range of familiar historian's themes: urban civilization, rural depopulation, mass society, representative government, public education, a global market system, scientific rationality, ideologies of progress, changing gender roles, new technologies.

I will not attempt to elaborate each of these themes here, nor even attempt to enter historian's debates which can rightly locate "the modern" at 1789, or even push it back to 1492. I will situate myself rather after Charles Baudelaire celebrated "modernity" in the mid-nineteenth century and will draw on the formulations of Matei Calinescu, which have the virtue of being admirably clear and apparently simple: modernity is an awareness of time as an historical movement that is linear and irresistible, directed toward the future. As he puts it, "modernity as a notion would be utterly meaningless in a society that has no use for the temporal-sequential concept of history."[15]

Reading time this way usefully locates "the modern" in political-economic categories. Hegel's unfolding of the historical spirit becomes Marx's directed chronicle of *acceleration* in which the old is replaced by the new, the past continuously obliterated to serve the logic of competition, markets, and ever greater productive forces. I have been speaking of reading the body politic as a variously degenerating or regenerated organism, propelled by an evolutionary biology of conflict between peoples and nation-states. More than a little of this evolutionary struggle is structured around the market logic of a system which I will recognize as late nineteenth-century capitalism.

The consequences of linking "memory" to "capitalism" should be evident: the past will seem to disappear, while the present will gain an ever increasing technical capacity to investigate, record, and generate references to that disappearance. Each moment will be overweighted with the possibilities of its own reproduction while being rendered immediately obsolete. This continuous disappearance of the passing moment will thus produce a dual effect: it will be experienced both as Baudelaire's celebration of modernity as "the transitory, the fugitive, the contingent," *as well as* Friedrich Nietzsche's tirade against the "burden of history." In Richard Terdiman's formulation, the "crisis" of nineteenth-century memory will be that there is simultaneously too much and too little.[16]

Perhaps the most evocative way to grasp this experience of memory, at once overdetermined and empty, is in Walter Benjamin's fragments on the Paris arcades. Benjamin read the landscape of the Baron Haussmann's Paris in the second half of the nineteenth century as a landscape charged with "the prehistoric impulse to the past."[17] Recall Frances Yates' thesis: memory obeys periods, thus Renaissance memory harmonizes intellectually with a certain kind of geometric architecture which is also its expression. What are the cathedrals and palaces of the late nineteenth century? Benjamin's answer was to be found in the articulation of the modern city itself, the expression of a civilization profoundly rooted in a logic of extinction and nostalgia. Structures were raised and leveled, piercing boulevards opened up spaces characterized by nothing but movement and agitation. In the commercial houses, the constant search for the ever-new transformed shop windows from displays into museums, housing yesterday's objects as fossils of an antedated fashion and technology.

What was new, active, part of history, was immediately nothing more than the prehistory of an eternally changing present. The ever-new instantly became an ever-same of objects and events relentlessly created and destroyed by an accelerated, sequential scheme of time. The persistence of memory was the record of things strangely familiar for being so quickly gone, only half-forgotten. As concerns with ontogeny and phylogeny were premised upon tracing origins and species inheritance, so Benjamin's writings on nineteenth-century Paris are instructive for the ways in which they say the same for urban space and capitalist exchange: modernity is deeply prehistoric.

The uneasy presence of the prehistoric and "primitive" haunted the late nineteenth century and defined its "memory." The memory of an organism, through the accumulated potential of its species, became the standard by which to measure its worth and destiny. As the French empire extended its political control over much of Africa and Oceania under the ministries of Jules Ferry, colonized peoples served to model not only different, but also *earlier* types of humanity, bounded within a degenerate or savage time against which the Europeans displayed their own evolutionary sense of supremacy.

Yet this was also the grand age when these same Europeans were theorizing their own racial memories and discovering the savage within.[18] Such thinking was not limited to France in this period: consider Sigmund Freud's interrogations of primal hordes, Jewish racial identity, totemism, and ancestor worship; Cesare Lombroso's atavistic typologies of Italian "born criminals"; the controversies among British naturalists about the descent of man. In France this was an era when Paul Broca led anthropology to the status of a legitimate science while dissecting the brain for centers of memory and language. Jules Ferry's colonial ambitions fueled an explosion of ethnological researches (and demands for financing) concentrated on an interest in what Jacques Le Goff calls "that collective memory of *sociétés sauvages*."[19]

Le Goff's statement is methodologically fascinating, for he designates his concept of "mémoire collective" specifically to encompass the practices, techniques, and knowledge of "people without writing." The anthropologist Marc Augé has defined "memory" for his profession as principally concerned with oral traditions or the "technical means" of remembrance; not the recollections of particular events, "but the memory of the ways in which they were transmitted."[20] Drawing on Le Goff and Augé, I have considered the "memory" of Canaque bamboo engravings, Argentine musicology, criminal tattoos, and vagabond hieroglyphics. Such elements help to define "modern" memory by outlining the boundaries of other traditions, and make possible analyses of different practices where they come into conflict, or are appropriated by each other. Such attention to memory-as-practice also pays tribute to the materiality of memory, that proliferation of tools, traces, and transmissions which prehistorian André Leroi-Gouhran has called "la mémoire en expansion."[21]

Tools, traces, and the expansion of technical means are a defining characteristic of late nineteenth-century European memory. "Modernization"—here including the decline of oral traditions in villages, the rise of the popular press in cities, and the extension of compulsory education everywhere—gave broad meaning for the first time to a civilization whose information and records were parts of a "print culture," a memory of serial events in block texts printed by machines. More, radiographic technologies and photography served medical and police archivists in recording names, dates, faces. Phonographs inscribed musical traditions on wax and made them portable. Drama critics and technical writers argued that the newly invented cinema camera was a sort of memory machine *par excellence* which would capture, register, and preserve forever great historical events and the passing moments of the present.

The machines did more than impress, inscribe, capture, and record posterity: they produced it. The record of an event would be not just a text or document, but ten thousand identical documents visible everywhere at once. Such proliferation took place within an estimation of time redefined by shrinking space, as technologies of speed—railways, early airplanes, and automobiles—conquered distances and reinvented geography for voyagers, explorers, and fugitives. If the memory I described earlier was beholden to evolving organisms, it also surged to electric, mechanical, and industrial rhythms, the whirling of the print-drum, the hammers of engines, and the charged signals of coils and telegraphs.

Why this concern in "memory" with bodies, machines, and especially their action and movement? One key, recurring word explains all: *accel-*

eration. Pierre Nora begins *Les Lieux de mémoire* under its sign: "The acceleration of History: let us try to gauge the significance, beyond metaphor, of this phrase. An increasingly rapid slippage of the present into a historical past that is gone for good, a general perception that anything and everything may disappear."[22] As History accelerates, the "lieux de mémoire" are designated sites which defy time's destroyer, the places of commemoration where memory anchors the past. My studies, rooted in the biology, technologies, and political economy of the late nineteenth century are somewhat differently oriented: they attempt to approximate Henri Bergson's understanding of memory as action and transformation. In looking to shattered monuments, financial markets, high-speed machines, and the nervous system, my subjects are not the memories preserved from an accelerating history, but histories of accelerated memory, subjected to the dramatic rhythms of an age.

Associating "acceleration" and "memory" helps locate my work historically, yet, more important, creates imperatives of meaning which neither term alone expresses. Milan Kundera has written of the rush of events, human and political tragedies, from Allende's Chile to Czechoslovakia, to Bangladesh, to the Sinai to Cambodia, "and so on and so on until everything is forgotten by everyone."[23] In Kundera's remark is not only an observation of time accelerating, but in the face of that very fact, a meditation on the importance of retaining a living past, indeed of a certain obligation to doing so. Kundera's memory is the other side of commemoration as affirmation and heritage; his memory rather pays witness to a history which Jacques Le Goff has grimly traced "from the gulag to torture, from Nazi extermination camps to apartheid and racism, from the horrors of war to those of famine."[24]

The powerful dimension of human responsibility associated with memory is not the product of a stunned twentieth century. As Frances Yates reminds us, Cicero in *De Inventione* considered "memory," along with intelligence and foresight, one of the three essential parts of Prudence, that is, "the knowledge of what is good, what is bad and what is neither good nor bad."[25] Prudence would be the first of the cardinal virtues, accompanied by Justice, Fortitude, and Temperance. Memory in the classical tradition was a point of evaluation and choice and carried with it an internal logic of moral obligations. Mere remembrance fails where ethics and decision are absent.[26] "Everyone complains about his memory, but no one complains about his judgment," noted La Rochefoucauld. He perceived better than most that the two cannot be separated.

If memory in the Ciceronian sense was necessarily and problematically about judgment, it was also dramatically about *speaking*. Cultivation of the memory was and is a necessary rhetorical skill for persuasive public discourse. Memory serves as a point of judgment not simply by recording the past, but by giving its re-speaking both language and gesture, creating the possibility for "ideal speech acts" and their opposites to contest one another.

Post-modern, post-colonial critics argue that belief in "history" in the western tradition can exist only by silencing (or appropriating and absorbing) disagreeable voices and testimonies, and call for new, personal traditions and genealogies. Opponents find such claims irksome and divisive. New genealogies mean new investigations of the past based on perspectives and politics which, by definition, will be concerned with abandoning claims to universality. Abandoning such claims will defy the possibility of a history of "humanity." A strategy of justice for the forgotten necessarily requires reading the past as conflictual, evidence as problematic, all positions as suspect. History as a positive or liberatory narrative gives way to a history of mnemonic traces, each endlessly recited, reiterated, recombined.

If history is the story, then memory is the part of the past which, in its intimate connections to things and people, seems to lend dignity to the identity of a group. Memory for France, Nora argues, has become the inner voice which tells each Corsican "You must be Corsican" and each Breton "You must be Breton." He also observes the powerful force of memory in the Jewish tradition, a theme extensively studied and articulated by Yosef Yerushalmi, who follows the history of "the people of memory."[27] One could make similar arguments for almost any group, ethnicity, heritage. Margaret Lourie, Domna Stanton, and Martha Vicinus have asked about their own works, "Did we mean that memory is gendered, that there are memories that can be described as specifically feminine? Who gives value to women's memories; who degrades or ignores them?"[28]

In other words, no history can be pure event, pure evolution; each is rather a repetition, a return to a story which must be retold, distinguished from its previous tellings. The past is not a truth upon which to build, but a truth sought, a re-memorializing over which to struggle. The fragmentary, disputatious, self-reflexive nature of such a past makes a series of "memories"—ever imperfect, imprecise, and charged with personal questions—the appropriate means for rendering the "history" of the present.

To return to the matters at hand: though I have called my subject France, the reader might argue that my observations describe a more European-wide fin de siècle. In the literature of this period one finds an obsession with all the themes I have put on memory: acceleration, transformation, permeability, and movement—largely in natural decay and decline, an age reeking with "Symbolism." This was the turn of the century, in belles-lettres, when Joris Karl Huysmans and Oscar Wilde seemed to live out the thesis of Max Nordau's "degeneration"; in history, when Peguy,

Taine, and Renan struggled with the legacies of romantic and positive histories; in biology, when phylogeny and evolution ruled scientific discourse.[29] As I have argued above, "memory" has too often become another analytic vocabulary to impose on the past; the point should be to re-historicize memory and see how it is so inextricably *part* of that past.

My study here invokes the fin de siècle in yet another way, that is, not merely to say it is about the end of a century, but that it is equally written at the end of one. Falling Napoleonic monuments, silent movies, Latin grammar and textbooks, dance crazes—my subjects, casting back a century ago, will perhaps seem obscure, but, as deserves any treatise on "memory," they should also resonate with an odd familiarity. The "acceleration" I have discussed above is not only a conceptual attempt to define the end of two centuries, but an historical reflection on how both past and present are drawn together by a collapsed sense of time. Marc Augé has noted, "In a certain way, history has caught up with us, history is on our heels; in other words, history tends to become current events."[30] This does not mean that historians should be journalists; it means that memory history will always in some ways be—by its own definition—a "history of the present."

Images of toppling statues of Lenin and Stalin in the former Soviet Union bore witness to the historical rupture of political and cultural revolutions which shook the Communist world in the late twentieth century. These falling monuments marked an age which has also seen the rise of global capital markets, an upheaval of democratic ideologies, and rancorous debate on "the end of history."[31] Such fractures have generated enormous social dislocations, and thrown light on "alternative" pasts and futures born from conflicts over cultural and national identities. From movies to music to dance, arts and fashions have crossed cultures and traditions, often propelled by virtual realities and information technologies.[32] (What is the stated difference in memory and power between the engineering of a silicon chip and the baroque dreams of Borges's universal library?) Celebrated court battles concerning war crimes, civil liberties, or male versus female testimonies have pitted witnesses against each other and against experts and contributed to the uncertainty of knowing past events. In the far corners of the world, the legacies of colonialism have not been forgotten by those who were subjected, or left to war against each other.

I will not insist on the parallels between then and now; such comparisons are as easy as they are hazardous. I maintain only that "memory" is a crossroads for many histories, of both stunning beauty and cruelty, always reminding of something else. From the brink of 1870 to the brink of 1914 two explosions of mistrust, hatred, bloodshed, scorn, and recrimination center the fin de siècle and the Belle Epoque. It was a seductive and deceptive period, framed by violence, a period which I will fitfully evoke in the pieces which follow. In "memory," we must make do with—yet affirm—traces, remnants, fragments, the incompleteness of the past. "Memory" always seems a sort of "mémoire," in the French sense, a personal reflection, a report, indeed a confession in history, like Bunyan's Pilgrim crossing the places of vanity and despair to say what he has seen.

Figure 3 Counter-commemoration: the fall of the Vendôme Column, 1871.
(*Source:* Bibliothèque Nationale)

1

Monuments: Idols of the Emperor

A strangled cry breaks the frightening silence which hangs over the crowd. The column shakes. All eyes are fixed on the colossus atop the huge cylinder of bronze and granite as the metal cracks. Oscillating its full length for an instant, the column crashes down. A muffled impact of shattering metal mixes with the breaking of brush and clouds of dust rise in the air. At that instant an immense clamor breaks out from the crowd, and cries ring out, "Vive la République! Vive la Commune!"[1]

The debris rains down on a site of mathematical elegance, a vast octagon, paved in stone. The architecture of the "Grand Siècle" is borne majestically around the perimeter of the octagon; the Roman arcades of the ground floor are crowned by Mansart's roofs, framed by silent windows and Corinthian columns. The space is an area stunning in the grandeur of its horizontal expanse, lines of sight unbroken—except for one feature: in the exact center of the octagon, a massive pedestal and, for more than half a century, a huge column, forty-three and a half meters high, bronze and granite; at the summit, a statue of the Emperor.[2]

May 16, 1871. A gathering of dignitaries, soldiers, and the curious takes place at the Place Vendôme in Paris; thousands crowd the available space, the exact numbers are disputed. "The crowd is enormous," reports one paper, remarking on the colorful mix of engineers and laborers, national guard regiments, officials positioned strategically along the balconies, throngs on the floor of the Place. Large barricades and embankments protect the area. A scaffolding rises in three parts around the center of the octagon, and laborers haul in cartloads of sand, brush, and manure to dump at the foot of the pedestal which is decorated with banners and red flags. Military bands play patriotic airs: the 190th battalion strikes up the Marseilles, and the 172nd the "Chant du départ." Then, an eerie silence falls over the Place.

The column is snared in cables drawn to the summit and back down with pulleys to a capstan. Portals around the square have been shuttered, and windows masked against a concussion. Soldiers turn the capstans. The cables tighten. At the fatal hour, a huge crack suddenly resounds. A shudder runs through the crowd. A capstan has broken, five or six guards have been thrown back by the recoil, miraculously none injured seriously. A half-dozen workers are back on the scaffold, diagonally sawing the stone and bronze at the base of the column. The afternoon passes. Another military fanfare. At 4:30 the clarion again sounds. At 5:15 the guard are again at the capstan, slowly winding down the cable. The column resists. "The attention is immense." The cables draw tighter.

The column shudders. The cry—"strangled" escapes the crowd. With a "slow oscillation" the column trembles and totters. Radical writer Maxime Vuillaume recalls, "A monstrous zigzag suddenly passed before my eyes, like the beating wing of a giant bird. Ah! I shall never forget that colossal shadow. . . ."[3] The column tumbles. One gravure shows it toppling in full length; others show it breaking into three sections as it falls. Some renderings show the scaffolding; others do not. The column crashes to the ground, with an explosion of dust but little noise, impact muffled by the cushion of dry brush, sand, and manure. The bronze shatters and collapses into its hollow core. The column is completely demolished. The Emperor strikes the ground, a globe and winged Victory fly out of his hand and are never recovered. Fragments are snatched up by the crowd. Dramatic illustrations show dozens of spectators climbing upon the now empty pedestal, waving red flags and cheering. The guard presses forward to the debris, taunting the fallen statue. The Emperor does not actually fall onto the branches and sand, but lies on the stones, head cracked, one hand shattered, face toward the sky.[4]

With the surrender of Napoleon III to the Prussians on the battlefield of Sedan on September 2, 1870, a new government under the politician-historian Louis Adolphe Thiers negotiated peace for France. Defiant, the city of Paris rejected the settlement, repudiated Thiers' authority, and constituted itself a revolutionary Commune on the model of 1792. In so doing, Paris set itself against not only the German forces, but Thiers' rival French government, now seated at Versailles.

The Commune would have only seventy-three days, and the toppling of the Vendôme Column would turn out to be among its last acts, a final spectacle of memory and resistance played out in a ceremony of destruction. What the column celebrated in imperial grandeur, the Communards tried to undo, bringing down an idol to proclaim a euphoric new order, shattering bronze and stone to rupture time and history. The ceremony at the Place Vendôme was an act of anti-commemoration, a stopped instant which released the exhilaration and struggle of seventy-three days' attempts to overthrow the past and initiate a European history of humanity.

Yet as the column fell, not one but many pasts were fractured by the impact, and the act of destruction divided and inflamed its observers, setting left against right, soldier against civilian, aesthetics against honor, liberty against patrimony, history against memory. As one commentator presciently wrote to a colleague on hearing of the fallen monument, "like you I fear that around this column, knocked down by the ones, rebuilt by the others, more and more ardent passions and hatred will be kindled."[5]

The object of all this attention was a triumphal column, consecrated to the memory of the military campaigns of 1805, decreed by Napoleon Bonaparte. To the painter Bergeret were confided the designs for the reliefs which spiraled up the cylindrical face of the column, a "suite of subjects which were like an historical journal of the campaign."[6] Importantly, the bronze for the reliefs was smelted from the cannons captured by Napoleon at Austerlitz from the Russians and Austrians.[7] More than gloriously symbolic, the column was the material commemoration of an historical event. The extravagant romantic reactionary author Jules Amédée Barbey d'Aurevilly proclaimed the bronze of the column a living substance for a living monument, steeped in and penetrated by the blood of soldiers. "The blood of France is there. The blood incorporated with the soul and honor of France!" Thus, "the Column is not a monument like others. The Column is part of the honor of France, and taken down, our honor is likewise degraded."[8]

Inaugurated in August 1810, the column rested on the pedestal of the former statue of Louis XIV at the Place Vendôme, which had itself been overturned in the Revolution. The new Napoleonic monument affirmed imperial greatness, while replacing the memory of one monarch with another. The name itself went through several evolutions: La Colonne d'Austerlitz; de la Grande Armée; finally, la Colonne Vendôme. A single, vertical projection, the column bore a colossal bronze of Napoleon designed by Chaudet at the summit, draped in the mantle of a Roman emperor, a globe resting in one hand from which soared a winged victory. Early renderings show the Emperor resting on an imposing broadsword, a feature later reduced and attached to his belt, where he grips the knob with a firm hand. Weighing 5000 pounds and costing 44,000 francs, the statue itself, interestingly, was not cast from the cannons of Austerlitz but from military pieces levied from the arsenal at Mayence. A distinction was always maintained, at least by some, between the different metals and representations. In the debate on the impending destruction of the monument, Jules Simon, Minister of Public Instruction, had favored smelting down the statue—but not the column.[9] Victor Hugo made the same point in verse:

> But it's France! Frenchmen
>   We are taking down
> What remained standing on our darkest horizons
> Great France is there! What does
>   Bonaparte matter!
> Does one see a king when one
>   looks upon Sparta?
> Lift away Napoleon, the people reappear
> Cut down the tree, but respect the
>   forest.[10]

The Emperor and his bronze double were deeply implicated in the political memory of the nineteenth century, for the imperial colossus atop the Vendôme Column followed its own history of triumph, misfortune, resurrection, and reappropriation. Inaugurated and placed originally in 1810, it was taken down at the Restoration and languished in a foundry at Launay for many years. From April 1814 the column was surmounted by the large "drapeau blanc" favored by the monarchy. Contemporary illustrations show the huge white flag flying serenely over the octagon. The statue was nonetheless no more forgotten than Napoleon himself. On April 6, 1814, the prefect of the Seine, the Count of Bondy, requested the reinstallation of the statue "in the name of the inhabitants of Paris." Lazare Carnot, then Minister of the Interior, noted the King's reaction, "His majesty responded that, as the statue had been placed on the column without his order, he did not wish for it to be replaced."[11] In 1831, with Napoleon long since safely defeated and the new Orléans dynasty in search of prestige, *Le Moniteur universel* reported an audience between Casimer Perier, the *président du conseil*, and the monarch: "Sire, the column at the Place Vendôme, that monument of immortal victories, lost the statue which crowned it fifteen years ago. This mutilation still continues; it is a sad vestige of foreign invasion."[12]

In 1840 Napoleon did return, in the Orléanist Louis-Philippe's management of the Napoleonic remains and mystique, to bolster the political legitimacy of his own regime. The Emperor's body, exhumed from St. Helena, was viewed and claimed to be in perfect condition. Returned to Paris, it made its way down the Seine on a black barge to be interred at the Invalides.[13] Along with the Emperor's exhumed body, his double found its place again atop the column. The new figure, by Seurre, was a popular Napoleon of "the little hat and frock-coat," in a familiar pose, one hand resting in his jacket. The "little corporal" was an extraordinary bit of political artistry—reaffirming Napoleon atop his column—but not Napoleon the Emperor. The Royal command which ordered the placement of the statue tried to be pragmatic: "the figures in the reliefs of the column being in French military costume, the statue should be equally attired in military costume."[14] The new statue had the intended appeal, at least with some. The publishers of a small guide, a "description" of the column, hoped the new Napoleon would be "part of the *solemnités* destined to celebrate for the third time the glorious and immortal July revolution," taking Napoleon for a general champion of liberty.[15] The great soldier and general, whose other body now rested securely at the Invalides, was the popular hero of French spirit ingeniously divested of the mantle which challenged the authority of the traditional royal lines currently ruling France.

The story does not end there. If troublesome to a few, the imperial Napoleon was a crucial political element to others. With his coup d'état and power consolidated in November 1863, Louis Napoleon, the nephew, regarded Seurre's "little corporal" lacking in grandeur for the background of his own imperial ambitions. As Emperor Napoleon III he ordered the statue replaced with a new version of Chaudet's original. Seurre's piece was thus taken down from the column and reestablished at the roundabout of Courbevoie. The toga of the Roman Caesars returned to the tower at the Place Vendôme, along with the winged victory, the crown of laurels, and the broadsword. So it remained undisturbed, until May 16, 1871.

As the column shattered, reactions were instantaneous—particularly from the military. At Versailles, Marshall MacMahon received the news and exhorted his troops to prepare for battle, raising the dignity of the invading Prussian army above the Communards: "Soldiers! The Vendôme Column has just fallen. The foreigner had respected it. The Paris Commune has brought it down. The men who call themselves French have dared destroy, under the gaze of the watching Germans, this witness to the victories of our fathers against the coalition of all Europe."[16] Only five days later the troops would enter Paris by the Point-du-Jour, beginning the final street-to-street warfare, the slaughter, execution, and burning of Paris of the "Semaine Sanglate"—bloody week. Tens of thousands died in the war of France against France. Vengeful mobs, ruthless commanders, wild female incendiaries crowd accounts of those days as barricades were defended and overrun, prisoners and hostages executed. Public edifices, including the Hotel de Ville, went up in flames. The last resisters were executed at the Mur des Fédérés in the Père Lachaise cemetery.

Military courts shaped the fate of those who survived the carnage. The military and the column in particular dictated the fate of one man who played perhaps the single most important role in the drama of the monument, Gustave Courbet. A renowned and often controversial realist painter, Courbet's major works, *Burial at Ornans, The Stonebreakers, The Artist's Studio,* had excited artistic and social commentary in the Salons and made him "the loudmouth of French painting."[17] As president of the Fédération des Artistes under the Commune charged, ironically, with protecting art in Paris during the siege, Courbet campaigned vigorously against the column. On September 4, 1870, he issued a communiqué suggesting that the column be knocked down, arguing that it was a monument "lacking in artistic value, tending to perpetuate the ideas of war and conquest of the imperial dynasty."[18] On April 12, 1871, the Commune issued its official statement, agreeing with Courbet that the column was a "monument to barbarism," symbolizing only "brute force and false glory, an affirmation of militarism, a negation of international law, a permanent insult of the victors over the vanquished, a perpetual attack on one of the three great principles of the French Republic, *la fraternité.*"[19] The Napoleonic monument was to be destroyed and replaced by a new figure symbolizing "March 18"—the founding date of the Commune itself.

The decision to replace one commemoration with another had perilous personal consequences for Courbet. Anonymous letters signed "a former soldier" or referring to Napoleon, threatened the artist with drowning and daggers if anything should happen to the column. With the return of the Versaillies to control in Paris, Courbet was arrested, jailed, tried for "complicity in the abuse of authority in the destruction of the Column" by a military court, and eventually charged with the full cost of the restoration—a clearly impossible sum. The charge included substantial payments to other artists, including Dumont for restoring the statue, and Mercier for the model of the Victory statuette. Courbet protested that he had acted with good intentions, intending only to take down the column and reestablish its parts at the Invalides or other appropriately museal site—though, in a pointedly ironic "rendering unto Caesar" he had also suggested melting down the commemorative reliefs and stamping them into money.[20]

Courbet's correspondence does suggest an apparently sincere respect for monuments and commemoration. In an "Open Letter to the German Army" of October 29, 1870, he had appealed, "let us have your Krupp cannons . . . the last crowned with the phrygien bonnet to be planted on a pedestal which we will raise together at the Place Vendôme. This will be our column, one to the other, the column of Germany and France forever federated."[21] Courbet would only inconsistently follow this line, for in his trial arguments he maintained that the verticality of the column disturbed the artfully horizontal lines of the Place Vendôme. "For me, this column obstructed. An individual thing does not have the right to block traffic. This column was badly placed. . . . at the Place Vendôme it was a miserable pretension as a work of art, which made foreigners laugh."[22]

As the internationalist monument he envisioned would also stand at the Place Vendôme, Courbet's argument against the Napoleonic column from a logic of spatial aesthetics was not his honest guiding principle, and it is intriguing that he would regard it as a form of innocence. What

Courbet tardily hoped was that Art would put him outside and above the real and explosive question: the control of historical memory. If his artist's expertise could prevail in convincing the court of the aesthetic merits of taking down the column, he might be beyond the reach of those—particularly soldiers and veterans—who did not wish to see the Napoleonic memory violated. The letter to the German army demonstrated, at least early on, that Courbet knew the hazards of destroying a military monument; he focused on forging cannons into commemorations—not effacing them. Under wartime circumstances, to destroy a military monument could not be regarded a virtuous act, not even by the Germans, not even in the name of art or brotherhood.

In destroying the column, Courbet's internationalism ran afoul of the traditions and glories of the military which Marshall MacMahon had suggested even the Germans could respect. As an institution charged now with dictating justice in its own name, the military was Courbet's judge and undoing. Harassed and threatened, Courbet fled to Switzerland, where he denied wrongdoing, saying little about the event, commenting on the increased value of his paintings. His friends began to plead his case and try to rehabilitate his memory in issues of a bulletin, *Les Amis de Courbet*. He subsequently died in exile, and his body returned to Ornans only in 1919 with a special "pass for cadavers" from the mayor of Vevey.[23]

I have called Courbet's case a struggle over "memory." The event which proved both his political triumph and undoing was well documented by witnesses, yet how much was the event remembered, and how much created in the records? The radical and not-so-radical press, the numerous personal memoirs, the histories and scholarship which center on the column recompose a torrent of words and images—both gravure and photographic—which complement and contradict. Karl Marx seemed to frame the event with the famous last lines of his "Eighteenth Brumaire." His image of the iron statue tumbling from the top of the column, coupled with his later analysis of the "Civil War in France," provided a well-known and defining interpretation of events leading to the Place Vendôme, yet his image of the falling emperor was drawn twenty years before the event, making him more prophet than witness.[24]

Among the journalists at the site itself, reports ranged fully across the political and rhetorical spectrum. To the left, Jules Vallès headlined his column in *Le Cri du peuple*, "It's fallen! The sentence of the people is executed, justice is done! It's fallen, this column made of cannons bought at the price of so many cadavers. . . ." *Le Salut public* of Gustave Maroteau published a biting polemic, "An Emperor on a Dunghill," declaring, "with him the cult of great men crumbles, those famous bandits whose image was hardened with the blood of the unfortunate." As for the monument itself, Maroteau described "the fall of this gigantic urinal."[25] Less enthusiastic was *Le Bulletin du jour*, whose criticisms were

Figure 4 Shattered history: the fallen empire. Note the separation of the imperial head from the body. (*Source:* Bibliothèque Nationale)

somewhat differently directed. In an otherwise prosaic account of the crowd scene, this biting line: "The numerous musicians of the national guard were summoned triumphally to celebrate the only incontestable victory of the Commune." *La Constitution* was not even so gracious in its interpretation of the event: "In the crowd united yesterday around the Place Vendôme there were explosions of hatred and rage. On your guard, members of the Committee and members of the Commune. . . ."[26]

The moment of impact was also witnessed differently by different observers—including photographic observers. Prosper Lissagaray, in his *Historie de la commune* (1876), comments, "the head of Bonaparte rolls upon the ground," leaving behind a "purified pedestal." Gravures also show the clean cut between the head and body. The rolling head is a telling image, since photographs taken from many angles, including one close group portrait of Courbet and his associates posing with the fallen statue, indicate that the head of the statue did not in any way separate from the trunk.[27]

Nonetheless the break was a favorite image of the reporting. *Le Reveil du peuple* played with the embedded historical references, "nothing remains but a heap of fragments. The Column is pulverized, the *tricolor* shrouds the decapitated Caesar, resting on a bed of manure." The image of death and the politics of the corpse was attended also by Vallès: "he rests there, somber and sinister, red flags at the four corners of the pile of sticks, as on an immobile catafalque containing the cadavers of imperial glory." Another press account from the Place noted a sailor taking up a paving stone to strike the head of the fallen Napoleon (he was, for some reason, prevented). Maxime Vuillaume also wrote in similar terms. "Caesar rests upon his back, decapitated. His head, crowned with laurels, has rolled like a pumpkin to the edge of the walkway."[28]

Photography and writing contradict. The head may have been reattached for the pictures, but more likely the journalists were writing less out of observation than political symbolism. The truth of the event was not the seeing, but the meaning of the act: the end of dictators, the head and the trunk, the ruler and the state, now separated, sovereignty returning to the people. Recent history was of course deeply implicated: by shattering Napoleon Bonaparte, the Communards proclaimed their liberty from the nephew, Louis Napoleon. Revolutionary memories would also evoke the statue of Louis XIV which had been overturned in 1792 at the Place Vendôme, or images from the Place de la Concorde, where the guillotine had severed the royal head of Louis XVI. In fact, in addition to the "decapitated Caesar," the "shrouding" of the figure was a determined choice of language. Not mere rage nor effacement of "symbols" was taking place, but a sacred transition, of both political and spiritual legitimacy.

Lissagaray's, Vallès's, and Vuillaume's imagery and the shadowy memories of the guillotine are arresting in view of a small historical action coincident with the toppling of the column. A *procès-verbal* from the National Archives relates the fate of the third Napoleonic body (after Vendôme and the Invalides), the "little corporal" resting at the roundabout at Courbevoie. On September 17, 1870, the very day the Prussians were to occupy Versailles, the government ordered engineers "to take down the statue called The Little Corporal at Courbevoie and deposit it in the Seine." A few days later, according to the architect in charge, the statue was taken down, during which the head ("in spite of precautions") was separated from the trunk. The whole was bound in 130 meters of tarred cordage, along with the head, which was placed at the feet. Transported upstream from the bridge at Neuilly, "at a distance of 37 meters from the corner (next to the end) of the rue du Bois-de-Boulogne," it was dumped into the river.[29]

The sacrality or desecration of the body ran throughout the tale of the Vendôme Column. Even the choice of May 16 for the ceremony resulted from technical difficulties the engineers experienced with the scaffolding and cutting of the base of the monument. The original date had been May 5—the day of Napoleon's death. After the fall, speeches were made from atop the debris itself. Citizen Henri Festrine declared to the crowd, "Citizens, we have seen this column fall, as well as the man who now lies on the excrements fated to receive him. This man, who stunned all the courts of all foreign nations, is at your feet, helpless." The broken body was also evoked by Vuillaume, who wrote, "The Col-

umn is on the ground, open, its entrails of stone open to the wind. . . ."[30]
The fall brought low the power and the glory of the Emperor to a corpse.
The editors of *Le Père Duchêne* make this point with their customary
glee:

> Having thrown down the little man of bronze
> That's not bad
> But that's not all
> And it's far from being enough
> Citizens members of the Commune
> Why only the bronze!
> The justice of the people has quite other relics
> To throw to the winds!

The "other relics" of course, were the remains of "the little man in
flesh and bone at the Invalides." *Le Père Duchêne* was unsparing in its
attack on the Napoleonic regime, and described an imperial corpse
"stuffed with spices in the stomach, for fear that it will spoil!"[31] Jules
Vallès also declared war on the injustices of the dead. Vallès, writer, journalist, poison pen par excellence, followed in the tradition of Marat with
Le Cri du peuple:

> The statue of the first Bonaparte as roman emperor is at the refuse dump,
> and that is very good, but it is not enough. The swaddled carcass of this
> master rogue is still at the Invalides . . . it must be burned . . . and its ashes
> scattered to the wind. Enough of these ignoble relics.

Vallès offered little distinction between the two bodies of the Emperor; the one shattered at the Place Vendôme and the other whose
remains rested at the Invalides, the "swaddled carcass." Here Vallès echoed *Le Père Duchêne*'s suggestions for Napoleon's remains: "Let's go!/
Fuck it in a bright bed of lime/ Or burn it/ Or throw the whole thing
into the Seine/ Or into the sewers!"[32] The drowning of the body was at
least partially accomplished as noted earlier. The burning of the body,
the reduction to ashes for *Le Père Duchêne* as well as for Vallès was no
consecration, but merely an efficient means to scatter dust so that no
more "relics" could remain. It was precisely the antiquarian "sacred"
powers of the relic which was the scene of the struggle for them.

The battle over memory and monument was not limited to wicked broad-
sides in the radical papers. The column had equally eloquent defenders
who on several occasions turned to verse to make their points. Poetry as
a location of political sentiment was common enough in the nineteenth
century (think of Lamartine or Hugo), and numerous small booklets proclaimed their own version of the events at the Place Vendôme. In a paen
to the column (1874), one Eugene Léveque allowed the monument to
speak for itself. At the side of the fallen column, the poet finds the Napoleonic statue declaring "in its vibrant voice resonating everywhere"

"the shame with which the crime here was committed."[33] Another defender of the column, Edouard d'Anglemont, in 1872 published *La Resurrection de la colonne*, a telling title to say the least. D'Anglemont lauded the column, and offered his stamp on the Communards, "Bible of our exploits/ popular monument/ you are no more!/ The royal brigands of Paris/ possessed of infamy and stupid hatred/ have laid down your epic debris in the gutter!" The column becomes proud victim, fallen to the "purveyors of death, kings of the guillotine, hideous profaners of the sainted word: liberty," a pointedly Jacobin imagery. When the column is finally restored, the resurrection image—the rising anew of the body from death—incorporates a new glorious France, "great again among nations!"[34]

The conjunction of resurrection and nation ran through the conflicts of the Commune. A few weeks after taking control of Paris, on June 7, Adolphe Thiers' new government had the body of the Archbishop Darboy (executed by the Communards) disinterred, embalmed, and commemorated with a grandiose ceremony at Notre Dame. A few years later came the grandest, though to its opponents, the most grotesque vision of expiation and reconciliation of the nation: the building of the basilica of Sacre Coeur, overlooking all of Paris from the summit of Montmartre.[35]

The poetic treatments of the column described not only the promise of the nation as resurrected body, but also the unfolding of history itself in which words and monument become one. Léveque's 1874 verses (above) open with an arresting laudation: "Standing with its glorious spiral against the sky/ a bronze monument dominates the city/ on its proud flanks it unrolls the history/ of the dawn of the century to posterity. . . ."[36] The description here of an unrolling history is noteworthy, for the Vendôme column, much more than other more pointedly allegorical statuary, actually *is* an historical mural, 425 plaques, unrolling some 840 feet, over a thousand if fully extended. The bronze spiral of the column unfolds, in multiple sequential tableau, Napoleon's campaigns and the victory of Austerlitz. The story begins August 24, 1805, with the march of the French armies toward the Rhine, features diplomatic encounters at Wurtemberg, Louisbourg, and Ulm, and episodes of battle leading up to Austerlitz on December 2. The spiral concludes with the cession of Venice to Italy, and the return of the Napoleonic guard to France.[37] The contemporary (Napoleonic era) costuming of the armies, their formations, and artillery, wind up and around a monument rendered in imitation of Trajan's victory column at the Forum in Rome, crowned by the Roman draping of Napoleon himself, after the Royal style made popular in the eighteenth century. By 1871 many layers of empire and memory were already incarnated at the Place Vendôme.

The story in bronze which the column unrolls is not only a documentary of Napoleonic military campaigns, but itself a treatise on historical consciousness. As an almost exact copy of Trajan's column, it was at once triumphal monument and funereal marker. In Trajan's case his ashes were deposited in a mausoleum in the base of the monument, associating his person, his memory, and his monument with the geographical center of Roman authority.

The subsequent embedding of the Roman example in the French was taken very seriously, as Napolon's self-representation as a Caesar indicates. In 1821, one Alexandre Goujon, a former captain of the artillery, had published a poetic pamphlet dense with the imagery of Napoleon's greatness, placing the general in the line of the "heroes of antiquity." The column was something more than a marker, for "standing upright upon the triumphal column, holding the Victory in his hand, he resembled commander of Europe!" The personal majesty which linked Trajan to Bonaparte through the column led to Goujon's unsurprising suggestion: "Yes, Napoleon, the column at the Place Vendôme is the only monument worthy of receiving your ashes. . . ."[38] To consecrate and mix the ashes with the material of the monument itself would unify the two bodies into one sacred relic, the ultimate repetition of Trajan's memorial.

The "memory" of the column was manifest in other ways as well. The iconographies of monuments like Trajan's column were not intended merely to glorify brutal military conquest, but to illustrate grand lessons in politics and morality deserving of respect and emulation. A great conquerer hero could not achieve glory merely through military victories, for the source of success was inextricable from worthiness and the exercise of the virtues of "courage, clemency, justice, piety." Like Aeneas leaving Dido to pursue Destiny, the great man was only the incarnation of these virtues, a part of an unfolding, ascending spiral of history. A triumphal column, with its continuous frieze, was an invocation of historical time, a series of images which, in one notable interpretation, "incarnates to our eyes the temporal dimension which draws together the past and the future," and translated to the viewer "the immense effort of the ascension of the Roman world." At a cosmological extreme, the spiral of time was a Dante-like history of the world, unwinding somewhere between the Earth and the moral system of Aristotle, and Paradise—the image of the Ptolemaic heavens.[39]

The destruction of the Vendôme Column was much more than an antimilitarist statement or attempt to mock one Napoleonic dictator by bringing down another. To break the column would break and collapse many different histories—those of the Napoleonic regimes of course, but also classical, cosmological, cultural, and national narratives. To efface one without disturbing the others was impossible. As the Emperor fell, so also did the patriotic genius of the French revolutionary armies. Tyranny conquered meant a cultural heritage endangered. Virtuous republics tumbled down alongside ambitious dictators.

The politics of memory thus shaped fiercely divided reactions to the

Communards' act. One document contemporaneous with the events in Paris neatly outlined the complex terms of the debate. In May 1871, Paul Brandat of a pacifist organization, the "Ligue Internationale et Permanente de Paix," wrote to his colleague Frédéric Passy, requesting an official position on the tumultuous events taking place in Paris. The entire exchange, which ranged over civil war, world brotherhood, working-class oppression, and the rule of law, was conducted around the singular event of the column's destruction, locating the act between "the art of producing and the art of destroying . . . the politics of life and the politics of death."[40]

Brandat opens the exchange by giving support to the action at the Place Vendôme and the right of "workers, condemned to misery by conquerers," to negate oppressive memory in the name of their own human liberation. He justifies the Communards' action by locating the column in a sinister lineage, drawing not on European history, but Asia and Africa as sites of unspeakable savagery to make his point. "A long time ago, Timour-Beg, an Asian Napoleon, built an edifice of human remains," he begins, matching this horror with an account of a voyage to "the coast of Africa" where he encounters the warrior King of Dahomey, elevating a funereal monument to the memory of his father—"a gigantic tomb of bricks hardened with human blood." Brandat unseats Napoleon from Rome and places him alongside non-European barbarians, neatly serving as signs of a primitive savagery counterposed to antique grandeur. The column, he claims, is nothing but "an immense pile of human debris."[41]

Yet Brandat's support is ambivalent; he finds the destruction of the column an unsettling act, a sign of "serious times." He was right about that: the immediate situation around Paris was explosive for a population trapped "between civil war and foreign war." By May 8 Thiers had already delivered an ultimatum to the Parisians, and by the 13th his Versailles forces occupied an important fort near Paris, just three days before the column fell. Brandat was careful to admonish the destruction of the monument as "the necessary consequence of the cult of force," which he abhorred.

The attack on the column raised a troubling question: was violence justifiable—even against monuments of oppression? For the Commune, what were the legitimate means of its own defense? Frédéric Passy, in his reply to Brandat, judged the events at the Place Vendôme a crime, even if they were directed against tyranny. The blow against the column, he argued, was criminal because it was effected by "a faction, no . . . a band without mandate, without authorization, without title or appearances of any kind of title."[42] The unacceptable fault of the destroyers was not their revolutionary politics, nor particularly their use of force, but that they did not act in the name of what he called "the nation."

But who could claim to speak and act in the name of "the nation"? Clearly, it was not the Napoleonic regime, for whom Passy had no sympathies: "it is not the statue of that great and sterile butcher which should take its place on the summit of this funereal monument, but the statue of his principal victim, *La France*."[43] The Communards had read the column as a monument to tyranny and militarism, thus deserving destruction. In Passy's view, the Communards should only have exchanged Empire for Patrie by replacing ruler's laurels with a symbol of the People's heritage. Breaking the Vendôme Column captured the political shift, yet also damaged the incarnated and resurgent nation. His argument has a perplexing circularity: only the nation could destroy monuments, yet the nation would be attacking itself by doing so.

The logic of this conundrum, and the thinking behind its origins, can be illustrated by actions taken at Versailles. On April 25, 1871, less than a month before the events at the Place Vendôme, Adolphe Thiers had presented a *Projet de loi* declaring all public and private property in Paris (especially if seized by the Commune) to be inalienable. The document begins with a declaration of urgency: "The insurrection which dominates Paris and disquiets France has taken on, in its audacious development, characteristics which no legislator could have forseen."[44] Thiers' bill opens by defending the bourgeois sanctity of property, yet expands this notion to declare the Commune a threat not to anyone's particular wealth, but to the cultural heritage of a nation.

> The monuments erected by our fathers, witnesses to our old glories, are threatened, the wealth of our establishments are taken and brazenly presented to the Mint. The hand of the ravagers does not hesitate before the sacred vases which the faithful have given to our churches to contribute to the pomp of their ceremonies. They covet and have begun to pillage all the art objects which the passion of a few amateurs or the enlightened taste of governments from different eras have been able to unite in private and public collections.[45]

The bill establishes as inalienable not only properties belonging to the state, department, and city, but also to churches, workshops, civil and commercial companies, and individuals. Arrest and condemnation await anyone acting in the name of, or under the orders of "one so-called Commune of Paris." The intent of the legislation is quite clear: to punish "plundering and theft" and to place "out of circulation all goods and properties upon which the insurrection would exercise its own accounts."

Behind the proposal however, more was at stake than punishing theft and trafficking. In his bill Thiers wrote, "Before this peril *d'un nouveau genre* which none of our too-numerous revolutions has ever before presented, the legislation appeared insufficient." Thiers, a good historian, was certainly familiar with theft and the willful destruction of icons, images, and art in revolutionary situations—what was "new" about this? His deputy M. Bertrand clarified the position of the Versailles government by denouncing the "pillage and devastation" of everything which "the nation, the department of the Seine, the great city and its individuals hold particularly dear," reviling the Communards as "adventurers without names, and more often without *patrie*."[46] In attacking the Communards thus, the government at Versailles saw "France" as the injured party, assaulted by outsiders, internationalist fanatics not even French.

Maurice Aghulon has argued that a new language was being shaped at the time of the Commune, a language of visual representations outside of politics. To destroy symbols of despotism was an expected act, "but to demolish one of the celebrated monuments of Paris! That was no longer politics, it was vandalism, barbarism . . . in this new language, Napoleon and the Column were no longer a political symbol; they had become works of art, to be preserved as such. One did not yet speak of 'patrimony,' but the idea was there."[47] Courbet, recall, had tried to defend himself by appealing to aesthetics. Alas for him, the column had itself already acquired a quality of temporal sacrality beyond his or anyone's artistic judgment.

Aghulon is perhaps too modest in emphasizing the historical lateness of transforming political symbols into objects of artistic heritage. Struggles over "patrimony" had begun at least with the French Revolution, and in his exchange with Brandat, Frédéric Passy had defended the column by arguing that "the monuments raised by our predecessors are a sacred patrimony."[48] On this point he was adamant. In Passy's vision, history and art, or better, history embodied in art, were the markers which resisted time's "incessant destructions." Each shattered monument was a forgetfulness, an oblivion, so to attack the Vendôme Column was to attack not merely Napoleon, but History itself. Such elegant arguments had been employed even earlier by Casimer Perier, who, in remonstrating before Louis Philippe for the return of the Napoleonic statue, had concluded, "Monuments are like history: they are inviolable like it; they must conserve all the nation's memories, and not fall to the blows of time."[49]

Yet shaping a patrimony is a process of selection and designation, and the difference between symbols of tyranny and grandeurs of a "nation's memories" is not always obvious. In their committee work, the Communards themselves were often at pains to know exactly what to destroy. One act of obliteration was decreed by consensus on May 10, 1871: "The house of Thiers, located at place Georges, will be torn down." The house of the chief of the Versailles government was completely demolished, but the total project was in no way simple. In a May 12 meeting, Courbet posed a problem to his fellow delegates: "Messr. Thiers has a collection of bronze antiques; I wonder what should be done with them." The delegates decided that a commission would be appointed to conserve and protect them. Demay remarked, "Don't forget that these small bronze artworks are the history of humanity, and we want to conserve the intelligence of the past for the edification of the future. We are not barbarians." Protot differed: "I am a friend of Art, but I am of the opinion that all the pieces representing the image of the Orléans should be sent to the Mint. As for the other artworks, they will obviously not be destroyed." Clemence added another category: "Thiers' collection is also composed of bibliographic riches, for whose conservation I ask that a commission be named." Grousset also: "There are also in Theirs' home pieces belonging to the Archives . . . it would be good if, on the commission we are going to name, there could be historians, men of letters."[50] So the Communards organized their own patrimonies by taste, politics, discipline. One thing was destroyed, another preserved; some useless or offensive articles were to be broken up or burned, consigned to oblivion, others protected, the history of humanity.

For the Communards, the breaking of time was the deep logic of their many ritual acts, including the destruction of the column, of Thiers' house, of Orléanist and Napoleonic imagery. The Commune attempted to establish itself in a revolutionary temporality, adopting the Republican calendar for *Le Journel officiel*, and declaring the Commune's founding date the consecration of a "rupture" and "negation" of previous history.[51]

    This negation of the past would prove to be one of the most fiercely contested points in the whole debate around the destruction of the Vendôme Column. The poet Léveque, cited earlier, had attacked the Communards for having "soiled forever the French name," raging, "They have pulverized Glory/and attempted to erase History!"[52] The war over the column was a struggle over representing the legacies of the past. Partisans of "patrimony" like Frédéric Passy were vaguely sympathetic to the Communards' anti-imperialism, but found their politics of rupturing time, space, and history anathema to his own. In condemning the radicals, Passy defined what was clearly the true offense of the Place Vendôme: "crime against the present and crime against the past . . . foolish and barbarous pretension to make a tabula rasa of the material works of our fathers as well as of our traditions, ideas, and the laws of human nature itself."[53]

    What Passy shared with the Communards was a certain internationalism, a humane and ideal politics based upon a federalist world order free from political oppression, dedicated to the rightful exercise of work and art. In this, the programs of a hundred Proudhonian, Marxist, Blanquist, Jacobin, socialist, and other workers' movements of the middle and late nineteenth century could find general philosophical agreement. Passy's position against the Communards on the question of the column was something else, however: it was a bulwark against the unsettling possibility that the past had no meaning. He could not fault deposing images of tyrants, yet if monuments could be destroyed, the "material works of our fathers," their embodied traditions, aspirations, and patriarchal lineages would be upset, and with them his attempt to define a "nation."

    Invoking the destruction of the column, Passy agrees that the nation has the right to decree such actions, yet only as a "purifying France" answering to a higher principle "like the dens of pagans converted by

Christianity given sanctuary by the God of justice and love." At the place of the destroyed column Passy would fashion a new monument. "I would, in the name of France, in the name of humanity, ask that the memory of those whose fathers gathered together the bronze and stone with their blood be sadly inscribed."[54] The moving eloquence of inscribing memories of fathers' blood equates the "name of humanity" with that of France in a patriarchal prescription. The transcendent, encompassing, eternal humanity which Passy invokes, the tears it weeps, the language it speaks is that of a French nation defined as generations of fathers inheriting the classical and Christian worlds. By defending "material works" Passy's reflections also underline another point: this inheritance is a defense of property, in much the way that Thiers' "patrimony" law sought to defend a nation defined through property and ownership. Passy's views on the column outline a bourgeois historical vision, couched as they are in a language of nation as patriarchal, propertied lineage, Christian redemption, and the defense of an abstract humanity in the continuities of a French tradition. Such historical narratives ultimately moved him to disdain the Communards' action in the name of "human nature."

Passy's history was extensive, drawing its power from the transmissions of an unrolling legacy of time. Other histories were intensive, fixed on the decisive meaning of moments. The moment of the falling column proposed a special historical scheme to Passy's interlocutor Paul Brandat, for whom the events at the Place Vendôme were less a threat to a redemptive, liberal history than an ecstatic expression of social justice and international politics as a unique instant of lived experience:

> Ah! It was a noble festival, a festival blessed by God, as if at that great council of work, the Universal Exposition, the French people had invited the workers of all the nations to tear down this symbol of war to the sound of a European orchestra, for peace, and peace alone, can emancipate the worker.[55]

The French, by their action against the Vendôme Column, set the example for the new world order. The character of this world order is breathtakingly characterized in the first lines "Ah! It was a noble festival, a festival blessed by God." The image of the "festival" (*fête*) in Brandat's vision is striking, and was revived forcefully and eloquently by historian Henri Lefebvre (1965) in his bold formulation: "The Commune of Paris? It was first of all an immense and grandiose festival, a festival which the people of Paris, essence and symbol of the French people in general, offered to themselves and to the world."[56] For both Lefebvre and Brandat, "festival" is a critical category in understanding the revolutionary actions of the Commune: the celebration of apparent disorder in the face of order, the "destructuring of society" attempted by the Commune's innovative legislation on worker's rights, women's education, and political liberties. Seen in this way, the overturning of the column was simply the most spectacular example of a society playing out festive rites of reversal, making a world upside-down out of politics, class, and culture. This meant inverting hierarchies and rupturing time in the present, creating disorder out of which could be born new orders.

The joyful image of the festival embraces both the excitement of workers' internationals, and the self-congratulation of the Universal Expositions—those late nineteenth-century showcases of bourgeois civilization. Shaped by the French revolutionary tradition of the nineteenth century, the Communards were true indignant believers in this exalted new world order, part Blanquist in taking the Jacobin past as a political and social model, part Fourierist in looking to a worker's society organized on scientific industrial principles. Framing this fervor in terms of the Vendôme Column, the *Journal officiel* of the Commune reported on memories of the future: "Let the world be convinced: the columns put up from now on will never celebrate some historic brigand, but will perpetuate the memory of some glorious conquest in science, work, and liberty."[57]

The Communards believed in many things, in justice, work, liberty, science; they also believed that revolution was necessary to achieve those goals, and that revolution was a struggle over memory. Marx had contemptuously denounced the operatic nostalgia of Louis Napoleon's coup d'état and later celebrated the martyrs of the Commune in his writings. The followers of Auguste Blanqui honored the cult of 1793, organizing their political activities around pilgrimages and mythic rituals commemorating the heroes of nineteenth-century insurrection.[58] Yet revolutionary memory triumphant required more than a cult of saints. It required war on the memories of the old order.

From the Place Vendôme, radical writer Félix Pyat delivered his attack: "The Column has fallen, victim of the United States of Europe. Sooner or later its fall will sweep away the Trafalgar Column in London, that of Blucher in Berlin, all the old royal and social forms, all the vestiges of war and hatred, of race and caste."[59] In London and Berlin, just as in Paris, fallen columns inaugurated a new federalist world broken from despotic history. Far from a nurturing and identifying tradition, Pyat recognized the past incarnated in the columns as monopolized memories, the false, intolerable glories of a decrepit order. Humanity would be possible only when such memories were destroyed, the old forms and vestiges crumbling as their props were pulled down.

Pyat's account separated past from future, and the column appears as a marker to conjure a series of rhetorical oppositions, an ethical map of political principles and ironic justice: "This monument of force against law, of empire against republic, of war against peace, of Caesar against the people, has finally been knocked down by the hand of the people themselves."[60] The column defined the moral space of a new history which lay at the base of ethical rule: the resurgent, recaptured justice of "the people." That space was also geographic, the mapping of an entirely new political order of Europe. Writing from the Place Vendôme, Pyat concluded, "It has fallen forever at this place which will henceforth forever be called 'Place Internationale.' "[61] At a reception following the events of May 16, officials in fact adopted this new name, but time was not on the side of the Commune.

One more report on the column gives an important variation on the spectacular overthrow of history and memory taking place at the Place Vendôme. Venting his rage against the "rigid, brutal, heavy and dumb" monument, Jules Vallès saves a good part of his derision for the ease with which it fell: "to bring it down, the calculations of an engineer and a few rounds of rope were sufficient." Vallès's sarcastic astonishment is tuned not to dramatic moments, but to the altogether commonplace way in which history vanishes:

> They thought that this column, that this glory could never fall without a shattering upheaval in the world, without the walls of Paris trembling like those of Jericho to the sound of the trumpets of the soldiers of Israel; the inhabitants waited for a shaking of the ground, at the exits of their homes, for the breaking of their windows. Illusion![62]

In wicked overstatement, the invocations of Apocalypse become comic-opera, inversions of grandeur and tragedy. The end of history— the crumbling walls, the trumpets of Israel—evokes not disaster, but mockery. The colossus falls, Paris does not tremble, the world of the ancients does not reel. Just like its muffled landing on the brush, sand, and manure in the Place Vendôme, the history encased in the monument crumbles without impression. Illusion! The grand tradition, the glory, the mythical past of the Roman emperors is overthrown by the modernity of a fugitive moment, an unremarkable instant.

Indeed, as history was momentarily broken and memory challenged at the Place Vendôme, the monument itself was desubstantialized, its sacred power of place and material rendered spectral and absent. Barbey d'Aurevilly had declared of the column, "Its bronze is more than simple bronze. The blood of those who perished before the enemy on the battlefield has been drunk in, penetrated, making it a thing human and living."[63] Such defenders of the sanctity of the metal were no doubt horrified by the reports of April 20, 1871, in the *Journal Officiel de la Commune*; giving Courbet's original remarks on hauling the column off to the mint a businesslike twist, the *Journal* reports, "The materials which compose the column at the Place Vendôme are for sale. The bronze of the cannons of Austerlitz is supposed to permit the fabrication of a million five-centime coins."[64] *Le Père Duchêne* equally proposed, "It is necessary . . . that this bronze end up by serving the commerce of men, that it be nothing more than a money of exchange representing real work and the force of the People circulating around the world!"[65] Infamy—the wreck of the column, the dignity of its cannons and statues was to be taken up and stamped into money! In the destructive moment of modernity at the Place Vendôme, the sacredness of material, of site were to see their final transformation into the anonymous exchange of the economy.

Regarding this brief moment when history turned at the Place Vendôme, it is hard not to read a disquieting resonance out of this exchange-value vision of the future. In his famous memoires of the Commune, Prosper Lissagaray reports "the people wanted to share in the debris of the Column," by running out after souvenirs as it shattered; "the Mint opposed them on the grounds of the money involved."[66] Even the champions of the monument use mockingly similar language. Barbey d'Aurevilly reports one enraged suggestion from a patriot of the column to capture and imprison Courbet in an iron cage on the pedestal of the fallen monument, ". . . and the man who suggested this added to the punishment all the filth and degradation of the modern spirit in adding: 'he can be shown for money.' "[67]

The plans to strike the new money from the shattered reliefs were never carried out: not enough time. Had they been, the coins would undoubtedly have shared the fate of other artifacts, subsequently enshrined in their own institutions of memory. Lissagaray reports: "The pieces struck by the Commune are exceptionally rare. I possess an example of a known type, the same as one can see in the displays at the Musée Carnavelet, where a series of everyday objects recalling the insurrectional period of 1871 are laid out."[68]

The reliefs were reconstructed and the entire column completely rebuilt by the conservative Republican governments in a few years. Photographs show the engineers and architects replacing the Napoleonic statue just after Christmas, 1875. Memories lingered even of this reconstruction project. Lissagaray: "One of the first acts of the victorious bougeoisie was to once again raise that enormous baton, symbol of imperial power. To place the master back on his pedestal cost a scaffolding of thirty thousand cadavers. Like the mothers of the First Empire, how many of our own time can look upon that bronze without weeping?"[69]

The Commune is annually commemorated by European leftists and guardians of the seventy-three days' memory at the Mur des Fédérés, the site where the last resisters were executed by Versailles troops against the walls of the Père Lachaise cemetery. At the Place Vendôme, the column is outfitted with the tricolor on national holidays, and, as a Napoleonic monument, takes wreaths for military commemorations.[70] The Place in the late twentieth century is the locale of luxury boutiques, great banks, insurance companies, and the Ritz hotel. The Commune is nowhere present.

Most of the documents reported above as "testimony" appeared in papers and journals on May 17, 1871, the day following the destruction of the column. Some eighty years later, on the same date, a small news article appeared in one of the Paris newspapers announcing a commemoration at the Place Vendôme. The piece, clipped out and filed away at the Bureau des Batiments, announced the forthcoming 250th anniversary of the inauguration of the Place by the Sun King, Louis XIV, whose own statue there had been overturned by the Revolution. The origin and ordination by monarchs had slipped far enough back in history to claim priority over attempts to break that history. The Place was to be adorned with bowers, and a royal mantle hung in front of the Ministry of Justice. Every night, the façades were to be illuminated so that the whole Place would be covered with a "luminous canopy." In the evening, there were concerts, the release of pigeons, and "an elegant and flowery dinner at the Ritz." "The Big Event," however, at the end of the festivities, would be "a carrousel of elegance in automobiles," around the Place and around the column, which did not even exist in the age of Louis: twenty-five luxury cars carrying young women presenting the latest dress styles "of our great fashion designers."[71] *Le Père Duchêne* would have to laugh.

Figure 5 *Non-lieu* of memory: interior of the Paris Bourse. (*Source:* Bibliothèque Nationale)

2

Numbers: The Temple of Time

Ten days after the fall of Louis Napoleon Bonaparte and the Second Empire, Karl Marx addressed a letter to a colleague: "The drama of the French, therefore also the workers, is in great memories. It is necessary that events put an end once and for all to this reactionary cult of the past."[1] That cult, Marx had once observed, was the French revolutionary tradition of presenting "the new scene of world history" in the "time-honored disguise" of Roman republics and empires, a parade of tribunes, virtuous consuls, and glorious Caesars. Since his *18th Brumaire*—that mordant analysis of Louis Napoleon's coup d'état and accession to power—Marx had warned of a Napoleonic regime legitimating itself by commandeering the "costumes" and "battle slogans" of the Revolution, brandishing them in the reflected glory of the first Bonapartist Empire. Louis Napoleon was the man who could be everything because he was nothing, an empty name easily filled by a people's nostalgia for his uncle's imperial greatness. "The French, so long as they were engaged in Revolution, could not get rid of the memory of Napoleon."

Yet, from Danton to Robespierre to Napoleon, Marx recognized that the revolutionaries had done more than merely parade in Roman costume; the trappings may have seized upon the grandeur of an ancient world, but the project was nothing less than "the task of releasing and setting up modern bourgeois society." The first revolutionaries had knocked the feudal system to pieces; to their inheritors remained the task of creating within France the conditions under which "free competition could first be developed, the parcelled landed property exploited, the

41

unfettered productive power of the nation employed." Ultimately, Marx argued, the borrowed costumes and phrases were not to be scorned because they foolishly honored Republican or Imperial ghosts, but because they were memories which granted heroism to the unheroic revolutionary project of the bourgeoisie which so fascinated and appalled him: to be "wholly absorbed in the production of wealth."[2]

Where are the "memories" of bourgeois wealth? In his grand epic of France under the Second Empire, Emile Zola had dedicated one volume to *Le Ventre de Paris* (the Belly of Paris), the ancient market center of Les Halles, with its "colossal breath, still heavy with the indigestion of the night before," a place of "things melting, of fats and greases," evoking the body, digestion, consumption, the weight of things and their values.[3] In 1899 writer Gabriel Mourey and his illustrators went in search of their own Paris to create a literary and artistic portrait of the city at century's end. Haunting the boulevards and cafés at night, wandering Montmartre in the morning, strolling the streets and passages at noon they inscribed and drew their notes and impressions into the fleeting sketches of *Les Minutes parisiennes.* They searched for, and found, a new center of Paris—not an ancient monument or market site, but a recent edifice existing only since 1808, whose cornerstone had been laid by Napoleon Bonaparte. Heading down to Rue Vivienne just at the end of Rue de 4 Septembre—a surprising coincidence? (it was the date of the proclamation of the Third Republic)—they came upon their marker. What they found was the stock exchange.

"*La Bourse!* The heart of modern Paris, as les Halles are the stomach. *La Bourse!* The cathedral of the new age, the temple of the only truly flourishing and sincerely practiced religion."[4] The language of the body of Paris was instructive. What they found was not a stomach, but a heart: that is, not consumption, not digestion—but circulation.

The movement of wealth defined the Bourse, and in its halls as nowhere else the most extreme, fantastic representation was given to the credo of a society propelled by a modern economy: time is money. Let me add: time is money is historical memory. In the decades after the Franco-Prussian War and the repression of the Commune in Paris, the corridors of the stock exchange were the stage for an extraordinary struggle over the representation of the past in which the vocabulary of the economy—growth, circulation, exchange—was wielded by revolutionaries as a language of tyranny, and by capitalists as a weapon against a past which they wished to forget. The power of financial exchange to shape or efface the imprint of political events was at the heart of polemics between ex-Communards and market traders, and is one example of what I call the "memory" of the stock exchange at the turn of the century: an accounting of the multiple ways in which financial markets affected different groups' consciousness of their own remembered pasts, and a description of the social and political dilemmas created by an accelerating sense of time definitively linked to a capitalist economic system.

The memory of the stock exchange: where capitalism reigned, where not only actors, but even the transactions of the moment were crossed by the strange remembering and forgetting of a money economy. Richard Terdiman has argued that "the enigma of the commodity is a memory disorder." Offered up on markets, commodities are objects whose economic values are established in the process of exchange, thus as bids and offers are made the objects are reified, sought for the values they command in transaction alone. Following Marx, the commodity seems enigmatic precisely because it forgets how it was produced, much as "profit," the grand principle of capitalism, forgets its origins in surplus value extracted from human labor. The more a commodity is exchanged, the more it loses its past. The Bourse generated such amnesias for capital itself. In 1900 sociologist Georg Simmel noted in his *Philosophy of Money* that stock exchanges existed simply to enable values "to be rushed through the greatest number of hands in the shortest possible time."[5] The frenetic nature of exchange which characterized the Bourse assured that money itself would be the ultimate forgetting.

The amnesia of the exchange took the shape of political struggles over remembering and forgetting—the polemics between capitalists and Communards. Strikingly, both sides could be said to be committed to programs of "modernity," understood as a commitment to breaking with the past, to acting out an originary moment upon which to build a new society. For the Communards, such a moment had been their seventy-three days to create a workers' paradise; for the capitalist partisans, the reopening of the Bourse and the brave new world of "business." Both sought to exorcise the past in the name of the future. But the Communards needed arms to overthrow the past; the capitalists did it with their "revolution in miniature" everyday of buy and sell. In order for the future to be built, the memory of the past had to be emptied out, absented from the task at hand. The Palace of the Bourse was the ideal theater for such a task. The Bourse was a site where only the latest information mattered, a place of contingency and moment where all was movement. Finance was an eternal clearing away of dead memories—and memories of the dead—in the name of a developing, progressive capitalist future. The work of the joint-stock company for the anti-Communard business historian H. Cozic (1885) was, "in a word," to "present everywhere the image of the rebirth of life on the ruins of the past."[6]

The polemics were strong on both sides. Despite his proclamations against Louis Napoleon's imperial nostalgia, Karl Marx was not opposed to exploiting the politics of memory—if they could be worked to his own advantage. That Marx proposed to substitute revolutionary memory for imperial memory was evident in the closing remarks of his pamphlet on the Commune, *The Civil War in France*, a work he concluded with an exhortation to remember: "Working men's Paris, with its Commune, will be forever celebrated as the glorious harbinger of a new society. Its martyrs are enshrined in the great heart of the working class."[7] Financial historians with similar sympathies linked such commemoration directly to attacks on the exchanges; one Auguste Chirac called struggles over the Bourse a "struggle upon cadavers," and grimly pronounced, "The populace is on its knees before the Bourse."[8]

If such critiques maligned the Napoleonic regime for its attachment to nostalgic symbols and offered up a shrine of martyrs to revolutionaries, French capitalists wrote their own visions of past and present to challenge the radical thinkers. Financial writer Georges Manchez (1897) characterized the transformations of his own time as constituting "the irrefutable proofs of a regime of liberty," remarking that "in this fin de siècle liberty has undeniably taken off. It is everywhere, giving life to all of human activity."[9] No less a visionary than radical thinkers like Marx, Maxime Vuillaume, or Felix Pyat, the liberty he spoke of was nonetheless of a completely different order than that conceived by the inheritors of 1789, 1830, 1848, and 1871. His liberty was not that of the working man, but of the financial markets. The parallelisms in language between financier and agitator are instructive. The rhetoric of the brotherhood of work could be, and was, appropriated by the stock exchange. In February 1893, future French President Felix Fauré addressed the Chamber of Deputies on the happy development of an "international solidarity of markets which will help contain too-sharp or accentuated crises." The "Internationale" of markets was built on the very words of solidarity and the brotherhood of work remapped into the supporting strength of international capital. "Where would we have been, and what would have been the results of the crisis called the 'Crash of 1882' if we hadn't had this grand international market which interlocks the shares one with the others?"[10]

Other writers attacked the revolutionaries directly. For financial partisans like H. Cozic (above), radicals and agitators were demagogic fanatics, unwilling to turn away from a past of hatred and conflict. Attacking Communist polemics and radical agitation, Cozic maintained that the increasing value of stock issues after 1871 had demonstrated "to everyone's eyes that these subversive theories are happily shared only by a small minority of *clubistes* who imagine themselves a great army as they carry their indictments of blood and fire from meeting to meeting." Cozic disdained his opponents as precisely those most enchained by the past, and he openly scorned "the frenzy of those who have nothing in their hearts except to ceaselessly recall the enemies and faults of the past in order to discourage the present."[11]

Cozic's text was a manifesto which played out a historical disengagement with a disagreeable past through the operations of the stock exchange. "Our century has begun a new life of work, production, wealth, and well-being," he noted, "whose expanding operations often have the Bourse as the motor." The Bourse for Cozic was an engine of modernity, the generator of a new history. The stock exchange promised a new order established beyond politics, an order of the end of history. If political and ideological struggles were burdensome, it was because they were things of the past. "The capitalists who sold at Austerlitz and bought at Waterloo were not attempting the least act of political animosity. They were concerned purely and simply about their savings and looking after their interests." On the financial markets, Cozic pushed history outside of moral struggle or national interest. His historical memory was not the commemorative grandeur of the cannons of Austerlitz, but the values sold and repurchased at Waterloo, not an event, but an "opportunity."

Events were a screen, a backdrop in front of which the real "business" of the world now went on. French speculators could not be expected to ally their interests in simplistic, patriotic ways by celebrating great military victories or defeats; their interests were not with nations, but with markets. "If the return fell at Austerlitz, it's because Austerlitz represented the continuation of the battle of the Empire against Europe, and consequently the continuation of war. On the other hand, if the return gained at Waterloo, it's because Waterloo represented the return of peace and the possibility to getting back to business." [12]

While radicals like Marx and stock investors denounced each other over the political-economic meanings of the recent past, the financial markets were also producing other memory shocks which must be attended to understand "modernity": shocks which resounded in the cities, in global trading networks, and in that most unlikely of places—the provinces. The Bourse was deeply implicated in the rural world, and the late nineteenth century was a profitable investing age for those who could afford it. As prices fell through the 1880s and mid-'90s, securities doubled or tripled in value. Property holders could expect about a 3 percent return on their landed investments, while stocks and bonds rose 12 percent between 1881 and 1895. Many land holders, notes historian Gabriel Desert, "sold out their already debt-burdened property, and put the cash they received on the Bourse."[13]

Yet what profited some distressed others. Conservative Catholic sociological journals like Frédéric Le Play's *La Réforme sociale* agonized over a vanished era when "the speculation at the Bourse was not in usage," not because of the anguish of brokers and speculators, but because the monetization of the French countryside allowed by credit and financial instruments threw all property into "the same vertiginous movement" of exchange and land speculation, disrupting traditional lines of inheritance.[14] Contributors to the journal condemned the circulation of money and titles as creating parallel movements of populations in the countryside, the "dispersion of persons, their affluence towards the cities," movements which depopulated villages and workshops.

"The distant era of the regional economy" became the subject of studies on rural worker cooperatives like that of researcher Jean Perruche de Vecna (1910), which portrayed melancholy small craftsmen dreaming up programs to "bring back to life the social forms of that era of peace, that blessed past time." De Vecna painted a sad, luminous portrait of the "former petit atelier where a few *compagnons* joyously went about their business to the refrain of an old bantering song." The workshop his subjects claimed to remember in their testimonies was a place of contentment, full of gay faces and diligence, where regular rhythms of work were interrupted only to joke with one's fellows or, naturally, "to have a glass of red wine."[15]

How to interpret and understand this ideal, backward-looking melancholy was a question which fascinated an occasional contributor to *La Réforme sociale*, Dr Raoul de la Grasserie. In 1911 he published a study, *De la nostalgie*, in which he attempted to capture the shifting and unsettled relationship between different experiences of time, memory—and money. De la Grasserie defined "nostalgia" in terms of space, as "the painful passion to return," and an "instinct of direction," not unlike that which motivated birds and other migratory animals. Like "pigeons and cats," human beings were constantly infused with "memory . . . the reappearance of the past" which acted as a sort of gravitation, a relentless pulling back of any body moving away from its point of origin. Unlike the migratory instincts of animals however, the nostalgic attraction of human beings was produced by social and economic upheavals, and conflicts between different schemes of historical time.

Nostalgia was most profound precisely in the man who "sees the future closed before him, of progress made for others, but not for his own class." Nostalgia characterized particularly the uprooted of society, those who had "no place even in the present." Notably, this unsettled present was characterized by movement and money, a world defined by a relentless "frenzy of locomotion," pushing forward a new race impatient of the past: "they march straight ahead, amassing fortunes, accumulating ruins to achieve their goal of incessant progress." To "the fallen Adam" these true believers posed "the progressive ape," looking to the day when sooner or later they would see arise "the superman of Nietzsche." These were beings whose sense of history was but "the instant, the day itself . . . the financial report, the course of an operation"; their kingdom lay not in the traditions of the countryside, but in "the trusts from the New World." [16]

De la Grasserie was alternately impressed and horrified by his own observations. Portraits such as his described a turn of the century in which commentators on work, law, and finance struggled to understand a world transformed by capital, and tried to valorize and protect it by counter-posing the promises of economic progress to the idea of a cultural heri-tage, an ideal of a glorified past greater than progress. Speaking of the cherished rural family holding, *La Réforme sociale* warned of the upheav-als of the century which carried along and threatened to break apart three inseparable units: "people, patrimony, and properties." More than money and family members were on the move in a dislocated France: "patri-mony, that shadow of the individual, has followed the same road, it has become prey to a mobility which contrasts with its former immobility."[17]

What did *La Réforme sociale* mean by "patrimony"? The term had both a broad metaphorical and a strict juridical sense at the turn of the century, both tied to the notion of historical memory. As a generalized concept, some medical professionals used it to talk about the human mind, and the acquisition of intelligence and experience. Interestingly and importantly, two psychologists, Drs. Joffroy and Dupoy, spoke about the "patrimony" of the mind in an utterly financial metaphor, reflecting on "our psychic capital," for which "a first deposit of funds is provided by our predecessors." This patrimony they suggested was then transmit-ted across generations by family members, gradually accumulating sen-sations and enriching itself to provide a wealth of "emotional and affective states in the memory."[18]

"Patrimony" as a heritage or legacy was a logical concept by which to talk about the complex relations between family, finance, and the pres-ervation of the past. The legal notion of "patrimony" was indissociable from that of "property," and under Roman law had been initially a title of transmission of goods from a father to his inheritors. Yet, as legal scholar Georges Plastra put it in a thesis of 1903, patrimony was a notion which historically came to be defined "with the development of civili-zation and especially one of its principal elements, commerce." In this way, patrimony was also recognized as a legal counterpart to "the eco-nomic notion of credit." Juridically, patrimony was a complex ensemble of goods, credits, and debts. This "continuation of the person" after death thus involved not only the transmission of goods to the inheritors, but also debts, a linking of responsibility across the generations. More-over, as Plastra noted, "patrimony is . . . a general universality, susceptible to being divided into many other smaller universalities." The notion of patrimony was at once general and particular, and the personality of an individual could be "completely absorbed by the family personality."[19] Juridically then, commentators on "patrimony" unavoidably evoked a generalized legacy from the individual transmission of properties, and the debts and responsibilities which each generation assumed from and bore for the last.

In the countryside, the property of smallholders was legally consoli-dated to this double notion of "patrimony." The concept rested upon both the financial basis of property and credit, as well as the idea of the obligations the present bore for the past in the name of the future. In

1897, legislators agonized, "if there is in our time a tendency which everyone agrees should be deplored, it is certainly the depopulation of the countryside." In putting forward a law of 1910, legislator Alfred Comat proposed the establishment of an agricultural savings bank to offer loans to failing farmers. More, he proposed a special legal status for the smallholders, establishing in effect that "the property of the *agricultural petit patrimoine* so constituted to be declared inalienable." In his discourse, defending the *petit patrimoine* was much more than delivering financial support to insolvent farmers. His project reminded the legislators that preserving "the countryside" and "the rural population" was part of the glory of France, the sources of strength for "the army, for colonization, mines, agriculture, all the great motors of national movement."[20]

Comat's project notably conceived of the "patrimony" of the countryside not simply as the symbol of a cultural heritage, but as a defining feature of a nation—more specifically as a "motor of national movement." In this he differed markedly from *La Réforme sociale*'s fear of finance. Patrimony in Comat's sense defended not only an image of tradition to be preserved and commemorated, but a past which contained an active potential for production, industry, and expansion. Patrimony as a "motor" of national movement tied to colonization, industry, and agriculture was an idea of a grand tradition and heritage projected on an active present preparing the future, a sense of history—not surprisingly—shared by operators on the financial markets. Business historian H. Cozic (above, contra Marx) echoed Comat's dynamic patrimony by identifying the French nation as the sum of its productive economic activities, a nation whose debt to the past and obligation to the future would be realized "when she applies herself to bringing fertility to her commerce and colonies, to multiplying her mines, forges, and factories, to circulating everywhere economic transports, credit, and capital."[21]

This was the project of financial partisans: to reconcile the profound tradition of the smallholder and the ambitions of the capitalists. Preserving the patrimony of the small workshops and the small farms did not contradict a desire to expand the influence of capital markets, according to promoters of the Bourse; some even suggested that stock and bond investments were, in effect, a way of preserving the honor of the traditional *petits patrons* in the face of a new, ruthless phenomenon in France at the beginning of the twentieth century: big business. As one financial writer, L. Page, observed, "more and more the *petits patrons* are disappearing and becoming simple wage laborers . . . more and more we are moving towards the 'trust' and disguised monopolies." Big business was destroying the small concerns, and Page warned, "the difficulties and necessities for life will only increase." Yet, as it destroyed, big business now offered up an opportunity—investment. Page argued that becoming rich in business or industry would become impossible for even the most gifted entrepreneurs, and he regretted that "many have lost their money when only a part judiciously placed on the stock exchange could have assured them of a good capital investment productive by itself."[22]

In an age of Republican ceremonies, commemorations, and pedagogies self-consciously seeking to link individuals and regions into a national historical identity, market-makers were already describing their own financial histories in which the "small universalities" of individual patrimonies were transformed into the grand patrimony of the nation—or on a more grandiose scale, that of humanity. "Without the Bourse, where would the railways be? Where would be found those grand and magnificent works from which we have so greatly profited?" demanded the market writer Condette, "where would be the exploitation of mines? Where would be the Suez canal be?"[23] Railway projects were often selected as emblematic of the creative power of the joint-stock companies, associations which transformed anonymous savings into the iron, steam, and speed of modern industry and commerce. One clerical defender of finance, the Abbé Deville, cited the example of one railway plan requiring five hundred million francs: "there is no capitalist capable of furnishing such a sum. So, what happens? A company is formed." Far from an exploitative or parasitic enterprise, "this common action, in effect, is the result of a million individual efforts, a million particular shares."[24] For the Abbé, an industrial or commercial project was nothing less than the solidarity of contribution realized into the common work of progress benefiting all. The financial markets were their own heritage of the people's labor, the work of millions transformed into one. Where patrimony was investment, money was the incarnation of national memory.

Such prescriptions did not go uncontested; the very notion of capital "productive by itself" was a call to arms for social reformers and revolutionaries who saw money gained without toil as disguised expropriation and fundamentally immoral. In polemics against the stock exchange, editorialists, pamphleteers, and satirical papers like *Le Père Duchêne* railed against the injustice of an institution where "a day of speculation brings in more than a lifetime of work and savings," and "ten million workers save their money, ten million speculators seize it and lose it."[25] In response, financiers made a fundamental case—the Bourse was neither gambling nor usury—it was work, and nobody could argue against that. To speculate intelligently was a skill demanding exhaustive study and effort.

Support for such views from a Christian perspective came in tracts such as the Abbé Deville's *Les Opérations de bourse devant la conscience* (1884) which judged that stock speculation could indeed be justified as legitimate and difficult work, as it required of the "man at the Bourse" an immense range of competences: "politics, laws of social economy, the poor or prosperous condition of a country, the development of industrial or agricultural wealth, supply and demand." For the Abbé, making money with money was neither avarice nor usury; on the exchanges speculation was the divination of time itself. "What is trade, industry, progress? It is Man dominating materials and rendering them useful by his work. What is the Bourse? It is Man trying to read and dominate the future."[26]

Yet what was the future? The "paper wealth" of the stock and bond markets was not like that of other investments. Stock-investment guides addressed to "the father of the family" offered sober advice about the real meaning of "security" in a securitized world, "a portfolio, excellent today and carefully locked up in a safe, can decrease in value . . . to the point of changing good papers into simple scraps."[27] How was the "father of the family," the patriarchal locus of generation-memory, to transmit his heritage to the great movement of a common patrimony while not also bequeathing personal ruin to the good name of his children? Patrimony, after all, was a legal ensemble of debts as well as credits. For the careful investor, the answer lay in appreciating the industry of the modern world, but placing one's money in the old. Stock adviser Alexandre Assier drew up a list of shares which "no prudent capitalist would ever have in his portfolio," a list which notably read like a roll-call of "the future," the technical and communications developments of the nineteenth century: "titles of coal production," "lighting and gas heating," metallurgy, spinning, railways, credit companies, newspapers.[28] Everything speculative or risky was fuel, metal, transport, credit, information, all the vaunted engines of progress and economic development. Where to place one's money then? Assier counseled sane investment in titles to real estate, or the debt of the city of Paris.

Perhaps investments in property and public works seemed more solid and secure than industrial or commercial ventures. They were perhaps more secure, but certainly not more solid—in the urban centers they were money spent for change. In 1893 *L'Illustration Universelle* presented its readers with an incomplete city plan of Paris and a reminder that the great projects of urban transformation wrought by Baron Haussmann under the Emperor Napoleon III were "far from over." The city would soon be floating another issue of public debt to continue financing Haussmann's most striking contribution to the Paris landscape: the boulevards. The issues traded at the Bourse were the tools to allow the continued and controversial works of "that intrepid demolisher."[29]

Financial markets did more than make and lose money: they altered time, space—and memory. "Haussmann's pickaxe has profoundly disturbed old habits," remarked one writer, pointing out the simple truth that a shaken sense of the past was not limited to provincial laborers reminiscing over their workshops.[30] Haussmann's grand scheme was a prolific generator of urban nostalgias—acerbic, in the Parisian style. Playwright Victorien Sardou lamented in one piece: "Dear child! It is the old Paris that is lost, the real Paris! A city which was narrow, unhealthy, insufficient, but picturesque, varied, charming, full of memories." Now,

lamented Sardou, there was "nothing left of the things which once constituted our own little world."[31] Capital was already creating new landscapes for memories, by dictating and circumscribing the size of the
hotels and width of the roadways, by fixing rents which forced the poor
out of the city center, by opening up commercial spaces to the businesses,
trading companies, services, and entertainments which attracted the public. The elements linked together by *L'Illustration* described a city transformed into the image of the Bourse, Paris as an urban landscape moving
to the rhythm of capital markets. The boulevards were more than lanes
of traffic and transport; they made possible the very materialization of
movement. In notes on *La vie des boulevards* (1896), writer Georges
Montrogueil reminisced about his former traditional walk on the old
Champs-Elysees, "the promenade without haste, without the rush." The
new boulevard was quite something else, a great "river of business" and
battle of interests, where "everything rolls uninterrupted in an intense
coming and going to gain some victory."

The façades which lined the boulevards were the visual expressions
of this relentless activity and its logic: the movement of money. Commerce was quitting "the gentlemanly hotels of the Marias," Montorgueil
noted, to establish new lodgings on the boulevards around the rue
d'Hauteville. There, behind coats of arms indicating not heraldry, but
brand names, business exchanges took place at a devouring pace, companies like The Universe buying up "everything which is sold, quick in
business, having the prompt once-over and the easy letter of credit." For
Montorgueil, the agitated, intense commercial activity made even his own
youth seem immeasurably far away. The elegant "exclusively Parisian"
promenade was a distant recollection of a world before the "revolution
presided over by beer" which had opened up the boulevards, taverns,
and shops with their rapid turnovers of merchandise. The next generation
of walkers, wanderers, buyers, and sellers in turn already belonged to a
new century which would "open onto a boulevard which our fathers have
never known."[32]

Consuming memories: with displays of fashions soon replaced behind
plate-glass windows and stocks of housewares changing hands across
counters, the typical boutique of Montorgueil's boulevard was "a kalei-
doscope of activity," an arena where buying and selling was marked by
"the feverishness of businesspeople, the perpetual coming and going of
strangers." New deliveries, new fashions and styles, new merchandise en-
sured a constant distancing of the immediate past in anticipation of the
new, a drama of telescoped time which the customer experienced as a
drama of changing objects, a spectacle from which the viewer reeled in
"a constant state of astonishment."[33]

Such shop windows told truths about the genealogies of modernity.
"In the window displays of beauty salons are the last women with long
hair. They have rich, undulating hair masses with a 'permanent wave'—

fossilized hair curls." Thus wrote Walter Benjamin, piecing together an archaeology of the Paris arcades, iron and glass galleries of specialty shops fated to commercial failure in the late nineteenth century by the rise of those spectacular merchants of mass-production material dreams: the Paris department stores. Such an extinction of early consumer merchandisers was part of the "natural history" of capitalism which Karl Marx had outlined in declaring the competition of industrial society the "prehistory" of communism. Capitalism, for all its productive energies, was after all still only a system of cycles, part of an evolutionary scheme in which fully "human" history had yet to appear. In the ruins of the arcades, in the abandoned display windows bearing outdated fashions and unsold objects, Benjamin found the fossils of earlier forms of bourgeois society, each artifact a trace of those early nineteenth-century creatures from "the pre-imperial epoch of capitalism," whom he called "the last dinosaurs of Europe."[34]

Benjamin's allegorical analyses attempted to get at the traces of primeval epochs which he believed still lay in the ruins of earlier commercial strata, species of merchants and buyers destroyed by the evolving natural history of capitalism. In his arcades and shop windows what once were goods were now petrified memories of another age. At the heart of French capitalism itself, the Corinthian temple on Rue Vivienne, the "memory of the stock exchange" was also a drama in which forgotten ages lingered to haunt the present.

The inaccessible Palace of the Bourse was a temple of time, a site where submerged epochs and mysteries surfaced again as ancient mysteries and rites. One essayist, Georges d'Avenel, described the edifice as an "idol—sumptuous and excessive," dedicated to "the glory of the cult celebrated there." What went on inside, according to d'Avenel, sounded like an exertion of heavenly powers between the columns of an earthly Olympus. "The legend would have it that in the heaven of the Bourse there exist mysterious gods, 'masters' of the market, saying one word: 'let there be a fall!' and the quotations crumble, or 'let the recovery begin!' and the market slowly rises."[35]

Journeying inside, writer Gabriel Mourey (1899) also read this institution of modern finance as a site of ancient mystery and revelation. The brokers and speculators he found to be keepers of a sanctuary, a divine throne, "sacred priests surrounded by glory, wealth, and pride; nothing would dare challenge their sacred sovereignty." Yet, apart from this singular image, he did not find them to be serene, imperious beings. The "memory" of the Bourse lay in its rites and daily rituals, and these were practices which could be described only as survivals of a pagan religion, "as savage, as bloody, as mysterious as the most barbaric cults, with its own strange rites, special language, sacrifices, categories of initiates, and college of priests."

The Bourse was a temple of atavistic savagery which guarded within its walls the primal ordeals of the marketplace. The new age of business was a hallucinatory vision of the trading floor as an agitated crowd in which the repercussions of the world markets, the fluctuations of the quotations, the relentless tensions of the exchange were all impressed deeply and physically on the traders who went "running in every direction with nervous gestures and somersaults of worry, anguish tightening their lips." Thousands, millions of francs were offered, exchanged, promised for a railway, an ironworks, a package of debt issues.

As Mourey watched, the trading activity on the parquet degenerated as it intensified, and the traders began to recapitulate in their very business the heritage of primitive ancestors. The rites of capitalism were played out in a "sinister atmosphere . . . heavy, charged with animalities, dry and brutal, extravagantly violent." Bodies collided. Faces reverted. The collectors at the Ecole d'Anthropologie or the Musée d'Ethnographie would have found interesting specimens of a living past on the floor of the exchange: "study these physiognomies: grimaces deform them all; there is a return to primitive animality. Masked features depress them, foreheads are crushed."[36] The combats of the Bourse recalled to Mourey the atavistic savagery which lay at the heart of capitalism, phylogenetic memories of a primitive "triumph of force" revived by the frenetic rituals of exchange and competition. The victors of this day counted their margins.

The Palace of the Bourse was a site which not only collapsed time, but also reimagined space. To treat the temple at Rue Vivienne as a *lieu de mémoire* is to try to understand not only *mémoire*, but also *lieu*—the place-ness of memory. Yet the Bourse was a center of absence, existing only to concentrate the wealth which was everywhere else. The financial heart of Paris, like the Louis Napoleon of Marx's *18th Brumaire*, was everything and nothing, an imposing structure housing no merchandise, goods, or treasures: an edifice of emptiness. Mused one financial writer, Condette (1884), "Commerce requires an appropriate locale to receive merchandise. At the Bourse there is an establishment, what can I say—a palace for nothing." Behind its pillared façade, what the Bourse defined above all was capitalist space, a site for a market which was not there. "The Bourse is, par excellence, the temple of transactions," observed Condette, "a vast and altogether special house of trade. One buys without taking delivery, one sells what one does not have."[37]

As a memory site, the Bourse was not like other locales, for the meanings of its rituals were not played out within its walls. As brokers engaged in savage combat, the author of a series of wicked observations on the financial markets, Emile André, noted, "This sort of struggle between Horaces and Curiaces is obsolete." In his mordantly funny *The Art of Not Being Robbed, Swindled, Cheated, etc.*, André supposed his readers might find peculiar the Bourse phenomenon in which "everyone buys and sells at the same time . . . and finally nobody wins! Can it be that so much money is lost by everyone?" André articulated what was perhaps the most striking characteristic of clashes at the Bourse: for all the immediate drama of the trading floor, it was important not to naively "believe one's eyes," for the challenge of outmaneuvering the best at the Bourse was not in vanquishing the warriors at Rue Vivienne at all; "the bottom line is at New York," among "the grand producers, the Yankee financial powerhouses."[38]

The financial world of the Bourse rewrote the meanings of space under capitalism; the market was everywhere, thus nowhere in particular. Writer Georges d'Avenel gave it a nod as one of the "mechanisms of modern life" (1905), characterizing the financial institutions of the early twentieth century by their "cosmopolitanism, the repercussions of the markets one upon the others. There are international funds like there are international trains." With a certain respect and astonishment d'Avenel commented on the shares of a copper company "unlisted in Paris whose headquarters is in America," which comes under attack on the New York stock exchange. "Immediately, the Rio-Tinto, a copper mine unlisted in New York whose headquarters is in Spain drops 100 francs in Paris."[39]

The breathless activity of global financial competition evokes a characterization made by the historian Pierre Nora of a modern era self-defined as torn from its past by an "acceleration of history." Such an "acceleration of history" could find no better expression than in the hourly activities at the palace on the Rue Vivienne, where all past disappeared into the present of immediate events, a phenomenon of "extreme acceleration . . . a commotion and compression," according to Georg Simmel, who in 1900 detailed his commentaries on financial markets by remarking on "the swiftness with which every factor affecting the situation is grasped and forgotten again."[40]

What Simmel called the "factors" driving the markets were none other than events, coming to the traders as rumors or pieces of news, each rapidly succeeding the next. The events which composed this forgetful accelerated history were not especially "economic" news centered on earnings reports or share prices. Noted financial journalist Lucien Revon, "The greatest source for the news agencies is political tension." At the fleeting heart of the financial markets were the most traditional of historical subjects: machinations of kings and kaisers, diplomatic dispatches, palace intrigues. "Assurances of peace, of threats of war; the appointment of a minister inspiring confidence, or his fall; such and such an alliance, the death of the head of state, or any other political event, happy or otherwise." At the Bourse, wars and rumors of wars agitated the traded values, and every piece of information seemed critical. At the Bourse the traders watched anxiously, wondering which events would return the world to "the fateful days of the Spanish-American War or the Russo-Japanese War."[41] At the Bourse, history was the history of the present, to be watched, anguished over, bought, and sold.

In 1892 social psychologist Gabriel Tarde watched with unquiet fascination the rise of a double phenomenon. On the one hand the financial partnerships with their "enormous development of liquid wealth," and on the other hand, "the prodigious increase in the consumption of newspapers."[42] In a sense, history at the Bourse was history without memory: events with no past, judged, traded, quickly forgotten. Yet the Bourse was equally memory without history: in daily speculation, the events which traced out the markets did not constitute historical narratives; each event drove the markets up or down, then was overtaken by another. Such moments were recorded in a medium which accepted a vision of the world as made and remade everyday. That medium, which rose to prominence in the late nineteenth century, was news—registered and imprinted as the daily popular press.

The rise of the popular press in the later nineteenth century is distinctly implicated in the "modern memory" which I have been describing. Questions of rural patrimony and depopulation, global information, and volatile financial markets are all linked together by a complex and essential phenonenon which defines so much of fin-de-siècle memory practice: the democratization of print culture. The nostalgia for abandoned villages and rural workshops which I sketched out earlier was not only an event linked to economic transformations, but an historical rupture between different kinds of remembrance—oral versus written, living tradition as opposed to externally recorded information, the latter mechanically generated and proliferated. A print culture organizes mnemonic skills not around oral transmissions, but around literacy, technology, and money.

Eugen Weber has noted that well into the 1880s ancient village or town gatherings (*les veillés*) continued to serve as institutions for passing on traditional wisdom in the French countryside. Talk, which accompanied communal spinning, laundering, cooking, and dancing, was "full of allusions to the past," tales of the Revolution, of legends and proverbs handed down by word of mouth and personal memories and recitation. In these last decades of the century, Weber also notes, however, that "the old tales were being replaced by stories from the schoolbooks," and cites a teacher's complaint against the villagers' old ways: "Instead of gadding about to *veillés* uttering cries that make one doubt whether they are men or wild beasts, they could go and read a book."[43]

The replacement of storytellers by printed texts marks a transformation which belongs to more than the history of civilizing rude peasants and spreading basic literacy during the Third Republic. A people increasingly schooled by the public education of the Ferry laws to read for information becomes a people whose memories and traditions are framed by the historical peculiarities of a typographic culture. The printed page addresses the eye, not the ear, and knowledge transmitted by print can be registered by individuals rather than recounted in communal settings. As narratives are fixed and transmitted in type, they are disassociated from speakers, gestures, and voice; memories lose their personal qualities, taking on a sort of authorless authority on the printed page. In transmitting information texts seem to speak for themselves in fragments; memory is "externalized."

Ink and paper become the representative medium for the memory of a typographic culture—one which reads and writes events and registers them in texts. By the late nineteenth century that medium, driven by the linotype and machine printing, made possible the reproduction and super proliferation of this printed memory in the form of cheap newspapers, the storytellers of a modern age. Freed by new press laws after 1881, papers like *Le Petit Journal* and *Le Petit Parisien* could each claim circulations of a million copies by the end of the century. My point is that though both reading and print have long histories, the commercial, mechanical, typographic memory of the late nineteenth century could be genuinely considered the first memory accelerated.[44]

The printed record contributed to the volatility of information as much by making news as by recording and reporting it. *Les Annales de la bourse,* January 15, 1893, commented, "The Bourse, in effect, moves according to news stories received from the daily newspapers—or rather, twice-daily papers, since we have the morning news to influence the official Bourse, and the afternoon news to disorient the *Petite Bourse* in the evenings." Moments and impressions rather than grand narratives composed the political record which was instantaneously translated into the movement of money. News, politics, and finance became registrations of each other, and as *Les Annales* put it, the rapidity of information operated in such a way that "the incoherence which reigns in the parliamentary and governmental spheres ends up by reaching the trading floor."[45] Successive events and crises were marked up and down at the Bourse. Noted Lucien Revon, "It is so much the barometer of prosperity and politics that every event which the country finds in some way interesting finds its expression in the level of the market."[46]

As the Bourse quoted values, so Gabriel Tarde noted, "la presse" quoted reputations. If the Bourse provided the mechanism for the instant valuation of companies, the press replicated this practice in the political sphere. With a wary eye, Tarde called the press "that steam engine for the fabrication and destruction of renown on a grand scale," and noted "one pen suffices to set a million tongues wagging."[47] In the background of Tarde's work politicians rose and fell like quoted values on storms of approval and disapproval, matching or motivating the uncertainties of the markets. "Foolish is the man who would dare give an opinion about what the Bourse will do this evening or tomorrow morning," advised one journalist, "in these disorderly times when the most solid ministers are dropped . . . in the wink of an eye."[48]

While brokers and agents read charts and quotations for the movements of money, Tarde recognized that the Bourse might be a model for

— 41 —

Plus hauts et plus bas cours

	1903	1904	1905	1906	1907
	pl.haut pl.bas	pl.haut pl.bas	pl.haut pl.bas	pl.haut pl.bas	pl.haut pl.bas
Emp. 4% 1865 .	572 » 545 »	562 » 544 »	565 » 548 »	564 » 526 »	544 » 520 »
Emp. 3% 1869 .	464 » 433 »	465 » 429 »	495 » 450 »	476 » 441 »	524 » 447 »
Emp. 3% 1871 .	416 » 405 »	415 » 402 »	414 » 404 »	414 » 394 »	410 » 399 »
Emp. 3%quarts	110 » 105 »	108 » 104 »	109 » 104.50	108.50 103 »	108 » 102 »
Emp. 4% 1875 .	580 » 555 »	575 » 547 »	579 » 561 »	583 » 525 »	548 » 522 »
Emp. 4% 1876 .	578 » 555 »	570 » 548 »	580 » 560 »	583 » 525 »	546 » 522 »
Emp. 2½% 1892	390 » 371 »	386 » 368 »	394 » 377 »	395 » 370 »	379 » 357 »
Emp. 2¼ quarts	101 » 97 »	101 » 97.50	104 » 97.50	101.25 97 »	101 » 95.50
2½% 1894-96 .	390 » 372 »	383 » 368 »	396 » 376 »	395 » 370 »	383 » 356 »
2½% quarts ...	102 » 96.25	100 » 96.50	97 » 100.50	96 » 98.50 93.75
Emp. 2% 1898 .	424 » 406 »	424 » 410 »	450 » 417 »	449 » 439 »	435 » 412 »
Emp. 2%quarts	106 » 102 »	108.75 103.75	113 » 106.50	117 » 106 »	110.50 104.75
Emp. 2% 1899 .	410 » 396 »	412 » 398 »	435 » 409 »	440 » 408 »	420 » 397 »
Emp. 2%quarts	103 » 98 »	» »	107.75 102 »	112 » 103 »	108 » 102 »
Emp. 2½%1904	» »	454 » 437 »	441 » 425 »	440 » 423 »	433 » 416 »
Emp. 2½%cinq.	» »	100 » 88.75	90 » 85 »	88 » 84.25	87.50 83.75
2 3/4% 1905...	» »	» »	380 » 370 »	385 » 375 »	440 » 418 »
2 3/4 % quarts.	» »	» »	95 » 89.50	93.50 90 »	88 » 84 »

Année 1908

	Janv.	Fév.	Mars	Avril
	pl.haut pl.bas	pl.haut pl.bas	pl.haut pl.bas	pl.haut pl.bas
Emp. 4% 1865 .	543.50 532.25	539.75 531 »	538 » 532 »	540 » 532 »
Emp. 3% 1869 .	525 » 480 »	527 » 511.75	530 » 521.50	530 » 480 »
Emp. 3% 1871 .	405.50 498 »	404.75 402 »	406 » 403 »	408 » 403 »
Emp. 3%quarts	107 » 104 »	106 » 105 »	108 » 105 »	107 » 104 »
Emp. 4% 1875 .	540 » 531 »	543 » 538 »	550 » 541.75	546 » 534.50
Emp. 4% 1876 .	540 » 530.25	542.75 537 »	547 » 540.25	545.50 533 »
Emp.2½% 1892	364 » 360.25	368 » 362.50	372 » 366 »	376.75 369 »
Emp.2½%quart	100.50 95 »	100 » 97.25	100 » 98 »	102 » 99.25
2½% 1894-96 .	365 » 359.50	369 » 363 »	370 » 366 »	376 » 368 »
2 ½% quarts .	98 » 95 »	99 » 96.50	99.50 97.50	99 » 98 »
Emp. 2% 1898 .	420 » 416 »	428 » 420 »	426 » 415 »	420 » 418.50
Emp. 2%quarts	111 » 105 »	112 » 110 »	111.50 109 »	110 » 108.50
Emp. 2% 1899 .	408 » 403 »	412 » 409 »	411.25 402.50	405 » 403 »
Emp. 2%quarts	106 » 104.50	107 » 105 »	107 » 105 »	105.75 104 »
Emp. 2½%1904	433 » 420 »	435 » 432 »	438 » 433 »	438 » 432 »
Emp. 2½%cinq.	88 » 86.75	89.25 88 »	89 » 88 »	89 » 87.50
2 3/4% 1905..	389 » 382 »	390 » 385 »	390 » 382 »	396 » 387.50
2 3/4% quarts	94 » 91.50	94 » 93.50	93.50 92 »	94 » 93 »

Figure 6 The memory of the stock-exchange: quotations from *Les Annales de la Bourse*, 1909. (*Source:* Bibliothèque Nationale)

creating tools to read the "mood" or temper of a time. As Tarde saw it, the rising quotation of an industrial stock or bond at the Bourse signified that "the number of those who believe in the success of the enterprise has become larger, or that those who already believed it believe it even more firmly, or that the number of believers and the strength of the belief have both increased at the same time."[49] By 1901 Tarde was writing about finance as well as the complex preferences and voting lines which crossed French politics, and beginning to conceive the analysis of what could have been the first efforts to quantify a sort of "collective memory," a numerical record of what people knew or believed at particular points in time. He called it "public opinion."

To take such stories as records of "collective memory" does require some caution. Historical records traditionally contain and are studied for the material they indicate about the reliability of the past. The stock records equally contained something else: reactions to every rumor, misinformation, speculation, or mistake. Because the Bourse always reacted, it recorded the swings of every major political event, but equally events which were anticipated or feared, but never took place. One financial writer, Rallovich, noted in 1891 that "the quotations of the Bourse are the numbered language of events as well as a sort of prediction, an anticipation of the future."[50]

Closely watched were the links between the signing of treaties and the physical health of statesmen. Connections between documents of alliance and respiratory or organ troubles (of special interest to medical historians) were closely observed by the market makers. So inseparable were the two that Emile André noted the inversion of cause and effect in the ritual language of the traders. Bourse traders and agents commonly spoke in formulas, remarking, "It's signed" upon noticing a sudden and inexplicable rise in the markets. An equally inexplicable drop in the markets was cause for the traders to murmur one to another, "He's dead."[51] Or consider again a random stock report of March 20, 1885, concerning news of combat in Afghanistan. "The political horizon becomes somber and the Bourse expresses its apprehensions by quickly pulling back, losing in a few days all the ground gained over the course of almost a year."[52] Under the heading of "False Alarms," another newspaper described a severe market plunge in 1887 in which "the fall was so rapid that financial houses were ruined in a few days." For what reason? "Bismarck had his subsidized newspapers publish the most alarming news stories." In the ensuing panic, "the German banks sold everything," a debacle and crash for financial institutions all across Europe.

French investors had much to be concerned about: fifteen billion francs abroad in 1870 rose to forty-five billion by 1914. Two-thirds of that total was placed in Europe and the Mediterranean, of which one-fourth in Russia. I spoke earlier of memory and Communards, of selling at Austerlitz and buying at Waterloo, of a world of financial self-interest beyond politics. The political past haunted this dream. In 1887 investment broker and adviser Alexandre Assier published words on international investment echoing bitter memories of the Franco-Prussian war. "It is with our money that Russia has the Saint Petersburg-Varsovie railway, Austria that of the Saxony to the Danube and that of Vienna to Bavaria." He also cited cases which applied to "Italy, the Romans, the Lombards, and the southern regions of Spain." Yet, he recalled darkly, "on all of these lines built with our money—often poorly compensated—how many men came to our aid in 1870?"[53]

Assier fumed over the emptiness of the obligations entrained, and in doing so stated a truth: in an increasingly international financial market-place, money generated nostalgia, but had no memory. As finanical writer M. Ploque put it, "from the moment that the money is accepted [on the market], no matter what its origin the capital acquires the predominant role—the individual doesn't count any more."[54] Money had only one quality: its quantity. This meant, according to Ploque, that even decisions of politicians and company directors were constrained by the sheer weight of numbers; their power "is replaced by the world of the shareholders, the true holders of capital, which constitute the aristocracy of contemporary society."[55]

The Bourse was a strange place, a temple of time without a sense of history, memory, or priority of events. Alexandre Assier, watching the traders with contempt, perhaps concern: "You believe perhaps that these men are concerned about these values, about what they buy and sell? You are wrong; they buy and sell with no worries at all, French securities or Turkish securities, French railways and Spanish railways." Capitalists had created an extraordinary non-lieu, a site which registered profound political and economic shocks, yet one "where they speak to you about the most serious matters, the dissolution of the government or the resignation of the President of the Republic, as if they were the simplest things in the world."[56]

The agent worked, in Assier's words, in a world "without any reflection," executing the orders of clients or superiors, "like a soldier executing his duty." Assier's military parallel finally was quite deliberate. The global financial market economy was a state of war, of strategy, rapid movements, execution, interrupted crises. The records of the Bourse show Austerlitz, Waterloo, and Sedan becoming the accelerated buying and selling of Central European tensions in the early twentieth century. Emile André related the telegrams which drove the markets: "The morning dispatches tell us one after the other of the Turks and the Bulgars ready to tear each other apart, of Serbia and Austria not arriving at any agreement." History was being made, an accelerated history of the present, bought and sold around the world. The Balkans were exploding. Perhaps it all meant something, but perhaps it did not. The speculators had only moments to judge. "All of Europe could be drawn into the conflict," mused André, "and some days the Bourse follows a most disquieting trend."[57]

Figure 7 The power of the image: early nineteenth-century mnemonic pictures, from *Traité complet de mnémonique*. (*Source:* Institut National de Recherche Pedagogique)

3

Words: The Grammar of History

From the world of accelerated numbers in the last chapter, I turn to the universe of words. My discussion takes me momentarily back to the events at the Place Vendôme in search of what I shall soon problematically call an "image" of memory. With the destruction of the Vendôme Column, a notable disagreement took place between two of the radical papers the next day. *La Commune* floridly endorsed the action, condemning "this monument which, in a word, was raised with nothing but French cadavers." This in itself was predictable, yet the report continued with a commentary on a suggestion by *Le Mot d'ordre* that *L'Histoire du consulat et de l'empire* by Adolphe Thiers should be taken to the debris and burned at the base of the column. The burning of the highly regarded history of the Napoleonic regimes by the chief of the Versailles government would have seemed perfectly justified—after all, the Communards had no problem about razing Thiers' home in Paris.

Nonethelesss, *La Commune* replied this way: "Giordano Bruno and Vanini were burned, Voltaire and Rousseau were burned; the hand of the executioner has sullied all the books of the future in the past. In burning *L'Histoire du consulat et de l'empire,* you do it honor by fearing that it might also be a work of the future. Your persecution, by analogy, is a tribute."[1] Why destroy the Napoleonic monument and not the Napoleonic book? Why does the "history" belong to the heritage of Bruno, Vanini, Voltaire, and Rousseau, while the monument evokes no such lineage?

Historian Krzysztof Pomian has suggested a way to think about such questions by tracing the Latin roots which distinguish "monument" from "document." *Monumenteum* is linked to *monere*, to "make remember," while *documentum* is tied to *docere*, to teach or instruct.[2] Though both monument and text locate and preserve the past through visual practices (seeing, reading), words have an explicit pedagogical function which is only implied by the veneration or celebration of commemorative imagery. Monuments guard the past, but words instruct the present and teach the future.

La Commune's defense of the word and erasure of the image could stand as an emblem of a nineteenth-century shift in mnemonic representation. The privileging of the word over the image as a memory site is a theme I wish to examine by turning to a literature which for centuries had valued both: mnemonic guides—those manuals and instructional volumes dedicated to the technique and art of memory training. The most immediate, and somewhat disappointing observation about the literature by the end of the nineteenth century is its suppression of images—the relative lack of the allegorical pictures which made Renaissance *ars memoria* systems so allusive and fascinating. Imagery continues to play a large role in commemorations and political symbolism in France—Republican banners, figures of Marianne—yet the complex mytho-allegorical world-system imageries of a Giordano Bruno or Robert Fludd appear to be gone, and with them the chance to explore the extravagant minds of their creators.[3]

Where do the memory palaces go? By the late nineteenth century almost all French mnemonic methods were based upon strategies of dividing words into syllables and assigning references to the phonemes themselves. Depending on the method, letters, vowels, or clusters of consonants would be assigned some number or value: 1=b, p; 3=f, ph, v; 4=g, j, ch; and so forth. A piece of information to be recalled, such as the death of Henri IV would be rendered first with a statement, "Mort qui fait à l'histoire une supreme epoque." With the method, "supreMe ePoQue" configures to MPQ, in which M=6, P=1, Q=0, thus 1610.[4] The enunciation of the words themselves contained the thing to be remembered.

The popularizer of this technique in France was a music teacher, Aimé Paris, whose work *Exposition et pratique des procédés de la mné-motechnie* (1825) abandoned the *lieu* method of placing striking images in imagined locations and championed the "number-letter codes" which allowed the practitioner to create correspondences between parts of words and numbers. Paris developed his method in admiration of a newly popular writing technique—stenography. Mnemonic systems based on number-letter codes had existed since the seventeenth century, yet none had ever fully abandoned the use of images, and none drew on the striking assumptions of stenography: writing at a great speed demanded a notion of language as a system of signs whose total meaning could be determined only from context and placement of the elements. Conceiving mnemonic method as a form of shorthand for the mind is central to understanding why Paris's word-number code-based system can be taken as a model of the "modern" genre. By abridging written language, stenography increased the speed of transcription. Coded in simplified signs, it was an accelerated writing, and on paper, an accelerated memory, framed by a logic of time productively employed. As a technique it was particularly appropriate to business and administration, developed to suit imperatives of commerce, transaction, and negotiation. Though I will not treat this aspect of the subject here, a catalogue of the mnemonic literature published during the nineteenth century would include relatively few original *ars memoria* "systems," and very many imitations of Paris's shorthand adaptations targeted at merchants and other seekers of quick, "practical" memory skills.[5]

Paris's mnemonic method was modern in yet another way. By thinking through stenography, Paris recognized language as a composition of acoustic, inscribed, and mental signs. Memory was analogous to an arrangement of traces made from phonemic units whose values could be determined only by difference and association as they were quickly scripted into writing. By conceiving of memory as this system of like and unlike, Paris located his mnemonics in an ability to distinguish and assign meanings to an otherwise random play of sounds and letters. By the beginning of the twentieth century such insights would be theoretically pursued by Swiss linguist Ferdinand de Saussure (1857–1913), whose *Cours de linguistique générale* (posthumous, 1916) elaborated language as a system of signs and provided the bases for French structuralism.[6]

Locating mnemonics in parts of words rather than images, Aimé Paris's system was linguistically bound, that is, it made memory and language inseparable. The method could be applied to any language, yet was also linguistically specific: the fund of sounds, and the system of rules and conventions which governed a particular language, would determine the possibilities of mnemonic expression. What Paris obviously popularized was the adapted memory of the French language.

The changing bases of memory training in the nineteenth century thus cannot be isolated from the meanings and uses made of (what would become) national languages. The embodiment of memorizing in the articulation of words would inseparably link mnemonic history to histories of literacy and textually based instruction in the same period; to cultivate one's memory was to be educated to read and speak "one's own" language with precision. My discussion thus centers less on tracing mnemonic systems in an intellectual lineage than examining the critical intersection of a method and an educational institution: the point at which mnemonics is distinctly memory *training*.

Following my general thesis that "memory" is historically specific, I will describe the mnemonic universe created at this intersection as "modern," after Aimé Paris, and, after 1870, specifically governed by a socio-

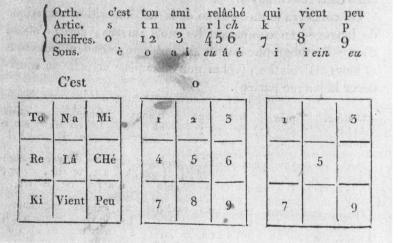

Attribuons à chaque articulation une valeur numérique, en rangeant dans la même classe les articulations relatives, ainsi qu'il suit :

se	te	ne	me	re	le	che	ke	fe	pe
0	1	2	3	4	5	6	7	8	9
ze	de	gne			ille	je	gue	ve	be

Les sons n'ont aucune valeur en chiffres; ils pourront donc être intercalés entre les articulations, sans rien changer au nombre représenté par ces articulations, dans la phrase suivante :

Orth.	c'est	ton	ami	relâché	qui	vient	peu
Artic.	s	t n	m	r l *ch*	k	v	p
Chiffres.	0	1 2	3	4 5 6	7	8	9
Sons.	è	o	a i	*eu* â é	i	i *ein*	*eu*

C'est   o

To	N a	Mi		1	2	3		1		3
Re	Là	CHé		4	5	6			5	
Ki	Vient	Peu		7	8	9		7		9

Figure 8 The grammar of history: the shift to memory as language. Aimé Paris's *Souvenirs du cours de mnémotechnie*, 1830. (*Source:* Institut National de Recherche Pedagogique)

political grand design appropriate to the Third Republic: the pursuit of an ideal correspondence between the French language and the progressive history of a republic borrowing its virtues from the classical world. Though the practices I will describe as mnemonic training—reading, recitation, declamation—are hardly specific to the late nineteenth century, the peculiar uses of mnemonic language will be adapted to an élite, ideal republicanism carrying forth an immortal French civilization by disseminating that language as part of a universal pedagogical project.

At an historical juncture when the notion of basic literacy is becoming widespread under the compulsory education system decreed by the Ferry laws, mnemonic writings capture both the classical ideals of an élite and the democratic ambitions of instructing a nation in a civic culture.

More, the mnemonic systems will betray concerns with physiology, the "memory" of the body, and the "judgments" of both which characterize bourgeois republican thinking of this period. As a function of pedagogical institutions, memory training was training in what some critics have called "high modernism"—the privileging of will, personal judgment, and cognition at the core of forging an "ethics of responsibility."[7] The late nineteenth-century mnemonic universe was all of these things; a look at the literature reveals a memory of the modern as richly evocative as its Renaissance predecessor.

Pedagogical intent resonates throughout mnemonic literature. One 1891 *Aide-mémoire* offers 470 memory formulas for the chronologies of the principal facts on the history of France, with the promise of "a practical and easy if not attractive method, accessible to all, even young students." A *Calendrier de mémoire* (1891) for calculating dates suggests that the method "should be taught in schools: the operations are simple, even recreational. This will accustom the students to reflect and exercise their memory."[8] In the promotion for the booklet *Mnémonie classique* (1874), the director of a professional school in Le Havre rhapsodizes about his "sincere admiration" for the method: "I was looking for a simple and easy means of inculcating exact and precise notions about History in children and young people."[9]

One mnemotechnical journal, the *Revue mensuelle de mnémotechnie ancienne et moderne et de l'art d'apprendre* (1886–88), offered its subscribers "the logical vision of the totality of human knowledge and the clear and distinct vision of each subject in its respective place."[10] In ambition, the series could not be wrongly likened to Diderot's *Encyclopédie*; volumes on science, history, art, and the breadth of scholarly learning, neatly organized in endless mnemonic variations. One distributor of the *Revue mensuelle* promised his readership an extraordinary education for twelve francs a year. "We have begun to memorize history, French grammar, arithmetic, geography, geometry, mechanics, astronomy, archaeology, political economy, industry, theology, philosophy, etc." The next lessons would be on literature.[11] The emphasis on instruction and training the memory was the *Revue*'s practical motive, but the texts reveal the dream of a universal book in which total knowledge is shaped through the lesson.

A mind trained in any art of memory is lost to us, but the texts which instructed it are not, and a selection can be particularly helpful in reconstructing the mnemonic universe of the turn of the century. I will present the following: the *Mnémonie classique* of P. Dugers and Felix Bernard (1874); *Exercises de mémoire* (1887) by A. Delapierre and A. P. Delamarche; *La Mnémotechnie* of Ed. Manteaux (1894); and *Le Syllabaire mnémonique* of Alfred Robichon (1905), with its revised edition, *La Mémoire littéraire* (1909). Ranging widely over different mnemonic styles,

these methods are united by the characteristics of "documentum": mnemonics as a form of teaching, in which the particularities of a national
language become the "memory" of historical instruction.

I begin with *Mnémonie classique* (1874), a "formulary method"
treating "inventions and discoveries" which is at once a mnemotechnical
manual—that is, a series of memory exercises, and a veritable history of
the technology, science, and material progress of the Occident. Dugers's
and Bernard's mnemotechnica operate as a series of elaborate memory
formulae patterned upon Aimé Paris's number-letter correspondences.
Properly trained into the memory, entire cultural universes are cached
away, to be invoked by the simple articulation of words. An initial training
establishes "mnemonic rapports," between numerals and syllables, that
is, 1=b, p; 2=d, t; 3=v, f, ph; 4=j, g, ch; 5=l; and so forth. Once
mastered, only a key word, and an ability to distinguish its parts gramat-
ically, are necessary to open up a wealth of historical information. For
example in the statement "Les cloches à l'eglise appellant les fideles"
(The bells of the church call the faithful), the key word is FiDeLes. Once
properly read or spoken, this key "FiDeLes" is rendered F=3, D=2; L=5
by the table of rapports, or 325—the date (they say) when bells began
to be forged and appear regularly in villages. The authors suggest, "With
these formulas, all difficulties with learning dates disappears . . . the date
of 'cloches' is *in* the word."[12] The word itself contains the memory.

Following Aimé Paris, the system can be applied to any language, yet
is also linguistically ("fideles") specific. Dugers and Bernard can thus use
French to describe a universalized history of progress. The section of the
work devoted to "Inventions and Discoveries" proceeds with a chronology of all sorts of useful inventions. Once the memory technique is mastered, any invention can be immediately correlated with the year it
appeared. If the word is properly trained to contain the memory, the
memory it contains is potentially vast. The "inventions" in the booklet
number over eighty, and include bells, the windmill, Arabic numbers,
Roman architecture, mirrors, the cannon, drums, oil painting, tobacco,
coffee, the daguerreotype, lighting, the barometer, the telescope, mechanical clocks, glass, porcelain, the printing press, steam engines, and
electrical generators. Biographical notes digress upon noteworthy names
in the history of science and technology, including Bacon, Papin, New-
comer, Watt, Jouffrey, Fulton, Franklin, Galvani, and Volta.[13]

As a veritable catalogue of technical and everyday wonders, the Dug-
ers-Bernard system has an evocative beauty. Mnemonically, the training
for the system is as mentioned above, 1=b, p; 2=d, t, and so on. These
form a sort of table of the elements out of which memory, and then
history, will be reconstructed. The letters are combined into syllables,
sounds—"it is necessary to explicitly articulate: beu, deu, feu, jeu . . ."—
whose syllables form a word or words, and those words form a mnemonic
phrase. The speaking or reading of the *word*, the articulation of the syllables evokes the code of letters which draws out the hidden numbers in

the word, thus the date. The date fixes the event or information in a proper chronology. With proper order and sequence, history is revealed. And what a history it is!

This is best explained by example. The table of inventions begins chronologically with the bells in 325, and more or less closes with the Transatlantic Telegraph Cable of 1858. The entry for the cable in the text reads thus: "Le Télégraphie Transatlantique. 1858.rlr." Keeping the mnemonic tables in mind (R=8, L=5, R=8), one remembers not the information, but this: "Deux mondes par un fil de fer se relierent." (Two worlds are joined by a thread of iron.) The key is not factual memorization, but the ability to articulate the French word "ReLieRent"; the speaking of the word syllabically evokes the code "R-L-R" which in turn evokes the date, 8-5-8. Tables of descriptions are arranged chronologically in the text, so the date locates the particular inquiry in its correct order, while the phrase "Deux mondes par un fil de fer se relierent" recalls the content of the recollection. This is done by imagery—not visual—but verbal. "Relierent" which is also "RLR" which is also "1858" carries in it the "two worlds" and the "thread of iron" which connects them. The articulation of the phrases evoke more words, presumably studied by the reader in neat little paragraph summaries:

> It was in 1858 that the first great attempt was made to join Europe and the American continent together by a submarine cable, 800 leagues in length, seven copper wires, gutta-percha, between Ireland and the island of Newfoundland. It was only able to transmit electric current for a few days. [14]

So, from a tiny point of distinctions between a few letters and numbers comes an entire description of a marvelous technological development. Nor is this all, for the example of the Transatlantic Cable would not have been studied in isolation, but in the context of the other inventions and their descriptions. In this case, the cable falls under a general rubric of "Electricity." Working in reverse while maintaining the proper sequence of dates, the cable entry refers back to "The Morse telegraph" and "The Chappe telegraph." These inventions in turn point to Volta and Galvani. Also carried along in this train are Franklin, Romas, and Dufay, each with an appropriate phrase, code, and description.[15]

The presentation of history here contained is a proud vision of science as a field of discovery, and inventions as the children of great geniuses. What the authors regard as science is clearly too complex for "des enfants," but instructing the memory of the latter in a particular historical vision of science and its role is not. Bernard and Dugers note, "We will give them an ample knowledge of the illustrious *savants* who have given their names to these marvelous discoveries." The memory of science is not the study of principles, but of "illustrious *savants*," and the *naming* of their work. The giving of the name is the advent of knowledge, and the circulation of the name is the expansion and internalization of that knowledge. It is "the names of these characters, so often set forth in books and spoken in conversation," which is to inspire in students (particularly "les enfants") a more individual, more "intimate" interest in science.[16]

The focus on great individuals is set within a framework of "inventions and discoveries" whose narrative of historical progress is both universal and pointedly nationalist. The invisible intentions of the volume rest in its prioritizing of technical developments across cultures. As an observation the authors concede, for example, that the windmill had existed in Asia "from times immemorial," but focus their own story on "the era when its usage was introduced in France." The general introduction, under the rubric of "civilization," plays with the presentation of barbarism and progress, struggle, and the ultimate historical affirmation of a distinctively French national identity. Thus the background for the story of science begins not with ancient China, but with Gaul and "the first Germans." Notably, these Germans are not only ancestors, but backward ancestors, who "had no other goals but pillage and destruction. Whatever they could not take with them they destroyed or burned," an assessment undoubtedly little helped by the recent Franco-Prussian War.[17]

To be fair, the barbaric portrayal of the Germans is extended to other early warrior clans, but with a telling distinction. "The Roman Gaul" is not a conquerer, but attempts to absorb the other clans, "to shape them in his civilization." The history of the Gauls, like that of France in the late nineteenth century, is a tale of loss to a brutal enemy and an historical overcoming to be marked by the ultimate success of a civilization: "the history of France proper makes known the series of painful struggles and political and religious events which will come to mark the renaissance of the civilization amid the chaos."[18]

The whole training of a "French" identity pervades much of the mnemonic literature. A. Delapierre and A. P. Delamarche's *Exercises de mémoire* (1887) is a sort of literary counterpart to Duger and Bernard's scientific history. Though it does not draw on Aimé Paris's system of codes, it nonetheless also illustrates my point about localizing mnemonics in language and institutional teaching. An anthology of poetry, prose, and dialogues, it is among the most colorful and beautifully edited collections of writings to fall under so prosaic a title. Over twenty selections of poetry are featured, including works by Hugo, LaFontaine, Corneille, Florian, Musset, and Racine. Some sixteen prose selections include excerpts from Bernadin de Saint-Pierre's *Paul et Virginie*, Bossuet's *Athènes et Lacedomone*, Buffon's *Le Cygne*, Chateaubriand's *Spectacle d'une nuit dans les deserts du nouveau monde*, Th. Gauthier's "Le Chat et le perroquet," as well as fragments from Voltaire and Rousseau. The dialogues are represented by Bornier, Collin d'Harleville, Coppée, Fénélon, and Molière.

Each reading is ordered around an excerpt, a "morceau," followed by a "maxim" or "reflection," and concluded by the editor's "pedagogical counsels," which feature explanations of key terms, and suggestions for reading and analyzing the text. The mnemotechnical method is the manual itself. Hardly two words need be said in this case about the role of selection of texts. A canon of renowned French writers is exhibited, a proud, carefully managed self-portrait of a literary tradition emphasizing national loyalty, prudence, and the spirit of finesse.

Frédéric Bataille's "The Lesson" tells of a teacher's role in inspiring a particularly patriotic young student, and occasions a declaration from Hugo: "Glory to our eternal France! Glory to those who died for her!" Th. Gautier's "The Cat and the Parrot," in which the bird saves its own life by confounding the cat with talk, allows a sober injunction from Regnard: "Events frequently confound predictions." La Fontaine's fable of "Phebus et Borée" is a familiar tale in which the sun and the storm wager to see which can make a traveler remove his cloak. The storm rages, but the sun, by its insistent warmth, resolves the contest and the question, "Which of the two is truly the stronger?" Though La Fontaine might be the last author ever to need a maxim added to his fables, J. J. Rousseau is made to supply one anyway: "Vanity produces nothing good, and from pride expect nothing but vices."[19]

Delightful and enchanting, this literary anthology is a "memory exercise" with distinctly pedagogical intent. Delapierre was an inspector of primary education for the Seine, and Delamarche a representative of the Association of Members of Teaching. If the point be missed, the opening epigraph to the book informs the reader, "To love the school is to love *la patrie*"—courtesy of Delamarche. The authors deliberately designed their manual for "higher and complementary courses in our primary schools, our higher level primary schools, and the elementary classes of *lycées* and *collèges*."[20] The authors also suggest that the program could not hurt the training at the *écoles normales*.

Delapierre made something of a small reputation for himself upon the programmatic aspects of memory training. In an 1891 awards ceremony at the Lycée Michelet he spoke to the graduating students on the "briefness" of lessons and recitations of the current generation, lamenting "poor memory, her beautiful days are behind her." Invoking the muses, he goes on to exclaim his astonishment with critics of memory in the educational system. "They accuse her first of making pedants! They accuse her of harming the development of the other faculties of intelligence and particularly judgment!"[21] In fact, argues Delapierre, the case is just the opposite—memory is the foundation of intelligence and judgment, thus also an active pursuit of the good, individual and public. Against the enemies of memory Delapierre retorts, "How many remarkable men would be assured of fame for the capacity of their memory even if they hadn't been owed more enviable titles!" His "remarkable men" include Mithridates, Themistocles, Hortensius, Caesar (dictating four letters at a time!), Richelieu, Pope Paul IV, Pascal, Racine, Condorcet (a veritable encyclopaedia in his head), Gambetta, Macaulay, Guizot.[22] With a phrase, Delapierre's "memory" creates a tradition which somehow manages to link Mithridates to Pascal to Condorcet to Guizot, casting all in an equal light of virtue.

Clearly, students should aspire to this tradition and to its memory. How? "Be attentive to the explanations of your masters in order to learn," recommends Delapierre, and "apply yourselves to retain your lessons, not only with your ear, listening to words you repeat like music, but with your mind." Discipline and study skills are the foundation of this memory-virtue. Reading notably plays a paramount role in Delapierre and Delmarche's method. "The students of the *écoles normales* must learn how to read." What should be read is reasonably clear from the selections of the exercises: the great body of a morally instructive French literature. The significant point for students is more than a familiarity with authors, however:

> They will obtain more than one benefit from this exercise. First is that of cultivating their memory, that master faculty which has been greatly slandered because it has been so abused; then they will make provisions for what they lack most—ideas—and with these ideas a vocabulary of proper terms, and chosen expressions to use them. They will learn to read well, because whoever recites well, reads well. [23]

A first observation about memory and words—especially the written word—in this passage is simply the remarkable conjunction of the two. History is not memory, yet history becomes memory because a carefully defined tradition of skillfully edited texts is presented to be trained into a generation of students through the rigorous practice of "*analyser, expliquer, diction.*" In the ideal cultivation of memory each student will have been carefully trained by disciplined readings, recitations, and discussions. Memories of history are not unique personal experiences, but parts of a collected series of references based upon a documented tradition—which depends upon what one is allowed to read.

More profoundly, literary and moral traditions concern not just what one reads, but how one reads it. A book or exercise alone is not evidence of a student's memory; training forms the essential link between memory and the medium of the printed page. For these inspectors, mnemonic reading is not based on passive impressions from the solitary searching eye, but expressions of body and morality. The literary texts are supported by the classical idea of memory as one of the essential components of good rhetorical and dramatic skills. Not for nothing do the editors call their program the "expressive recitation of selected texts in prose and in dialogues, of scenes borrowed from the classics."

The point of rhetoric in the classical tradition meant public expression, especially after the model of the ancient Roman orators, in particular Cicero. Mnemonic training was defined by education in civic character. For Delapierre, attentiveness to memory was not only mental exercise,

but also "the best lesson in taste and judgment."[24] Delmarche and Delapierre discourage untrained, uninspired readers from destroying the Ap-
ollonian "wise harmonies" contained in the manual's verses with a
graceless monotone or "lifeless eye."[25] In introducing recitation exercises, the manual lauds the famed tragic actor Talma, who transformed
recitation from mechanical to "natural," "in exactly translating the
thought of the author."[26] To read (and thus to speak) is to become again
the thought of the writer, to become identical through memory with the
text as a living past. Here, mnemonics is inspired selection and the reem-
bodiment of past virtues.

Delapierre and Delmarche's focus on "exercises" in poetry, prose, and
drama aims to incorporate language as memory into the body of the
student through gesture and dramatic expression. Memory training is
thus not only an effort of mental, but also physiological capacities. The
"physiology" of memory, particularly its neurological variants, was widely
discussed and debated in the savant literature of medical science and philosophy at the turn of the century, involving such figures as Sigmund
Freud, Pierre Janet, Alfred Binet, and Henri Bergson. Yet the neurophysiology of memory also appeared in the instructional literature of mnemonics—admittedly not as "science," but translated into the disarmingly
practical vocabulary of "health" and "hygiene."

    La Mnémotechnie appliquée aux sciences elementaires (1894) by
Edouard Manteaux, an instructor at Clermont-Ferrand, is a splendid example of how mnemonics mediates between clinic and classroom. Manteaux begins his treatise not by elaborating a mnemotechnical method,
but by establishing some physical "conditions of memory" on which to
proceed. Memory training for Manteaux is the effective application of
"attention," repetition," and "the association of ideas." The point is to
register strong impressions of the things to be remembered as inscriptions
in which the state of the body plays a significant role. "Memories are
inscribed by emotion," says Manteaux, an ancient metaphor of writing
or impression, concerned in this case with the proper regulation of those
memories and emotions in terms of "health and the waking state." Good
health or *hygiène* is absolutely essential not only for the well-being of the
body, but for the moral health of the person: "If the man suffers, the
mind is more or less asleep, it languishes; the nervous system is more or
less weakened." The clinical vocabulary of the nervous system serves as
a useful descriptive language for social and moral commentaries; as Manteaux suggests, "a bad memory is slow, lazy, fugitive, rebellious."[27]

    Memory training is an intellectual discipline, "regular and serious,"
which requires good health, so it is not odd that Manteaux should offer
prescriptives on how to maintain that health. Nor is the nature of his
advice surprising: "As far as nutrition, follow a uniform regime as much
as possible, no special foods, moderation with alcoholic drink. . . ." Such
council is structured around an imperative of moderation, from eating

and drinking routines, study habits, and even a directive that "the working room should be filled with pure air, neither hot nor cold."[28] Effective remembering may operate by remarkable signs which "strike us sharply," and engrave themselves on the memory, but the person him or herself ought always to avoid extremes.

The proper physical and moral character of the subject once established, the actual training of memory can begin. Here the practical side of mnemonics reappears: "How one must study" is the majority of the text, concluded by "advice for exam prepartions." Manteaux surveys poetry, grammar, history, geography, mathematics, and sciences with an eye to classification and taxonomies. History is a particular problem because of its "irregularity": its division of reigns and historical events do not correspond equally to the centuries and time divisions it establishes for itself, so many genealogies, analytics, and synoptics must be employed.

Manteaux ponders the process for fixing "the important dates" to "the succession of facts." He favors no particular method, though some are wonderfully evocative. For history, he describes a "Légende des Signes," a geometric grid whose coordinates locate boxes filled with letters indicating "Acquisition," "Alliance," "Expedition," or "Festival," a veritable map of historical memory. Another system plays with numbers, so that "48" groups together "1248—7th Crusade, 1348—Black Plague, 1648—Peace of Westphalia, 1848—2nd Republic," an unusual and thought-provoking determination of number over event.[29] The "Méthode Franco-Polonaise" is the familiar conjunction of numbers, letters, and mnemonic phrases in which codes simultaneously evoke dates and events.

Less enthusiastic than other memory writers about systems, Manteaux nonetheless shares with them the creed that memory is located in language, specifically in words. The more distinct a single part of speech, the more it can be unfolded to reveal the entire content and structure of thought. Training memory through language is important because it reduces the burden of remembering:

> a single word, a single formula . . . embraces a multitude of objects and particular facts. To lift oneself into the sphere of generalities as much as possible without falling into vagueness, to set out everywhere ideas of the whole from particular details, this is the way to learn and to retain a lot. [30]

The focus on the evocative power of words in not an end in itself. Memory as acquisition of poetry, grammar, history, mathematics, and sciences is only knowledge. The fundamentals of memory training are not about "the nature of things," but those things "worked and refined by good sense and reason." The goal of memory training, as it was with Delapierre and Delmarche, is to give the student the means to exercise "judgment, the most precious of our faculties." Again, the repeating theme of "judgment": memory not as recollection of the past, but the past as contained in the moment of decision and decision-making.

Manteaux takes pains to emphasize that his guide is "only a guide, alas quite modest," and disavows any pretension to "speak of the great proceedings of Cicero and other philosophers of antiquity." His denial only invokes the implicit: an indebtedness of late nineteenth-century mnemonics to an exalted view of the world of the ancients, great orators and rhetoricians embodying the virtues of the Republic. In French mnemonics, this link is played out through the ways in which the "judgment" of memory can be located in a continuum through language between modern French and its Greco-Latin ancestors.[31]

At least one mnemonist was absolutely sure about the intercalation of classical and contemporary memories. Lawyer and writer Alfred Robichon's *Le Syllabaire mnémonique* (1905) and its revised edition *La Mémoire Littéraire* (1909) openly draw upon a mythological classicism in a "new art of analyzing words." In Robichon's work the full flower of the ancient world is reborn.

Le Syllabaire mnémonique: a little volume on pronunciation and aspiration, whose intention is to correctly apprehend the combinations and order of the superimposition of vowels. The tables, the exercises are all to the point of learning to "penetrate the secret of the origin of words," to find within them "their harmonies, their literary power." As above, Robichon's is a mnemonic system without images, without grotesque or striking emblems—the *lieux* of memory have been distilled into the history located in words themselves. A word is neither a fixed sense nor a "thing"; rather, "its elements divide themselves and enter into movement." What one grasps in language is not essence, but "a succession of sensible forms," so that "we learn one thing by another proceeding it."[32]

As Aimé Paris had proposed, language has no "things," only syllables and sonorities which are distinguished, differentiated; each makes sense only by reference to the others. Yet where Paris saw random syllables, others like Dugers, Bernard, and Manteaux saw that in a constructed language words and parts of words referred to each other not only spatially but also temporally. For his part, Robichon suggested that words "are engraved on the memory by the character of the roots which represent these words, and by the ideas which they signify to the mind." A word, in effect, is apprehended according to the memory it contains already in its own differentiated syllabic bases. Robichon insists upon what he calls "an audacious theory": French has the "same roots as LATIN and GREEK."[33]

Few etymologists would think this particularly "audacious," in tracing the bases of the French language. Emile Littré's scholarship, for example, had well established some of the origins of French in Latin and Greek by the mid-nineteenth century. Robichon's originality is not as a language scholar, but as a thinker applying grammar to memory. As the "laws of Latin rhythm and stress apply themselves to French," so the articulation of each French word bears an "internal language," an exacting correspondence between the articulation of the word, and the "origins" enfolded within the historical memory of the word: the classical world which created it.

That world—in a familiar theme—is a world of oratory. "The harmony of words, which enters into prose as well as in poetry, always corresponds to Latin and Greek roots; these are the roots which, by their choice and coordination, give force to the dignity of elocution." [34] The emphasis on the correspondance between memory, eloquence, and public speaking recalls Delapierre, Manteaux, and the general pedagogical strategy of inculcating memory training as an exercise in civic morality.

Rhetoric means more than Latin studies. Robichon is no philologist; to him memory is not the scholarly past of languages, but a present resonating in the speaker. By shaping his mnemonic system around the essentials of language, Robichon raises a basic point about speaking the past—its "formation in the mouth," the *sonorité* of language. Memory is in part literary and intellectual, but in the speaking of that memory, the articulation of words is the act which links the past with the moment. "Memory," in effect, means memory of the body—its fundamental act is the operation of the "tongue and larynx"; as he puts it, "one memorizes thus by the organs of the voice."[35] Memory, deep and weighted with ancient civilization, is most perfectly realized when words are expressed—as Henri Bergson would appreciate—as the actions of the body.

Mastery of this corporeal yet ephemeral act is not simple. Proper articulation, "the length of sonorous intensity determined by its mode of organic formation," requires attention and discipline. The great enemies of memory—"the inattention of the mind" and "the aversion of the heart"—are gradually trained away by rigorous application of verbal exercises. In the revised edition of his treatise Robichon is blunt about what constitutes success. Something stronger than mere effort is required:

> Exercises of memory are equally exercises of the will. Thus, the Greeks were right to say that the act of memory is the result of an act of intelligence united to an act of will.[36]

Robichon's text is hardly isolated in its fixation on the "will" and "memory." Théodule Ribot, one of the pioneers of clinical psychology in France, had already well publicized the connection some twenty years earlier in his *Maladies de la mémoire/ Maladies de la volonté,* and I will explore the links between moral politics and physiology more closely in the next chapter. Fears of "degeneration" and "malaise," as well as calls for *volonté* (will) and *hygiène* were recurrent in French social thought between the disaster at Sedan and the Great War, when the ability of the French nation to be the standard bearer for a classical civilization was shaken.[37]

Robichon's *Syllabaire* defends France through the exercise of grammatical and articulate memory. Moral qualities are developed through

speech exercises. Robichon's diagrams of proper pronunciation emphasize the auditory and muscular aspects of speech, so that the "internal
language" becomes "weighted in the nervous system," the impression of
memory—and moral health—in the organs and expressions of the voice.
Despite the emphasis on speech, writing is not distant from this physical
memory. As a student studies a text, practice with syllabic exercises transforms the written page into a writing on the body. The end is the identity
of body, memory, and word: by regular practice with the exercises, "the
words of the text in this way are imprinted on the larynx."[38]

The training in the exercises of the *Syllabaire* casts the reader in the
model of the classical past. Every syllable is the perfect control and evocation of deep historical references: one "lives" ancient virtue, wisdom,
and learning. "It is in the passages of vigorous sentiment that one sees
the best parallelism between our syllabic prosody and that of ancient prosody." To speak the ideal life of the ancients! Through the discipline of
words and memory training, past and present become manifestly the
same, and the "mnemonic power is spread throughout our entire being,
like the soul of antiquity."[39]

At the center of these exercises is one man's perspective on the status of
the classics in his own age, in which classics are an insight into class. By
his exercises and memory training Robichon maintains an attachment
which some Third Republic historians have called "the aspirations of a
bourgeoisie faithful to eighteenth-century bourgeois ideal of living 'no-
bly' and devoted to a Latin civilization of 'lawyers' not 'producers.' "[40]
Since 1871, reform movements in French secondary education favoring
scientific and technical instruction had attacked classical education as elit-
ist and ill-suited to a complex, modern society, blaming it for the
humiliation of France by Germany. A government body, the Ribot Commission, was established to consider reforms and pursued hearings and
depositions from 1899 to 1902, inciting long debates between Ancients
and Moderns. Robichon was an unapologetic champion of ancient wisdom, yet managed to circumscribe carefully his pedagogical objectives
within a timely political program.

The student of his method first achieved a certain beauty of mind:
"We have created here an exercise of the mind and of style, until now
inapplicable in French, which when employed by the Greeks and the
Latins, prepared them to write their masterworks with the greatest perfection of form." In this discipline of a literary art of writing, the broader
"perfection of form" was the achieved unity of memory, grammar, literature, and moral philosophy, finally manifesting itself in the mind, soul,
and body of the "masterpiece" of Robichon's system—"the best citizens
of the Republic of Letters."[41]

Any part of this inscription could be emphasized to different ends,
yet all form a unity: citizens, Republic, letters; all embody a particular
perspective on political identity, civic virtue, intellectual traditions. Such

training passed from antiquity to turn-of-the-century France by way of the Revolution, when Camille Desmoulins, Saint-Just, Danton, and Robespierre had made public speaking synonymous with public power. The model of antiquity weighed heavily upon the orators of 1789, who self-consciously emulated Cicero in evoking Republican Rome as the historical age of public virtue married to individual courage, frugality, and patriotism.[42] The soul of such a citizen speaks and acts the ancient world while maintaining a firm "attention" to the judgment of the present. These qualities are transmitted through studies—the memory of print and perfection in writing, then fully incorporated in the sensibility of the individual when impressed in the activity of the body itself, the organs of speech.

To articulate French syllabically is to invoke Latin and Greek, and this is to speak the ancients and to speak a civic morality. Memory, words, and civic morality—the goal of the *Syllabaire* is to create in a generation of students a unity of intellectual, ethical, and political responsibility based on a common tradition extending back to the Revolution, and then to legendary republican ancestors.

Read through mnemotechnicae, this then was the mnemonic universe of the turn of the century, a universe whose "memory" was rooted in the French language and bounded by progress, great traditions, and a complex unification of classical oratory and physiology in expressions of disciplined moral judgment. Memory training was training in the "high modernism" of independent will, judgment, and civic responsibility to *la patrie*. "Memory" was the agreement of virtue and language under the sign of a bourgeois republicanism.

I return now to the beginning of this chapter where *La Commune* disagreed with *Le Mot d'ordre* about burning Adolphe Thiers' *L'Histoire de la consulate et de l'empire* in the debris at the base of the Vendôme Column. *La Commune* refused to martyr words in the same way that it supported the destruction of public monuments, arguing that burning writers honored them as prophets of the future. In nineteenth-century mnemonic literature, words resonated with the soul of the past which prepared the physiology and the ethical action of each moment and the next. Words were "the future in the past," the site of the printed page and the voice turned to action, the bearers of knowledge, virtue, and an ideal republic of citizens.

In 1891 historian P. Gachon wrote bitterly, "Wasn't it Condorcet, passionate champion of progress, liberty, pure and generous dreamer, who at the legislative tribune proposed the destruction of the archives of the nobles? Nothing could be more contrary to the scientific spirit."[43] Condorcet had called the aristocratic archives places of "vanity," but to destroy the words was to contradict fatally what was sacred to the Revolution and its legacy: the promise of instructing the future which the memory of language contains.

La Commune had defended Thiers' Napoleonic writing while agreeing to destroy Napoleonic statues; his words were the "memory" which
deserved to survive. That defense of language was, notably, carried out
before Thiers' final assault on Paris and the loss of thousands of Communard lives. Years later Delamarche and Delapierre's *Exercises de la mémoire,* that charming schoolbook of verse and prose discussed earlier,
included a small excerpt from the "Serment de Jeu de Paume" (The Oath
of the Tennis Court), a rousing piece of writing which captured the birth
of the National Assembly. What would *La Commune* have made of the
official place in memory accorded the author of this text, Adolphe Thiers,
who is remembered this way?

> President of the Republic from 1871–1873. He wrote *L'Histoire de la ré-
> volution française* and *L'Histoire du Consulat et de l'Empire,* two masterpieces
> of the genre for their impartiality, their clarity, their style, and rigorous ex-
> actitude of facts.[44]

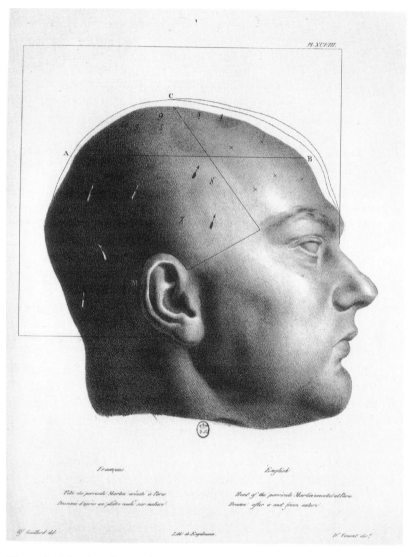

Figure 9 Mapping the mind: nineteenth-century phrenological image. (*Source:* Bibliothèque Nationale)

4

Bodies: The Third Convolution

Two days before Christmas, 1877, Madame H. was admitted to the medical clinic in Yonne. Eighteen months before, she had been stricken by attacks of apoplexy and aphasia. At the end of a year, the paralytic episodes had partially subsided, though without any improvement in her aphasic condition. Her specialist, one Dr. Rousseau, noted that she remained completely lucid and took care of all her own affairs, but that when she went out, she needed to be accompanied by someone "to serve her as an interpreter." Rousseau's clinical reports, circulated under the title *Observation et autopsie d'une aphasique* (1882), went on to trace the gradual mental, emotional, and physical decline of a woman afflicted with what would ultimately prove a "destructive lesion" on her brain. After periods of intermittent melancholy, weeping, hallucinations, and agitation, Madame H. fell into a perpetual sadness. The doctor reported: "Her vocabulary is composed of only a few words; in writing she can only sign her name no matter what phrase is dictated to her; her dumb show is vivid and expressive; she reads her prayer book continually, without us being able to say whether or not she truly understands the texts before her eyes."[1] The clinical descriptions describe well Madame H.'s particular malady: aphasia. Between the interpreter who accompanied her, the loss of vocabulary, the terrifying limitation in writing to her own name, what Rousseau traced in the degeneration of his patient was a strange and complex disorder whose symptoms could nonetheless be simply described: a gradual isolation from language.

In 1896 the philosopher Henri Bergson wrote, "Anyone who approaches, without preconceived ideas and on the firm ground of facts, the classical problem of the relations of mind and body, will soon see this problem as centering upon the subject of memory, and, even more precisely, upon the memory of words." In a series of lectures at the medical faculty in Bordeaux (1898), one Dr. A. Pitres reminded his audience that "memory is one of the essential conditions of the formation of language."[2] What Dr. Rousseau's Madame H. was losing according to the neurological wisdom of the day was both language and memory, or better, the memory of language.

Language and memory, the embodiment of the one in the other—and the disorders of both—were inseparable in clinical literature at the end of the nineteenth century, studied in detail by such greats of neurology as Carl Wernicke, Jean-Martin Charcot, and his Viennese student Sigmund Freud. I will work around such figures to piece together a constellation of texts and observations by French clinicians and anatomists with lesser-known names such as Fauvelle, Pitres, and Ferrand, drawing my discussions not from Charcot's spectacular dramas of hysterical patients, but from anthropologist Paul Broca's investigations into one very particular organ, the brain, and one particular malady, aphasia. The historical study of aphasia helps explain how memory and language came to be located in the brain by clinical psychologists, and clarifies what they thought they would find by subjecting the cerebral tissues to a particular tool: the scalpel. If memory as expressed through language could be materialized, perhaps it could be cut up and inspected like the parts of any organ.[3]

As the title (*Observation et autopsie*) of Dr. Rousseau's report suggests, Madame H. finally succumbed to the advanced stages of her illness. Rousseau had then the chance to search for the sources of that illness, to find the seat of the troubles which had destroyed his patient. He did so—and this is important—by autopsying her brain. In his notes, he left behind a compelling image of the "memory object" of my discussion. Aristotle, in one of the first texts on the subject, had likened "memory" to imprints left in soft wax or clay tablets. Here, from Rousseau's autopsy report on Madame H., the most advanced procedures of medical science left their representative mark. "The brain is small, discolored, and atrophied . . . its consistency is diminshed. It spreads out on the table where it is examined, and it conserves the imprint of fingertips."[4]

As a report on late nineteenth-century brain science, Rousseau's description is at once compelling and misleading. If he and his colleagues replicated the materialty of ancient images by irresistibly impressing their fingers into the substance of Madame H.'s brain, what I will argue is that the logic of their own clinical researches by scalpel was leading them to a conceptualization of language and memory as utterly *in*substantial, immaterial functions composed of links and connections, activities and operations, a memory of *movements*. As Dr. Pitres (above) told his students after explaining the new conception, "these operations have a real existence: the 'memory' does not."[5] Ultimately, aphasic amnesias would cease to be considered effacements of impressions in brain tissues, and reimagined as "ruptures" between "centers of communication." The faculty called memory, classically envisioned as a seat of remembrance in the brain, would be replaced by multiplicities of movements and transmissions, "pathways" of the "transcortical" mind—a memory for a modern world. By the first decade of the twentieth century the eminent experimental psychologist Henri Pieron would be writing of the "acceleration" of memory, figuratively comparing the operations of the brain to those of new communication networks and printing presses. Other savants made the memory of language into a marker by which to measure the progress of a society, comparing the grunts of primitive "monosyllabiques" to the "more perfect inflections" of peoples endowed with evolved brains, politics, transport, and industry. The brain and its dissection finally measured not only disorders of language, but the ultimate historical memory: the evolution of human civilization. The clinical literature on aphasia read both the pride and the paradoxes of that civilization.

What then was this "aphasia"? A frequently cited definition comes from an 1875 clinical thesis published by one Dr. Legroux: "Aphasia is the diminution or perversion of the normal faculty of expressing or understanding ideas by means of conventional signs, in spite of the persistence of a sufficient degree of intelligence, and in spite of the integrity of the sensory-nervous and muscular apparatuses which serve the expression and perception of these signs."[6] Aphasia was a curious affliction, a negativity, a disorder defined by an inability to comprehend ideas and signs "in spite of" what would seem perfectly "normal" intellectual and neuromuscular functions. Here was the aphasiac mystery: how could a patient lose language ability while still possessing unaffected intelligence, nerves, muscles, organs of speech?

The anatomical foundations for addressing such questions date back to April 1861, when an elderly patient at the Hopital Bicêtre, Lebrogne, came to the attention of Dr. Paul Broca, surgeon at the hospital. Broca, who would become famous and notorious for promoting racial theories based on cranial capacities (favoring European males), had been developing a theory of language and the brain, and was fascinated by the case of this man called "Tan," named for the only sound he was apparently able to articulate. No organic cause could be found for the man's apparent linguistic dysfunction. When Tan fortuitously died ten days later, Broca autopsied his brain and discovered one part, "on the front left lobe, the lower half of the second and third frontal convolutions, whose substance was replaced by an infected pocket."[7] A second, similarly afflicted patient and a second autopsy resulted in similar findings, which Broca reported to his Société d'Anthropologie. Broca believed himself to have discovered, in the brain itself, a center of language. More important, this faculty could be demon-

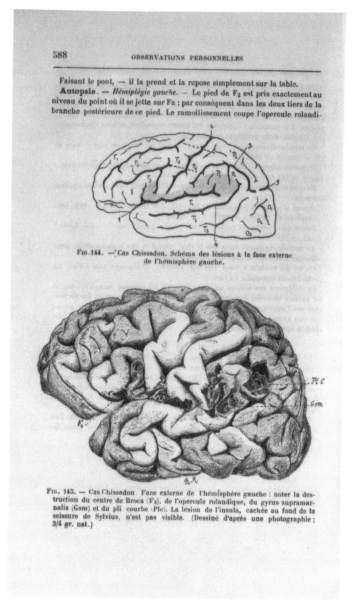

588   OBSERVATIONS PERSONNELLES

Faisant le pont, — il la prend et la repose simplement sur la table.
Autopsie. — *Hémiplégie gauche*. — Le pied de F₃ est pris exactement au
niveau du point où il se jette sur Fa ; par conséquent dans les deux tiers de la
branche postérieure de ce pied. Le ramollissement coupe l'opercule rolandi-

FIG. 144. —'Cas Chissadon. Schéma des lésions à la face externe
de l'hémisphère gauche.

FIG. 145. — Cas Chissadon. Face externe de l'hémisphère gauche : noter la destruction du centre de Broca (F₃), de l'opercule rolandique, du gyrus supramar-
nalis (Gsm) et du pli courbe (Plc). La lésion de l'insula, cachée au fond de la
scissure de Sylvius, n'est pas visible. (Dessiné d'après une photographie ;
3/4 gr. nat.)

Figure 10 Broca's brain: autopsied left hemisphere of the brain from F.
Moutier, *L'Aphasie de Broca: travail du laboratoire Bicêtre*, 1909. The third
convolution is indicated "F3." (*Source:* Bibliothèque Nationale)

strated to have a distinct localization in a particular convolution, the third
left frontal, to be precise. Disorders such as aphasia could perhaps be generally characterized as the deterioration of this center.

Though localization theories had been popular at least since Franz
Joseph Gall and his pseudoscience of phrenology—reading bumps on the

head—earlier in the century, Broca's discovery was the first widely accepted surgical evidence that functions of the human organism could be linked to specific centers of the brain. Yet what exactly had Broca located—had he discovered the oft-speculated "memory of words"? Some definite link existed between memory, language, and organic material—this no one denied, but the nature of that link remained in dispute. A generation of anatomists and neurologists tried to define the significance of Broca's discovery. The key legacy of Broca's convolution, oddly enough, was ultimately not the precise, well-delineated mapping of the brain he might have sought, and which remains the image of "localization," but the beginning of an ability to think of the brain as an entity discontinous, disaggregated, interrupted. Broca's disciples did indeed attempt to map the brain, to order and classify its areas, but something else is also true: the more precisely the Broca school mapped the brain, the less its operations could be localized to any particular center.

By physically pinpointing the areas of sensorial (visual, auditive) as opposed to motor (graphic, verbal) dysfunctions, Broca and his successors revealed the awesomely complex multiplicity of ways in which the brain and body remember. The royal seat of language was challenged by studies of patients who could understand but not pronounce words, or vice versa. More studies recognized and defined the multiple physiological habits necessary to produce the movements and reflexes of speech or gesture. In 1889 psychologist Dr. Georges Surbled summarized the new complications in brain science by dismissing the old conception of the seat of language: "the memory of words does not belong to Broca's center . . . what is lacking in the aphasiac is thus not the memory of words, but the faculty to verbally express his ideas."[8] The ability to use language was located not in an exceptional storage center of words, but in an ensemble of actions and processes.

In his original report on Tan and another case to the anthropological society, even Broca himself had suggested as much. Despite the powerful attraction of pinpointing a "center" of language or a "memory of words" in the brain, Broca suspected that the third left frontal convolution would prove no entity of remembrance in itself. His concept of the memory of language was not as a fixed locale, but as a series of coordinations and activities.

> What has perished in them is thus not the faculty of language, it is not the memory of words, it is not even the action of the nerves and muscles of speech expression and articulation, it is something else: it is the faculty of coordinating the proper movements of articulate language.[9]

Broca conceived the "memory of words" not as an entity, but as a capacity for *movement* and arrangement. Aphasia was a curious disorder; one victim might lose the ability to read, another the ability to speak while maintaining his reading, a third, like Madame H., might suffer from a complete collapse of all language functions, one at a time. By reading localization studies in terms of aphasia, Broca and his successors were

compelled to record many different kinds of language failure and to recognize "memory" as a ceaseless contingency of different sensory and
physiological functions. One student, Mathias Duval, summarized the
concept simply, remarking, "As Broca said so well, there is no single
memory; there are different memories."[10]

Duval's statement could perhaps serve as an emblem for the fin de siècle,
and as a profound description of what I call the "modern" qualities of
memory in this period: a framing of experiences and observations in a
language of disappearance and change, moments, movements, and multiplicities. For the historian, such language can be read in Baudelaire's
celebration of "le transitoire, le fugitif, le contingent," or seen in the
picture images of the Impressionist painters, records of a world transformed by urban living with its shifting spectacle of daily life, commerce,
mass transport and communications. The "memory" of such a landscape
should be itself fugitive, formed and constantly re-formed by rapidly
changing impressions—many memories for many perspectives. At the end
of the century, writers on the brain obliged this image.
    At the Société d'Anthropologie, anatomist and anthropologist Dr.
Fauvelle (1885) argued that memory was the perpetual *activity* of cerebral elements, a notion which explained the brain's ability to accumulate
an incalculable number of ideas despite "the restricted number of sense
organs." Rather than being limited by the storage capacity of a fixed
memory, the neurological brain had the power of arrangement, citation,
and re-citation. The consequences of such a conception were profound:
memory or specific "memories" could no longer be strictly defined or
evoked, for each was only the fugitive linking of a certain number of
neurological elements. Fauvelle argued that "the same sensations can be
combined in a thousand ways to take account of the objects which surround us."[11] What fascinated him was the alarming logic of such a statement. An object, to take the simplest case, would not actually be
"remembered" as it had been perceived; it would always be reconstructed, re-combined by elements which could as easily have been combined in a thousand other ways. The brain housed not the past, but the
elements of representation, responding to contingent circumstances—the
present. Another aphasia writer, Dr. J. B. Bouchaud, conceived a phrase
to capture this startling vision: he declared the brain not a repository of
experience, but "a *virtual* organ."[12]

Mapping the brain did not localize memory in particular fleshy lobes, but
abstracted and extended it in time and space. In his 1898 lectures given
at the hospital St. Andre de Bordeaux, Dr. Pitres argued, "There is no
more a memory than there is a respiration." The latter, he suggested,
was simply a categorical term to express the totality of "gaseous exchanges," which passed through the body; equally, "memory" did not
exist "outside the activities of anatomical elements which serve the exe-

cution of memory-operations." In effect, memory could never be truly localized in the physical brain, could never operate from "a unique center, autonomous, and autonomously distinct."[13] Pitres' comparison of memory and respiration was quite intentional. Breathing depended upon the lungs, but was not the lungs; memory depended upon parts of the brain, yet was none in particular. Like a breath, memory could be said to exist only as the ceaseless activity of links and connections not to a "center," but between "the thousand centers" of the brain.

In destroying brain tissue and creating "amnesias," what aphasias degenerated were not entities or "memories" stored in the brain, but connections. Pitres explained that the aphasias did not act by destroying a specialized center, but in "breaking one part of the paths and junctions which unite the centers." Pitres' conclusion was a stunning and sweeping evocation of memory as a cartographical communications network, a map and global web of signals and circulating sensations lodged nowhere in particular. From this point of view he proposed that memory and language disorders would well merit the name of "transcortical aphasia . . . the rupture of communications between the sensorial cortex centers and the equally intercortical neurons of the psyche."[14]

Pitres used a vocabulary of "breaks" and "ruptures" in the cortical centers as a means of explaining aphasic amnesia disorders. As he well knew, however, the memory of language was not limited simply to the brain. Though investigations of Broca's center had determined that it did not contain the "memory of words," it was nonetheless presumed to contain a sort of *pouvoir interrupteur*—a switching power—to stop or release nervous current to different groups of muscles. Articulate language depended not only upon the powers of the brain, but an effective coordination of brain, nerves, and muscle into reflex operations. Language— Dr. Legroux's "expression through conventional signs"—was a function of the memory of the body entire. Recall that Broca himself believed that the third convolution contained "not the memory of words but those of movements, necessary to articulate words."

Cases like that of Paris physician Dr. Paul Garnier (1889) well illustrated this conception of memory language as body movement. Garnier's aphasic patient, Jules G., was evidently tormented by hallucinations and oneiric enemies which attacked his ability to communicate with other human beings. Unable to understand his patient, what baffled Garnier was not Jules G.'s lack of ability to express what had happened to him, but his disassociation of ideas from motor abilities: he could not say what he meant. In place of the usual coordination of words with tongue, lips, or gestures, Garnier noted, "each of these two mechanisms acted apart from the other . . . the word wanted by the idea en route to being projected is not juxtaposed with it. Another is substituted by the chance of verbal encounter."[15]

The "scene" of memory as defined by aphasia was only incidentally the brain, for in aphasia, memory was "localized" not more and more specifically to particular brain tissues, but more and more generally to different links and connections with organs and muscles which manifested and expressed speech and gesture. Medical-legalist M. J. Lefort called aphasia "a symptom of diverse afflictions, but in no way an affliction in itself," in that it was an aberration in the "synergy of muscles concurrent with the act of speaking."[16]

Lefort described muscular synergies in terms of speaking, yet the extension of memory into the physiology of the body also raised language questions about another complex communicative gesture: writing. Dr. Georges Surbled (1889) noted that along with the "memory of words" of the brain, anatomists had long postulated a "graphic center" which was supposedly "the memory of writing." Localization studies declared this to be incorrect—as memory was no longer a particular repository of language, there could be "neither a graphic center, nor graphic images" in the brain. Once again, "movement" became the defining characteristic of a reconceived memory of writing. The mythical "centre graphique" was in fact "a motor center . . . which enters into relations with the language centers to actuate the muscles of the fingers and the hand necessary for the complicated play of writing."[17] The activities of the arm, hand, and fingers manifested "memory" no less than the brain.

The memory of writing differs from that of speech and other gestural expressions in an important way: it is a motor activity which generates its own external record. Two memories operate in writing: that of the arm, hand, and fingers, and that of the traces, loops, and lines left by pen and paper. The links between the neurological memory of the brain and the traces of the ink and paper were a particularly charged subject for clinicians, for the failure of memory in this respect was not only a psychological or medical problem, but also a legal and moral dilemma.

M. J. Lefort (above) reported how aphasia had created dilemmas of legal responsibility hardly studied or understood except "very lately." He noted the case of a former merchant from Valence who could write perfectly well to express his ideas, but then could not understand "the lines traced out by his hand," a disorder which gravely affected his business.[18] Such neurological puzzles call attention to the status of writing in the nineteenth century and the essential role it played in framing the boundaries of an abstract, responsible individual. One medical and legal scholar, Dr. Charles Mills, drew on this point by examining French laws concerning testaments, documents, and contracts, noting that the signature was the affirmation of a legal act. Oral proofs of agreements did not carry the same weight as writing, which alone constituted "the criterion of competency and responsibility." The logic of giving such status to writing is complex and deeply linked to memory. As an externalized and inscribed language, the written word has a certain fixed continuity through time, unavailable to the ephemeralities of speech. Moreover, writing can be detached from its author, thus becoming its own author-authority as a record, a piece of interpreted evidence which its creator may then be forced to confront. Writing—especially the signature—thus carries an internal promise of responsibility.

In legal testaments, writing was itself a memory, carrying to the future the desires of a man or woman after death. Legal scholar Charles Briand (1891) noted, "The will and testament is the most solemn act which a man can undertake; he makes arrangements for his property for a time when he will no longer exist; he dictates his will to future generations." I raised such issues in an earlier chapter. The memory of writing was not merely a psychological issue; it was an issue of patrimonies and judgments, of the "memory" of generations and the transmission of heritages.[19]

Writing was more than signs and representation for neurologists and legal scholars, it was evidence of judgment linked to memory, a way of ensuring responsibility for past acts. These issues were thus played out not only in the clinic, but in testimonies and courts. Consider for a moment an event as notorious as the Dreyfus affair. The tale of the Jewish captain falsely condemned for treason which divided France at century's end is a grand epic of French anti-Semitism, military cover-up, and bitter polemics about Republican principles and national interest, individual justice and the dignity of the *patrie*. A surprising choice to talk about writing and memory? The role of the press was significant, as was the pen of Emile Zola. In many ways the press *made* the Dreyfus Affair, as Zola's "J'accuse" to reopen the case ably demonstrates. But most of all, and well worth remembering, is that the Affair was, at least initially, entirely based upon a question of handwriting.

The use of writing to establish responsibility for past acts was, at least juridically, what the Affair was all about. Dreyfus and the *police judiciare* fought not over the partisan political issues which came to consume the case, but over the significance of establishing guilt through written traces. According to the transcript of the trial, October 26, 1894, Dreyfus was interrogated about the famous incriminating letter which indicated he had sold military secrets to the German enemy. "How can you explain that a letter, announcing to the agent of a foreign power the sending of confidential documents, has been identified as having been written by your hand?" Dreyfus responded, "I deny, as from the first day, having ever written to any agent of a foreign power." One officer described Dreyfus's confrontation with evidence: "Extremely defiant, he always remained vague when I presented him with isolated fragments of writing." Dreyfus denounced the fragments, arguing in effect that written proof depended upon a wholeness of expression; the prosecution was showing not writing, but only that someone had taken "detached pieces of my manuscripts and put them together." His defense was always to disassociate himself from the identity of writing: "I can only imagine one thing: *c'est qu'on m'a volé mon écriture*"—"They've stolen my writing from me."

Language and writing experts followed the case closely. Alphonse Bertillon, famed for his systems of criminal identification based on anthropological techniques (he was a family friend of Broca, and will be discussed in detail in a later chapter), was a handwriting expert at the trial and declared the incriminating documents authentic. On October 18 the Commandant du Paty interrogated Dreyfus: "How do you explain that the experts find your writing the same as that on the document . . .?" Dreyfus denied authorship ("the experts have made a mistake"), despite the fact that he himself was nevertheless often at pains to distinguish his own writing from the documents he insisted were false. He was, predictably, subjected to dictations in which his own writing, though he attempted naturally to alter it, was astonishingly similar to the incriminating documents he denied. In such cases, report the judicial police, he had but one familiar explanation: "On m'a volé mon écriture."[20] The political and ideological storms which came to surround the trial gradually obscured the fundamental point about the Dreyfus case: the judgments were based upon accepting the premise that a man's guilt or innocence, honor or treachery could be decided by the disputed evidence of written traces.

"The memory of writing" in the Dreyfus affair was framed, juridically, by the examination and interpretation of characters and symbols—Dreyfus's own handwriting. Worth recalling, however, is that "la mémoire de l'écriture" for clinicians was, more often than not, "the memory of the *movements* of writing" (G. Subrled). A stroke was an image, but also a transit of the hand across the page. Writing was movements—ascending, descending, lateral, spatial, the repetition and combination of directions. Memory could be extended anywhere that the motor centers of the brain could coordinate the spatial work of writing. Though no one would rightly call a pen "memory," the movements of a pen were evidence of memory in action. Why not the operations of a more elaborate tool, the printing press, and after the mid-nineteenth century, one fitted with a mechanical motor?

Dr. Henri Pieron, who would make an international reputation for himself as an experimental psychologist, proposed such an argument in a detailed thesis, *Mémoire et evolution* (1910). In a work of extraordinary drama, Pieron drew together the "memory of writing" with that of "movement" to fashion an image appropriate to the dynamic "modernity" of the early twentieth century. His image was the printing press, the machine which permitted "the fantastic acceleration of mnemonic progress in modern societies by multiplying the prints and traces of memory."[21] The printing press, with its seemingly endless impression of texts, not only created a typographic memory of events, but made possible the rapid circulation of an increasingly multiplied quantity of printed words. Fixed on paper, widely distributed, separated from the presence of a particular speaker, Pieron's accelerated explosion of printed traces was the homologue to the aphasic memory described by Georges Surbled in 1899: "The memory is not a unique and indivisible faculty, special and autonomous, as the old psychologists like to think and teach; it is a faculty which multiplies itself to infinity."[22]

In "memory" literature, Gutenberg's printing press has been a favorite image around which to concentrate the historical triumph of written records over oral traditions.[23] The fin de siècle deserves its own image of the typographic and neurological in collision, and one is provided by an oddly appropriate medical anecdote. In a bizarre case from 1901, Dr. Gilles de la Tourette (of Tourette's syndrome fame, a nervous disorder) reported an autopsy at the hospital of Saint-Antoine in which the printed word literally substituted for the neurological organs of the body.

One day, after examining several cadavers during a busy morning, the doctor in charge of the autopsy theater was astonished to discover that the brain and spinal cord were missing from one of them. Despite an obligatory search, the parts had apparently been confused with those of another corpse, mislaid, or stolen. To his consternation, the doctor found himself confronted by a "body without organs" and a strange spectacle: the brain was definitely gone, and the spinal cord had been replaced "by a newspaper subscribed to by the *garçon* of the ampitheater." The image is arresting: the governing nervous distributor of the body and main organ of memory were missing in the corpse, mysteriously replaced by a typographic news record. To aggravate this metaphor, let me note Tourette's report that the situation became a great scandal precisely due to "la Presse," which attacked the doctors for incompetence, leading one to complain to Tourette bitterly of insults and criticisms "which will certainly seem to you unjustified."[24] The journalists seemed intent on ensuring that the hollowed-out body would nonetheless generate its own series of reports and writing.

However one may read Tourette's imagery, it can serve as a useful mnemonic in portraying a split between the corpse as a social body emptied of organic, "living" traditions, and the newspaper as the external, hyperproliferated typographic culture of the late nineteenth century. The links between memories of body and writing in the machine age were so overwhelming that maladies of forgetting were accompanied by shocks of too much memory, an unsettling perception of senses overloaded by excesses of information to decipher without logic or coordination. Pieron warned that "one risks losing oneself—and one almost begins to wish for the ancient destructive amnesias of the fire at the celebrated library of Alexandria."[25] The image Pieron offered was not of amnesia as a deep well of forgetfulness, but of obliteration and destruction. His *société moderne* accelerated the technologies of memory, but ultimately had no control over them. The reactive blindness he proposed against too much writing, too many words, drew upon images which came out of the neurological clinic: fragments, sensations, erasures, language, and images without sense or coordination—modern civilization was becoming aphasic.

Images of an age read out of the body—particularly the language-memory centers of the brain—were regularly evoked by anatomists and neurologists for whom clinical aphasia studies were opportunities to speculate on broad questions of historical change. Pieron's were only the most dramatic examples, illustrating an externalized "accelerated memory" which ended up by unsettling its own creators. Many of Broca's disciples at the Société and Ecole d'Anthropologie followed their master into the "natural" histories of polygenesis and cranial development by formulating evolutionary narratives to trace the biological destinies of the human species. The measuring stick for such speculations was often, predictably enough, the third frontal convolution.

The anthropologist Fauvelle argued that Broca's center measured not only disorders of language, but the ultimate historical memory: the evolution of humanity, in which the passage from lower to higher species was motivated by the third convolution. In a commentary on men and apes, Fauvelle noted about his simian cousins that "they have also the muscles which, in Man, create articulate language, but they lack the third frontal convolution, that is to say the group of volitive cells whose connected actions produce language." Fauvelle did not define "language" merely as an ability to produce sounds or gestures. At a time of free education (Ferry Laws), expanding railway networks (Freycinet Plan), and Republican governments waiting for the arrival of the petit-bourgeois "nouvelles couches" to electoral power, "language" was nothing less than the extension of *civilisation, egalité,* and *fraternité* to all of France, and perhaps the world. The third convolution was a small section of brain marked by the political, pedagogical, and material progress of a society extending its "perfections" to "the mass of the people."

> Today regular and correct language is no longer the prerogative of the ruling classes: the inhabitants of the countryside speak as well as those in the towns; means of transport are available to all. Industry, in multiplying, has popularized the means of improving nutrition, clothing, and habitation.[26]

Taking "regular and correct" language as a marker of evolutionary progress was an argument for placing Broca's convolution at the center of historical explanation. Just as apes were defined as having no third convolution, the raw inarticulateness of aphasics set them back in the scheme of primitive and modern to a period in the history of the evolving brain "when the group of cells in question didn't exist except in an undoubtedly incomplete state. I would speak of the Chellean prehistoric epoch." The primitive brain was recapitulated in the attack of the illness itself; to be stricken with aphasia was to go backward in time, to experience brute language in the process of formation. The afflicted individual manifested this regression in his or her own life history. In an 1888 appraisal of Broca's localization theories, one clinician commented that the victim of aphasia, stricken by loss of "the very complicated art of coordinating a great number of muscles in the production and articulation of sounds," was deprived not only of language, but was returned "to the state where he was in his earliest infancy."[27]

Why should the neuro-physiological centers of language and memory have been the record of "civilization" in the body? Part of the reason lies in the way language functions were one part of the human organism which could be trained to "progress." To make this point, one Dr. Ferrand compared "the ruling nerve centers of language" with other organs which, "once formed, act according to their organization," such as the liver which produced bile, the stomach which digested, the heart which beat automatically and naturally. The nervous system which coordinated speech was unlike these organs, being principally reactive; as such, it was sensitive to external stimuli, susceptible to alteration. The human species, because of its highly developed brain and nervous functions, was graced with a special capacity for such alteration. For Ferrand, this meant the possibility of *improving* the organism. The nerve centers of language did not function automatically, but in accordance with "the activity which education imposes upon them, and the adaptation which use makes them undergo."[28]

The unique human use of memory, determined by the third convolution and highly developed nervous system of the species, was ultimately a question of education. Ferrand was not alone in presuming essential rapports between the physiology of language and memory in the clinic and the pedagogy of the school system. On the same theme Henri Pieron had cast a jaundiced eye upon "a young man 14 years old" from "the old French school . . . glorified for its pedagogical successes because it has succeded in graduating some of its imbeciles, who furthermore remain incapable of rendering the least service." The heart of this diatribe was a double attack: clearly against conservative, often Catholic "old school" institutions, yet also against a model of memory as accumulation and storage, a model appropriate only to a pedagogy based on pointless indoctrination. As Pieron complained, "a surcharge of memory makes new acquisitions more and more dificult, succeeding only by diminishing the force of previous memories." Far from improving the mind, learning through brute quantities of rote information was debilitating. Pieron argued for a new conception of memory as movement, dynamic, mobilizing, and selecting "the useful at any given moment."[29]

Memory was charged with a vocabulary of "service," of what was "useful." Pieron's memory played with a double language, constituted between medicine and the human sciences by a dual practice: the surgical

technique of the clinic, and the rhetoric of a civic politics. Other neurologists and anatomists presented a similar "memory" in clinical reports.
Examining convolutions and hypothesizing the thousand nerve centers
of memory was more than good medical science; it was an attempt to
write a morality of the nervous system. The brain and neuromuscular
activities described, presented—created—by the savants were more than
the objects of medical curiousity; they made language into progress,
memory into responsibility, and nerve centers into the redoubts from
which to battle over a territory divided by religion, profession, and political ideology.

Pre-neurological conceptions of memory had been based on a twin notion: that memory was a sort of faculty or quality of mind (like "imagination"), and that it operated by storing impressions somewhere in the
brain. Fauvelle was among the strongest critics of this received wisdom,
remarking, "This word *faculty* is absolutely improper; faculty, power of
whom, of what? A center is necessary for a faculty." As I have argued,
clinical theorizing and practice was based upon *de*centered memory, fixed
areas replaced by "the forced results of many felt impressions, of nerve
currents, more and less active." In this phrase of Fauvelle's, with its vocabulary of force, nerves, and activity, lay a singular conception: memory
was the firing of one nerve rather than another. This, in itself, was perfectly consistent with the image of the transcortical network of the brain.
Yet a neurologically conceived memory determined that something more
be true: memory functions would operate according to principles not of
impression and accumulation, but distinction and differentiation. Fauvelle
argued this point with a didactic image of a man placing his hands in
buckets of hot and cold water; "it is impossible to have at the same time
the sensations of hot and cold . . . without there being a comparison, that
is, a judgment by the simple fact of their simultaneity."[30]
    "Judgment" was a strong key word; Fauvelle mocked traditional psy-
chological philosophers, "foreign to physical and physiological knowledge," for maintaining that reflexes and actions of the body were due to
"a species of memory." Memory was not an entity, not a site, but a series
of distinctions endlessly made by "the primordial property of nerve elements," a memory of *difference*. "Judgment" was not a sign of divine
authority, but a *necessity* carried in the memory of a body ceaselessly
confronted with change and the "comparison of sensations."[31] As a neu-
rophysiological entity rather than an abstract faculty, memory was fully
functional in the human organism, open to medical investigation, a subject proper to a clinic or scientific society. Dynamic rather than static,
adaptive to the present rather than concerned with keeping the past, it
was a scene of political morality not by reliance on traditional knowledge
or appeal to abstract powers, but by the natural functioning of nerves
and muscles revealed by anthropological research: distinction and action

in every reflex, scores of judgments—each useful, individual; a memory of pragmatic *service*.

This anthropological conception could be savagely polemical, and stands as a small marker in the great nineteenth-century debates over the evolutionary questions so resoundingly articulated by Charles Darwin— whether "Man" was part of or apart from nature; whether humanity was a "species" like other living organisms; whether a divine human soul and unique human faculties separated men and women from other lower animals. Those favoring the divine dignity of Man took a generally dim view of the materialist tendencies of anatomists and anthropologists, whose claims seemed to reduce all proud human qualities to a rather ignoble series of biological functions in the name of something called "science."[32]

Moreover, allowing groups of such like minds to associate and share ideas could have dangerous political consequences. The founding of the Société d'Anthropologie during the reign of Napoleon III in 1859 had raised such questions. Broca's initial petition to establish his scientific society had worried the Ministry of Public Instruction, as Broca's biographer notes: "anthropology suggested subversion and the spirit of 1848; something vaguely degrading to man's immortal soul, possibly conflict with the teachings of the Church and the interests of the Empire, perhaps even a threat to the precarious security of His Majesty."[33] Police agents attended the first two years' meetings, and discussions of religion or governmental matters were strictly forbidden.

If an anthropological, anatomical, medical "science" of memory can be said to have existed at the end of the nineteenth century, it was the product of decades of political and intellectual battles. Under the Empire such battles were shaped by the uneasy relationship between anthropology as a discipline and the politics of the Church and imperial government. A generation later, the triumph of "science" as a mainstay of republicanism may have put the Church on the defensive ideologically and made the idea of police agents at the Société d'Anthropologie laughable, but disputes among the savants over doctrine and institutional politics were vivid.

These disputes were as much part of the forging of the modern memory of the brain as the doctors' own clinical reports, since they could determine whose science would rule the profession and the public. Aphasia, which shaped the contours of so much of memory research, was not only a medical entity, but a political point of struggle. Some attacks of one party against another were of the sort which Pierre Marie and his student Moutier launched against "the clinic of Broca." Marie, a distinguished former student of both Charcot and Broca, disparaged the inflated importance given to "Broca's aphasia," using his own anatomical researches to establish himself as successor to his great teachers. Most of all, he wished to wrest away the preeminent authority which Broca's closest students exercised over so much of anatomical and anthropological work in France.

Marie argued that Broca's science rested effectively on the identification of a "clinical entity," which was in fact "the simple juxtaposition of two very distinctive problems" in the articulation of language: words and physical processes. Having failed to make this distinction, Broca's students had satisfied themselves by creating all sorts of different "mixed" and "total" aphasias which were in fact only degrees of the same syndrome. What Marie defied was the Broca school's strategy of extending its competence over all of neurology by way of the prestige of the third convolution. Marie argued for the place of his own research and theories in medical journals and practices by declaring the third frontal convolution "an accessory fact, banal, lacking all clinical significance."[34] His work ultimately inaugurated a new stage in aphasia research.

Conflicts were strong even within the walls of the schools themselves. In 1889, as the Paris Universal Exposition commemorated the Revolution and affirmed the Third Republic, memory struggles were taking place at the Ecole d'Anthropologie. In that year Paul Topinard, Broca's successor at the Ecole, published a pamphlet dedicated, ostensibly, "to the Memory of Broca: the Society, the School, the Laboratory, and the Broca Museum." Topinard's work was a *mémoire* dedicated to the *mémoire* of a man and all of the institutions which remembered and reminded of him. It was also a transcript of the multiple and contested memories within the central praise of the master, and a meditation on whose version of science would control the future. Topinard wrote on the occasion of his own expulsion and exclusion from the Ecole and of his struggles with Fauvelle. The latter belonged to a faction described by Topinard as "materialist and intransigent from every point of view," extremists desirious of publishing "the natural history of the Supreme Being." Fauvelle's faction attacked all dissenters from its own point of view (including Topinard and the moderates at the Ecole d'Anthropologie) in a series of polemics, and planned to publish a "Dictionnaire du combat," a manifesto of positive science and anti-clericalism.

In the struggle to control the direction of the Ecole, Topinard played his memory card, denouncing his enemies by cloaking himself in the shadow of his predecessor: "I believe my duty is to save the works of the master. . . . I've not had but one goal: to recapture a measured and tolerant anthropology, non-systematic, as Broca would have wanted it." Fauvelle and company played their own memory card, hosting dinners not to the honor of Broca (whom they respected), but to commemorate other appropriated figures, emblematic of their politics. Perhaps the most important was "the dinner which took the initiative of celebrating the centenary of Voltaire and Diderot," on which occasion several volumes of papers were published.

Topinard and his vision of science in the memory of Broca were finally forced out. In his account of the events he noted how the new masters inaugurated their own rituals of commemoration, and recorded with some perspicacity the inexorable links between memory, commemoration, and the dissection table, and the politics of all three. "They didn't forget themselves either. As soon as one of them died, they organized a subscription to raise a monument to him and have a medallion made. Every civil burial was a triumph. The medallion, procession, and autopsy were all connected."[35]

The history of memory in the late nineteenth century is one of intellectual and political struggle: a scientific reconceptualization of the brain embroiled in the conflicts between its investigators. What the investigators proudly called their "science" was a field crossed by innumerable disputes, not all of them tied to ascertaining the truth of positive knowledge. The differences between neurologists and psychological philosophers were one source of division. Professional rivalries between anthropologists, anatomists, and neurologists themselves were another.

If anatomists, anthropologists, and psychologists seemed to be turning their science into political positions and moral philosophies, proper philosophers were returning the compliment, showing how grand concepts (real/ideal, mind/matter, determinism/freedom) could be imagined in the language and assumptions of the latest clinical debates. The greatest monument to this interlocking of disciplines appeared in 1896, several hundred pages of fluid argumentation whose last word was *liberté*. In *Matière et mémoire*, Henri Bergson laid out the philosophical plan for an evolutionary, ethically charged dynamic materialism, and I use his work alongside the aphasic brain as a site where the meanings of a truly "modern memory" are located at the end of the century.

Bergson begins his plan by arguing that his body is something which he calls an "image" which is curiously a "center of action." As an image, it is halfway between a material thing and an idea, having physical qualities, yet being characterized principally as an aggregation of positions, simultaneously and instantly again different. To grasp this concept, consider a way of seeing introduced just a year before Bergson's writing: the cinema—independent still pictures which moved, each distinct, yet defined only as part of a sequence.

Memory was the record of *this* sort of body, not a faculty of storage and recall, but a series of moments seized and inserted into a continuous "present action." As Bergson argued it, "the brain does not act as a reservoir of images." Memory was rather "the act of choice of a resemblance among many resemblances, of a contiguity among other contiguities." Like a flickering celluloid band, each instantaneously seized and selected moment of the past would become present and be the potential of the next. Memory was always "that which no longer acts but might

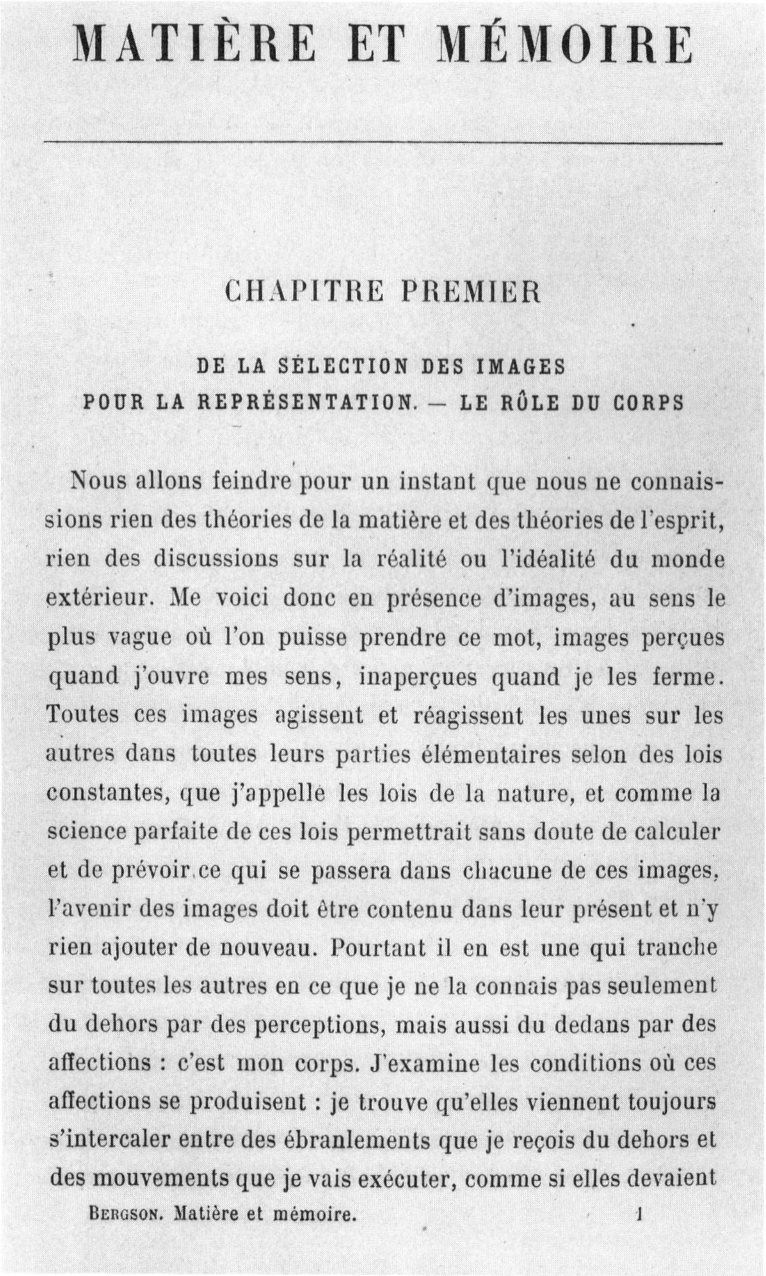

MATIÈRE ET MÉMOIRE

CHAPITRE PREMIER

DE LA SÉLECTION DES IMAGES
POUR LA REPRÉSENTATION. — LE RÔLE DU CORPS

Nous allons feindre pour un instant que nous ne connais-
sions rien des théories de la matière et des théories de l'esprit,
rien des discussions sur la réalité ou l'idéalité du monde
extérieur. Me voici donc en présence d'images, au sens le
plus vague où l'on puisse prendre ce mot, images perçues
quand j'ouvre mes sens, inaperçues quand je les ferme.
Toutes ces images agissent et réagissent les unes sur les
autres dans toutes leurs parties élémentaires selon des lois
constantes, que j'appelle les lois de la nature, et comme la
science parfaite de ces lois permettrait sans doute de calculer
et de prévoir ce qui se passera dans chacune de ces images,
l'avenir des images doit être contenu dans leur présent et n'y
rien ajouter de nouveau. Pourtant il en est une qui tranche
sur toutes les autres en ce que je ne la connais pas seulement
du dehors par des perceptions, mais aussi du dedans par des
affections : c'est mon corps. J'examine les conditions où ces
affections se produisent : je trouve qu'elles viennent toujours
s'intercaler entre des ébranlements que je reçois du dehors et
des mouvements que je vais exécuter, comme si elles devaient

Figure 11 A matter of memory: opening arguments of Henri Bergson's
Matière et Mémoire, 1896. (*Source*: Central Research Division, The New York
Public Library, Astor, Lenox and Tilden Foundations)

act, and will act by inserting itself into a present sensation from which it borrows the vitality."[36]

I have treated cinematic questions in a separate chapter. What concerns me here is what a careful reader would recognize in Bergson's formulations—the language of the Société d'Anthropologie: the rejection of the brain as "reservoir," the "choices" of memory, the activities, "sensations," and actions of the body. In denying the possibility that "memories were truly deposited in the brain," Bergson was only following what savants like Broca or Pitres were arguing. Consistent with clinical studies, Bergson maintained that, "in the diverse aphasias and disorders of visual or auditory recognition, it is not determined memories which are torn away from the place where they are located."[37] As localization had oddly demonstrated, memory was not a site, but a coordination, an activity. Aphasic amnesias had demonstrated not effacement of words or language, but damage to coordination, the loss of contact between mind and body, an inability to arrange and to "use" the past (experience, education, habit) effectively. The challenge of an effective memory lay "in discovering in the present situation that which resembles a former situation, and then in placing alongside of that present situation what preceded and followed the previous one in order to profit by past experience."[38] In aphasic disorders, problems of memory were the disjunctions between the vitality of memories and "la situation presénte," instances in which past and present could not be unified as act.

The classic example of such dysfunction from a clinical point of view would be a patient unable to communicate because of a complete disassociation between linguistic idea, articulation, and muscular movement, much like the Garnier case cited earlier. The parallel philosophical problem for Bergson was that of reconciling the freedom of the human spirit with the scientific imperatives of considering the human being a biological organism. This philosophical dilemma of mind and matter, determinism and freedom, would be solved if the body itself could be demonstrated to act out *liberté*. The disorders of aphasia pointed to the resolution. The key was a neurological philosophy of memory, for in this schema what was memory but the experience of the past adapted to each singular moment expressed in the nervous system? Aphasia studies showed that language was both idea and act, that memory was the fine coordination of concepts and muscular movements, invoked and instantly expressed as speech or gesture. Bergson could thus present memory as both necessity and pragmatism, the choice and imperative of *expression*.

In 1881 experimental psychologist Théodule Ribot had proposed a "law of regression" by which amnesias destroyed memories. Bergson later wrote commentaries on this law, noting that "in general, words disappear in a determined order, as if the affliction understood grammar. First eclipsed are proper nouns, then common nouns, then adjectives, and finally verbs." Why verbs should be the last parts of speech to survive a destructive amnesia followed a logic which made perfect sense to Berg-

son: "It's simply that the verbs express actions," unlike linguistic concepts which required "a more and more complicated artifice."[39]

"Memory equals verbs" could be a shorthand for Bergson, with this
critical footnote: the verbs were selected and adapted to the present situation. Memory was not the blind instinct of generations. By transforming the moment of nervous reflex into an act of judgment, memory
instantaneously materialized the past acting in the present as a morally
defined activity. Each moment which "facilitates language and favors action" was the employment of memory as "bon sens"—the manifested
experience of deciding the right thing to do. In an academic address
Bergson described "good sense" as "that which gives to action its reasonable character, and to thought its practical character," a formulation
which ultimately was an imperative to ably "orient oneself in practical life
. . . not only in one's own affairs, but also and above all those of the
country."[40] To summarize, "memory" was not recollection of the past,
but choices made of the past applied in the present—each choice bearing
a logic of obligation to oneself, others, and the reasonable truth of the
situation.

Bergson, like his colleagues in the clinic, fashioned a new memory and
generated a new vocabulary to talk about it: dynamism and transformation, decision and judgment. The link between memory, neurology, and
the new vocabulary was aphasia. Aphasia research linked the expressions
of writing and speaking to the nervous system and the physiology of the
body through mappings of the brain. This meant, ultimately, that memory would be reimagined from a faculty of impressions or storage to a
dynamic play of nerve centers, movements, and actions. This "new"
memory was fashioned by the practices and disputes of clinicians and
thinkers with historical visions of evolution, science, and civilization at
times attached to republicanism and civicism. Through aphasias and convolutions, anthropologists and anatomists grappled with the accelerated
typographic memory of the machine age, driven by the printing press and
a growing reading public. Ideologically, neurological memory was partisan in educational, legal, and religious controversies. Upon "memory,"
the odd philosopher even made his reputation, reading the legacies of
the aphasic brain to create a moral philosophy to serve *la patrie* from the
act of remembering.

The new memory also left behind its own monument. Here I return
to Broca's autopsy report from "Tan," whose case began the whole transformation: "The patient died April 17, at eleven o'clock in the morning.
The autopsy was done as soon as possible, that is within 24 hours, the
temperature was not very high. The cadaver did not present any signs of
putrefaction. The brain was shown a few hours later to the Société
d'Anthropologie, then immediately immersed in alcohol. This organ had
been so greatly altered that great precautions were needed to preserve it.
It was not until the end of about two months and several changes of

liquid that the piece began to harden." The thousand nerve centers of contemporary neurology floated in Tan's brain, a monument to the history of memory. Broca's final words cannot fail to impress: "Today it is in perfect condition, and it is deposited in the Dupuytren Museum under number 55A, "the nervous system."[41]

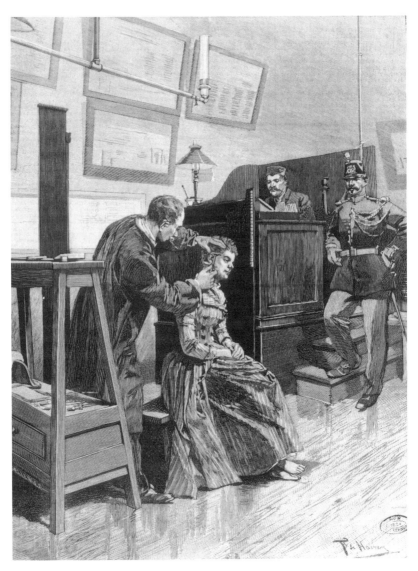

Figure 12 The measure of woman: the Paris anthropometric service (see Chapter Six) classifies a suspect, 1890. (*Source:* Bibliothèque Nationale)

5

Testimonies: Deserving of Faith

The case was dismissed—declared a "non-lieu"—by the judge. The archives remember them, a man and a little girl, in a dusty file from the Ministry of Justice. This one is titled "L'Affaire Cayotte, 1908."[1] It contains prosecutor's reports, scrawled notes from inspectors, yellowed newspaper clippings marked with orange wax pencil. Cayotte was a public school instructor at Francheville and he had been at his work for twenty-two years when his prosecution began. He was married and had a son studying medicine at Nancy. His conduct, according to the investigator's reports, had always been "irreproachable." A clipping from *La République* of September 19, 1908, relates what happened that year. "The odious news was carried by word of mouth: the teacher had called in and raped a young girl . . . the anger of the teacher's enemies knew no limits. Numerous 'witnesses' paraded into the chambers of the investigating judge. With a word, the magistrate confounded each of them . . . the clericals responded in their own fashion." The prosecutor's report details the accusation: "22 April 1908. Having lifted the skirts of the young girl, he would have touched her sexual organs with his hand, and have sent her off after a half-hour, recommending to her not to say anything, and threatening her. Such is the declaration of Lucienne Vuillaume, *sole witness* to this scene."[2]

These were the elements: a man of reputation, a girl, a sexual crime, a republican press, a clerical faction. This was the issue: both the newspaper and the prosecutor's report centered on the question of the *temoin*, the witness. The case rested upon the testimony of the little girl, the "sole witness." How the testimony was read was the critical factor in the judgment.

In his report, the chief inspector noted, "The Vuillaume child, heard many times over the course of the investigation has always, it is true, made an identical deposition, without variations . . . which appears sincere even though it has the appearance of a lesson learned by heart." The deposition was affirmative, consistent, and apparently sincere; oddly enough it was this very regularity which invited the suspicion of the inspector. Questioned on this regularity, the little girl was sure about the crime, but imprecise about when and where it had taken place. "She is very affirmative on the subject of the facts about which she would have been the victim, but she cannot bring any precision to the time at which they took place." Moreover, she was unable to give an accurate description of "the furniture adorning the room where the crime would have taken place." Pressed by the investigating judge to "tell the truth," the little girl began to fall apart, pronouncing a singular, critical phrase, "I'm afraid for my father to go to prison!"[3]

What follows is a history of the possibility of the past, indicated by three observations taken from the judge's and prosecutor's files in the Cayotte affair. The first concerns the investigator's questions about the hour and the furniture in the room where the alleged crime took place. What invited the prosecutor to challenge the child's story was the apparent disparity between the precision of the events of victimization and the ambiguity of their context. The importance of this point was not simply an obsession with detail; the furniture and the hour were at the heart of accepting the reality of the event. The young girl's narrative of events was intact, but not the coordinates which would have made it a true event—that is, having a location in time and space.

History or fiction?[4] Despite consistent depositions, the criteria of truth as established by the judge revealed the inextricable historical assumptions which linked testimony and memory. The girl's testimony was a tale recited like a story, a compelling narrative, but lacking the essential qualities of a true past—the historical dimension of uniqueness in time and space. In a commentary on historical practice, Henri Bergson had once written, "The unique question here is to know if the event had truly taken place at a given moment of time, at a determined point in space, and how it was produced."[5] Between story and history the prosecutor demanded an irreducible search for presence in the past; it was this historical imperative which divided the past between the memory and the lie.

The second observation is based upon the investigator's comment, "a lesson learned by heart." In a discourse before the Court of Appeals of Bordeaux (1902) lawyer J. Maxwell noted that of all the elements assembled to constitute a legal fact, "there is one . . . of particular importance, especially for the witness, the accused, or the plaintiff: that is the integrity of the memory."[6] Integrity and memory: the testimony of the little girl appeared finally not to be an act of memory, but memorization, and therein lay the difference. Struggles against forgetting are one dilemma for the witness who creates evidence through memory. In the Cayotte case, another dilemma was equally important: the possible falsification of the past.

"False witness" was a subject of considerable interest around the turn of the century, and research in the subject was seeing "an historic evolution," according to examining magistrate Emile Fourquet in 1901. The question of "false witness" seemed to Fourquet "an interesting chapter to join to that grand history of human lying which I am astonished to see has never been treated by the historians of our institutions."[7]

The materials for Fourquet's history of lying were already developing all around him. Psychologist Ernest Dupré summarized a growing literature (much of it written by himself), including specialized journals devoted to the fallibility of testimony, commenting that the most elementary considerations about legal testimony had rested "until very recently" in a "vague and imprecise state."[8] In 1912 one Dr. E. Paulus wrote of this new domain for his colleagues, "It is only over the course of the last twenty years and under the impulsion of a group of doctors, alienists, neurologists, and psychologists that this germ of a science is developed—today documented and flourishing—the *science of testimony.*"[9]

The new French "science of testimony" was not an isolated phenomenon at the turn of the century, but part of a developing pan-European interpretive framework centered upon what philosopher Paul Ricoeur has called a "hermeneutics of suspicion"—the idea that people do not say what they mean. What Marx had called "false consciousness" shaped by class would be elaborated into a staggering psychological science of "the unconscious" by the end of the century, fueled by studies of hypnotism and mental suggestibility. In clinics, psychiatrists' offices, and legal proceedings, the certainty of language as an expression of human intention was rendered suspect, sincerity interrogated as a guise, words a code for something else. The psychological investigation of testimony was an attempt to shape a science to interrogate a modern, indeterminate "self," driven by inner, unsuspected motivations.[10]

In 1885 Dr. Jean Martin Charcot, eminent head of the Clinic for Nervous Diseases at the Salpêtrière Hospital in Paris, commented that he'd had no contact with his German translator since the Franco-Prussian War. His guest Sigmund Freud took up the task of recording and translating Charcot's lectures into German, while trying to interest his teacher in the "cathartic" methods for treating hysteria developed by his colleague Breuer in Vienna. Freud was already building his "seduction theory," arguing initially that his patients' neuroses derived from episodes

of sexual assault, then in a later controversial turn, that they had fanta-
sized their victimization.[11]

The French study of false witness was also an attempt to get to the
heart of a real past, to know the limits of memory and to define a historical reality by interpreting stories with a practiced skepticism. As with
Freud, much of the science centered on analyzing and judging the reality
or unreality of sexual abuse. What the literature on scientific testimony
demonstrated both deliberately and unwittingly was that juridical truth
depended very much not only upon what was remembered, but upon
who spoke and who was believed. The result was a multiplication of
divided visions of reality which I will treat in sequence: science against
religion, expert against witness, child against adult, male against female,
and public against private, each declaring in its own way to speak the
truth.[12]

A third observation I would like to draw out of the Cayotte affair comes
from Freud's questions about fantasy, and a closing note added to the
declaration of a "non-lieu" in the case. In the wake of the girl's revelation, a note from the bureau chief appraised the testimony of the young
witness. "First of all, to suppose that the young Vuillaume lied, as I
believe, it would be necessary to demonstrate that she repeated a lesson
suggested to her by her parents . . . she could, all the same, have lied
spontaneously."[13] The child, the girl, the accusation, the suggestibility,
the spontaneous lie, all these elements were easily associated by the chief.

The vocabulary of the note demonstrates a particular fact about the
literature of "false witness": it was a field of investigation overwhelmingly
concerned with the female gender—girls and women. In clinics as well
as courts, the belief was quite plain. Ernest Dupré wrote: "the influence
of sex is preponderant, and little girls have much richer and more marked
tendencies to lie and invent than little boys. Furthermore, this etiological
influence of sex will distinctively mark the adults."[14] Emile Fourquet was
equally precise in making his distinctions, exclaiming, "How the feminine
false witness alone merits her own monograph!"[15] In France at the turn
of the century such statements were backed by research involving clinical
experiment and physical examination. Primary subjects were women and
children, and sexual crimes, rape, and molestation. As read by the specialists, these subjects and those crimes indicated that the credibility of
memory was distinctively gendered, and that in the sinking world of un-
truth, women and children would be first.

Let me address the three observations in order, beginning with the links
between testimony and history and a statement by scholar Ernest Naville,
who in a study dedicated to *L'Importance logique du temoinage* (1887)
maintained, "It is evident that in History, testimony alone furnishes the
material of the science—the past escaping all direct and personal observation." The parallel is of course not exact; originality in court testimony

would not have obeyed the same imperatives as originality in historical writing. The historian was presumed to reconstruct, synthesize, speculate based on the best available evidence. Not so the witness. The witnesses' relation to the past was very strictly defined by the condition of presence: the power of witnessing was to have had an absolute relation to an event. As Dupré put it simply, "judicial testimony is the deposition of a person who attests in court to have seen or heard something."[16]

Witnessing depended upon presence, yet presence (like "experience") was itself a problematic category for establishing the truth of the past. Naville outlined different orders of truth, basing his work on the theories of the mathematician-physicist-philosopher Euler. The first order characterized "the perceptions of our senses," reality as immediately perceived and experienced by the physical senses. The second order comprised "truths of reasoning and proof"; in this field, the work of mathematical logic especially operated, rendering the "proof" of scientific principles. Finally, there remained a third order of truth, distinct from these first two: "the third class is formed from truths which rest upon testimony, and their proof always comes back to this: "this thing is true because one or more persons *dignes de foi* have assured it."[17]

What means this "dignes de foi," a truth not grasped by experience or reason but by the acceptance of what others assure? Translated according to sense, the term would describe and define someone deemed trustworthy, reliable, credible. Literally understood, the term is composed of two elements, of which "foi" is the most notable. "Foi" suggests sincerity, word, evidence—and faith. Lawyer M. Duverger wrote essays on witnessing as nothing other than "an exhumation of memories."[18] The use of "exhumation," of a "dead" past returned to a living world, is an allusive image, for as appeals court lawyer Georges Gagnebe (1900) noted in his examination of the French legal system, false witness was not "a crime against the administration of justice," but "a crime against religion." The former system was characteristic of the Belgian and Italian penal codes. The latter religious interpretation, however, "is that of French law. Under our law, in effect, testimony in the legal sense of the word is a verbal declaration made in justice under *la foi du serment.*" The oath in France was taken "before the Divine," and as such all depositions affirmed the speaker's sincerity in front of "the God of truth who knows all."[19]

God, in the time of Gagnebe's writing, was under challenge. The religious oath was more than a promise to tell the truth, it invoked the long antecedents of the Law of Moses and recognized truth spoken not just as words, but as The Word attached to the people of The Word. The "good faith" of speaking under oath was allied with the "testimony" of the Christian believer who professed to "witness" the truth of God. The promises (and perils) of the *oath* were centered on a non-human justice whose signs of judgments all pointed to God, depending upon a faith in things unseen. Gagnebe noted ruefully that this threat of "all the vengeance of Heaven" was "no longer our conception today," and drew a distinctive historical break between ancients and moderns, commenting, "one can easily conceive how among the peoples of antiquity for whom religious belief was very ardent, perjury would have been considered one of the greatest crimes imaginable."[20]

At stake in the definition of perjury was a contested conception of the human person as a willing being, conscious of responsibility. The religious and ethical vision of credible testimony depended upon the sincerity of the witness under oath. Not so for practitioners of the "hermeneutics of suspicion." Noted the Italian criminologist Alfred Niceforo, "the unreliability of the deposition very often might not depend upon the bad faith of the subject; errors committed in good faith often present themselves in the form of a precise and exact memory."[21] The moral conception, argued Ernest Dupré, had to be discarded and replaced by one recognizing that "the conviction with which the witness makes a deposition is in no way proportional to the exactitude of the asserted facts. The assurance of the witness depends a great deal more on the suggestible nature of his mind."[22] Testimonies could not be judged in terms of the intentions of the speaker.

Such views had ideological roots and consequences. Disputes over the oath were part of a prolonged struggle between the Church and the (most recent) Republican government which would be marked by their official separation in 1905. Lawyer Pierre Farcet (1902) tracked this developing conflict in the meetings of the Chamber of Deputies. "Some twenty years ago even the institution of the solemn oath was attacked in the Parliament. One day, a newspaper article appeared: this was the point of departure. The next day a group of deputies, belonging to the extremists in the Chamber, formulated a project."[23] Such political maneuvering would find champions in clinicians like Dupré: "The sacramental formula of the oath which enjoins the witness to tell the truth and nothing but the truth dates from an era when positive psychology was not born, and it appears today in flagrant disagreement with the psychology of testimony itself."[24] Declaring individuals *digne de foi* appealed to ancient categories of argument from authority. The question would now be, whose authority? Fear of the Almighty—and respect for the Church—was at odds with the faith of positive science—and respect for the Republic.

The conflict was not limited to the use of the oath, but spilled over into the use of testimony in criminal cases as civil authorities sought to extricate themselves from the clergy in education, administration, and legal procedure. The Cayotte affair, recall, had engendered the remark, "The clerics responded in their own fashion," from *La République,* whose political sentiments are evident from the name of the paper. In the investigation, the testimony of the little girl wound together several strands about the politics of accusation. Piecing together the evidence of the case, the prosecutor concluded his report on Cayotte with some political observations about the village: "the former municipality had held him (Cay-otte) in very great esteem, but since the last elections, with the arrival of a clerical and reactionary majority in the city hall, he had been subjected to all kinds of interference . . . he was reproached in the clerical party of being, in the village, the champion of Republican ideals." The report of the chief inspector notes "the strange attitude of Vuillaume" (the father), who "by his own account had only one goal: to obtain the removal of the teacher . . . moreover, he neglected to have his child examined by a doctor."[25] The dismissal was granted not only because the girl admitted to lying about the crime, but on the judge's ultimate decision that the girl's testimony had been invented by the father in collaboration with the anti-Republican elements of the village government.

The polemics of sexual abuse and politics were always strong. When a priest was accused of molesting a girl, *L'Action* of March 6, 1908, gleefully headlined "A Clerical Scandal," with the ironic subtitle "suffer the little children to come unto me." Remarkably, the prosecutor's report in this case noted that the alleged victim was examined by "Doctor Du-pré, medical-legalist," who observed that the victim presented "no traces of violence resulting from any immoral offense." The paper nonetheless reported only that "the priest of Blandouet took flight in order to escape the gendarmes."[26]

Harsh words were reversed when the accused was a public instructor. In a case similar to the Cayotte scandal, "l'Affaire Marchand" (1908), another school instructor was indicted and condemned to three years in prison after two girls claimed he had molested them. Here, the concur-rent testimony of two witnesses convinced the judge: "the precision and the agreement in the declarations of the children seemed to leave no doubt about the question of guilt." The press quickly reacted, each paper brandishing a particular element of the case. *La Petite Républicaine* (Jan-uary 6, 1909) took up the outrage to reputation: "Marchand has been arrested, dishonored!" *Le Radical* adopted the framework of false charges, calling the Marchand affair a case "lacking a guilty party . . . in the Marchand affair this party has been invented, arrested, judged, and condemned." *La Lanterne* focused precisely on the psychology of testi-mony, with a clear and familiar bias against the witnesses: "Who are the witnesses upon whose depositions the jury based its verdict? Children." *La Lanterne* reminded its readers, "How easy it is to make children say what we want; how easy it is to influence them to the point where they themselves consider facts which never existed as having really been pro-duced in their presence." Nor did the polemic end there. If children were to be regarded de facto unreliable, it was not only because of their im-pressionability, but because of the ease with which they could be politi-cally manipulated. *La Lanterne* made clear where the real danger to justice lay, calling the case a "beautiful victory for the clericals . . . chil-dren are their most precious auxiliaries."[27]

Psychologists like Dupré were sympathetic to such skepticisms about the testimony of children. The reliability of testimony, he felt, could not (or should not) depend upon an idea of truthful speaking, for testimony was a "production" shaped according to "the age of the witness, sex, intellectual level, totality of qualities and psychic aptitudes, and emotional state at the moment of observation." The witness had to be dealt with as a "modern" self—that is, indeterminate and changeable, like the world of political, economic, and social flux he or she inhabited. In the face of such a dispersed and contingent psychological reality, the role of the medical expert was proposed by Dupré as essential to legal procedure. To the old soul, the priest; to the new mind, the expert, a specialist adapted to contemporary experience and qualified "to participate directly in the administration of justice." Notably, and ultimately, this direct participation in justice was conceived as the authority to question not only the value of testimony, but the truth of the speaker—whether he or she was "digne de foi." The expert, by excavating meanings rather than hearing confessions, would become "the nearly indispensable auxiliary of justice."[28]

Defining a new profession demanded staking claims to specialized skills and knowledge, and medical-legal practitioners legitimized their interest in testimony by anchoring it to practices they considered rigorous and scientific. "Testimony" would not simply be an arena of polemical dispute between Church and Republic; made into a science it would be analyzed by a modern experimental method, held to standards of proof, judged by the criteria of evidence. Testimony in the laboratory was a series of controlled experiments in which subjects were exposed to images, texts, or cinematic representations, reconstructions of familiar locations or staged scenes. Each situation was repeated, and altered to achieve a series of depositions by the same witness about a slightly differing set of views. Through difference and repetition, each successive test permitted the researchers "to study the influence of testimony on memory, the mechanism of consolidating remembrances, and in this way the progress of the crystallization of testimony."[29]

What the researchers unexpectedly ended up studying were their own assumptions about "science." A major experimentalist, Dr. André Fribourg, noted that if a subject were placed in front of a test object—say, an engraving—the resulting description of the image would never correspond to what the same person might say in a more realistic situation, "having seen the same gravure by chance on the wall."[30] "Real" witnessing took place, according to Fribourg, in situations of inattention. "Every day in the tribunals, people are called to make depositions on facts about which they were witnesses, but which at that time left them indifferent." An individual unconscious of the importance of unfolding events would later produce testimony "much inferior to that of a forewarned witness."[31] This distinction was a caveat to the psychological laboratory and the archive, where consciously or not, both the researcher and the research subject paid undue attention to finding what they expected. Ernest Dupré agreed that making a science out of the past was a dilemma, for the shape of that past depended upon the questions asked of it. "The value of a response depends upon the question which has provoked it. The response and the question form an indivisible system, a veritable couple, whose elements serve each other reciprocally."[32]

What did the experimental past look like? Fribourg noted a scene staged by another psychologist, Edouard Claparède, in which "a masked and disguised individual enters suddenly into the room . . . gesticulates, pronounces incomprehensible words and heads for the door." Asking his subjects to recall the details some two weeks later, Claparède found that the improbability of the situation had not improved their recall, nor could they identify the mask when it was presented to them. Surprised, he wrote, "strange, isolated facts, which should be the most striking to people who witness them, are not those which are best remembered as is commonly believed." On the contrary, he argued, "the mind refuses to admit that which is strange, contrary to the everyday and the routine."

Less and less did Claparède find that events were recalled "as they happened," and more and more that they corresponded to familiar narratives, images by which his subjects organized and expressed their experience. His conclusion was that the past—even of a simple event—was less a record than a sort of taxonomy. Not perceptions, but categorization of familiar types was the major function of the memory. "Our testimony depends much less on our memory, than on the mental image that we possess of a type or a class in which we arrange facts." The reliability of past events was shaped less by experience than by the structure of expectations by which they were investigated.[33]

Could any form of testimony, any deposition about the past be reliable? Notarial testimony addressed this question by depending upon the principle of a "large number of witnesses." In such cases, the notary played a fascinating role of substitutability, in which an act of public testament could be received by two notaries and two witnesses, or one notary and four witnesses. One notary had the existential legal value of two witnesses—the minimum of two establishing the truth. This principle also applied in history. Claparède commented that in good historical works "facts" were reported "in different ways by multiple narrators." In this way "one of the versions is supported by a greater number of witnesses than the other." To make his point, Claparède cited the argument of the historian Bernheim, who reasoned that multiple observers were a "means of control and protection against the exclusivist character and insufficiency of the faculty of individual observation."[34]

One evening after a lecture, Claperède put this principle to the test by asking his students if they knew of a window outside their room which overlooked the main corridor of the university. The problem was posed to refer to something undeniably familiar to the students, who passed by it often on their way to the lecture. In theory, as in historical practice, the multiplicity of observations or opportunities for observation should either have supported the correct response or at least canceled out the incorrect by the weight of majority. Claperède reported: "In spite of all these favorable conditions, its existence was denied forty-four times out of fifty-four persons; eight subjects responded 'yes,' and two declared they did not know." The conclusion: "In numerous cases, not only is the value of witnessing not proportionate to the number of witnesses, but a small minority can be right against a strong majority." Many witnesses, in effect, could agree in very good faith upon the same mistake.[35] The majority was consistent and undoubtedly sincere in its testimony— but wrong.

The question of the science of testimony remained unresolved: who was trustworthy, credible, "deserving of faith?" The notary, in limited instrumental proceedings, was charged with this responsibility, but in all other cases demonstration showed that neither good intentions, nor even numbers guaranteed accurate testimony. Reliable witnesses were defined by a principle of exclusion. Under the law, any number of psychopaths, imbeciles, or others typed and declared mentally deficient were deemed not witnesses of reliable quality. They were not alone. Emile Fourquet in 1901 wrote, "Age and sex also exercise their influence on testimonies; we have seen how, in the course of this study, women and children figure in the first rank of false-witnesses . . . for both it costs much less than for the man to alter the truth."[36] Fourquet was not alone in his judgment, and his basic point bears repeating: "memory" was not the same for male and female. Between the past and its retelling were a series of fractures which divided man, woman, adult, and child. Psychologist E. Paulus wrote, "Testimony by men is less comprehensive and less assured, but more true than that of women." Ernest Dupré's own clinical studies suggested to him the following conclusions: "Of testimonies taken under the sacred oath, 11% are false. Women swear much more easily than men, and in sworn responses are twice as often mistaken."[37]

The distinction was not a simple matter of considering women less credible than man; at issue was the definition of credibility itself. Women, like children, were probably more perceptive, and apparently more sincere than men in giving testimony. The problem was, under the assumptions of the science of testimony, a particular logic operated—the suspicion of sincerity. "The sincere assurance of the witness does not guarantee anything about the value of the testimony. Good minds are less affirmative than others," wrote Dupré. Unreliable adults were "in the large majority of cases, women," and if they should happen to be male, they bore the "corporeal marks of psychic infantilism or feminism." The afflicted male displayed not his own masculine symptoms, but those of women and children. Sincerity—and the propensity to lie—were "feminized."[38]

Women, like children and especially small girls, were considered abstractly by the experts as a class of creatures defined in opposition to what was essentially "Man," the truths of purity of conscience and intention fitting incompletely into those of controlled observation. Untruthfulness, to the scientist of testimony, was not essentially an ethical dilemma, but a fact of anthropology and evolution. "Memory" could be modern or not, and as feminist critics of nineteenth-century psychological science have argued, the woman "signified the disavowed irrationality of the male psyche of modernity."[39]

The science of testimony sought to define "natural" characteristics and roles for men and women. Yet natural roles would still mean that the researchers were male, their subjects for the most part female, and scientific practice would operate with an implacable logic: the higher form of life studies the lower. Females were characteristically children, and a child was "a veritable primitive . . . the existing representative of prehistoric periods of the human mind, that is, a modern specimen of paleopsychology," as Dupré put it. In the child the trace of the primordial species remained. Lying, which women did so automatically, was characteristic of a being "without experience, without judgment, lacking the basics of comparison and control which form the critical mind." Fearful, imaginative, and suggestible, the cerebral functioning of a woman/child operated according to "a natural and incessant mythical activity."[40]

Women and children were "suggestible" creatures of permeable nerves, lacking an internal moral core or structure of intellectual resistance to immediate sensations. Impressionable, they recapitulated what they absorbed as confused, personal realities. Fourquet wrote of women, "Their duplicity, their propensity to lie seems to be part of their weakness and of the predominance of the nervous system over the muscular system in them."[41]

Whereas grown men had "common sense" and a certain morality based on the strength of their constitution, women and children suffered from passions, tumult, disorder, and an "excess of joy and hatred" as a result of a physiological state which recklessly absorbed and personalized the external world. For the male experts, such personal recollections based upon honest, agitated emotion were of doubtful value to a justice concerned with the objectivity of seeing and speaking. Women were undoubtedly sincere, yet in matters of testimony, their memories were "private"; in court and clinic men would be the keepers of the "public" memory.[42]

The easy association of lying with infantile and feminine qualities was notable in medical-legal literature. Lies, fabulations, and distortions of truth were "the weapon of choice employed by children and women to satisfy either their need for protection, or their innate penchant for aggressivity and self-destruction in case of a perversity of instincts."[43] While the broader field of legal medicine concerned crimes and pathologies of all kinds, works dedicated to "testimony" and "false witness" consistently returned to women and children as subjects. Moreover, as numerous clinical cases and prosecutions such as "l'Affaire Cayotte" demonstrated, this was a field dominated by controversies involving moral and sexual crimes. Dupré commented on "the self-accusing liars, the other-accusing criminals, the false martyred children, the alleged victims of dramatic vices, the denouncers of imaginary abuses," noting that the complaints of these "mythomaniacs" almost always tended to concern "immoral offenses and rapes." In fact, he went so far as to say that "rape is almost always the crime of choice pronounced by the accusers."[44]

That this crime, "particularly odious," should be the central figure of an entire theory of lying, may appear disquieting or shocking, hardly commensurate with a science which spent so much time doing rather academic memory experiments in the lab and classroom. Yet the focus is not entirely surprising. Struggles over the truths and meanings of sexuality, violence, and victimization resonated in France in the decades after 1870. France had been brutalized by an invader. The rape of Marianne and the seizure of her children Alsace and Lorraine were the torments of a violated woman, a sundered family, and the shame of the men who could not defend her from the enemy they themselves had challenged. To the degree that memory research into questions of sexual violence is, as one scholar has put it, "at least partly about a family in pain," the "crime of choice" at the turn of the century would obsess not only mythomaniacs, but medical and legal men searching for principles to recharacterize gender roles in an age when both male and female had been "victimized."[45] In the same decades feminist groups militating for political rights debated whether women were duty bound to save France from a "depopulation crisis." The Parisian "New Woman" defied the bourgeois female's circumscribed territory of hearth and home by pursuing education and public life. Men seemed more and more demoralized and "diminished"—by the Prussian defeat, by the working-class menace symbolized by the Commune, and now by the assertiveness of women themselves.[46]

Rape was an outrage and a socio-political issue at the heart of an unsettled sexual protectorate. Who should protect whom? Who was a victim? Notably, medical-legalists studying testimonial situations did not portray women as passive victims of male crimes. Rape cases were battles: if women were indeed the victims of male sexual violence, in many cases men were equally the victims of female false accusations. The "crime of choice," as Dupré called it, was interrogated through the category of "victim" itself, becoming a test case for who was truly victimizing whom.

For the experts, rape cases turned upon constituting both a clear perpetrator and a reliable victim, and in a vaguely ironic way, the *sincerity* of the woman at the moment of the alleged crime. Had she truly been violated, and had it been against her will? Ernest Dupré's investigations centered on definitions of the female character, which he attached to a syndrome of his own invention, mythomania: "the tendency, more or less voluntary and conscious, for the mind to alter the truth, to lie, and to fabulate."[47] Though paying tribute to Charcot and the dominant school at the Salpêtrière, he maneuvered his diagnoses so that his patients "no longer belong to hysteria," but were attached to "vice, perversity, to what is generally heard about under the name of simulation." For Dupré, hysteria was a form of unconscious irresponsibility. What he sought was the logic of an infantile female character which drove women to accuse men of phantom crimes. This suited his thinking that rape accusations were not simply cases of women incapable of accurate testimony; it was a suggestion that women had a misguided and dangerous power: they could and would invent their own victimization.

Dupré did not mean that women invited sexual assault; rather, they told stories about it when it had not happened. Within this framework of the woman as storyteller, Dupré evaluated what he considered the most frequent variety of "malignant fabulation in the adult," that is, *l'heteroaccusation genitale*. This particular form of accusation was a detailed production of an entirely false event with a characteristic form: "it deals as such with a rape or a rape attempt with strangulation or mutilation of the victim, or an immoral offense with violence committed." Particularly striking about Dupré's description were the details with which he presented the crime as a managed event, a set-piece complete with props. "In almost every one of these cases, the mythical-pathological story is framed in a dramatic setting: disorder of furniture, broken glass, traces of struggle on the victim who is discovered fainted, bound and gagged."[48]

Dupré's typology attempted to show how false accusations of rape followed a determined story line, a predictable and identifiable narrative. Yet his analytical framework had a few curious echoes of its own—broken glass, disorder of furniture, a bound and gagged victim—he himself was ordering a reality which had already come to him originally as a story. In the details he was repeating a case which would have been familiar to most practitioners in legal medicine: the celebrated (and oft-cited) condemnation of Emile de la Roncière in 1834. De la Roncière had been a candidate at the Ecole de Cavalerie de Samur, accused of writing threatening letters to the sixteen-year-old daughter of his commander, the general Baron de Morell. The letters were cryptic, "I am neither man or women, neither angel nor demon, and so bring as much evil as good." The writer claimed to have destroyed the happiness of three women, and to the daughter vowed, "if I could chop you up, kill you, I would do it."

De la Roncière was presented with expulsion from the school, and despite protestations of innocence and "strong indignation" decided to leave Samur. He wrote an ambiguous letter explaining the difficulty of his situation and retired to his family in Paris. The mystery did not yet end in Samur. One evening, hearing strange noises in the daughter's bedroom, the attendants forced her door. They found her on the floor; "a rope was bound around the waist of the poor child, and a white kerchief was tight around her throat; drops of blood were visible on her chest and on her nightshirt." Shards from the shattered pane of a balcony door were strewn about. Brought to her senses, the daughter indicted de la Roncière, "I've come to avenge myself," she reported him to say. She claimed that he struck her repeatedly. " 'Ah! they've insulted me. They've chased me away from here,' he said, 'Well! Now I'll have my revenge.' " Arrested and tried for the assault, de la Roncière was sentenced to ten years' imprisonment.[49]

This would seem to be Dupré's syndrome, not a reflection on clinical types, but line and detail taken from a notorious scandal. These notes come from Emile Fourquet, one of many legal scholars who studied the case. In his own assessment he asked, "What did the accusation rest upon? Only upon the declarations of Marie de Morell and the letter of explanation of de la Roncière"—the letter explaining the accusations against him and his reasons for leaving Samur. "There was thus nothing but the testimony of the young girl, and this testimony prevailed, in spite of the conclusions of experts charged with examining the incriminating letters, in spite of the impossibilities of fact."[50]

Fourquet's conclusion is instructive in its certainty. A detailed study of the case is in fact much more ambiguous in terms of whose writing appeared on the letters; true, some "experts" said it was Mlle. Morell's, but others had apparently confirmed it as de la Roncière's. Fourquet leaves unexamined the role of other cavalry officers like M. d'Estouilly who may have been rivals, perhaps jealous rivals of de la Roncière, and misses the codes of military honor which among other things had once led d'Estouilly and de la Roncière to a duel. Fourquet interpreted the case so that everything rested upon "the testimony of the young girl." The male suffered, the female lied. The conclusion of a misjudgment based on false testimony is presented as evident: the letters forged, the glass broken, the attack simulated, all by Mlle. Morell, an iconographic figure of the female as false witness. Ironically, the eminent medical-legalist Brouardel also commented on the case with a note about a much older Mlle. Morell in his own work, "Mlle. de Morell is married and has become one of the most faithful clients of M. Charcot."[51]

Like Fourquet's interpretation, Dupré's clinical formulas were supported by a specialized literature of disbelief, carrying titles such as the *Medical-legal Report on a Judicial Inquiry Motivated by a False Accusation of Rape,* by one Dr. Laennec.[52] The Laennec investigation can be read in terms of a profound dilemma which arises for interpreters of rape cases: how to "recuperate what has too often been left out: the physical violation and the women who find ways to speak it." In the myth-story of Tereus and Philomena, Tereus rapes Philomena and cuts out her tongue to prevent discovery. She weaves a tapestry which tells the story and in doing so makes her silenced voice into a visual image of pain and anger. [53]

Yet finding "voice" alone assures neither credibility nor justice. In the Laennec case, the doctor was called to a small town to examine a young woman who had been found lying, gagged, some distance off the road. The doctor's report began by establishing the coordinates of presence: an accounting of the date, time, location of the events, and a presentation of the woman when discovered. "N——— was lying on her back; her clothing did not present any disorder; her hair and bonnet were in no way disturbed; her arms lay at her sides; her legs were extended and together." Working from the testimony of witnesses, the doctor's acceptance of the language of "order" in the woman's appearance suggested to him nothing unusual except the fact of her being where she was.

When the woman began to talk, the doctor kept a transcript of the interview. She spoke and he listened, he heard a victim—but was she *credible?* Her story was strange, spoken in the third person, recounting a young man with gloves and a tall hat who had followed her from her work: ". . . he dragged her into the meadow, in spite of her cries and prayers. He beat her like a dog, gagged her with the kerchief she'd had in her hand . . . she fainted . . . he had his way with her."

To make sense of the deposition, the doctor counterposed the woman's spoken testimony with his expertise of seeing: "quickly we were able to observe that on no part of her body did she present even the least trace of violence." What Dupré had called a "genital" accusation now admitted of a "genital" resolution in the Laennec case; truth descended not upon listening, but upon specific anatomy—which denied a crime. "Genital organs: the large lips are not swollen; the small thin lips are rudimentary; the urinary meatus is pale and in no way swollen . . . the hymen is intact." Neither the woman's words nor her body validated her claim of physical violation. "We can thus affirm that at no time was a rape consummated, and that N——— presents no trace of the violence of which she claims to be the victim on last July 20."[54]

Here then was the dilemma: how to reconcile the divergent testimonies, "the absolutely negative results of our examination," with "the revelations of N———, the precise accusations which she brings against a young man." This case is particularly fascinating because of what seems too obvious; the doctor dismissed the woman's accusation because physically she manifested no signs of abuse. Physical injury composed a system of signs from which evidence could be taken; absence of these signs invalidated the woman's spoken claims. Her body—as read by the doctor—contradicted her voice. A particular way of seeing transformed a possible victim of violence into a perpetrator of false accusations.

Was there a victim? Laennec did not think so, and if he did, it would not have been the woman. Even before examining her, the doctor commented, "one cannot consider without shuddering the disastrous consequences which this sort of accusation could have," particularly when inflated by "the impressions of witnesses and public rumors." "Impression" and "rumor" already doubted the reliability of the victim/witness. Laennec's doubt was not patronizing, but grimly defensive; he feared the effects of the testimony spreading. In his report the woman finally appears as a figure "dangerous to the public security, which she troubles with her chimerical complaints."[55] In these observations, Laennec articulated the expert's common belief: not only were women unreliable witnesses, but their "sincere" testimonies were disruptive and potentially dangerous to civil society and the realm of the "public."

Could the most "private" of evidence have supported the woman's case? Would a serious and sympathetic talking through of the woman's "memory" have been helpful? For specialists like Dupré, Charcot's work had demonstrated the dangers of such an approach. The interrogation of patients by the doctor was "one of the most common sources of the alteration of testimony by suggestion." Referring pointedly to the school at the Salpêtrière, Dupré criticized the theatrical symptoms of hysteria, the grand part of which were "created by the doctors during their research on illnesses."[56] Who could say that even the most highly regarded professionals were not simply inventing maladies or testimonies for their patients?

Better to rely on physical evidence. The notable point about the Laennec report is that he dismissed all of the woman's testimony because of his conclusion that her genitalia had not been violated. Notwithstanding crimes of traumatic shock which she may have suffered, the lack of physical proof seemed irrefutable. Yet consider again the ambiguity of physical signs—would the woman's claim have been supported if she had shown definite signs of physical aggravation? Would the body, in effect, have "restored" the truth to her words? Although Laennec dismissed the accusations based on a lack of physical evidence on the woman's body, he might have reached the same conclusions even with clinical observations of pronounced irritation, swelling, trauma, or discharges.

Impossible? Here lies the dilemma of making the body the scene of evidence. Professor and clinician P. Brouardel, head of the Société de Médecine Legale de France, had addressed these issues by painstakingly ennumerating the many organic or biological disorders which might result in symptoms appearing consistent with sexual assault. His *On the Causes of Error in Expertise Relative to Indecent Assault* (1884) was a veritable catalogue of organic genital dysfunctions and infections, with a strong injunction for the unpracticed medical-legalist to err on the side of skepticism when confronted by even the most evident signs of aggravation. Most young doctors, he recalled from a case where he had to correct an inexperienced colleague, could not even correctly testify on whether a woman had a hymen, having never actually seen one themselves. The intern in question testified that he would have been accused of a crime himself had he actually the experience of knowing what he was looking for. In this case, the legal judgment against a man was reversed when the two doctors together reexamined the woman claimed victim and found her hymen where it should be.[57] The imprecision of expertise was a sentiment echoed by another medical-legalist, Dr. Ducor (1898), who regretted lack of study about the hymen, and asked for a medical museum to begin "an accumulation of forms as well as alterations of this membrane," so that detailed studies could be made about "the different results of traumas" in the genital region, and the genital malformation of both men and women.[58]

Insufficient information, experience, and resources of the profession were all admissions, oddly enough, which defended the doctors. The expert proceeded as prudently as possible so as not to indict an innocent man, and a doctor who erred did so by honest ignorance. The distinction between male and female testimony was again particularly pointed in a generalized case presented by Brouardel, in which a little girl was the presumed victim of sexual molestation. Unlike the real "Affaire Cayotte," which centered on the machinations of the father, Brouardel's model described the way in which an excitable woman sends an innocent man to punishment because of her wrongheaded insistence on perpetuating a crime she herself has invented. Speaking about discharges and genital irritations common to little girls, Brouardel commented:

> Every now and then it happens that an impressionable woman is alarmed by the discovery of a discharge and suspects that her child has been maltreated. She goes to find the doctor, who unfortunately could not know of this infection, and so declares that the child has a venereal discharge. What happens in this circumstance? The mother demands of her child, "who's played with you? Who had you on his knees recently?" The child responds innocently, "no one mother, I swear." The mother then reacts, "oh don't tell me such lies, I'll whip you if you continue."[59]

The child tells the mother what she wants to hear, and when the father comes home, is made to repeat the story "just as she told it to her mother," each time reinforcing its logic and believability. Dupré, echoing a similar case and using the same phrase as the inspector in the Cayotte affair, explained, "the child learns by heart" the story she has been made to invent, and "not wanting to forget anything in telling it, remains invariably faithful to the version fixed in her memory." Based on the child's spectacularly reliable testimony, a culprit is named, an investigation pursued. The doctor, in his ignorance of diagnosis, "gives his testimony and the man is punished for a crime he never committed." The doctor was ill-informed, but the responsibility for this travesty was clearly supposed to rest with the females. By the criteria of intentionality, "only the little girl has lied," but the mother was clearly presumed responsible. "The mother furnished the bases of the accusation, and she by her questions gives an appearance of truth to a story which the little girl easily fills in."[60]

The literature of the medical legalists did not deny rape or sexual crimes, nor do I wish to suggest that rape and abuse cases were never pursued or prosecuted (note the Marchand case, above). Demonstrating the psychological and thus legal unreliability of women and children was not the goal of the science of testimony, but rather its consequence from first principles. Autonomous subjects with critical judgment were "always, already" male. Women and children were defined by the *other* category of the female. The "science" of testimony operated through a logic of reasonable masculinity and "modern" disinterested observation, thus requiring a way of seeing weighted to disbelieve a woman who had no physical signs of assault; to suspect a diagnosis which demonstrated physical signs by possibly attributing them to other maladies; to emphasize the "impressionable" character of the female, and her questionable ability to discern and judge situations.[61]

The experts never simply portrayed women as victims; women, they thought, did this to themselves—and threatened men in doing so. The memories of "false witness" were struggles over who could possibly be believed, and how credibility was to be determined. What drove the testimony professionals was not a strategic plan to discredit victims of sexual crimes, but a suspicion of sincerity (read: personal, sensitive) and an uncontested belief in the reasonable, rational male as the essential creature of judgment and public life.

If priests had once kept the secrets of the confession, the experts were the men who sought to fashion a true "public memory," in their own pronouncements and in the ways they attempted to control the transformation of others' memories into testimony. I have examined the distinctive gendering of such expertise not to overtly condemn one or the other (much less the reasonable, rational male), but to address in a compelling way the question which remains at the heart of this chapter: who is "deserving of faith"? Women for their female sincerity when circumscribed within the world of family and children where "digne de foi" resonated with emotional senses of belief and piety. Men in the "public," where law, code, and contract reigned, and "foi" signified "trust" and "credibility." Above both the arbiters of faith and truth: notaries, and once upon a time the priest, now more the institutional practice of the professional expert.

A closing note: experts shaped "public memory" not only by pronouncing on male/female distinctions, but by assuming the role of judging *all non-experts*. Shrouded in science, culture, and the authority of his profession, the medical-legal expert was truly a figure trustworthy, credible, deserving of faith. Alexandre Lacassagne, the dean of medical-legal studies in Lyon, commented, "The witness, whether he be a savant or an ignorant pupil, can inform Justice. It is sufficient for him to have memory. The expert on the other hand, must have made special studies and above all demonstrate intelligence and judgment."[62] The witness—male or female—had memory, but the expert was defined by intelligence and something more: judgment. Dr. Ducor, secretary of the Société de Médicine Légale at Paris, rather haughtily proclaimed, "The *savant* called by the accused is only a simple witness, whose authority weighs little for the judge compared to the expert, who benefits from the advantages given him by his official investiture."[63]

The witness, the presence of the one who had heard and seen, was challenged, or justified, by the one who never heard and never saw, but who nonetheless could render commentaries on the experience of the other.[64] The role of the witness remained central to jurisprudence, assuredly, but that role was to be expertly managed, and the opinion of the specialist was its judge. Perhaps this was nowhere clearer than in the articles and statues of the medical-legal profession, in which the Société defined its role in testimony. "The medical experts called to make depositions before the courts and tribunals for medical-legal operations in which they are involved shall be always considered as experts, and will never be called upon as witnesses."[65]

Figure 13 Vagabond murder in the popular imagination: Vacher strangles
Eugénie Delhomme. (*Source:* Bibliothèque Nationale)

6

Identities: Doctor, Judge, Vagabond

Writers Joris Karl Huysmans and Max Nordau were not the only ones to talk about the "fin de siècle" in the 1890s. Joseph Vacher also used the term on his way to the guillotine.[1] The sensational and grisly case of Vacher as revealed by Emile Fourquet, a *juge d'instruction* at Belley, and the medical-legalist Alexandre Lassacagne implicated the "King of Assassins" in a series of brutal and violent murders of ten adolescents—four male and six female—and one older woman over a period of four years. Fourquet called Vacher a "criminal vagabond," a fascinating designation in which the definition of *vagabondage* (vagrancy) itself was part of the crime. The particularity of the Vacher case rested in the extreme difficulty the investigators faced in tracking down the murderer, then retracing, reconstructing, and linking his crimes together. Vacher's relentless wanderings, his movements, his "rapid movements and counter-movements" were, according to Fourquet, "a splendid demonstration of the extreme elusiveness of vagabond criminals." The Vacher case was a search not just for a killer, but a killer who incarnated relentless movement. What to do of a murderer "who accumulates kilometers between himself and the place of the murder before the crime is even discovered?"[2]

What finally trapped Vacher was what I will call the memory of the state, not "memory" as a series of sponsored commemorations, collective ideologies, or historical patrimonies, but as a series of documents, practices, and institutions. The "memory" I suggest here is what Max Weber would refer to as the "domination through knowledge, specifically rational," which characterized modern bureaucratic organizations—the

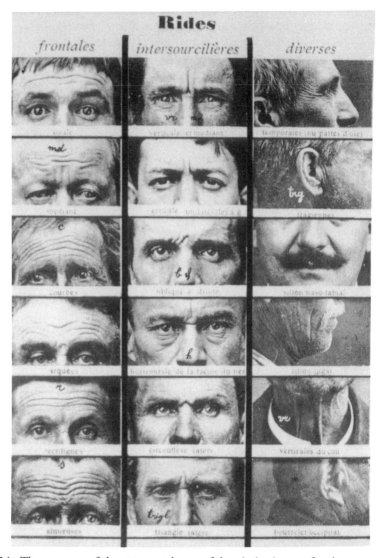

Figure 14   The memory of the state: catalogue of descriptive images for the "speaking portrait." (*Source:* Musée et Archives de la Préfecture de Police de Paris)

knowledge of the *file*. Part of this "memory" functioned on the classical metaphor of a faculty which stores information: the archives and record rooms of the Prefecture of Police. But "memory" meant more than a depository. To recall a name or a face, individuals search personal memory; for the state, accumulations of documents and images form part of a series of practices which involve specially trained photographers, measurement experts, and pathologists, charged with the task of arranging

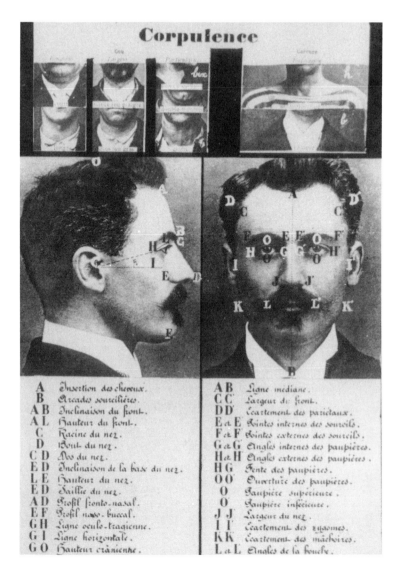

Corpulence

A	Insertion des cheveux.	A B	Ligne médiane.
B	Arcades sourcilières.	C C	Largeur du front.
A B	Inclinaison du front.	D D	Écartement des pariétaux.
A L	Hauteur du front.	E et E	Pointes internes des sourcils.
C	Racine du nez.	F et F	Pointes externes des sourcils.
D	Bout du nez.	G et G	Angles internes des paupières.
C D	Dos du nez.	H et H	Angles externes des paupières.
E D	Inclinaison de la base du nez.	H G	Fente des paupières.
L E	Hauteur du nez.	O O	Ouverture des paupières.
E D	Saillie du nez.	O	Paupière supérieure.
A D	Profil fronto-nasal.	O	Paupière inférieure.
E F	Profil naso-buccal.	J J	Largeur du nez.
G H	Ligne oculo-tragienne.	I I	Écartement des zygomes.
G I	Ligne horizontale.	K K	Écartement des mâchoires.
G O	Hauteur crânienne.	L et L	Angles de la bouche.

descriptions, clues, and correlations, ultimately collapsing the distinction between "identity" and "identification."[3] Such information was exploited, circulated, sent by rail and transmitted by telegraph. Ultimately it formed part of a network of technologies and judicial mandates which moved with the criminals it hoped to track down. The "memory" of the institution did more than remember—it was a memory which acted.

The Vacher case in its details would prove to be more than a series of sadistic crimes and the disciplined workings of police science. Reconstructed by journalists, administrators, and legal and medical specialists, the case became a statement about the changing landscape of late nineteenth-century France, a landscape of displacement, dislocation, and the acceleration of history. Unlike spectacular crimes centered in Paris, Vacher's wanderings traced out a geography of deep France, a geography of surprising and unsettling movement, a disrupted world of isolated villages, local communities, and somber farmlands abandoned by depopulation and migration, the peregrinations of rootless clans endlessly and increasingly traversing the regions by railway. Criminal vagabonds were the master "malfaiteurs" of this shifting landscape by their experience with flight and escape. The threat the vagabonds posed struck at the heart of French "identity," the constituent elements of a people, the assumptions about an orderly and stable society. How to control this massive, moving population? Social laws, identity cards, passports—each act of legislation grappled with changing rural traditions, each document an attempt not only to establish identity and domicile, but to replace the testimony of communal witnesses, and finally to divide the bearer of French documents from the bearer of any other nationality, to save and defend the "memory" of a people.

Vagabondage was, of course, hardly a new phenomenon in the late nineteenth century. The social psychologist Gabriel Tarde (1905) tried to place vagabonds against the background of a vast and colorful historical panorama. "Vagabondage, in its thousand current forms, is essentially a plebian crime; but in going back through the past, it would not be wrong to attach our vagabonds, our street-corner singers, to noble pilgrims and minstrels of the Middle Ages." Psychologists Marie and Raymond Meunier tied the rise of vagabondage also to the Middle Ages, the period of the "great Norman invasions," traversed by sellers, voyagers, seekers of relics. "From the tenth century, we enter into what could be called the poetic and mystical period of vagabondage," the great epoch of pilgrims, troubadors, jugglers, and knights-errant.[4]

The language of law at the turn of the century was somewhat less poetic. Reports from the Prefecture of Police to the Ministry of the Interior (1902) emphatically designated "vagabondage as a fact." The penal code "does not look for causes or for origins . . . there is nothing to demonstrate in the past to demonstrate a case of vagabondage."[5] The penal code itself (article 270) asserted: "Vagabonds or individuals without means are those who have neither a certain domicile nor means of subsistence, and exercise neither a habitual craft or profession."[6] Vagabondage was a crime in law, but an odd crime of negativity, of not having, of not doing. The first part of the code made criminal a lack of address, or of fixed location. Vagabonds were errants who made all territories their own, whose status allowed no fixed point of identification, who erased personal history, and could invent themselves anew in each encounter. This in itself was unsettling. If such were also a dangerous criminal, how would he or she be found? Fourquet complained, "The secret of impunity resides precisely for them . . . in the essential mode of their existence: knowing the wandering life eminently appropriate to misleading searchers," a life of passages in "rarely traveled roads in the deserted countryside." Keeping track was moreover complicated by the democratization of new technologies: "today, bicycles permit wrongdoers to escape even more easily from pursuits," not to mention the problem of "thefts committed in moving trains." The vagabond criminal was a double threat, a figure which wound together the timeless menace of anonymous wanderers with the accelerations offered by machines and mechanical transport. Fourquet observed, "They find a marvelous source of alibis in the rapidity with which they are able to cover large distances." [7]

On the road, the aimless unpredictability of the vagabond was cause for anxiety and fear. Difficult to check, perpetual threat existed in petty crimes, or as in the case of Vacher, aggressive violences. Vacher's own testimony said much about the terror of vagabond murder: "On the road crossing Le Var, I encountered a young girl who seemed to me eighteen, coming towards me along the way; without saying a word, I threw myself on her and cut her throat with a knife I had found in an isolated cabin." The notable element in Vacher's testimonies was his insistence on the precipitousness of his actions. He gave no word, no indication, evinced no motive. The crime itself was a movement of violence pressed into a single impulse. "A rage pushed me to march straight before me and commit my crimes," Vacher avowed. "I never looked for victims, it was always chance encounters which decided their fates." His crimes were contingent, unmeditated, spontaneous, marked by an aggressive speed of which he was modestly proud. Vacher offered this consolation to his victims: "The poor people have nothing to complain about; between them all they didn't suffer more than ten minutes."[8]

Few vagabonds of course were actually murderers, yet suspicion pursued them as a "social danger" and a "plague," for vagabondage in general was not an act, nor even a series of acts which could be carefully examined, but a condition—one which cut to the heart of organized society. Neither pilgrim nor mystic under the law, the vagabond was "rebel against social discipline." At the court of appeals in Paris, the lawyer Alfred Lagresille argued that every constituted society was composed of members each charged with particular roles and duties. A civilized people understood, honored, and preserved these roles and duties in their institutions. Every man or woman was obliged to acknowledge the foundations of human society: "A family situation created by marriage, offering company and relations of affection; an establishment, a habitation, a place of habitual residence which will constitute for him relations of friendship and neighborliness, and make him test the desire to maintain the esteem of those who know him; work, an employment of his faculties, or at least acquired wealth or some resources which will be brought to the common fund in exchange for what he takes."[9]

The vagabond upset all these: marriage, family, neighbors, friends, work, and place of residence. Each element was interconnected and the vagabond respected none. Location was paramount, for it allowed one to be known, to have identity in a community. Family and work were presumed to be the foundations of responsibility. Wealth insured the esteem of one's familiars, contributed to the common fund, and guaranteed the future. The vagabond's frightening indifference to all made him worse than a common criminal who, when detained, at least had a social conscience linked to a personal past. The vagabond was a deterritorialized figure, and as such one utterly lacking this binding quality of a moral individual: the conscience created through memory. According to Lagresille, "during his detention, he does not have sorrowful thoughts about the punishment, of the misery of a family clamoring for his presence; he doesn't have to suffer being separated from anyone whose company would be habitual and necessary."[10]

The crime of vagabondage, with its mythical lone wanderers, cannot be understood historically without grasping the threat it was presumed to pose to the family as a fundamental institution in French society. Though the solitary male was often the representative vagabond, fear of vagabondage in general respected no age or gender group. The threat had two faces. The first, above, was the vagabond's refusal or indifference to live according to the rules of human society defined by affective units of husband, wife, children, parents, relatives, bound by traditions, patrimonies, and other customary memories. The second was even more troubling. If the vagabond rejected the family, social and economic change reserved for some families an even more terrible fate: that they themselves would be transformed into vagabonds. Dislocation and social-economic fear of falling were real and powerful concerns at the end of the century. Deputy Mabille du Chêne (1892) outlined an all too familiar story: "Many households come to establish themselves near the cities, and do not find there the work and means of existence which they have counted upon. The household comes apart; the husband wanders to find employment, the wife and the children go to beg, and often this material misery is joined to moral misery, which ends finally in divorce and a condemnation for vagabondage and begging."[11]

The sources of these upheavals, according to Judge Fourquet, lay, extraordinarily, in the great institutions of modernity: industry and transport, public schools, the national army. Between 1870 and 1914 the national railway network of the Freycinet plan, the compulsory education edicts of the Ferry laws, and the obligation of military service slowly assimilated peasants and other countryfolk to a national idea of France. [12] Within this broad history of the forging of a common identity, however, lay a shorter term, a history not of a nation drawing together, but of one part destroying the other. Far from creating a sensibility of unity, the railroads, the schools, and the army were ambiguous engines of progress, the bearers of knowledge and opportunity, but also the sources of disintegration and misery, the origins of vagabondage and crime.

Fourquet's thesis, framing his analysis of the Vacher case, was a moralist's history about the price of progress. The great projects of rail and steam had crisscrossed the countryside, true enough, but they were dominated by "big business and industry, born from the federation of capital," which were the ruin of "the small artisans and sellers." The pressures of economic hardship and the specter of starvation unleashed "a current of emigration from the villages towards the cities."[13] Vagabonds were no more the picturesque pilgrims, minstrels, and wandering sellers of an earlier age, bearing their faith and plying their crafts and trades from village to village. Vagabondage was the sign of an unsettled modernity, of a money economy whose logic of competition and exchange put not only goods, but uprooted people into relentless circulation.

Industry alone was not to blame. Rural emigration, the key factor in the "increasing of vagabondage," also resulted from "mandatory military service for everyone and the expansion of instruction." If the schoolhouse was practical in teaching the sons of farmers how to read and calculate better, it had also the "fatal" effect of turning many young people away from the farming and merchant life. The result was the birth of "la classe declassé," rooted in the countryside, yet existing in no particular world, incapable of carrying out agricultural work, or exercising artisanal crafts.

Army service also gave each recruit a double-edged blade. Oddly, going into the military was not such a fatal step; it was the return which was a devastating transition, according to Fourquet's argument. The identity of the national state was forged at the expense of the local. "There are regions where, out of ten youths entering military service, one can affirm at the very least five or six having but one concern upon returning home: that of returning to the cities." Dreaming of the "promenades du dimanche," the village was a site of a perplexed reverse nostalgia: that of the countryside dreaming of the city. Upon the return to the family, suggested Fourquet, "their home seems more miserable, their village more grim, deserted, silent."[14]

Fourquet was hardly alone in portraying the countryside in such melancholy tones. Demographer Arsene Dumont suggested that even "the most dead city" was preferable to rural life, since the typical peasant farmer "didn't aspire for himself anything but a situation like his parents." Attorney General Paul André evoked a mythical peasantry "closed in its tight circle of immutable traditions . . . a perfect immobility." Yet if the countryside appeared hopelessly static, Dumont's own studies suggested a rural population living under an opposite reality, "the necessity imposed upon each individual to move around endlessly."[15] Dumont's statistical data (for 1886) purportedly showed that 53 towns had recently absorbed over 300,000 new inhabitants, leaving fewer than 238,000 residents to spread across a remaining 36,000 communes in the countryside.

The numbers on emigration were disturbing enough, but they became terrifying when correlated with the increases in crime and vagabondage. Numerous commentators sounded this alarm. In his study on "nomad vagabonds," Lawyer P. Le Roy intoned, "the number of vagabonds increases without end, and at this moment [1899] more than 100,000 individuals wander illegally each day on the main roads." Deputy G. Mabille du Chêne reported (1892): "Begging and vagabondage . . .have become at this time a veritable social plague. Some claim that out of an average of sixty-thousand individuals brought to the police stations, those arrested for vagabondage and begging figure to be about a third." The lawyer Lagresille concluded the existence in the French territory of "a vague population of thousands of vagabonds . . . their number increases rapidly year by year. There is certainly a peril for public security."[16]

Not all rural emigration was motivated by economic misery and the attraction of "more remunerative work." Equally commented was something not quite so obvious, consonant only with the development of transport, information, and a new experience of capitalism as consumerism: "the need of excitation."[17] Fourquet offered judgmental examples of a rural society gripped by "the irresistible *entrainement* toward luxury," the abandonment of prudence and savings in the face of the desire to purchase, to chase fashions set in the capital. "The poorest girl in the most miserable village" now needed "hats and dresses of the latest fashion."[18] Changing material and status desires, markets given and taken away by industrial manufacture, and the facility of roads and railways were the interwoven elements which Fourquet saw at the heart of a modern vagabondage.

The ultimate created need was movement. Critic Alexandre Bérard pointedly linked the increasing number of vagabonds to "the development of the means of transport." The two phenomena were inextricable. "With the increasing facility of travel, all the lazy and slothful of our cities, towns, and villages are invited to distance themselves from their birthplace."[19] This will to movement, this separation from the village, the town, the neighborhood, was not purely or even principally the result of economic hardships. Lawyer Adrien Sée, a specialist of travel documents, saw a society of displacement, a population obsessed with "an imperious thirst always to discover the new." New moralities, "so different from the older," were leaving "their special imprint." The new ethic was an agonized, agitated modernity, solitary and individual. Fourquet wrote of the inveterate wanderer preferring anonymity, escaping from remembrance and identification, chasing adventure and the "mirage of the unknown and faraway."[20]

The fantastical, unsettled, and agitated individualism by which legal scholars marked a vagabond civilization excited the interest of another group who thought it might be a disease: medical professionals. Paris psychologists Drs. Raymond and Marie Meunier devoted a special study to vagabondage, suggesting that "before depending upon legislation or political economy, vagabonds belong to psychology." In a medical science teeming with psychotics, hysterics, and mythomaniacs, the doctors

were enthusiastic to create their own typologies, but they found vagabondage confounding, not an easy syndrome to possess with labels.

> Examine during a day ten well-socialized men, ten teachers, ten factory work-
> ers. You will quickly find common traits, often a community of origins, even
> more often a community of tendencies. Examine on the other hand ten vag-
> abonds and you would find ten individuals having each a different personality,
> coming from different backgrounds, and having the most divergent tenden-
> cies.[21]

What the observer would find, suggested the doctors, was that "a
first will vagabond for economic reasons; another to catch up on his
thinking or reading; another because he cannot live otherwise, either to
escape his enemies or for simple fantasy; a last finally, afflicted with a
weakening *dementia*, will wander unconsciously without purpose like an
automaton, etc., etc." Vagabondage was at once juridicial, social, and
medical, crossing over and confusing boundaries of motive and responsibility. Vagabonds were figures of uncertainty, imprecision. They lived a
sort of transgressive reality, giving their own status "a value much less
precise than the clinical entities, hiding uncertainty and heterogeneity
under the apparent precision of definitions."[22]

Clinical studies of vagabondage attracted the grand names of fin-de-
siècle psychiatry, including Jean-Martin Charcot. In 1888 Charcot created a syndrome to summarize his thinking on vagabonds and
vagabondage: "automatisme ambulatoire," which located vagabondage
in an automatic quality of the body, the action of muscles and nerves
responding to unconscious impulses. He named his syndrome to describe
the behavior of a patient "subject to flights accomplished in a secondary
state of which he had no memory once returned to his normal state."[23]
As legal scholars had condemned vagabonds for having no conscience
tied to memories of family and community, Charcot notably described
"automatisme ambulatoire" as a disorder of a mind functioning in a secondary state without consciousness or remembrance, specifically defined
by an alternating presence and lack of memory.

Another grand figure of French psychology, Pierre Janet, noted that
"amnesia is the essential reason" for the condition described in Charcot's
theory. The "état second" of "fugue," or sudden flight, was a condition
in which movement and forgetfulness of self operated together. As Janet
saw it, the sudden flights of Charcot's patients were amnesias motivated
by a return to the deep strata of a "primary personality."[24] Vagabondage,
more than a penal infraction or "social plague" of beggars and highway-
men, was a somnambulism, a moving sleep of the body forgetting itself
and reacting to an impulsive and "primordial" abandon to distance and
wandering. Returned to primary consciousness, the subject of such tendencies moreover could not remember how he had arrived at some usu-
ally unfamiliar locale. The impulsive vagabond suffered from precisely an
inability to coordinate memory and mind in the material action of the

body.[25] In the impulsive vagabond, the reflex, the instinctive primordial imprint overwhelmed the "representative" coordination of the memory-will, the *volonté*, which made individuals responsible members of human society.

The vagabond was a modern primitive, a figure of rootless perigrinations, attached less to human society than to the driving impulses of a state of "nature." Psychologist Emmanuelle Regis explored this affinity by uniting literary and clinical talents in a study dedicated to the "dromomanie" (tendency to wander) of the noble savage himself, Jean-Jacques Rousseau. Regis led off his study with a totemic image of nature versus culture: "We saw Rousseau fortuitously leave Geneva forever one night because, late by a few seconds, he sees the gates of the city close in front of him just at the moment he is about to come back in."[26]

Regis's study called Rousseau the first of the great "dromonanes thirsting for nature," arguing that Rousseau's spontaneous, impulsive wandering was the expression of a special "constitutional" relationship with nature particular to vagabonds. "It is a remarkable thing that many morbid itinerants have an invincible taste not only for the open road and great outdoors, but also for the beautiful spectacles of the universe."[27] The poet Jean Richepin similarly set his own wanderer out on a road of timeless symbols and the eternal grandeur of nature. In his adventure, Richepin's hero crossed "the honeyed ground, the wild canyon; the songs of the wind along the face of the riverbanks." He was a man who knew the living world: "and the sun, and the shadow, and the flowers, and the waters/ and the forests with all of their birds."[28]

In Regis's thinking the vagabond could be not only an observer of birds, but himself a sort of man-animal, absorbed anthropomorphically into the non-human world. He noted strange images: "I observed a vagabond so wild and so completely returned to the state of nature that he slept often at night in the branches of trees in the fashion of birds."[29] Marie and Raymond Meunier commented on the confinement of vagabonds in hospitals as "an illusion" and an important cause of error in their treatment. The official hospital definition made the wanderers economic victims, "simply the unemployed going from one village to the next to have themselves hired." As such they were examined cursorily and released to pursue their errant courses. In fact, they were men and women apart from such rational considerations as work, existing in intimate and ancient relations to nature, inhabiting the woods and pastures during the summers, sheltering in valleys and caves the winter, content to hide out in "the hollows of rocks." The vagabond lay down and assimilated nature, the mineral and the vegetable, the elemental. "We knew of a vagabond in the Alps who, being used to sleeping on the gravel of riverbeds, could not sleep in a bed offered to him out of pity, and returned to his river the very same night." Between the bed and the river-bed, the vagabond was a sort of natural creature. Arrest statistics showed the increasing movement of vagabonds to the south of France in the winter months. The Meuniers argued that between the fields of summer and the crevasses of winter the vagabond followed "a seasonal human migration, analogous to the annual migrations of certain species of animals."[30]

The Meuniers invoked the "migratory impulse" as more than a disorder, but a force at once "hereditary, innate, precocious, durable, irresistible." Vagabonds were imprinted with the phylogenetic memories of ancestors. The Meuniers saw vagabonds recapitulating the flight of humanity before the progressive freezing of the Earth's northern zones, movements which characterized "the glacial period of the pleistocene." As the vagabonds headed for the temperate zones of France to search for food, to steal, to beg, in each muscular movement they conjured the prehistoric moment when anthropoid ancestors gradually ceased swinging from trees, when hands became useful instruments and "the foot acquired the force for walking." With upright posture, wandering began, a migration of "detours beyond number," of encounters with mountain ridges and the great barriers of the oceans. Another psychologist, Pagnier, respected the "prehistoric instinct" of the nomadic tendency: "it has existed in all times, one could even say that it is one of the oldest in humanity. Man is naturally and necessarily a nomad."[31]

The nomads of modernity recapitulated the primordial migrations of a dispersed clan or tribe, leaving behind even the same sorts of traces and inscriptions which immortalized their ancestors. Vagabonds had their own obscure language, a language of signs scratched on posts and stones to indicate a hospitable lodging, an unsafe locale, the presence of enemies or friends. The language of the vagabond was pictographic, figurative, symbolic, a communication of signs—animals, bone shapes, loops, hats. To track down criminals on the road, investigators entered into a strange symbolism. Like the primordial mind of the wanderer, the signs were "veritable hieroglyphs."[32]

These pictographs, inscriptions, and cave paintings of a later date were the counterparts of another kind of pictorial writing inscribed on the skin itself, what the medical-legalist Alexandre Lacassagne called "a speaking scar," that is, tattooing. A tattoo could betray its bearer's origin, crimes, beliefs. "It is necessary to learn to read it, because tattooing is an eminently symbolic writing, and it sometimes represents conventional signs which are not understood except by the wrongdoers," wrote Lacassagne, who also offered up a bit of etymology: "the word *tatouage* is of Oceanic origin (tatou, which the natives pronounce tatahou) to designate marks on the body, according to the reports of Cook and de Dumont d'Urville." Lacassagne easily associated vagabonds and South Sea Islanders. While he readily admitted that in his own time "tattooing is observed among all peoples," his point about the practice was clear: "if one undresses the civilized, one often finds the primitive."[33]

All across a France gripped by the "modernity" of disruptive and increasing movements, the "primitive" killer wanted by the doctors and judges was on the road. Violent, impulsive, unpredictable, Vacher moved. Files and police reports accumulated behind him. Stopped along the road he presented assorted documents to satisfy gendarmes and was released. At one point he was imprisoned for minor assault charges in one jurisdiction while police searched for the unknown murderer in another. Local innocents were often accused of his crimes, sometimes condemned. The imprecision of documents, the lack of a central fund of criminal files dogged the investigators. Judge Fourquet consulted with Lacassagne at Lyon about the possibility and utility of creating "a service charged with centralizing the files of unpunished crimes and working out the connections between them . . . permitting the discovery of striking similarities existing between the murders [and] the circumstances which preceded them."[34]

Fourquet's proposal highlighted one of the foundations of modern criminal investigation: the beginning of projects to link together the technologies, procedures, and institutions of the state by organizing and systematizing the dispersed records of the prefectures, prisons, and courts of law. By the means of centralization, association, and identification, Fourquet was establishing the groundwork for an institutional memory, a memory of identifications: testimonies, descriptions of physical features, reports on locales and situations. Eventually the criminal would be recognized, placed in the vicinity of his crime, linked to the evidence of other crimes by the bureaucratic knowledge of the file. "This is exactly the method followed in the Vacher affair," according to Fourquet. Ultimately, anyone claiming to have a French "identity" would see that identity shaped through a French "identification."

The doctor and the judge collaborated to promote new systems to identify individuals. The most basic element of identification was documentary: papers which were registered, stamped, recorded. They were the memory of the state at the point where the gendarme physically stopped the traveler on the road. This was the sort of confrontation evoked by Guy de Maupassant in his short story about a vagabond. In his pitiless tale, a carpenter looking for work sets out on the road "carrying papers and certificates, with seven francs in his pocket." Arrested for begging outside a small town, he is brought before the local judge by a brigadier who announces him as "arrested in a state of begging and vagabondage, carrying good certifications and papers in good order." Before anything else, the mayor says, "Show me these papers," and "he took them, read them, re-read them, and gave them back."[35]

Why this consuming attention to papers? Documents assume necessary connections between print, words, memory, and responsibility. Vagabondage, identity, and documents were thus inseparably linked. Reforms for vagabondage legislation were common at the turn of the century, and documents were always central to the debates. In the efforts to track down vagabond criminals, lawyer P. Le Roy in 1899 commented, "Among the new measures, the most important is the creation of identity cards. It is the most radical and surest means: one avoids long searches, false allegations, and suspicious declarations." A standardized card was considered not only administratively efficient, but democratic. "The evil is attacked at the root," because everyone having to justify his or her identity would have "a special card, the same for everyone." The negativity of vagabonds would be combated by a rule of negativity. Just as vagabonds were criminals by their absence of having done anything, or having nothing to do, so the simple fact of "not carrying the card would constitute an infraction." The crime was to not have it.[36]

Behind such projects lay an interest at the heart of all modern bureaucratic institutions: standardization, an attempt to regularize the mass of papers which constituted identity. Residents of France already had a confusing choice of ways to prove who they were, including voting cards, military papers, passports, certificates of domicile and of birth, and work attestations. A new world of movement and displacement demanded easily identifiable documents. An early twentieth-century passport historian, Adrien Sée (above) described how passport law demonstrated not only the State's desire to control the movement of its citizens, but the dilemmas of identification engendered by a new national landscape. In 1907 he wrote of "the modern habit of devouring space in a frenzy of speed," commenting, "we live in the century of the automobile—and of voyages across the world following the development of means of communication: steamers, railways, etc." The development of transport meant the changing structure of an entire civilization. Like Fourquet, Dumont and other commentators on the decline of rural France, Sée noted that "the old custom of resting in the family home" was more and more lost. For the younger generations, "they desert the village; they leave for the big towns."[37]

What was identification in such a shifting society? How to establish oneself in new places, in a world of constant displacement? The law did not indicate the passport as simply a document of safe passage—rather it held it as proof of identity in default of a communal group. Avoiding a condemnation for vagabondage depended, in essence, upon one's familiars, the good testimony of others. Documents were a compensation for this social circle, which at one time would have been constituted by the village or commune. Displacement and documents were inseparable for the traveler. "When he is torn away from the small circle where he is known," argued Sée, "the individual, is marked with suspicion. He erases an instinctive distrust by producing an official piece of identity, destined to reassure those in charge of good order and a correct adminstration."[38] In effect, the role of the village, the assurance and authority of the "small circle" of familiars who could attest to the good name of an individual, was replaced by the distant authority of an "official" document, the assurance of an encompassing administration distilled down into a card. In an era of movement, the passport was a reduced, imprinted substitute for a communal identity now ruptured by distance.

Documents defined not only individuals, but the boundaries of identity—national identity—by creating declared members and ineligible foreigners as opposites within a framework of "territorial closure."[39] By the twentieth century suspicion of others was not limited to, nor necessarily even concentrated on, occasional strangers in villages and communes. The real question of the day, according to Adrien Sée, was, "How to make the distinction between what should be properly national, and what could be accorded without danger to foreigners?"[40]

Overwhelmed by vagabonds, monarchs under the *ancien regime* had periodically resorted to "the expulsion, individual or *en masse*, of foreigners found inside the realm." In the era of nation-states, conducting the unwanted to the borders of the royal territory was no longer such a simple solution. The new vagabonds were feared not for threats of brigandage or thievery, but differing standards of work compensation. The common danger, argued Sée, came from a situation in which "foreign workers, working for very low salaries, become competitors with the national workforce." Not the expulsion of one's own undesirables, but the implicit protection against the incursion of the others was the motive behind laws of restriction, voted into law in France in 1893. Such laws were adopted so as not to put foreign workers in a "better condition" than that of French workers. The new threat from without was not from criminals, but from immigrant workers, the human face of a struggle between nations—an economic struggle.

Sée noted a strange historical contrast—as political barriers which once divided territories were disappearing, nations were defending themselves ever more "against foreigners, with an objective of economic expansion." In the competition of nations and markets, each player moved "to close to the others the doors that he opens to himself." The traditional limits of identity, the borders, were fortified by fiscal measures, taxes and tolls to stimulate national production at the expense of foreign competition, pushing the states to economic war, "incessant, without quarter, without mercy."[41] Passports as memory documents were the individualized identities of distinction in this all-encompassing political and economic struggle of the nation-states.

Markets, exchange, circulation—modernity. Documents, registrations, impressions—memory. All movements of goods and workers were to be sanctioned by documents, verified by border guards and bosses. There was, alas, an exception to this legitimation, noted by lawyer P. Le Roy: "Only vagabonds, insubordinate to the law of work, those who in a word should be tracked, do not have these papers."[42] The vagabond sought no official crossing points, searched for no regular work. The vagabond, the one who should be tracked, escaped identification. The simple equation of identity and card was insufficient. Speed also accelerated these

uncertainties of identity. In an age of rapid displacement, of the multiplied traces of the printing press, printed documents were not sufficient to
insure identification or identity. In the case of criminals, such were evidently insufficient to the task of control. The Ministry of the Interior in
France in 1885 wrote to the Prefecture of Police of the dilemmas posed
by "the increasing facility of means of communication, the rapidity of
moving about, the multiplicity of relations between the diverse parts even
of the same country," in trying to track and control criminals, particularly
of the "habitual" variety.[43]

In tracking Vacher, Judge Fourquet called on Lacassagne, and the
medical-legalist consulted with his adviser and collaborator, a man to
whom he would later dedicate an entire study: Alphonse Bertillon, handwriting expert at the Dreyfus trial, son of an eminent demographer, family
friend of surgeon and anthropologist Paul Broca. As a low-ranking em-
ployee of the Prefecture of Police in Paris, Bertillon had been charged
with recopying descriptions of individuals in arrest reports in the hope of
matching up names with a repeat offender. Motivated by the pointlessness
of his work, Bertillon conceived of making his task more "scientific." This
meant borrowing some techniques from Broca and the specialists at the
Ecole d'Anthropologie who had made careers autopsying, measuring, and
quantifying the body.

With a trial budget, Bertillon established a "measuring room" at the
Prefecture de Police. In this atelier Bertillon set up an array of instruments
to measure the height of suspects, the diameter of their skulls, the length
of their forearms and feet, and a fixed, precisely callibrated camera to render full facial and profile portraits. Bertillon also measured and painstakingly noted the features of the human face, eye color, shape of nose, ears,
forehead, mouth.

Bertillon's work made the popular press. *L'Illustration* (November
10, 1887) visited the atelier and presented its readers with a panorama of
men standing on pedestals, inclined over callibrated iron tables, seated on
bolted-down chairs.[44] Bertillon's team carefully guided and noted the
measurements, but the real testimonies of identity now were in the lenses
and engraved scales of the camera, meter stick, and calipers. The witnesses
of a former age were replaced by the memory of instruments. The system
proved astoundingly effective. In 1883, having made his first 7,336 measurements, Bertillon was able to identify 49 repeat offenders; the following year, 241. Bertillon's superiors were impressed, and Bertillon found
his way to the head of a new "Service d'Identité Judiciare."

Bertillon's system owed much to anthropological techniques, particularly those of Paul Broca, who used his passion for measurement and bril-
liant imagination to reach many specious conclusions. In addition to
declaring feminine mental inferiority a function of small cranial capacity,
Broca had also hypothesized the retarded intelligence of non-white peoples relative to Europeans for the same reason. As a criminological tool,
Bertillonage was not exempt from such scientific prejudices, nor from the

class and race assumptions which informed such projects as the Italian
Cesare Lombroso's pursuit of the face of the "born criminal," or the ty-
pologizing of Jews as a degenerate race by anti-Semitic groups in France
and Central Europe. Bertillon's technique would be a superb marker of
modernity: an identification system conceived as a rational instrument of
state, founded on and deeply implicated in the racial and gender assumptions of the fin de siècle.

I have addressed such questions of race, gender, and memory tied to
anthropological and criminological questions in other chapters; my concern here is to read Bertillonage in terms of its role in creating an institutional memory. The heart of Bertillon's system was the *fiche signaletique*,
a card offering specific correlations of descriptive words and precise measurements. In its exactness for identifying criminals it was clearly superior
to the written *fiche d'état civil*, or passport, which had been designed for
travel. The *signaletique* was, however, a curious record premised on the
idea of fragments, pieces, individual features. The memory of the state:
complete identity was about taking the face and body apart. The fiche
permitted the investigator to "decompose" the human face "into all of its
traits." Rather than consider the subject as a story, the fiche was a record
of the subject as an arrangement of descriptive parts. The investigator's
task was "to analyze each of these traits separately and, consequently, to
compare each isolated trait with the corresponding trait of another
face."[45] Only after separate study were these "decomposed" pieces finally
shaped into an individual, a suspect, an irrefutable identity—the subject as
composite.

A very particular scheme of perception and memory lay behind "Bertillonage." In 1903 *Le Matin* paid a visit to one of Bertillon's training
classes. His philosophy was written in large black letters on the white
walls: "The eye sees in each thing only what it is looking for, and it only
looks for what is already an idea in the mind." In effect, cognition dominated perception, and the eye searched for what it expected to find, that is
"resemblance." Bertillon challenged his students to truly see, to think
around quick associations, to identify pictures of the same man with and
without a beard, or different men with apparently similar features. Inspectors were trained to conceive visually of measurements and vocabulary
when looking at a face. The nose, for example, was divided into three distinct features, its height, width, and projection, each part precisely designated and numbered. Anatomy and physiognomy were forms of writing
to memory, and Bertillon maintained that as long as a particular anatomical feature had not received "a name permitting the form and descriptive
value to be stored in the memory," it would remain "unperceived," as if
it "did not exist." Seeing a face was a fine thing, but such memories were
easily tricked. Better to concentrate the identifications of memory in language. As Bertillon put it, "it has been said for a long time: we only think
that which we are able to express in words."[46]

As it assembled individuals, the criminal portrait was also its own best

Figure 15 Memory-men: training the agents of criminal identification. (*Source:* Musée et Archives de la Préfecture de Police de Paris)

evidence for developing taxonomies of generalized identities with historical resonance. In the collected measurements of noses, ears, eyes, hair, and body shapes and sizes, Bertillon fashioned geographies of bodies, regional typologies, maps of territory and ancestry. One admirer commented on Bertillon's work:

> It is with the aid of the *fiches anthropometriques* collected in his service of judicial identity that he has drawn up the geographical map of height, cephalic index, bizygomatic diameter, eye and hair color in France, canton by canton, contributing thus to the study of the races which populate France and their geographical distribution in the French territory.[47]

In addition to identifying criminals, Bertillon's police archives thus also functioned as a resource for "collected" memories of the regions and communities of France, a fund of materials allowing the reconstruction of local ethnic and cultural histories which composed the nation. By measuring and indexing the features and proportions of the body, Bertillon's memory of the state identified individuals, but also outlined identities.

Bertillon's interest in mapping France by physiognomy is a good reminder that one of the imperatives of the state was not only to centralize information, but to project that information across space. In the case of criminal investigation, this additionally meant to speed and circulate it through outposts and contact points. To this end, Bertillon's deconstructed body of the offender was transformed into a veritable mnemotechnical number series by investigators, the police science version of the pedagogical formulae of school manuals which transformed knowledge into a logic of codes.

In 1907 medical-legalist Dr. A. Motet described a method of identifying, describing, and transforming bodies into sets of numerical correspondences. "The method consists in attributing to each individual physical feature . . . a classifying number based on the recognized elements most characteristic of their physical person, and inscribed in some ways upon their organs."[48] In 1912 another doctor with a system, Severin Icard, proposed bodies as figural landscapes to be plotted cartographically. "The way to proceed, especially on the surfaces, will most often consist in determining the placement of a mark on an organ or region as one determines the placement of a town on a geographical map." Identification was literally a matter of describing the latitudes and longitudes of a body to find its "median line" and "chosen reference points."[49] Each location and feature would be described by a compact combinatory formula. Consider: a man of about forty, large forehead, nose, atrophied right ear, clouded left eye, tattoo of a man and woman on the front of his right forearm: 40173–1048–118395–1350–3213–4863+2017–3907.

The truly astounding point about the Motet or Icard systems was not their reduction of bodies to coded references, but their ability to circulate those references as a system of signals. Dr. J. Vucetich, famed for his pioneering work in fingerprint classification, commented on the utility of the Icard system by noting that "one could not imagine anything better for the determination and telegraphic transmission of individual marks and features."[50] The body of written reports and photographic images materialized in the "fiche anthropometrique" and "portrait parlé" could become an electric body of speed, transmitted telegraphically. This was a body to be read in many cities, provinces, across borders and regions, a body sent and received as transmitted numbers, then transcribed, translated, and reconstructed, a body whose materiality was print, wire, electricity, and transcription.

Bertillon's instruments and measurements had resolved much of the problem of vagueness in identity papers for criminals. Industrial and electrical technology were now adapted to attack the deficiencies of central record depots and the dilemmas of steam-powered fugitives. Just as Broca's work had inaugurated a transcortical brain science, so now the techniques of his follower Bertillon created their own accelerated memory: telegraphic information could be both centralized and circulated across an electric memory web with the speed necessary to make arrests. Identification and evasion were an ever accelerating contest. In 1876 *La Ré-*

publique Française had already reported on a series of experiments undertaken by the Prefecture of Police to establish a system of "photographie télégraphique"—the transmission of images themselves by wire. Four months later *Les Droits de l'homme* (February 1, 1877) took these images of electricity and ink to speculate on a criminal pursued by "the fluid which will draw his physical likeness at a distance." Though the criminal might even flee the continent, the fluid could, "without appreciable loss of time, dive across the channel or ocean by means of submarine cables and arrive before the guilty party at Folkstone or at New York."[51] Such experiments were only attempts to keep up with change. Gabriel Tarde remarked on the relentless struggle to stay ahead of criminals, keen exploiters of a veritable catalogue of technologies of the late nineteenth century. "The wrongdoers have found more or less the same resources as the police or the judges in the development of roads, postal systems, railways, telegraphs, photography, the press, and medical-legal knowledge."[52]

What of crimes such as Vacher's, crimes of blinding speed, movement, disappearance, leaving endless tracks and trails? Medical-legalists operated with a profound assumption: nothing takes place without leaving some sort of imprint, track, or other indication. All events have their witness, their memory: the trace. In 1907 Lacassagne lent his authority to the publication of *La police et l'enquête judiciare scientifique* by the noted Italian criminologist A. Niceforo, a detailed work which described many of the procedures of French investigative work. Niceforo neatly summarized criminological work as a science of "traces." He defined this principal term as "every vestige left by a man or by an animal, which could serve either to discover its author, or to establish some of its individual characteristics."[53]

The most basic of trace studies, he maintained, was "the examination of prints," in particular the footprint, the elemental contact of human locomotion with the earth; the most singular evidence of the vagabond. Remarkable things could be read out of the soil. The tracks were indications not only of bodies and impressions, but of actions, directions, movements. The first thing a print revealed of course was whether its author had been standing, walking, or running. From that, perhaps even the sex of the disappeared could be determined, given that "the print of the woman is smaller and the toes of the print appear less separated," when compared with the tracks of a man. Extraordinarily, the synthesis of the brain and nervous system could also be resolved down to the track in the earth, and an expert (said Niceforo) could sometimes distinguish the staggered prints left by victims of paralysis, stroke, or other nervous afflictions.

The trace also comprised photography. Not only the portraits of Bertillon's "fiche anthropometrique," but "the photography of the invisible," that is to say, "la radiographie." Roentgen had not long discovered the x-ray effect before the miraculous revelation of living skeletons excited the public imagination. The implications and promises of the new technology for identification were not lost on specialists such as Dr. Foveau de Courmelles, who suggested a new procedure for police science: "next to the external description card of the criminal we will have, to complement the first, his internal card—the least easily changeable."[54] The proposition was striking—a criminal might change his appearance, but could never escape the transparency of his own body, the x-ray of his own skull and skeleton. In fact, not only the invisible body, but the past of that body could now be rendered by the technical scrutiny of seeing. If a criminal could change his face but not his bones, he should also be made aware that radiography could even read "the knowledge of old fractures and bony antecedents." The "rayons-x" were a time machine, peering into the strata of the body's past which the changing surface of the skin disguised.

As a time machine, radiographic instruments also found their way into the circle of historical tools. De Courmelles recounted a notable controversy from his time, the dental x-ray of the "presumed Louis XVII buried at the cemetery Saint-Marguerite," in 1913, which revealed a set of teeth not suitable to a young corpse. The revelation "put into doubt the authenticity of the corpse presented as that of the son of Louis XIV." De Courmelles did not know what the final judgment on the whole affair would be, but his overall conclusion was noteworthy: because of forensic science, because of technology, the past was ever harder to know. "Yesterday's history is today's anguished, macabre reality."[55]

Macabre realities were indeed the stuff of the history of identification. Vacher's murderous course placed grisly killings at the center of investigations which crossed the judicial world of Fourquet, the medical expertise of Lacassagne, the police science of Bertillon. Vacher, accused vagabond murderer, vagabond citizen, was directly and indirectly pursued by the archives, records, and actors which constituted the memory of the state; memory as a network of administrators, techniques, specialists, and their departments. Not yet knowing who he was looking for, Fourquet acted as a central judge to collect and review the files of "all unpunished crimes whose authors are unknown," grouping and arranging them according to descriptions of facts, injuries, analogous crimes. Relying on Bertillon's technique, he circulated a "fiche anthropometrique" based on a description of his likely suspect, describing the beard, nose, scars, and eyes of a man witnesses had seen or confronted on the road near violent crimes. Each report ended with the imperative to "telegraph me, in case of discovery."[56] Fourquet followed many false leads, but continued to circulate more descriptions and pictures, reconstructing more scenarios from what evidence and what witnesses he could find. Finally, the story of responsibility pointed to one Joseph Vacher, fortuitously locked up on minor charges in the provinces.

Vacher was accused. Lacassagne served as chief psychological expert at the trial, judging that it was "the question of responsibility which will dominate all of the debates." Ultimately, Lacassagne determined, "Vacher is not an epileptic, not an impulsive," but rather an *immoral violent*, thus responsible for his crimes.[57] Lacassagne and his team reached their decision after many interviews with Vacher, though their presentation at the trial notably did not depend upon their psychologizing, but upon traces of physical evidence. Vacher claimed insanity, declaring that a "fit of rage" had pushed him to tear off the genitals of one victim with his teeth. Lacassagne's team demurred, demonstrating how the scars showed clearly that "the wounds had been made with a cutting instrument." Vacher claimed to attack his victims suddenly, cutting their throats quickly in blind fury. The pathologists concluded he had surprised them from behind, wrestled them to the ground, and killed them methodically and precisely. Blood from a ripped throat they noted, would normally spurt 1 meter 50 centimeters from a standing or falling victim and leave "very characteristic spots of projection." Vacher claimed to have a fragment of a bullet in his head which deranged him and made him irresponsible. Drs. Lannois and Destot x-rayed and found part of a "foreign metallic body" in Vacher's right ear, but noted that it was far from where it would cause anything except occasional deafness or local paralysis. On the throat of the young victim Eugenie Delhomme, they pathologists also found "revealing prints," which they claimed matched Vacher's hands and nails.[58] Each of Vacher's protestations of innocence was met by a description, a reconstructed trace of physical evidence, sometimes a witness. Lacassagne concluded that, as for the victims, "all perished in the same manner," the work not of an impulsive madman, but a calculating killer.

Vacher was guillotined on the last day of the year, 1897. His brain was divided up and delivered to interested parties. One section was sent to the Italian clinic of Cesare Lombroso, whose chief claimed to find elements of criminality in it.[59] At the end Vacher is reported to have said, "Ah! *voila*, the great victim of the faults of the asylums." Psychologists Marie and Raymond Meunier reported: "at 7:03 the blade dropped: true as always to its instincts, the crowd applauded loudly."[60] Vacher had slaughtered almost a dozen people; he was captured and condemned by the memory of the state. That memory was a composite of bureaucratic logic and the resources and technologies available to a doctor and a judge: investigative networks, files, identity cards, expert in reading bodies and signs, all organized to operate in a world of accelerations and displacements. Fourquet reported Vacher's words as he was prepared for the guillotine, words which captured the excellence of the new science, and—as Vacher protested his innocence—also its disquieting and agonizing possibilities. "You think to expiate the faults of France in having me die; that will not be enough; you are committing another crime; I am the great victim, *fin de siècle*."

Figure 16 Islands of memory: an eighteenth-century vision of family and land in New Caledonia. (*Source:* Photothèque Musée de l'Homme)

7

Distances: In
the Revolutionary Garden

1889, the Universal Exposition at Paris; amid the spectacles and wonders
of the Pavillion of Electricity, the Gallery of the Machines, and the stu-
pefying achievement of the Eiffel Tower, the casual visitor to the Exposition might be forgiven for not having spent much time at the Musée
d'Ethnographie, with its superb collections of artifacts from Europe, the
Pacific Islands, Asia, South America, and Africa. To establish his exhibition at the Galeries du Trocadero with its fabulous display halls, the director Dr. Ernest Hamy requested and received contributions from
regional and private collections all over France. Oceania was admirably
well represented, in particular the islands of New Caledonia.

One piece was of notable interest. Borrowed from the Museum of
Caen, it was described as a "long engraved bamboo stick" etched with
the images of some sort of encounter: "we see the Caledonian men and
women, a chief wearing a hat and bearing an axe on his shoulder; a naval
guard with rifles; finally, the Commandant of the colony with his wife
and his two daughters."[1] In his studies of the Caledonian archipelago
(1900) the Marist missionary Père Lambert noted that the bamboo engravings were a sort of picture archive for the local peoples, the "means
of transmitting certain local facts to posterity."[2] A storyteller would display the engraved stick while recounting tales and chants of the village
and islands. As one scholar has noted, the bamboo served "the memory
of recitation, which as it takes place, associates graphic and phonetic expressions."[3] What would have been the memory of this bamboo, this
encounter?

143

Thirty-two million people attended the Universal Exposition. In a pavillion across the esplanade from the ethnographic halls, Edmond Bruyant, a lawyer, invited his readers to go down to contemplate an exhibit quite different from the display of Oceanic objects: two small commemorative sculptures, "extremely ugly and vaguely recalling the exhibitions of certain carnival shops, but still very suggestive." The first statuette he described as "livid, in tatters, bent by the weight of chains and dragging the iron ball"; the second, "strong, in fine shape, properly dressed, tool in hand, as much a good family man as reputable worker."[4] The statuettes aimed to celebrate the progressive style of French justice: the old, enchained prisoner exchanged for one redeemed, upright, tool of trade in hand, the image of the worker, provider, protector. The exhibit housing these sculptures was described in the catalogue as "penitentiary."

Different objects, different memories: a bamboo stick which recalls an encounter of two peoples, sculptures celebrating a man transformed by enlightened justice. Between the Caledonian bamboo and the statuettes, within the evocations of punishment, authority, family, redemption—and memories of a tropical locale—are a series of remarkable historical links. The *Larousse grande dictionnaire universel du XIXe siècle* (1877) described New Caledonia in a way which makes the connections admirably clear: "Island of Oceania at 1,300 km east of Australia in the great Pacific Ocean. To the southeast of the Coral Sea, this island, a French possession since September 24, 1853, serves today as the site of transportation and deportation."[5]

New Caledonia was a prison island, part of France's far-flung penal system which included the notorious Guyana. Yet New Caledonia and its penitentiary colony of Bourail were more than colonial outposts; they were also sites of an extraordinary experiment devoted to fashioning what—in my last discussion—I called "the memory of the state." Here my focus is not on technical systems of identification, but the ways in which penal-colony administrators sought to shape within their prisoners an *identification with* a state-planned program of patrimony, heritage, tradition, ritual, and longing for an ideal rural France. Redemption for the prisoners meant effacing personal memories and replacing them with an organized collective memory: the state's own glorious, nostalgic portrait of a golden age of patriarchal farming households.

According to the administrators, this transformation could not take place in metropolitan France where the condemned would "fall fatally back into the same mistakes," but only in a new land which canceled memory, which "removes the *malfaiteur* from his past."[6] The condemned would be born anew in the Caledonian isles, redeemed by the primal soil and the goodness of working it. Here then was the imperative of distance; New Caledonia was necessary as the uncorrupted past of "Nature," the site of the prison as primeval landscape. The prisoners would find not walls and bars to confine them, but the same untamed lands which had challenged their ancestors, whose roles they would now adopt.

The bamboo stick and the storyteller figure in this tale to mark the many dilemmas which bounded this experiment, and one in particular: the moment when the dreamers of the noble savages of Europe come face to face with the noble savage as native Melanesian Canaque. For the one, obliterating memories and building sanctioned historical traditions were keys to freedom, morality, and progress. For the other, pressed by the coming of the Europeans, losing memory meant the extinction of a living culture. The hatchet and the rifle, the Commandant and the Chief proved to be the inscribed witnesses not only of encounters, but of two memory traditions which would come violently and fatally into collision.

The policy of condemnation to New Caledonia was never organized around the axis of simply distancing the criminal element; it was distance with a purpose. Legal commentator G. Pierret, writing in 1892 for the colonial administration, credited the French Revolution with having introduced to modern penal legislation "the sublime and fruitful idea of redemption upon which is based the current policy of transportation." Pierret traced the change to a decree of October 15, 1793, noting that until that time the only purpose of transportation had been "to assure the security of the metropole; little thought was given to the future of the condemned. For the first time, the legislator was to advise on the means to assure the regeneration of the guilty one and his reinsertion into society."[7]

French criminal specialists like Alexandre Lacassagne and social-psychologist Gabriel Tarde had maintained a running debate throughout the 1880s and '90s with the Italian school of the "born criminal" headed by Cesare Lombroso. Key in Lombroso's argument was the theory of criminal atavism, which anthropologist L. Manouvrier defined for the *Archives de anthropologie criminelle* (1886). "Ataviques" were those who, rather than inheriting the instincts of their parents, "have inherited the savage instincts of distant ancestors."[8] Against the determinism of heredity in shaping criminality, the French argued the predominance of "milieu"—social and environmental factors, keeping in the spirit of progress and the possibility of human improvement.

Properly presented, the Oceanic isles as a site of transportation well supported this thinking. The prisoner was above all to be integrated into a completely new milieu. Far from condemned to his past, he would be rather the most dramatic expression of the salutary effect of environment on the individual, in the most encompassing sense. At the Court of Appeals in Paris, the lawyer Alfred Lagresille wrote: "The milieu, in effect, and the external circumstances, influence character and morals. This is a psychological truth: a change of land and climate, of objects and shapes in the surroundings transform the man himself."[9] Here, in transportation, was the hope not only of a reforming ideology or morality, but the radical transformation of the being whose bases were the encompassing effects of climate, soil, perceptions, and natural sensations. If prisoner redemption was a psychology, it was also a physiology, a permeating and integrative play of geology, botany, meteorology. For this, the imperative of distance: it was necessary to go away.

Most critically, distance was forgetting, a cancellation of the past which the passage of time alone could not hope to attain. This was the sentiment which the deputy de Miral had expressed on March 31, 1854, as a justification for the founding legislation on the colonial penitentiary system. Speaking of a typical fictional prisoner, de Miral argued that "in France, he was fatally doomed to desperation and crime. In the colonies, on the contrary, hope returns to him; he becomes a new man." The cancellation of memory was the motivating logic behind de Miral's legislation. The condemned is "carried away from the old world," where he fortunately leaves "the theater and the memories of his former existence and, in the new country where he will be transported, will not find the opportunity to surrender to them again."[10]

Former French Minister of Justice and historian Robert Badinter has suggested that the Third Republic—updating de Mirail's ideas—consciously invested in the idea of a "Republican prison" shaping institutions of punishment in the image of ideologies. Transportation policy was perhaps the most extraordinary expression of this thesis in ideal and practice: a project devoted not only to the organization of repression and control, nor even to the rehabilitation of criminals, but that rehabilitation by the administration of natural and human history. The Caledonian penal colony was a site for forgetting one's own past and replacing it with the "memory of the state": a return to a point zero of primal, innocent existence and the gradual recapitulation of a moral civilization patterned after rural France, one untainted by old faults. This meant recreating earlier stages in history—or even prehistory—as a sort of scientific experiment administered in the name of colonization and progress. In an 1874 report before the National Assembly, the Baron d'Haussonville had argued that transported criminals would be the founders of "a nascent society, tormented by needs, eager for a workforce . . . a society just being born."[11] New Caledonia was the site of an experimental history in the fullest sense, the offering of a "second chance" to an unfortunate humanity to reinvent a society from the beginning of time: from a garden.

If parliamentarians evoked the good of the prisoners and the good of colonial interests as motives for transportation policy, criminologists used the quantitative language of their science to explain why transportation was such an ideal penal policy from an anthropological point of view: prehistoric conditions were the only way to deal with criminals whose phylogenetic memories marked them with the behavior of ancient ancestors.

"Anthropometric" was a key word surrounding relegation and deportation debates. Alphonse Bertillon at the Service d'Identité Judiciaire—part of the police of Paris—composed albums of thousands of criminal portraits, arguing with a disarming logic, "to condemn a repeat offender to relegation, the first condition is to recognize his identity."[12] Identity through anthropometry meant, above all, measurement of physical features, a practice much in vogue at the Ecole d'Anthropologie, cofounded by Bertillon's family friend, Paul Broca. Broca's particular interests were brains and skulls which he patiently and painstakingly measured and weighed to demonstrate various favorite theses: the evolutionary superiority of Europeans over non-Europeans, moderns over ancients, men over women.

Bertillon's criminological interests and Broca's hierarchical anthropologies were drawn together by Broca's disciples from the Ecole d'Anthropologie who, following their master's lead, used quantitative information to articulate elaborate natural histories, some of which used their data to justify the deportation of criminals. One such study by Dr. A. Bordier was published in 1881 as a long article in *La Nationale*. Based on a detailed anthropometric study of the skulls of thirty-six guillotined criminals, Bordier concluded that in all thirty-six cases, the skulls were abnormally large and heavy compared with what was "normal"; in this they displayed characteristics which were "proper to prehistoric races." The criminal, particularly the repeat offender, was not a simple moral degenerate; he was a victim of a phylogenetic "force of centuries," of an atavistic morphological memory "which leaves its imprint even in the shape of the bones."

By the logic of Bordier's study, even the enlightened "rehabilitation" of criminals imagined by the Revolution would be a waste of time. A criminal of natural history would have to be reformed in kind. The most efficient punishment for an *atavique* would be "to place him in a condition comparable to his rudimentary state . . . *en plein terre*, in the primordial conditions of the birth and beginning of societies." For the atavistic criminal, an atavism of conditions; no central prison in France, no work house however severe could meet these conditions. No isolation cell, no threat of punishment or promise of reward could be counted on reliably to alter the behavior of what was in effect a prehistoric man. The answer—as dictated by science—was evident: the government must be willing to suppose "a desert island upon which will be placed all of these men who are still, in the nineteenth-century, prehistoric savages."[13]

If the d'Haussonville commission offered faraway islands as the site of a society to be born, Bordier's anthropological science promised that criminals were its proper inhabitants. What becomes of the French "preference" for milieu over hereditary determinism in criminological debates?

Bordier's proposal remarkably played both sides of such disputes: though he found the prehistoric savage imprinted by heredity, a completely new milieu could, over time, alter the human organism. Placed in their "milieu naturel," the criminals, those prehistoric relics of an earlier age, survivors of their ancestors, would face the rigors of the struggle for existence; they would, promised Bordier, be compelled not to reform, not to repent—but to "evolve."

The island—the seductive power of the image of distance and isolation—the island was the essential element in the scheme of reinventing civilization. Anthropologist Bordier had suggested, "if the desert island of a new Robinson no longer exists, the numerous archipelagos of Oceania or even Guyana—but an island is preferable—will offer a sufficiently large, equitable, and protective territory."[14] New Caledonia fulfilled this vision.

To geographers the island was a longish stretch of land with an agreeable climate. In the imagination of its chroniclers, it was a garden of times past, a prison built up in a paradise recreated, a nature bound by waves, populated by the shipwrecked, forested by groves and fruits, waters teeming with fish and sea creatures. To go there was to cross backward to the beginning of time. Famed radical, anarchist, and teacher Louise Michel, deported for her role in the Commune, waited for deliverance and wrote in 1875 at the Bay of N'ji, "tell old Europe these accounts of the childhood of humanity."[15] Naval doctor M. A. Legrand captured such sentiments well on departing the islands after his assignment: "Aideu to the vast horizons, to the grand places, to the forest strands and picturesque rocks! We are returning little by little to the world of the Europeans, we are returning to civilization."[16]

The island was a land onto itself, fulfilling the profoundest criterion both of the prison and the New World laboratory: isolation. The *Larousse* noted: "New Caledonia is almost entirely surrounded by reefs of white coral . . . this navigation is quite perilous and only captains, aspiring captains, and indeed the natives dare to try it." Within this ring of coral, the man-made captivity crowned the natural, a prison compound surrounded by the expanse of the Pacific. Beyond the confines of the prison lay another world, savage, impenetrable, beautiful. "The interior is filled with virgin forests, with extremely beautiful canopies; one can see many streams which rush into waterfalls and which form great pools around which immense kauris, fiery branches, date palms and great acacias are clustered."[17]

The interior of the island was a primal land of imagination even, or perhaps especially, for those who knew it well. Witness the raptuous testimony of Leon Moncelon, Conseil Supérieure de Colonies. In popular lectures before the Geographic Society, Moncelon evoked the legendary origins, the "shipwreck of one or several couples of exotic Adams and Eves," of these islands, and the "ocean navigators" who found their way to populate it. One can easily imagine the trunk of a fallen tree, "exposed along the coast of India, carried by the monsoon to the different island groups emerging from the ocean." In Moncelon's imagination a vast panorama of tides and ocean geographies unfurled, and it was with "the aid of thousands and perhaps millions of years and successive shipwrecks that the Canaque could appear in these fertile islands . . . on this great land so sudden, so strange, but also so poetic and seductive in its own savagery—New Caledonia."[18]

New Caledonia was a land of splendid natural provisions, whose richness was transplanted to the Ile de France for a Parisian public by the Universal Expositions. In his report on the islands for the Exposition of 1878, colonial adventurer Jules Garnier wrote, "The sea offers abundant resources; the fish is of good quality and forms the nourishment most available to all; one notices that our exhibition can only present a small number of specimens, but the visitor is compensated by a beautiful collection of sea shells." Here, the harmless and tranquil beauty of the islands was presented as a series of collections, images which might please a naturalist or a child. The soil itself was bountiful, "We would cite also the grains which are exhibited, wheat, barley, sorghum, oats, buckwheat, rice, indigo."[19]

The twenty-odd native cultures were denominated, collectively, "Canaques." They were peoples like the nature which they inhabited. Marist Missionary notes published about the Ouagrap tribe in 1890 described the locals. "Are they lazy?—they should be. They have need of so few things, are content with so few, and the earth easily produces everything necessary to them."[20] More aggressive colonialists complained of such reports, and the use of "eloquent and sentimental pages from the philosophers on natural men, the immortal dissertations of J-J Rousseau on these sweet and touching beings."[21] Yet, according to Moncelon, Europeans themselves would be little troubled to live other than as creatures of nature. "There, everywhere, from the edge of the sea to the heights of the mountains, an eternal and splendid vegetation covers the fertile soil, and the colonist has literally only to clear and plant to be sure of his harvest, what can I say?" What indeed: "In the grass he has only to take the coconut which falls from the tree and dry its oily pulp in the sun to establish a business sufficient to support his existence!"[22]

The islands beckoned. Far off in gray Paris, the Chamber debated their future. In different epochs, different measures had allied the fate of prisoners in France with the Pacific shores. Some of the measures had been expedient, based on the decision of military courts to distance dangerous political opponents in large numbers. After the civil war in 1871, thousands of members of the Paris Commune were deported to the Caledonian islands. Sentences were served out, but any hopes that the prisoners might have been seduced by island living were sorely disappointed. In October 1881 *La Nationale* regretted that the Communards "considered themselves caught but not punished, counting always on an amnesty." By 1880 most had returned to France.

Nonetheless, the project of transportation and reform of criminals did not die easily. A more deserving and appropriate class of prisoner would be sought. In the 1880s the dream of paradise regained fell upon the recidivist, the repeat offender, the career criminal. In the metropole of the Belle Epoque, the daily press clamored over the insecurity of the streets. "The truth is that Paris remains the most propitious and favored refuge for *malfaiteurs*, their safest sanctuary," cried one editorialist, expressing a common sentiment. Indignant letters from the Prefecture of Police to the Ministry of the Interior complained that "to read the newspapers, one would think that the police had the power to arrest, release, or relegate whoever they want." "Relegation," which the Prefecture defined as "the lifetime internment of convicts in the colonial territories or French possessions," was the hue and cry of the day.[23] An 1883 bill targeted habitual criminals with arithmetical logic in such categories as "convictions, within a period of ten years, for four offenses punished by at least three months' imprisonment each."[24] After contentious debate the Société Générale des Prisons and the deputies lined up in 1885 to designate New Caledonia a penal colony which would serve a newly voted relegation law.

The distant islands had long shaped the imaginations not only of prison boards and parliamentarians, but even of prisoners and accused criminals themselves. Here, two conceptions of nature diverged. If the deputies and anthropologists spoke more about struggle and work and new civilizations, prisoners in the central jails paid close attention to reports of coconut palms and leisure. Life in the islands was imagined to be a sort of idyll, and hard-line critics of the Caledonian penitentiary system were vociferous when they saw this idyll becoming suspiciously and intolerably real. In one report on the Caledonian penal system, writer Edmond Bruyant noted that newly liberated prisoners at Noumea often refused work engagements "under the pretext that at the penitentiary they were fed, lodged, and dressed without being submitted to overly difficult work." Another report by legal commentator G. Pierret lamented, "The former discipline of the penitentiaries was much too soft; under that regime it was much too easy for the convicts to obtain salaries, work, and concessions of land, and the detainees of the central prisons, enticed by the lure of such favoritism, dreamed of voyaging to Guyana or New Caledonia."[25]

The attraction of the exotic lands had, at times, been too much for the prisoners of the central prisons. Lawyer Lagresille commented on the fashion of convicts to commit "a serious crime with the intention of obtaining a condemnation to transportation." This was a practice which Pierret confirmed, and noted with alarm. "To reach this goal, many have murdered their guards, and the government was quickly obliged in 1879, faced with the multiplication of such attacks, to propose a law to deter these odious calculations." Colonial administrator M. James-Natan recorded a case of one Louis Bossaut, twenty-two, who wandered into a Prefecture of Police one day and viciously murdered a secretary to the police commissioner, simply to be condemned and sent overseas. An incredulous investigator Jacomet inquired, "Is it only to be sent to New Caledonia that you committed this crime, or also to take vengeance on the police agents?" Boussaut responded that what he expected above all, was a change in his life: "I was tired of being always put in prison, it was impossible to be at ease with this 'sacrée surveillance.' I wanted to escape from this situation."[26]

Ironically, it was exactly this desire for "change" with which transportation policy gambled. Attorney Lagresille wrote, "Undoubtedly the change, the adventure, the attraction of the far-away seduces them; but isn't there also at the same time a true instinct which makes them recognize the possibility of their redemption under new conditions?" The island was a chance to begin life over, to know again the "true instincts" of a life in accordance with nature. Yet what was it the murderer longed for? What were the basic instincts, the primary desires and attachments which, once satisfied, would make the criminal an honest man? Lagresille thought he knew, articulating the formula which I have called "the memory of the state": "Giving the convict work, property, and family will be the surest way to effect his moralization and return to society."[27]

In defining criminal "instinct," administrators, savants, and commentators articulated not the particular experiences and desires of their prisoners, but a collective story they determined to have the prisoners take as their own. The "memory of the state" was a sketch of an ideal of French society at the turn of the century: a society of close-knit families, of patriarchal authority, of small property-holders; precisely those institutions most shaken by urbanization, rural depopulation, agricultural depression. For the prison administrators, the ideal portrait of work and property was framed by a nostalgia for a glorified world of family and patriarchy—a world to be uprooted from the unsettled French countryside and transplanted to the land of the bush and coconut palms. In the new terrain, the prisoner would recapitulate on a small concession all of the stages which had built the cherished institutions of European work and social life, rising again to the identity of a productive citizen. That had been M. de Miral's project in establishing the first laws on transportation: "Property, family, social relations, self-esteem. Everything becomes possible for him again."[28]

In transportation policy, the invocation of such totems as "property" or "family" were not merely embellishments on parliamentary rhetoric. They were budgeted, administered, and supervised by colonial authorities. Article 11 of the law of May 30, 1854, had long established the right of prisoners to enjoy "a concession of land and the necessities to cultivate it for their own account."[29] This emphasis on reform through the working of the land was both practical and ideological. First of all, the prisoner would learn to produce his own food and become self-sufficient; his goods might even someday contribute to the commerce of the colony. Second, planting the land obeyed a vision of real work which integrated the prisoner into French history by following the same cycles and harvest patterns of generations of villagers and cultivators. Third, labor was inherently a moralizing practice tied to Christian toil. To these, add the perspective of the Société d'Anthropologie: the cultivation of the soil was the bridge between the life of the savage and the beginnings of human society. The passage from the nomadic to the sedentary by way of an agricultural revolution was "the greatest step ever taken by humanity . . . the veritable point of departure of civilization." [30] Isolating prisoners in a virgin territory, providing them with tools and land: the mythic sedentary stage of the development of human societies was recapitulated in the concessions. The nomadic impulse was to be trained out of the primitive and atavistic criminal not by restraint and threat, but by reinventing the moment when wanderers became cultivators.

With land came worth and responsibility, with cultivation, the end of savage society and the beginning of material progress. In the history of humanity, the evolution of fixed agricultural enclaves allowed the development of a certain material base. Colonial undersecretary M. Michaux had championed the development of the prison colony at Bourail and the works of the prisoners who had "transformed a savage land, put up buildings, levelled hills." Anthropologist Charles Ploix noted the next step: "Men could construct more spacious habitations from more durable materials . . . which could continue to serve other generations."[31]

Generations meant continuity, and the patrimonies, lineages, and heritages which would define the father and his someday descendants. This was the "memory family" of New Caledonia: an institution which authorized prisoners to ultimately be ancestors of the future, re-inventors of kinship and keepers of a new civilization. "Memory" in families is a matter of defining rituals, traditions, establishing successors. In his memoirs of the islands, former colonist Henri Rivière surveyed the entire evolution: "The son sets up his tent next to that of his father, takes a family and takes stock in his own time. Thus is born the station, then the village, then the town . . . these habitations scattered across the bush are the future of free men in a penal colony."[32] From the first scratchings in the earth, the birth of settlements, a human geography evolving into urban life was to be born.

Land was a matter of legislation and tools; likewise, the organization of the family. The primary importance of family institutions in the new territory to colonial administrators meant first a policy "to authorize families left in France to rejoin their head of household if he has proven himself deserving by his repentance and hard work."[33] Encouraged by such thinking and policy-making, emigration to the South Pacific indeed took place, though not always without conflict from local governors. Letters from prisoners and families in New Caledonia to the Parisian press attacked the local colonial authorities for keeping wives and children apart from the *pater familias.* Not wishing to complicate their budgets and administrative duties, the island administrators complained to Paris of the arrivals. When the governor argued to send back this influx of immigrants in 1885, the Ministry of Colonies in Paris made a strong reply: "Monsieur le Gouverneur . . . the measure which you propose to me is contrary to the interests of colonization and to the line of conduct followed until now by the Department." Further, noted the ministry, "as far as the family members of convicts, their support and permanent establishment in the centers can only profit the penal colony, and the administration has the duty to aid them with all of the means at its disposal."[34]

Not every convict had an eager wife and children waiting to join him from another part of the world. No matter; if families were not waiting, they would be created. In setting down the transportation policy in 1854, M. de Miral had been forthright about this necessity, morally as well as politically: "As the principal need of the man is the family, as the principal objective of transportation is colonization, we will provide wives for the convicts." But what woman would travel to the edge of the world to marry a criminal? Attorney Lagresille suggested what seemed to him an obvious solution. Wives could be easily drawn from those women "lost according to our morals." Women that is, who would consent to change their lives of "misery and shame" in France for a new life in the colonies.[35]

The island project was an experiment which sought to erase the past of the condemned and replace it with a selective story of work, land, and patriarchy. The family was the institution for reinforcing this vision, the site where the state's nostalgic "memory" was realized in the form of prisoners' harvests, household rituals, and patrimonies. Creating families was not an abstracted repentance; it was an engineered redemption—codified in laws, contracts, and agreements. At Bourail, the male convicts who applied themselves to agriculture signed standard documents which entitled them to a concession of arable land, a ration of basic supplies for thirty months, and a selection of agricultural tools. If their agricultural efforts were judged reasonably successful, they were entitled to certain other advantages:

4—the right to chose a wife at the convent of Bourail

5—basic supplies for the wife

6—a marriage trousseau including: a folding bed, a mattress, a bolster, a blanket, one pair of cotton sheets, six cotton napkins, ten meters of fabric, two head wraps, two handkerchiefs, two pocket handkerchiefs, two pairs of underwear.

Other incentives were added. According to penitentiary agreements, "the concessionaire receives 2 hectares of land; this property is doubled if he is married, and tripled if he has two children."[36] The engineering of families was a serious business, and its objectives were institutionalized by a neat alliance between Church and State. For the women prisoners, life was to be devoted to a singular role. Noted one report, "What distinguishes the convent at Bourail from all other penitentiary establishments—and all other convents—is that there *les pensionnaires* are prepared for marriage." The role of the sisters of Saint-Joseph was not only to purify the hearts of "their poor, unfortunate students," but also to prepare them specifically and as completely as possible for the role of "wife and mother of the family."[37]

Criminal anthropologist Bordier had argued for leaving the prisoners to their own devices on the island, with the idea that in "two hundred years, our grandchildren will see a new civilization arising from the ocean." The state did not intend to wait quite so long. A telegram dated July 30, 1885, and signed by the under-secretary of State for the Navy and Colonies notes, "I remarked with very strong dissatisfaction that despite formal orders, the majority of female convicts (35) who arrived at New Caledonia aboard the Dupuy-de-Lôme were still to be found in the convent at Bourail at the end of December 1884." The minister very specifically goes on to warn, "I would like to think that I will not notice a similar state of affairs in the future, and I would like you to make all efforts to marry . . . without delay all the women convicts who have been sent to you from France for this purpose."[38]

One wonders what sort of mothers, fathers, and families might result from such a program. The men were thieves, vagabonds, and—as noted earlier—murderers. Colonial reporter Charles Bertheau noted the lot which ended up in the islands, criminals of "rebellion, violence against civil servants and agents of the law . . . outrage to public morals, assaults, rapes, . . . false testimonies in criminal matters, fraud."[39] The reports of women convicts are particularly fascinating given their assigned wife and mother roles, and might give pause to the most enthusiastic of colonial proponents: "Catherine, 24 years old, background: debaucher, mother of three children out of wedlock. New crimes: strangled her child at birth with her apron strings." "Marie—background: unheard of depravation; three lovers at a time; party to doing away with children. Condemned to twenty years hard labor." "Elisabeth E. cut the throat of her child with scissors before throwing it in the latrine."

The administrative reports following these women's progress in the penal colony were often wishful narratives of the whole system of reform. Catherine's evaluation, for example, records "Hard worker, excellent conduct; takes good care of her housework." "Marie soon put her house in perfect order and helped her husband with the farming; she is industrious, and devoted to her duties as a wife." "Elisabeth" equally ends "une bonne mère de famille." If the official reports strain credulity, they point up at least what the administration saw as the ideal "memory family" of its penitentiary program: man, wife, household, children, pointed toward the promise of generations. Skeptics like M. James-Natan wondered if "the penal colony, like love, recreates virgins."[40] Lawyer Edmond Bruyant lamented a rather more depressing reality, notwithstanding occasional "marvelous examples of regeneration," that in general the marriage plan had "pitiful results" due largely to "the poor quality of the couple." The truth, as he mordantly observed, was somewhat less than the moralizing expectations of work and family: "Actually, the most frequent pitfall of these unions is the temptation the husbands have to traffic in the prostitution of their wives."[41]

Without a biologically sound base of reproduction and family unit the whole grand scheme of generations and patrimonies was doomed. Was this to be the final blow to the great dream of recreating civilization on the island? Not at all. Statistical studies on infant mortality in Guyana showed the way out. Naval doctor P. Oregas conducted lengthy studies on the health and development of prisoners, colonists, and their offspring in that other notorious French penal colony. Oregas, in his rather pessimistic conclusions, intended his work to demonstate the maladaptation of Europeans to the tropics. In one year he reported, "out of 353 live births of white children 117 died in the first year of life, thus 33%, while of 26 children coming from other races (pure or mixed) only 4 died after a year, thus 15%."[42] Such studies, which for Oregas scientifically demonstrated Europeans' non-tropical nature, oddly enough encouraged colonial enthusiasts disappointed with the limited success of prisoner intermarriages. If anything, such medical reports from the colonies "corroborated every day" the opinion (scientific!) that in default of prisoner intermarriage, the best way to organize a family in the colonies would consist "in marrying and crossing the convicts with the indigenous women." The conclusion of European mortality was to encourage more reproduction with local women: "The most plausible opinion is that of doctors who affirm that the surest way for the white race to acclimate and to perpetuate itself in the hot countries is to mix with the indigenous races." After a bit of reflection, not medical science alone, but history justified this: "Their theory is confirmed by the history of South America, of Mexico and the French Antilles, peopled with Spanish and French métis."[43]

Such proposals were enthusiastically championed by colonial supporters. Colonial propagandist M. Ben-Mill opined, "These marriages will assure the development of the colony. It is a good policy to encourage them." Naval doctor Legrand agreed: "The administration of New Caledonia would pursue a truly national and patriotic goal by encouraging in all cases legitimate unions between Europeans and Canaque and métis women." The mixing would of course have a certain limit. In New Caledonia the local women would contribute a certain hardiness of bi-

ology, but "the children are always brought up in the European style by
their father, whose name they legally bear, and whose language they
speak. In twenty years, all the métis will form a very beautiful and intelligent population, the future of the colony." The only real blockage,
apparently, would be that suggested by Edmond Bruyant's particular
view: "the Canaques are of a truly repulsive ugliness and their primitive
garments do not allow even an instant of illusion." To be perfectly fair,
he allowed, "On their side the Canaques and the women of the New
Hebrides are repelled by the thought of marrying Europeans."[44]

Yet marry they did, and it is perhaps emblematic of the whole New Caledonian experiment that it was the household of one such couple which
proved to be the point of contact between worlds in collision. I have
spoken of engraved bamboos as picture archives and the stories they told
of cultural encounter to Parisian fairgoers in 1889. Expositions mark the
history of the French in New Caledonia. A decade earlier, at the 1878
Universal Exposition in Paris, Jules Garnier had perused another collection of Canaque objects and artifacts. He noted particularly the Canaque
"primitive arms which correspond to the lowest level of civilization." The
same year, the Canaques revolted against the French presence. Well employed were the "pointed wooden spears simply hardened in the fire,
hard and heavy wooden clubs, slings and oval projectiles."[45] Over a hundred of the French were slaughtered, eviscerated, sometimes eaten. A
thousand or more of the Canaques were massacred and executed in the
repression. The chief Atai ("ferocious and bestial," wrote Garnier) won
notoriety as the principal leader of the rebellion, which had begun on
June 19, 1878, when the Canaques of the region of Dogny slaughtered
a French former convict named Chêne, his wife, and child. Writer Edmond Plauchut noted for *La Revue de deux mondes:* "Chêne was a freed
convict who had many years ago taken a native woman with him; he had
had two children with her. Tired of this first wife, he repudiated her and
went to the tribe of Dogny to chose a second."[46]

Debate raged about the causes of the insurrection: racial jealousy,
woman-stealing, explosive resentments from the appropriation of lands,
the destruction of taro fields by European cattle, the desecration of grave
sites and tabous. How to understand, how to make "friends and allies of
these men?" demanded the authorities with consternation. Leon Moncelon made his recommendation in a letter to Admiral Peyeron, Minister
of the Navy. "Give each native, as has been given to each colonist, a title
to property." To make of the Canaques "definitive property holders"
was to create for them what they lacked: private self-interest aimed at
preserving the gains of the past in the name of the future. Whether in
the name of penitentiary redemption, or colonial policy toward the indigenous peoples, Moncelon's letter underscored the sameness of imperatives of memory as patrimony and continuity tied to the inseparable triad
of work, property, and family in the French vision. "Each title-holder,

sure of his future and of his family, will attach himself to the hand which gives him that security."[47]

Some commentators had a special perspective: among those trapped between the colonial authorities and the Canaque rebels were thousands of special prisoners altogether familiar with rebellion and savage repression: the deported members of the Commune. In the face of the violence, the champions of the brotherhood of work and democracy had no common cause with the "savages"—with the exception of Louise Michel, who gave the rebels her last Communard flag. Deportee Victor Cosse maintained his revolutionary sentiment that "insurrection is the most sane of duties," but insisted, "we are after all part of a European society lost some six thousand five hundred leagues from our France, subjected to all of the brutalities of a people a bit too primitive." Simon Mayer, the commandant of the Place Vendôme under the Commune, rallied patriotically to his jailer's cause: "We thought in the presence of the Canaque insurrection that it was our duty not to sleep a cowardly sleep, but to defend the French government."[48] The Communards circulated enthusiastic petitions asking for weapons and volunteering to fight. The government politely declined their offers.

Why could most Communards not support the insurrection? For the Communards, struggle was an issue of class—and of the *patrie*. Cosse reaffirmed his "European" identity; both he and Mayer rushed to defend an idea of France against all attackers, as they had against the Prussians in 1870. Later, Amoroux and Henri Place recognized that what had divided their own loyalties was something which the Europeans, even in good revolutionary conscience, could not understand or overcome: "the antagonism between the white and black races."[49]

The memory of the other: though framed in terms of black and white, such arguments about "racial" antagonism were not exclusively about skin colors or physical features. While Paul Broca at the Ecole d'Anthropologie in Paris was busy establishing rankings of superior and inferior morphologies and races, the Marist Père Lambert in New Caledonia was carefully citing Broca's colleagues Quatrefages and Flourens for their clear declarations that "the skin of the black has exactly the same composition as that of the white," and "there is no difference, absolutely none, between the brain of the white man and that of the black."[50] The worlds in collision in New Caledonia exploded over race—defined a particular way; not only as a discrimination of color and culture, but a biology of time and space.

"Race" was defined for the colonialists in the shadow of that great totem of the nineteenth century—civilization. Race and civilization were inseparably knotted, and it was the specter of "civilization" which haunted the European interpretation of cultures. Since mid-century, racialist thinkers like the Comte de Gobineau had equated race with vitality and civilization, fearing the degeneracy of the latter if the first were debased in its bloodlines. More optimistically (from a European perspective), the scholar Ernest Renan argued that although the inferiority of certain peoples had been proven by the "onward course of civilization," they could yet be redeemed by infusion with the "noble blood" of the advanced races.[51]

Civilization was not a plateau; it was above all a movement, an unfixed, relentlessly transformative acceleration and advance, a movement with a goal—the perfection of the species. In a statement with long echoes back to the Revolution, anthropologist Charles Ploix defined the term for the Société d'Anthropologie, "Civilization is nothing other than the normal development of a humanity which will continuously perfect itself from the triple point of view of intelligence, sentiment, and activity." All societies were parties to the same point of departure, and all ran on the "same track." Distinctions between races were a matter of the "differing speeds" attained by each at the moment they were comparatively considered. Surrounded by coral reefs long away in the Pacific islands, the indicative sense of time for the Europeans nonetheless was an historical biology of acceleration. The diversity of races and cultures had no significance: "Societies are more or less civilized, they are not differently civilized."[52]

One Dr. Victor de Rochas recounted an anecdote in his travel journal that well captured this singularity of historical vision. On an ocean voyage to Australia (a former penal colony whose success French officials envied), a Canaque was taken to Sydney and asked his impressions of that "great and beautiful city," with its evident signs of industry, commerce, and progress. The Canaque replied, with a "disdainful" air, "it's true there are a lot of houses, but no trees and grasses." Such views were annoying and inexplicable to the Europeans, as de Rochas complained: "As he had not the intelligence or higher education to reasonably appreciate the superiority of our industry, it made little impression on him, and he thought himself superior, or at least equal to us."[53]

What the Canaque defied principally was the inexorable demand of the European mind for "civilization" to be a single history, a linear evolving law of change and transformation in a progressive, accelerating scheme of time. To be outside of European time, according to the polemicist Ben-Mill, was to stand in the way of a greater purpose. Multiplicity and diversity were not watchwords of the day. The renegade Canaques were "rebels against civilization, hostile to progress." Ben-Mill challenged the Canaque sympathizers: "In these times of social transformation, I defy the most ardent of negrophiles to maintain seriously that progress, science, industry, commerce, all the bases of our modern society, should have to stop before the Canaque and negroid nationalities." Ben-Mill argued from an evolutionary natural history: "During this course *à la vie*, all of nature tends naturally, fatally, ceaselessly, to transform itself, to modify itself, to perfect beings and things, to destroy that which is, to raise up that which should be."[54]

This sense of present time favorably destroyed in the name of the future was not universally shared—least of all by the Canaques themselves. Yet if documents show that European-represented pasts were building into a dynamic scheme of evolutionary destiny, questions remain of how to know the "memory" of the islanders. Studies such as those of Père Lambert and the deported Louise Michel suggest ways in which such memory might be situated in local stories, sites, objects, and ritual practices. Michel collected Canaque tales and songs, and Lambert described the islanders' material universe, from dwelling construction to costume- and mask-making. For the Canaques, both tale-telling and working with materials were activities infused with the presence of the past. Stories told, wood carved, fibers taken for weaving, tubers cultivated for feasts guarded ancestral spirits which manifested themselves in daily activities; respect for the dead was an obligation to a past and present inextricably bound in everyday practice. By clearing land, destroying totems, and trampling taro patches, French colonists and administrators upset the living memories in rites and routines which linked the past to the order of the island's universe. Threats to the landscape meant threats to sacred places, to the boundaries of clan organization and kinship—and to the authority of local chiefs. The Christian interests of the missionaries also meant that the rites and traditions of the Church would challenge the cosmologies and creations carried down in the Canaques' own lore.

Although the spiritual, temporal, and material worlds which constituted Canaque traditions and practices were thus embattled by the French presence, those worlds persisted in other kinds of memory. Despite the authority of European institutions and ideologies, islanders and their descendants would retain a sharply distinctive sense of what was important to transmit across the generations. Two traditions of creation and descent illustrate this point. In search of memory strands and traces I return to the bamboo stick and the storyteller. An analysis of Canaque oral traditions by the folklorist Eliane Métais makes possible a reading of "memory" in which a Canaque myth of origin demonstrates a vision of history distinctly different and opposed to that of the French:

> The history of the beginning of the world, of Adam and Eve, was in France, but not here. If really everyone had come from Adam and Eve they would be all the same, they would be all white, they would all have the same language and the shrubs which are in all the countries, they would all be the same. . . . It is necessary to believe in a different creation for everyone.[55]

Two histories collided in the cabin where Chêne and his family were slaughtered. The tale of an Adam and Eve from France, "but not here," underscores a critical point: the original men and women imagined by the colonial administrators were sharing a garden with original men and women as Melanesian Canaques. Attorney Alfred Lagresille had declared the Pacific islands "still unoccupied . . . empty of all civilization."[56] By his own definition, he was half right. Yet not one, but two original peo-

ples were there, face to face. If there was only one "civilization," whose
would it be?

In the "memory of the state," the dignity and redemption of the
prisoner was to depend on productivity and effort, yet the Canaque defied
this. As Moncelon noted, "the Canaque is generally occupied by doing
nothing; he wanders with his long hatchet on his shoulder and his spear
in hand. He spends hours wandering about, waiting for some big fish to
come by." To the European, this was a behavior suitable only to the
most disreputable of vagabonds. Lagresille, as part of the relegation debate, had argued, "The judge does not say to the vagabond, you've done
this which you have no right to do—he says, the law of work being
imposed on humanity, if you live in the state of nature you will not find
the means of your subsistence except by the fruits of your own labor."[57]

The state of nature was one in which to labor or perish. Colonial
policy dictated that the New Eden be a paradise of production; as such,
none had the right to accept nature indulgently as a gift. The inoffensive
Rousseauist contentment of the Canaque was no longer grace. According
to naval doctor Legrand, the Canaque was a creature of "nonchalant
apathy." If the island had a future, it was to be in "its commercial and
industrial development, which does not permit the natives to live in their
usual state of bestial laziness."[58]

All French commentators, whether sympathetic or hostile to the Canaques, agreed on this singular point: the islanders had no choice but to
accept the inescapable progressive logic of European history. Never mind
that that logic—"to make the Canaque a civilized man"—was a fatal
prescription. Resistance would make no difference. As the fighting of
1878 became ferocious Amoroux and Henri Place drew distinctions between the combatants: "to the fires lighted by the savages, civilization
responds with other fires." The victory would come finally and legiti-
mately when the "miserable savages" recognized the futility of challeng-
ing European "intelligence aided by science." Violences and rebellions
according to pro-colonials like Jules Garnier were only the last efforts of
a fatally condemned race, efforts which, far from delivering it, would
merely "tighten the noose and hasten the day of its complete disappearance." Former colonial Henri Rivière agreed: "The great cause of the
insurrection . . . is the antagonism which has always existed between a
conquering and a conquered people. It is necessary that this latter be
absorbed by the other, or that it disappear."[59]

The Canaque did not live in history, but in a sort of exotic living
past like that of Bordier's "prehistoric criminal," a virtual being, already
condemned by the future, "destined to disappear by the incessant law of
evolution which carries humanity to progress." Even as sympathetic an
observer as Louise Michel, who alone among the Europeans supported
the insurrection and studied the language and lore of the Canaques during her years of exile, looked upon the culture which impassioned her as
a sort of museum piece: "The leap from the stone age to us will be

Figure 17   The memory-family under attack: Chêne's household, 1878. Note the (French) illustrator's narrative elements—a man at his dinner, a wife fleeing with her children. (*Source:* Musée de la Marine)

curious to study . . . later, when the tribes are extinct or mixed, we will perhaps regret not having taken while alive these notions of the past."[60]

Between the panicked French and the chiefs led by Atai, the rebellion exposed the real historical meaning behind the island experiment with its mythical families and recapitulation of agricultural society: triumph for the few, extinction for the rest. The dramas of Chêne's cabin were struggles over a memory family: Chêne was French; his wife Canaque; their children métis. Chêne was a rehabilitated free colonist, a former prisoner of the state's island experiment; he had put away his own past and taken on the mantle of French history by building up his plantings and his farm, crossing his blood with the local women, and producing offspring with them. He was the civilization dreamed by the penitentiary and colonial authorities. He embodied their race; his farm and children were their history. That history, that "civilization" spelled doom to the Canaques.

More men like Chêne would take Canaque women and infuse, according to Legrand, "a new blood from which would spring a strong and vigorous Franco-Caledonian population which will replace, advantageously experience shows us, the last debris of the indigenous element." Henri Rivière, in a similar vein, argued, "The race of métis that is germinating in New Caledonia will be more conscious of its real interests

. . . interests to be those of its new blood and turned towards the whites."
As Place and Place explained, such mixing was not exactly racial acceptance; it was an affirmation of the dignity of the other as the same. The
inferior beings of New Caledonia would be gradually transformed by the
superior racial histories which ran in European blood, preparing the way
for a more intelligent race, "that of the métis, destined one day to merge
completely into *la grande famille blanche* [the great white family]." [61]

For the Europeans with their dreams of families, villages, and towns,
many pasts produced but one story of progress—their own. Above, I
cited the Canaque tale of separate creations. The deepest meanings in the
Canaque narrative come not from the consuming trajectory of a history
which must ultimately totalize the past, but from that past as a series of
living, intimate legacies carried from one generation to the next. As the
Canaque tale makes clear,

> The point of origin, it must be what the old communicate to their children,
> and the children to their children in order for them to know it. It is a history
> which is not written. It is what is kept in the head . . . it is necessary to have
> a good head, a good memory, no?[62]

The recited, spoken memory of the Canaque, an oral tradition of the
bamboo stick and "different creations," came up against a European history of "mémoire-famille" driven by patrimony, property documents, and
evolutionary assimilation. For the French, this meant the gradual extinction of the Canaque. The chief Atai, among others, did not plan to suffer
this fate. He, like the Canaque in Sydney, did not see the evident superiority of the Europeans and declared war on them. He made his attitude
toward "la grande famille blanche" clear in a famous encounter with the
French governor of the islands, Pitzbuer. Affronted by the chief's hat in
a meeting of local authorities, Pitzbuer commanded him to uncover his
head, to which Atai—noting the governor's ceremonial helmet—responded, "When you take off your hat, I'll take off mine." Atai was to
lose more than his famous hat in the struggle of 1878. Surprised at his
camp by rival tribes loyal to the French, he was speared several times,
then beaten to death with the famous Canaque long-handled hatchet.
His death was a significant loss to the insurrection. European civilization
carried the day. His attackers celebrated with a large and feverish ritual
of dance and sacrifice, the *pilou-pilou*. They finished by decapitating the
bodies which surrounded them and bringing the severed heads to the
leader of the French forces, Commandant Rivière.

Here, with these severed heads, these reflections on islands, history, and
the memory of civilizations come full circle. The trophies were sent first
to the New Caledonian capital of Noumea, and then to Paris. Atai's head
made the trip—in reverse—which had brought and would bring so many
prisoners to the shores of New Caledonia in search of redemption in the

harsh cradle of an island paradise. One such prisoner wrote in 1878 that Atai's head would probably reach Paris "before the Universal Exposition closes."[63] It went to the Museum of Natural History and in the twentieth century would go on to visit a newly established Musée de l'Homme, Place de Trocadero, with its very fine collection of engraved bamboo sticks.

Figure 18 Historical illusions: filming a scene in 1907. (*Source:* Collection
Roger-Viollet)

8

Spectacles: Machineries of Magic

One day by chance, journalist Michel Georges-Michel found himself at the cinema with the world's most famous living philosopher, Henri Bergson. "It is thus one day that we found ourselves in a movie theater where he spoke to me of these spectacles which have such a large role in modern life: 'The philosopher should be interested in everything,' he said, 'in everything which influences the masses as well as everything which touches the elite.' " Sharing what he has learned from the cinema, Bergson evoked the racecourse images of the Romantic painter Gericault, famous for incorrectly rendering horses' legs fully extended while running. "The cinema taught me that the vision of Gericault was the exact apparent vision . . . and from that you can imagine what a philosopher could deduce about the apparent exactitude and the *exactitude réele*."

Invited to the philosopher's garden at Clermont, Georges-Michel takes in the afternoon sun while Bergson tends his roses. In the calm of the garden Bergson speculates on the nature of thought: "The soul, that is to say the mind, is it entirely tributary to the body? That is to say to the brain?" The philosopher fashions his own reply with an image, describing thought neither as mind nor brain, but as a "succession of films created as they appear," an endlessly changing series of visuals, "rolled up into a store called *memory*."[1]

The memory cinema, the cinema as memory: Bergson's musings described a medium whose singular quality lay in creating the "exacte vision apparente"—images of what was most perfect in what *seemed* to be. To understand what this could mean, I turn from Bergson to the brothers

Lumière (who invented the cinema camera in 1895), and especially to another man and incident a few years later. In the spring of 1898 at the Place de l'Opéra, Georges Méliès—professional illusionist and owner of the magical Théatre Robert Houdin—made his historic transformation of a public coach into a wagon, and men into women. For those unfamiliar with the story, Méliès recounted the incident later in his memoires:

> One day as I was prosaically photographing the Place de l'Opéra, a minute was necessary to unblock the film and put the apparatus back into working order. During this minute, the passerby, omnibus, and carts had changed positions, of course. In projecting the film strip, spliced together at the point where the rupture had taken place, I suddenly saw an omnibus Madeleine-Bastille change into a hearse and men into women.[2]

Not the camera, but the camera jammed stands at the center of Méliès's story—the "rupture," the interruption, the discontinuity of the jolted panorama which created the fantastic. The intriguing histories of Edward Muybridge, Thomas Edison, Etienne Jules-Marey, and the brothers Lumière, their workshops, studios, and laboratories are the background for the birth of the cinema, but my concern is principally with Méliès, for my interest is not in the technical history of mechanisms, but in the language of discontinuity and deceptive persistence which Méliès saw at the Place de l'Opéra. Méliès was a magician. He did not invent the cinema, but with him as impresario, the prestidigitator, the trickster, the illusionist stepped center-stage into the memory of the modern.[3]

My own particular interest lies not in the plots and images of Méliès's films per se, but in the very categories of reality and illusion generated by his camera. In an essay on postmodern thought, Andreas Huyssen has asked, "How, then, do the technological media affect the structure of memory, the ways we perceive and live our temporality?"[4] Sketching out a twentieth century characterized by a quickening pace of material life, media images, and information, Huyssen describes what I would call an "accelerated memory," a relentless telescoping of time in which the boundaries between past and present appear to dissolve, and all time and space are rendered apparently simultaneous in the present. I raised this issue earlier in discussions of Walter Benjamin's phantasmagoric readings of nineteenth-century capitalism, where prehistory is a category of modernity. As I will show, "phantasmagoric" was also a term employed by commentators on the early cinema as they struggled to describe what they were seeing: projected images of a past more immediate than their own present.

The invention of the cinema camera was the invention of a memory machine, a technology for witnessing and preserving both great events and daily rituals. Yet the machine did more than preserve the past; the authenticity of the moving image was so authoritative, so *real*, that filmed subjects seemed to exist not as records of a point in time, but in the present of projection. Sensibilities of temporal depth and sequence which gave reality to the past were dominated by the spectacular immediacy of the image. Striking images would become the viewer's memory of events, shaping recollections to the measure of filmed and projected scenes. Citing physiology, ethics, and the impressionable nature of what Bergson called "the masses," critics of the new medium debated the accuracy and morality of the cinema, and raised questions about the virtues of screen memories, as opposed to those of the printed page.

With its ability to capture and collapse time, the cinema camera was an utterly modern marker for the accelerated memory of the late nineteenth century, a machine which generated superbly real living records while simultaneously creating its own fantastically unsettling perceptual and temporal frameworks. If the inventors of the machine—the brothers Lumière—thought of their creation principally as a scientific and documentary instrument, artists like Méliès saw it as part of a mechanism of dreams, a chance to capture absolute unreality and create effects and visions far beyond what his theater could imagine. What follows then is a double narrative: an examination of the essential realism of the cinematic image as record and document, yet also a critical look at the processes by which moving images were rendered fantastic by the technical language of filming and projection, so that the "exactitude" which Bergson sought in the memory cinema was from its very inception that of a medium of illusions.[5]

The mechanism of this magic had originally been developed by Auguste and Louis Lumière, scions of a Lyonnais industrial family, and displayed to a select public on December 28, 1895, in Paris. Père Lumière stood in for his sons (who remained in Lyon) and made the legendary invitation, "What are you doing tonight, about five o'clock?" to an audience likely to appreciate the family invention: impresarios and men of the Paris theater with names like Gaumont, Pathé—and Georges Méliès. The seance in the basement of the Grand Café, Boulevard des Capucines, began with a projection of a street image—like a lantern slide—which convinced the unimpressed Méliès that he had wasted his time. Suddenly, the image began to move, and Méliès stared, as he said, "jaw dropping."

His reaction would be repeated by dozens of other viewers over the next few days as the Lumières began projecting their films to a paying public. As tramways, cars, and passersby made their way across the screen, movement itself was truth. *Le Radical* of December 30, 1895, reported these first moving images as "astonishing"; rolling waves and seaside bathers "excited enthusiasm" and were commented to describe "a marvelous realism."

One enthusiast for the new technology, writer and publicist Boleslas Matuszweski, noted in 1898 that "animated photography has a character of authenticity, exactitude, and precision which belongs to it alone," and proposed the creation of a national historic film depot. Matuszweski's comments are notable in that he did not limit his appreciation of the cinematic image to its ability to *represent*, but also realized its power to *preserve* a visual reality. The new medium not only framed space, but captured—rather than stopped—time. By imprinting its images on moving celluloid bands, the cinema camera automatically generated records of complete scenes in temporal extension. "Ordinary photography," which in any case was wanting in its susceptibility to the "retouch," was poor cousin to the new moving picture, "par excellence the true and infallible ocular witness."[6]

The privileged relationship of memory to vision in the late nineteenth century is a theme I have examined in my discussions of medical-legal examinations and identification systems. As in the latter, "memory" in the cinema would be displaced from persons to instruments.[7] Acting as a "witness" the new machine would be, in effect, the dispassionate eye of history, a scribe whose power was rooted in the recording of time through seeing. As a technology of memory, the cinema camera was thus closer to other forms of visual recording—such as print—than it was to speaking. Matuszweski in fact argued that the camera "could control the oral tradition," and presented his analysis with an evident suspicion of the spoken as opposed to the visually reproducible as a medium of historical evidence. "If human witnesses contradict each other about a fact," he suggested, the evidence of the camera would enforce agreement, "shutting the mouth of the one who's lying." Not only was the machine the site of accuracy in memory, but the visual record, blessed with an objectivity of seeing, acted to close off biases of individual speakers. Matuszweski cited an 1897 state visit to Russia in which allegations of "a mistake in protocol" on the part of the French President were discredited by a film record of the event. The seeing of the cinema camera appeared to guarantee that much of "History" would "henceforth escape from the fantasy of narrators."[8]

Convinced of the *verité* of cinematography, Matuszweski nonetheless did not intend to consider the records of the new medium to be "historical" unless they could be arranged into a system of preservation commensurate with what he already knew: "For cinematographic proofs having a historic character it will be sufficient to assign a section of a museum, a wing of a library, or a section of the archives." The institutional location of the film depot insured that its contents would attain "the same authority, the same official existence, the same access as other archives already known." Between the memory machine and the archive, the dream of history "wie es eigentlich gewesen"—as it really was— seemed dramatically possible. As Matuszewski argued, "if only we'd had reproductions of scenes which animated photography can easily bring to life for the first Empire and for the Revolution . . . how much uselessly spilled ink would have been saved."[9]

Matuszweski's vision of the cinema camera as a technologically objective, faithful mechanical witness was not to last long. Within moments of seeing the Lumières' moving pictures at the Grand Café, Georges Méliès, dreaming of illusions, had promptly offered to buy their apparatus. The famous refusal—"the cinema has no future"—was the father's vision, shared by his sons, of the industrial, scientific, and documentary applications of the tool, but its inadmissability (beyond a season's fashion) as a truly popular medium. Recalled Méliès, "Lumière refused to sell, desiring to consecrate his invention to science, principally the study of movement as (Etienne-Jules) Marey had done." Undeterred, Méliès learned what he could about the Lumières' instrument and wasted no time building his own. Within a month he opened his magical Théatre Robert Houdin as the "world's first public cinema."[10]

Between 1896 and 1912, Méliès produced over five hundred films, including his signature piece *Un voyage dans la lune* (A Trip to the Moon). After imitating the Lumière camera operators by spinning out scores of short films of babies, trains, steamboats, city views, market days, and small staged scenes, Méliès and his theatrical troupe turned from such "realism" to develop a body of original works which both replicated and extended the detailed, fantastic spectacles of his magical acts. In 1902 already, Louis Lumière agreed, "the owner and director of the Théatre Robert-Houdin is the creator of that class of cinematographic films which are composed of artificially prepared scenes . . . he was the first to have the idea of reproducing comic, magic, and fantastic scenes, and until now has never been successfully imitated."[11]

For Méliès, the cinema camera would be nothing but an exalted instrument of illusions. In his works he voyaged to the moon, conquered the pole, and sailed 20,000 leagues under the seas. His was a staggering history of an industrial age—a titanic cannon throws a projectile through space to the lunar surface; a winged bus flies to the top of world; an underwater boat delves the submarine gardens. At the same time, however, Méliès applied his craft to make technology disappear. Chorus lines of maidens attend the cannon, water fairies add visual grace to the iron submersible. Méliès's set-pieces, his mechanical men, his optical effects, his staging for the camera were logical extensions of the engineering behind the trap doors and armatures which supported his illusions at the Robert-Houdin. In cinematography all the effects and emblems of science—projectile, submarine, dirigible—were present to the audience, yet all the industry which produced the magic—rail, harness, gears, glass plates—and especially the cinema camera itself, were invisible.[12]

In a 1907 essay Méliès recorded his division of the filmed world into four distinct types of scenes, of which the last was his own invention. "Four great categories of *vues cinematographiques* exist, or at least, all views belong to one of the categories. The views called open air, the scientific views, the *sujets composés*, and the views of transformation." At

first, Méliès argued, "the views were exclusively subjects taken from nature; later the cinema camera was employed as a scientific apparatus, finally becoming a theatrical apparatus." The most exalted "vue" was that
which surpassed both nature and science to enter the realm of the fantastic.[13]

For Méliès, the realism of the cinema was neither science nor "objective"
witnessing, but a truth of illusions, a reality of tricks and simulations.
Some of the simulations were breathtakingly mounted. Méliès was among
the first to conceive of fictional-documentary re-creations of "historic"
moments. His version of the coronation of the King of England, Edward
VII (1902), occasioned praise from the monarch himself for his impersonation. Reviewers of the film were amused or dismayed by the public's
credulousness, mocking especially the British for believing they had seen
a record of the actual event. In several reels Méliès also restaged the
Dreyfus affair, including the trial, imprisonment, and vindication of the
wronged officer.[14]
     If coronations and news events could be restaged or completely sim-
ulated for the camera, the new machine could also shape meanings and
opinions simply by the way it framed events. One film writer recounted
a woman's testimony of a military ceremony at Roubaix in which French
clergy maintained a respectful distance from visiting German officers in
honoring their war dead. The German officer in charge pronounced his
homage, asking that "we cease to consider ourselves enemies." With
these words, "he seized the hand of the French clergyman next to him,
and began to shake it warmly to the great stupefaction of the horrified
priest." Here the machine interceded: "At the same instant, a camera
began to roll . . . it was taking a film to be shown to neutral countries!"[15]
     The Roubaix incident was considered a disturbing precedent in
France where police, judges, and prosecutors were presumed to "not yet
have the boldness and effrontery of the authorities in Prussia and Bohemia." The Roubaix writer warned of the day when filmed images of an
event would become an element of proof in justice: "How many abuses
there will be." Why this fear? "Nothing is simpler than doing tricks with
films, and the secret police could put a whole team of operators to work."
With a justification Méliès could easily admire, the writer noted, "We are
not talking about those tricks dear to Robert-Houdin, tricks of spirits
and hindu priests. We want to speak here of tricks inherent to the cinema
camera . . . effects obtained by photographing movement, thanks to in-
genious combinations."[16] Reversals of movements, substitutions, tricks
which only the grammar of the cinema could effect could be combined
to confound, delight—or falsify memories of the historical record.
     Clever or devious operators who could stage or distort events were
only one threat to historical memory and the truth of cinematic seeing.
Another, perhaps even more unsettling, was the directness of image and
compression of time which the camera itself created, an immediacy which

annihilated temporal order, distance, and reflection. In matters of reporting events, the printing press multiplied the news, but "often the cinema camera itself overtakes the newspapers; it acts in any case with a disconcerting rapidity," according to film writer J. Rosen, who offered readers this extraordinary spectacle: "Witness the tragic airplane accident which took place in December 1910, resulting in the deaths of the aviators Laffont and Mariano Pola . . . the Gaumont company was able to film the crash of the aviators second by second and a few hours after the accident the Gaumont theater situated on the Paris boulevards projected fifty meters of film reproducing the tragic event."[17] Before the events were scarcely comprehended by those at the scene, they were witnessed by a distant public viewing "the last word" in *actualités*. Image preceded understanding; the experience of tragedy and the memory of an event was the shared viewing of the projection itself, all the more striking and apparently real for its immediacy.

Soon enough, Rosen noted, news events would be framed and transmitted instantly, reported not even as they had been witnessed, but as they were *being* witnessed. The element of time which had depended upon distance in reporting information was being destroyed. Reported Rosen on the British reception of cinematographic news: "one of their newspapers even let it be known that the cinema camera will be superseded in the near future by cinema-telegraphy, which will permit the showing of scenes taken the same day over long distances." To this possibility of transmission, Rosen could only remark, "don't shrug your shoulders."

Why indeed be surprised by this infant reign of visual media, where the latest was everything, when a sort of evening program was already possible: "The Pathé Bros. Company has even created what is happily called the *Pathé Journal*, the cinematographic newspaper which projects the most important events of the day or week each night."[18] The document of the camera operators was a sort of "instant history," not assembled, worked, and judged by historians, but captured with an astonishing directness, drawing its credibility not from analysis and reflection, but from quickness of presentation. Speed and immediacy were all; the camera allowed the past—or what used to be the past—to be almost instantly displaced into the present.

The cinema camera did not simply record; it *produced* new schemes of time. Though the writer Matuszweski (above) may have erred in declaring the "ocular witness" to be "infallible," he did appreciate the cinema camera as the ideal tool to capture the tension between history as a grand traditional lineage of posed encounters and a history which could now be taken "on the wing." What the new moving pictures could capture was not only painterly scenes and grand portraiture, but "the beginnings of action, the initial movements, the unexpected occurences." The "events" of history need not be given by "solemn occasions, organized in advance," but seen in those captured moments always beginning, un-expected. This could mean the "news" of the cine-journalists, but also the recording of everyday scenes. Matuszweski saw in the intercession of technology the ability to record a new history suited to his own times, a history based on the principle that "the historical fact is not always pro-duced where one expects it."[19]

The movement-image was more than a technical triumph—the dy-namism, the activity spoke a language of life to chroniclers at the turn of the century. A new machine had captured the changeable flux of time, the sensibility of ceaseless transformation which so profoundly affected commentators on capitalism, evolutionary anthropologists, and Impres-sionist painters alike. The defining quality was summarized in a medita-tion on the new art in *La Revue des deux mondes*: "It is by the reproduction of movement that the cinematic image differs from the for-mer charming magic lantern. Movement is its triumph and essence."[20] The Parisian press read these sensibilities into the birth of cinematogra-phy. *La Poste* of December 30, 1895, began its report, "photography has ceased fixing immobility. It perpetuates the image of movement." The moving image drew together the technical possibilities of producing and endlessly reproducing life and memory. The reporters of *Le Radical* sug-gested, "Already, words are collected and reproduced; now life is col-lected and reproduced. We can, for example, see our dear ones again long after they would be lost to us."[21]

As *Le Radical* suggests, words were already subject to record and reproduction, in script, typography, or by this time even phonographic registration, and I have discussed elsewhere the mechanization and pro-liferation of popular literacy and print culture in the late nineteenth cen-tury. Cinematic images in turn further revolutionized the possibilities of the meanings of a "modern memory." The idea of capturing lost time through the moving image resonates strongly in press accounts detailing the reception of the very first cinematographic images. Pierre Bourdieu has noted how photography initially democratized the aristocratic portrait gallery by allowing people of simpler means to enjoy their own "family album," an album generally arranged according to "the memory of time and chronological evolution."[22] In this the family album was not only portrait gallery, but personal archive, genealogical record, and keeper of the family history. The cinematic image pushed this personal sense of time and heritage one step further. The recording of the image in still photography was a registration of memory, but it was a fixed image, distanced by the camera. "Cinematography" was different. The memory of the cinema camera was (as Bergson might have appreciated) charac-terized by movement; it was movement which constituted the remem-brance which could lay claim to life. To remember was to retain emotional ties to beloved friends and family as living beings, recognized through their actions and familiar gestures. The point of memory was the longing for not the image, but the image alive. True memory was movement forever lost to time, life recaptured by the camera. *Le Monde illustré* of January 25, 1896, made this point with a lesson in etymology: "*Cinématographe* is a compound Greek word signifying the registration of movements. The object of the apparatus is in fact to reproduce life and movement in all of their appearances."[23]

In a way no still picture could capture, the memory of the cinema camera kept the record of the everyday, the fugitive: "the road which bustles, the laborer who works, the child who smiles, the bicycle which passes, the cigarette on the lips. . . ." Much more than merely a moving form of photography, the cinema camera captured and recaptured at each instant both change and the location of that change in each precise experienced moment, whether the panorama of a street, the smile, the gesture. The cinema camera gave to the present "a living portrait, instead of those cold, languid images which never look right in their attempts to represent the fluid grace and charm of certain beings."[24]

When the first moving images were originally projected, *La Poste* had immediately advocated the cinematographic apparatus be made available to the public. In a particularly striking passage, *La Poste* confirmed the status of the new machine as an instrument of remembrance, a machine whose role would be to forever preserve beloved family and friends in the ultimate act of memory—overcoming the tyranny and separation of death:

> When this apparatus is made available to the public, when everyone can photograph his dearest ones, not only in their immobile form, but in movement, in action with their familiar gestures and with words shaped on their lips, death will cease to be absolute.[25]

The cinema camera captured lost time in its living essence. If typography and photography distanced friends and family from their oral traditions and intimate activities by generating fixed records of the past, perhaps the cinematic image could heal the separations by restoring the past as living, moving memory. To live forever in memory—the proposal of *La Poste* was immortality as produced by a machine.

The cinema camera inscribed, documented, and reproduced the rhythms of life, but the new machines also produced that life in a strange form. The continuous moving picture, born into a nineteenth century more accustomed to print, paintings, drawings, and at best photography, was a transparency of seeing a bit too real: "It surprises our gestures, it records our most spontaneous attitudes, and sometimes this can seem audacious," noted one writer. The cinema camera seemed to capture everything, and the very invasive and immediate power of the lens rendered it "even more indiscreet than journalism."[26] The presence of the subject was overly direct. Not properly censored by the play of words, the artistry of the brush, the hand of the engraver, the pose or arrangement, the cinematic image lacked the distance which time created in painted portraits and other artistic scenes. Even photography fixed a particular past moment. The cinematic image seemed rather to reproduce actuality, to invade the present.

Cinematic memory was a world of affronted senses and collapsed time. What the cinema camera did was replicate gestures (again, activity defines) with such accuracy that being and reproduction, the subject and its image were confused. Shortly before introducing the cinema camera in Paris, the Lumière brothers had already presented their invention to the Société pour l'Encouragement de l'Industrie and the Congrès des Sociétés Françaises de Photographie in Lyon. The press account in *Le Progrès* from the summer sessions is worth noting: "We saw ten lifelike animated scenes, absolutely intense: men walking, jumping, streetcars rolling by in such a way that there was an absolute illusion of reality." Referring to filmed images of two members of the group, Messrs. Janssen and Lagrange, who were also in the audience that day, the paper reported: "The gestures were reproduced with such accuracy that one could have supposed behind the screen the complicity of two characters playing a fantasmagoric story, and yet there they were in the room."[27]

As the passage indicates, Messrs. Janssen and Lagrange were not merely "captured" by the camera, they were its co-conspirators, collaborators in a fantasmagoria of impersonation in which the actors astonishingly appeared to be alive on the screen, yet were seated nonetheless in the audience, watching themselves. In a piece strikingly similar to the Lyon reports, writers in *Les Annales* of April 28, 1896, described the moving image as possessed of "an unimaginable realism. The power of illusion! Face to face with these scenes, one wonders if it's not a hallucination—if one is a simple spectator, or really an actor in these scenes of astonishing realism."[28] Was one observer or observed? As the cinematic image moved it had "actors," yet unlike the theater, the actors were alive—in most cases—by being absent from the scene. The realism of the moving image was always a record of the past displaced into the present. To see oneself would be an impossible exteriority, a doubling of bodies, of presences, a simultaneity of past and present in time and space. The memory of the cinematic image was a "hallucination," an illusion, perhaps best explained as a secret collusion between the parties, the unsettling sense that something was going on not like science, but more like prestidigitation and magic.

The first "memory" imputed to the cinema camera rested in its technical ability to capture and reproduce movement, to restore life in temporal dimension to events and faces from the past. Within months of the first projections, however, critics found the mechanism wanting as cinematic images raised troubling questions for what they excluded: language. As artistic forms, neither dance nor mime were presumed to require a spoken or textual base. Yet as the cinema camera captured "life," it forced a reexamination of the categories of experience and expression, and compelled its critics to wonder whether words were or were not an originary form of creative expression upon which all culture was patterned.

Matuszweski, noted earlier, had called the cinema camera an "ocular witness" and championed the accuracy of the eye against the ear, but others were equally partisan against images deprived of words. In July 1896, six months after the first public showings of the Lumière's work, a distinguished Paris visitor, Russian poet Maksim Gorky, recorded a strong reaction to the cinematic image: "It is terrible to see this movement of shadows, nothing but shadows, specters and ghosts; one thinks of legends where some evil genius captures an entire town with a perpetual sleep."[29] What Gorky notably loathed in the Lumière's images was the silence of the screen, and behind his grim description lay the question of the speaking voice. What the cinema evoked for Gorky was not images of life, but figures with lifeless smiles: "You see their facial muscles contract, but the laughing never comes out." The memory machine was a false witness. Without the voice, the expression on the screen was a mask, the laughing figure a mute mockery of itself.

For critics like Gorky, a partisan of words and voice, the collected images of the cinema camera would be forever incomplete, gray shadows awaiting reconciliation with voices. Technically he was half-correct, for if the voice was grimly silent on the screen, filmmakers like Méliès knew it was nonetheless present and essential in the studio, where ear, eye, and limb were inseparably linked to words in the duties of a brand new craft— that of the camera operator. "A mistake of the crank, forgetting a number in counting out loud while shooting the scene . . . one second of distraction and everything is lost."[30] Only absolute attention, a disciplined physical and mental presence could correctly coordinate the simultaneity of actions by hand, eye, and voice required to create *ciné-mémoires*.

For filmmakers like Méliès, waiting for the voice was beside the point, for the silent medium was a language in itself, a new language of movements. As a performer and as director, what Méliès recognized in the new medium was the primacy of physical ability and discipline—on both sides of the camera. In his notes on acting, Méliès wrote of "well-known actors" unsuitable for his productions, lacking the indispensable abilities of a film actor, "the perfect play of the physiognomy, the right attitudes." Body consciousness and bearing defined the cinema actor and defied the theatrical player. "Accustomed to speaking well, they only employ gesture as an accessory in the theater, whereas in the cinema speaking is nothing and gesture everything."[31] Méliès was not awaiting the amelioration of an incomplete technology, but grasped the dynamic, physical modernity of the moving image and adopted a language of action with no obeisance to the authority of the word. After viewing some of Méliès's work, one journalist summarized his own skeptical impressions, "Certainly you'll be shown something, but that something will be—what is the word—a sham, a trick of the light, low class theater . . . 'words! words!' said Shakespeare, 'gestures! gestures!' says Méliès."[32]

The arguments between the partisans of word and gesture raised questions which put the cinema at the intersection of social, political, juridical, and epistemological issues. The undeniable popularity of cinematic programs troubled critics; how was the viewer affected by the new images—was he or she edified by the medium, or were the entertainments of the screen merely vulgar and sensational? Was the cinema an original art form, or simply a mechanized version of older arts? As a machine the cinema camera registered its impressions on a physical medium of celluloid bands. As the practice of taking scenes became increasingly commercialized, legal scholars drew together many of these questions by asking, Who should control the films? Were they essentially narratives based ultimately on words? Could cinematic images have "authors" or did they capture "experience"?

Summaries and commentaries on early cinematic legal work, such as *Le Cinematographe devant le droit* (1908) by E. Maugras and M. Guegan, and *Du Cinematographe dans ses rapports avec le droit de l'auteur*, (1912) by Jean Marchais, tried to establish the legal limits of rights and protections accorded the new medium. What after all was the cinematic image? "Should it be considered as a drawing? As some sort of an engraving? A production of the mind?" As a physical record, as a memory or historical witness, the filmic image was legally appropriated to the status of a gravure. The judicial metaphor was film as inscription. Gravure was first of all established as "the art of producing figures on a plane surface. Either by incisions, ordinarily not very deep, or with the aid of files, or finally by means of chiseling or sculpture." The cinematic image added another dimension to this engraving processing—the developing bath—for "the negative impressed by light contains the image in a virtual state; the developing bath is simply a corrosive which, in destroying certain salts, makes the image appear."[33]

Just as Aristotle's wax block of memory, the cinematic image was established as an impressed, inscribed, traced, and finally revealed form of record. Yet the metaphor required something new, something tied in particular to the instruments of the late nineteenth century. The cinema camera, more than merely the engraver of a photographic negative, was also legally admitted as "a mechanical apparatus" of some sophistication. The important point was not the technical capacities of the industrial world which produced the instrument, but the way in which the instrument registered its record: "The eye of the spectator is deceived by the rapidity of movement and does not perceive the distinctions in the continuity of the image. The cinematic image is one more proof of the imperfection of our sense of vision."[34] The cinema camera, like an engraved plate, registered and preserved images. But unlike the gravure, the light-struck celluloid it pulled through the lens gate created its prominent effects precisely by illusion, by fooling the eye of the spectator with sequential images, misperceived as continuous. The moving image was lifelike, yet it was a kind of authenticity reached only by playing on the "imperfection" and limits of human perception, a literal *trompe l'oeil* of movement and physiology.

Such dilemmas over illusory perception and physical record form the points of contention in a famous test case of cinematographic jurisprudence, "M. Fourcade against M. Torres." From 1903 to 1904 Fourcade pursued an action against Torres, the former claiming for himself the rights of "auteur" over a series of scenes realized in collaboration with the aid and technical apparatus of M. Torres. A decision at Lourdes was upheld at the Court of Appeals in Pau holding Torres harmless, and dismissing Fourcade's claims of ownership, as "auteur," over the films. The higher court ruled that Fourcade could not claim the status of "auteur" over the material with emphasis on the following points of decision:

> Understood that the meaning of "dramatic work" shall be a direct representation of characters acting and speaking on a stage in a real or fictitious situation.

> The movement which characterizes cinematographic images is not due to the auteur, or to the performers, but to the special machine by means of which this movement is obtained and the optical illusion occasioned by the uninterrupted succession of scenes passing before the lens and their projection on a screen.[35]

The court's decision turned upon two remarkable interpretations. First, the action in the films could be "real or fictitious," but Fourcade could not claim to be auteur of a dramatic work, because a dramatic work required "characters acting and speaking." Language lay at the heart of legitimate claim to creation. The second point of the decision made clear the court's view that the idea of the work rested not with directors or players, but was identical with the perception of movement, and thus "the special machine" which produced it. Only with the master of the apparatus, and his ability to trick the eye itself, could rest the true claim of the "auteur." The owner of the images was the owner of the camera.

Reactions to the decision were divided. On the first point, legal commentator Jean Marchais agreed, for the very silences of the cinema camera meant that its productions would always be secondary to the authority of the word. Marchais's interpretation played upon a logocentric reality in which the image, the movement offered by the cinema camera would always be a "reproduction" of the primacy of the written word, which alone could render the vision "integral." Marchais's commentary is worth a few words of its own, for what he described in the Pau case was not just a complex property dispute, but something important in considering historical memory: the signs of a newly visual culture eroding the standards of a literate one. Using the figure of the mime to stand in for the cinematic image, he noted skeptically, "the evolution of a sentiment, a state of the soul, which a novel analyses for an entire chapter, is reduced

in pantomime to a few gestures."[36] A partisan of the richness and inte-
grality of written works, Marchais was concerned not only with the de-
centered authority of printed and spoken language in the new medium,
but the threat it posed by extension to the values of a literate culture. In
earlier chapters I described the transformations of a civilization increasingly dependent on print culture for its memory, and explained the hegemony of the word in mnemonic practices. The spectacular popularity
of the movie screen challenged that authority with its images. Writers like
Marchais were not pleased, insisting on the primacy of words before pictures. "The cinema camera, a mechanism essentially mute, is only good
for reproducing movement, and cannot make an integral reproduction of
a purely literary work."[37]

In other commentaries, the Pau judgment met heavy criticism. On
the first point, Maugras and Guegan argued, "If the projection of the
voice alone constituted a show, ballets and pantomimes would not be
protected," which in fact they already were by laws of 1862 and 1875.
Unlike mime or dance, the cinema was somehow prefigured to encompass not only the domain of art, but the possibilities of experience, and
the court had interpreted this to mean that the mute must give way to
the spoken to be fully realized and worthy of protection. Maugras and
Guegan reminded the court that expression rested also in gesture and
movement.

The two lawyers were equally skeptical about the Pau court's definition of what constituted a "work," though here their critique is not so
easy to embrace. If the decision were correct, "it would be necessary to
say that it was the apparatus which directed the action, which indicated
the gestures, which built the sets."[38] Maugras and Guegan made a direct
poetic substitution of the apparatus, making the machine act an absurd
human role. Though impracticable, the court's decision was differently
based—not on establishing scenes, but on defining the essential quality
of movement. In effect, the complaint of Maugras and Guegan was already conceded—human players do indeed arrange and indicate the
scenes. The interpretation of the court was that the essential characteristic
of the cinematic image was not scenes, but the control of the illusion of
motion.

Jean Marchais's reinterpretation of the case centered on this disturbing insight and decision, the court's apparently unreal reversal of original
and copy: "The court at Pau confounds the work itself with its mode of
reproduction. To appraise the character of a work, it is the work itself
which must be considered and not its mode of reproduction."[39] Marchais's interpretation, like Maugras and Guegan's disputes over establishing scenes, was based upon understanding the cinema camera as a creator
of reproductions, whereas the court read the apparatus as itself a producer
of originals. None of the commentators appreciated the modernity of the
court's position that cinematic expression was its own medium and could
not be translated or reduced back to another reality. Disagreements over

ownership of the cinematographic movement-image were locked in a shifting epistemological vision: an older, human-centered reality which copied and represented the world to itself was giving way to a startling new machine-driven multiplication of unrepeatable moments—copies with no originals.

The new vision would affect more than legal commentators. Henri Bergson, in his evocation of the memory cinema, had called the new art a form which interested not only the elite (like himself), but "the masses." Analyzing cinematic movement took on the quality of social-juridical judgment as writers, publicists, critics, and legal scholars attempted to explain the popularity of film programs and the class status and moral imagination of the filmgoers. That the cinema was an immediate popular, perhaps vulgar success after 1895 was not surprising to the elite; the moving picture was from the beginning a technical development ideally adapted to broad public spectacle. The lawyers Maugras and Guegan argued:

> Without speaking of the moderate price, which many appreciate, the cinema is easy theater. There, no complicated or laborious situations. The drama, the vaudeville, the comedy, unroll in a few minutes. Intrigue exists, but is only sketched out. The characters have just enough time, hastily sketched, to establish their characters, and immediately there is a happy ending, sentimental, always moralistic, which satisfies the spectator no matter his state of mind.[40]

What makes the passage so arresting is not Maugras and Guegan's judgment of others' tastes, but the way in which that judgment was inseparable from an accelerated rhythm of time. Rapid meant "simple," impatient with complicated situations and character development. As such, the movement-image read its own public: the cinema was the theater for "people in a hurry, who don't like long passages and fastidious monologues."[41] Critics of simplification, such as Jean Marchais (above), complained, "The action itself which is the object of an entire volume finds itself reduced to a few scenes which unroll in a few seconds." The essence of the cinematographic image lay in an unrelenting compression of time and activity, in which a spectacle comprehensible to the public was the product of a promoter's desire "to abbreviate, to shorten, to recut, to reduce the action of the piece to its general lines."[42] Another critic explained how reserving tickets, being properly dressed, and studying texts was part of the ritual of going to the theater. On the contrary, "one enters the cinema by chance, as one enters a café." The cinema was everything the bourgeois ritual of the theater was not—an experience of accidental and spontaneous time, "a half-hour," at a low price.[43]

The obsessive shortening of time which seemed to accompany all aspects of the cinema from abridged narrative to casual projection hall was re-embodied in the spectator facing the screen by the flickering of light, and the sensation of images impressed and retained in the nervous system. The cinema camera reduced the sentiment and emotional experience of stories into an acceleration of perception, a physiological reaction which agitated the body to emotional re-action by drawing on an intensity of collapsed time. Méliès stated a truism when he remarked upon the nature of film production: "A complicated scene sometimes requires two or three days of consecutive shooting. It's not unusual to spend eight or nine hours to execute a scene which will last two minutes when projected."[44] Cinema condensed and intensified effects which would be played out before the viewer in seconds, the particular rapidity of image and scene engendering a constant immediacy of sensation in the spectator. The memory machine accelerated time. Critic René Doumic predicted the future of the medium with a fitting description of the end of the century: "The perfect cine-drama, if we have it one day, will incarnate perpetual motion."[45]

The power of the movement-image to agitate the senses directly raised questions which demonstrated the inseparable links between perception, memory, and ethical judgment. The cinematic image was after all a sort of gravure on the mind, a form of impression into memory. Writer and critic Edouard Poulain cited the dangers of the projected image in a cautionary tract, *Contre le cinema* (Against the Cinema): "Observe the child. Study his psychology. He is the perfect imitator, a being of impressions and impulsions." The child especially was a malleable surface, easily imprinted with sensations and impulsive to act on them. The visual image could deform the moral and physical health of such a young being, undiscerning in replicating images and sensations. "He reproduces in his games the adventures he has witnessed. Thus when he watches shows where theft takes place before his eyes . . . where robbery is celebrated in scenes of violence, pillage, and murder, oh! shortsighted parents, on your guard!"[46]

For adults, the cinematic movement-image was also a means to mark ethical judgments. In a September 1913 issue of *L'Intransigeant*, one Fernand Nozière wrote his opinion of the filmgoer. "At the cinema, he comes looking for easy satisfaction. He has no shame about laughing out loud when he sees a farce, or pouring out tears when he attends a great drama . . . in truth, he abandons himself to his true sentiments."[47] In his portrait of the (male) spectator Nozière evoked a figure vaguely ridiculous for the shameless public display of his "true sentiments." Social distinctions bounded by surfaces of shame were broken by ignoble laughter and tears. As the eye was impressed by the image, so the body physiologically reacted with social transgressions in the explosive, accidental voice and the pouring out of tears. By his crude reactions to sentiments uncontrolled and easily satisfied, the spectator only revealed his own vulgar moral character.

Though admittedly plebian, film stories were nonetheless also praised for their sentimental, satisfying, affirmative qualities, "always moral"; if simple-minded, at least they were not corrupt. In an instance of pitting modernity against modernism, the lawyers Maugras and Guegan even defended the screen against the stage: "In the middle of the ambient and always growing immorality of the theater, it seems that this art wanted to throw off the yoke of the depraved tastes and dangerous ideas of modern literature."[48] The very dynamism of the form, with its appeal to a broad audience and apparently uncomplicated emotional cues, could be morally virtuous against the "scaborous scenes," "ambiguous situations," and "depraved tastes" of decadent theater and prose. With its happy endings, film in one way resolved the dilemma of moral judgments at the level of the story. More important, morality under the eye of the cinema camera was a kind of a rhythm—rapid actions and quick resolutions embodied in instant sensations. These sensations of body and feeling, laughter and tears, were "common," but honest and declarative, thus "memories" of ethical behavior.

The first posters to the original Lumière showings in 1895 are worth a word on the concatenation of image, rhythm, and ethics. Was the cinematographic spectacle a new form of scientifically rendered morality? In his acerbic review of the Lumières' rather innocuous early short film, *The Train's Arrival in the Station*, Maksim Gorky had imagined the locomotive transformed into an engine of righteous destruction, hurtling off the screen to crush the audience, "and reduce this room to dust, along with this entire building, full of wine, music, women, and vice." Gorky feminized the cinema and debased its pleasures to that of a brothel. For Gorky, popular halls, licentious women, and drink were the immoral and unfortunate showcase for "the latest conquest of Science."[49] The Lumières' publicity contested and reversed this image, transforming the projection hall into a site of solid moral comfort based on bourgeois images of family.

In the first poster commissioned to the painter Brispot, the fashionable crowd jostles for entry to the theater under the bold legend "Cinematographe Lumière." The titles are arranged so as to frame a lamp suspended from the ceiling, and the central part of the image is washed with light. The clamor is such that near the entrance a man's hat is knocked off. Canes are raised. No image or explanation of the "Cinematographe" is offered, only the anticipation and the mystery guarded by the shaded entryway. In the foreground, a firm, uniformed officer of the law faces the crowd. He is positioned so as to try to contain the overflowing enthusiasm of the throng, yet the figure he directly confronts is a priest, Bible tucked under his left arm. The officer engages his attention, yet also directly refuses him entry to the spectacle, while the crowd surges around the two of them. Why this choice of iconography? Has irresistible technology conquered religion as the new source of morality and the miraculous?

The second Lumière poster by Azuolle reveals the mystery behind

Figure 19   The secret of the cinema: poster for *L'Arroseur arrosé*. (*Source:* Collection Roger-Viollet)

the portals. The viewer moves inside of the projection salon, to regard the men, women, and children in all of their finery (including their hats and bonnets) viewing the spectacle itself. Here the image re-created on the screen is not the avenues and tramways commented on by early reviewers, but a jet of water in the face of the hapless gardener from the Lumiere's first cinematic "gag" film, *L'Arosseur arossé*. The women, children, men, the usher all laugh openly. The little boy in blue rises from his seat and gestures to the screen; a man extends his hat in hand; the elderly woman in the second row registers surprise with a colorful gloved hand. The two posters, counterposed one against the other, frame the inside and outside of the cinematic spectacle. Outside, the restless throng, the mystery, the interdiction of the black garbed priest await the miracles of modern technology. Inside, the scene is framed by the luxury of the entertainment, the smiles, the laughter breaking from the lips of all observers.

Generations are invoked by the figures—the girl resembles the mother, the little boy the father, the other two figures appear to be grandparents or relatives. The public in this picture is far from a collection of vulgar strangers; the image is an edifying portrait of the loved ones whom the first cinema journalists had wanted to memorialize forever with the new machine. Laughter, the images would seem to suggest, is not shame at all; laughter and joyful family company are the very experience of the cinema. These "memories" are the secrets guarded within these darkened salons of cinematic illusion.[50]

Laughter was something Georges Méliès knew well. His 1898 Place de l'Opéra epiphany had taken place at the moment the broken scene of men becoming women flickered by and he reacted in the only manner possible to him: he burst out laughing. Laughter and the fantastic would always be inseparable to him.

In later years he would laugh perhaps less. After years of enchanting confrontations with demons, living planets, and ice giants, real conflict— the First World War—moved into the background of Méliès's universe. The war and the expenses of maintaining theater and studio drove down his magic. Financial problems forced his retirement from the cinema to a small wooden stand at Montparnasse where he sold toys and amuse- ments to the passing public for a decade. The boulevards with which the Baron Haussmann had reshaped the Parisian landscape, and which had in turn shaped Méliès's visions, were changing. New capital investments, a new city plan, the increase of traffic and circulation required new pas- sages and motorways. The quarter around the Place de l'Opéra where the jammed film had created the "transformation" of modern cinema was reshaped. The "boulevards of the cinema" which had defined the early urban physiognomy and rhythm of the art were changing again, pressed by transport, population growth, and development. Blocks were pushed back, old structures razed. Old theaters, the staging grounds of early twentieth-century entertainment, redolent with memories of magic and cinema, went down. Among these was Méliès's beloved Robert- Houdin.

The memory of the machine had presented the turn of the century with a new way of seizing the passage of time, of registering and keeping the impossible: movement itself. With the cinema camera the decay and flux of time could be arrested in fleeting moments of intense movement and imagination. Creative visionaries like Méliès saw in the cinema a the- ater in which each performance would always be the first, the finest. He wrote of an immortality for artists photographed by the cinema camera, playing out their roles "imperturbably and unfalteringly," recorded per- formances which could never be "unequal, good one day and bad the next." The unrepeatability of the first peformance, registered, captured, fixed as a singular memory, unfolded into the breadth of an immortal, extended time: "If they have performed well the first time, they are ex- cellent forever."[51] But not all memories are equal. In 1923 Méliès's Théa- tre Robert-Houdin was destroyed in order to achieve the final passage of the Boulevard Haussmann.

Figure 20 A dance of love and death: "Tea-tango," by Ernest Desurmont, 1914. (*Source:* Collection Roger-Viollet)

9

Desires: Last Tango at the *Académie*

In March 1914, "the celebrated metaphysician of the Collège de France," one "M. Balgson," delivered a lecture on a subject previously unexplored by the world's most famous living philosopher: the tango. The lecture, reported more or less straight-faced by the satirical Paris journal *Le Sourire*, played on many of the themes which had brought such renown to Henri Bergson, whose weekly lectures on consciousness, memory, and the creative energies of the *élan vital* attracted overflow crowds to the Collège de France. The fictitious lecture of *Le Sourire* might have occasioned a laugh, as it lampooned the dance fanaticism of the 1913–14 season by equating the rage of the ballroom with the darling of popular intellectual fashion.[1] The conjunction of one of the Académie's Immortals, arbiter of classics, and the tango, a popular folkloric dance from Argentina, could be counted on to raise a few smiles.

In Paris, 1911 to 1914 were the grand first years of "tangomania." Fashionable themes for dining, drinking, and gathering sprung up around the dance music, as high society rushed to organize tango teas, champagne tangos, even chocolate tangos. The new dance was adopted by the spectacular Parisian department stores, which attracted and entertained customers in their tea and lunch rooms with hired musicians and dancers. *L'Illustration* of August 1913 featured a large spread of caricatures of the mad Parisians of "Tangoville," including Rodin dancing with a piece of statuary, and reported, "it is at the seaside this summer, in the country-side and the mountains. Everywhere the Parisians go, to the four corners of France, they carry with them the germ of that dancing sickness which

comes to us, it is said, from Argentina."[2] In Buenos Aires popular mag-
azines published reports coming back from Paris-based journalists: "The
tango is the fashion, in Paris above all, and shows no signs of letting up:
on the contrary, in the salons of every party, show, or theater piece . . .
in every diversion or pastime the Argentine tango inevitably figures."[3]

What was this madness which, for a few frenetic years, set fashionable
Paris dancing? In the tango, Parisians had their steps and gestures trained
to dance a fabulous sequence of appropriated pasts, as the taste-makers
of the French capital invented a rage from an Argentine dance which the
aristocrats of Buenos Aires had disdained. In Paris, the tango was an
astonishing concatenation of the folkloric and fashionable, a history in
rhythm and step of the wrenching modernity of two continents. The
tango was a dance born in Argentina out of burgeoning urban centers,
the rise of capital markets, shifting immigrant populations, and social
dislocations. It was a dance of upheaval, separation, and exile from family,
community, traditions, a dance of modernity and memory, of change
frustrated by nostalgia. The Paris tango in its turn was a dance of Europe
looking upon Latin America as a new world destined to challenge the
old, a continent hurtling with primal force toward unimaginable economic and political destinies. On the eve of the Great War, the aggressive
character of the dance would incarnate a desire to recapture a patriotic,
glorious France, shaken since the disaster of 1870. More than a season's
amusement, "tangomania" was a rage for a dance whose every step was
memory, a grasping for energies of revival in a degenerating old world,
while at once a longing across time and space for the promises of returning home.

The "memory" of the tango was in the literature and music which the
tango produced, but more, it was in the movements and glances of the
dancers themselves, stepping to the propulsive rhythms of the guitar or
piano, and the melancholy airs of the bandonéon. The music was at once
African and Latin American, yet familiar to a European ear: eight or sixteen measures, a mix of classical and popular instruments. The original
harp was gradually replaced by the guitar, then the piano. The violin and
the flute were used to draw out melodies, and the bandonéon—from
Germany—gave the tango its distinctive air. Each step of the dance
sketched out an ever-widening historical geography.
    Some scholars traced the word "tango" back to the latin "tangere";
others found in it an African onomatopoeia, "tango/tambo," the articulation of the rhythms on the "tambour." In Spain from about 1870 the
words "tango" and "tanguillo" definitively appeared in written commentaries on music, though the precise transmission to or from Argentina
is not clear. Sailors and members of the merchant marine or other immigrants were the likely bearers. Far from the more classical orchestra-
tions of dances like the waltz, the sources of tango music were part

Argentine "milonga," part African "candombe," part Spanish "haba-
nera."[4]

The tango drew on all without being exactly any. Born as an original
form somewhere in the great river delta of the Plata in the late nineteenth
century, the image which most commonly reached Europe was that of
the tango as a music of the grand pampas and that mythic figure of
Argentine identity, the gaucho. Such easy associations of tango and gaucho were disputed by music scholars such as Juan Alvarez, who in his
Origines de la musica argentina (1908) bluntly called the tango a dance
which was "never known by the gauchos." Despite the range-rider image, Alvarez's eye for invented traditions discerned a rather different historical reality: "Our cities disdained gaucho music, and launched
European styles into the countryside, together with immigrants and foreign products."[5]

Such critiques frame my own point: from the beginning of its popularity, the tango was a dance not of the countryside, but of cities looking
at the countryside and grasping for a lost world. The tango was the first
dance to know wide international fame born out of urban social dislocation, a dance of burgeoning neighborhoods, demolition, and migration
at the end of the century. The tango began as a harsh, yet melancholy
music, and as it became dance, it was dance neither of court nor country,
but of shifting populations.

The tango made its way from countryside and settlement to the popular quarters of Buenos Aires through the mediation of the cabaret, the
public space where high and low culture met, where the crowd may have
been half-elegant, but the songs told of prostitution, the community
blocs of the *conventillo*, and the distressed existence of the outlying dis-
tricts, the *arrabales*—three themes inescapable from life in Buenos Aires
between 1870 and 1900.

Estimates based on the interpretation of immigration records suggest
as many as 20 to 30,000 prostitutes worked in the Buenos Aires area,
many of them European women 17 to 20 years old, seeking work, husbands, often finding bordellos, plying their trade by following the steady
and largely male immigrant and migrant population of the burgeoning
port city. The *conventillos* were basic lodgings, flat blocs of single rooms
built around a central courtyard, whose well was the meeting place where
anguishes, arguments, and talk circulated the news of the daily life of
immigrants and displaced ranchworkers. The *arrabales*—often impover-
ished suburbs—were tied into the massive growth and displacement of
populations of the years 1880 to 1914. A federal republic from 1853,
the capital at Buenos Aires grew over the rest of the century in an extraordinary pattern of urbanization and economic transformation. In the
1880s the creole oligarchy dominated the rural economy, and the con-
tinual rise of the price of a hectare forced out many small farmers and
ranchers, often immigrants, who repaired for the towns, especially Buenos
Aires.

If some gauchos were fierce, independent range riders, many more were the hired hands on the latifundios. The tango was a form whose sounds and expressions were incidentally folkloric and definitively inseparable from the economics and politics of agricultural markets, urbanization, and the social boundaries of drinking and entertainment. Argentina around Buenos Aires was a world where British capital investments were encouraging market ranches concentrated on exports of grain and beef, and urban space was restructured by boulevards and streetcars. A vertiginous sensibility of exile and dislocation accompanied immigration policies which between 1875 and 1905 dramatically pushed the estimated population of Buenos Aires from 230,000 to over one and a half million. The movement created the nostalgia for the gaucho.[6]

The earliest tango was a form which carried with it an "ideology of the night," a lament and respect for the hardships borne in the urban centers of Buenos Aires. The evolving tango was thus never the music of a mere wistful nostalgia, but the agitated expression of a world in transformation. In its rhythms it expressed confusion and separation—and the proud desire to master the torment of a changing world. Strange that fashionable Paris would later adopt versions of this world which had at its heart an often grim, despairing world without God:

> My Lord, if Life is an inferno
> a lake full of tears
> What is the good of struggling
> in your name
> Why be proper and pure
> When Infamy leads the dance
> and Love kills in your name?[7]

The tango was a memory in dance steps of Argentina, but only incidentally a vision of the mountains, the lakes, and the sea, the land of the pampas; only in a picturesque vision. What the tango remembered was the modernity of city and demography, displacement and hardship, a longing for the years before the passing frontier.

In Europe, the great era of the tango was yet to come, led by a figure rooted in two continents. In the 1920s Carlos Gardel, the elegant Argentine, took Paris by storm as the "eternal lover" who had invented the expressive singing art of the "tango-canción" with "Mi Noche Triste" (My Sad Night) in 1917. The embrace of the French was attributed to the ever-accommodating character of the fashionable capital, the cosmopolitan "mondaine" of the interwar period, as well as to the fact that Gardel had been born Charles Gardes to a single mother in Toulouse, France, before emigrating to Buenos Aires at the age of two, where he was to make his career in the local taverns and theaters. But the early years of tangomania before the war were not marked by the tango-canción which made Gardel an international celebrity (and film star) and raised his 1935 death in an unexplained airplane crash to the level of myth.[8] They were measured perhaps more by the writer Ricardo Guiraldes—later to write the gaucho epic *Don Segundo Sombra*—who interpreted the tango in Paris as early as 1910. He and his companion Roberto Levillier frequented the salon of the celebrated singer Jean Reské, where, as legend has it, one night they stunned the fashionable crowd when asked to present a dance or song "representative" of their country. The performance was "astonishing," turning around "the embrace . . . as if one body were the negative of the other," an embrace of "the impossible."[9] What the audience saw that evening was an original form, at once sad, violently passionate, and astonishingly sensual. Guiraldes summarized his vision in concluding verses from his own poem "Tango":

> Fatal tango, superb and brutal
> Notes of misery, idleness, and a stifled
> piano
> Tango severe and sad
> Tango of menace
> Dance of love and death.[10]

Paris would become the first great capital of the tango. Guiraldes's poem, though published in Buenos Aires in 1915, had in fact been written in Paris in 1911, and it was in Europe that the tango first received international attention. The "dance of love and death" attracted the attention of Monsgr. Amette, the Archbishop of Paris, who forbade the tango "in Catholic families," triggering disputes between the high church, parishioners, and local clergy. The controversy ultimately reached the ear of Pope Pius X, who ordered a private performance. Though discreetly presented by two young aristocrats in Rome, the Pope told the dancers that it was not the sort of thing which one should be enjoying. News reports later indicated that the Pope had counseled a preference for "the Forlane, a colorful Venetian dance." A displeased Vatican denounced the reports, but the Forlane became popularly knows as "the Pope's dance" anyway.[11]

The controversy involving the Archbishop and the Pope was one way in which the tango divided a skeptical, sensuous "modernity" from an authoritative, moral "tradition." As the popularity of the dance grew, French writers and journalists could satirize or appreciate in the tango a strain between generations, finding in youth—particularly the "young ladies"—the frivolous pursuit of something exotic. Following Gurialdes's "dance of love and death" in the Parisian versions, some also read the tango as a "danse macabre," the whirling lament of a civilization recklessly accelerating toward war. Some saw it both ways.

Journalist and interviewer *extraordinaire* Michel Georges-Michel was one such writer, making of the tango a figure for the modernity and tensions of the early twentieth century. Georges-Michel assembled his alter ego's *Cahiers d'une Comedienne* under the collective designation *L'Epoque Tango* (The Tango Epoch). The three volumes, which trace *mémoire*-style "la vie mondaine" before, during, and after the war, are humorous, ironic, and often spiteful reports on a life whose events are bound together under the sign of the dance. What the tango embraces, first, is a self-portrait of a guardedly optimistic world. Volume two begins just on the eve of the war, where the announcement of hostilities occasions a refusal to believe, steeped in the imagery of the everyday. "War? . . . It's not possible."

> But the dresses are in the trunks, the trunks are in the automobiles. The season has begun; the weather has been reported superb. In three days Blathy inaugurates a *tango princier* and Foranze launches those umbrellas—you've even bought one for me. There's the horse races. Counuche is building a circular jetty and American style swimming-pools. The *aeroplane* service has opened its windows for excursions between Rue Gontaut-Biron and the races at Dieppe with supplements to Ostende.[12]

Georges-Michel's tango is a world of fashion and a certain privilege, the pleasures of the well-to-do. It is also a world in which dynamisms of economics and lines of flight have been embodied in a rhythm of life, in which the idea of tango embraces the possibilities of transport and technology. The trunks are in the autos, the "aeroplanes" are opening up new routes of services. In this is a certain adventure, a dynamism, and an impulsion to movement. One part of movement is contained, attached, coupled to another. The trunks containing the necessary costumes are transported by automobile to the expanding aerial topography of flight. The ability to move, to unrestrict oneself from the familiar, and yet to be linked to a common culture of tangos and "American style swimming-pools" is no longer excluded by distance. Simultaneous yet common worlds are possible. It is a frenzied and technical world, keeping a rhythm which overlays machines and communications with pleasures.

In a plaintive way, it is also a world straining to keep its order together. "War? . . . It's not possible," plays against "the weather has been reported superb," as if the attention to and invocation of multiplicities of details, tangos, swimming pools, umbrellas, horse races, and airplanes will deny the political decisions. Georges-Michel castigates the "priggish diplomats" for balancing the threat of European conflict above his heroine's head, "that sword of Damocles-William above the tea-tangos."[13]

The illustrator Xavier Sager created his own iconography of the tango in a series of postcards, 1910–14, which might have decorated Georges-Michel's memoirs. Thin men and women in gowns and tuxedos occupy a world of dance floors in which waiters move away from the tables in step, glittering female creatures drape on the steady arm of their partners, and bathers in striped costumes frolic at the seashore to the accompaniment of a smiling guitarist perched on a lifeguard tower. In many ways the world of the tango is a world foolishly at leisure.

What is striking about the graphics in Sager's work is the angular geometry and the vibrant colors of his characters. The melancholy of the music is sinuously drawn into a fury for action, at once fierce and restrained. In one notable montage of six images, Sager separates one couple by placing them at opposite ends of the card, each keeping the movement of the dance, but gesturing with empty arms. The poignancy of the image, however, is transmuted into something comic by the intercession of technology. The couple are joined by the scurrilous wires of the telephone, and keep their movements as the man holds the receiver up to the large horn of a phonograph.[14] Later, when Carlos Gardel became famous, his records were offered free to any customer who would buy a *concertola de mesa*, a small mechanical record-player. Music, machine, and commercial enterprise intersected the birth of the tango. In the Xavier Sager card, the dance, far from the simple nostalgia of bodies and music, becomes a yearning registered by the phonograph. The machine reproduces the music at will, and the dancers keep time across the urban networks of wires and electricity. In the center of the card, the seated lumpen image of the gaucho, smiling broadly with his guitar, seems to laugh.

The registration and inscription of the tango extended to all new media. In my last discussion I noted the inextricable links between cinema, memory, and modernity. Between 1907 and 1911 the first short filmworks began to appear in Buenos Aires, some 60 to 80 meters long. Essayist Claude Fléouter has commented that these short films "appeared more or less in direct relation with the tango." The projections for audiences were conducted "in a manner approximately synchronized with a record," so the rhythm of both music and film were experienced simultaneously.[15]

The early pieces, *Bohemia criolla, El soldado de la Independencia, El cochero de Tranvia,* were, perhaps, sentimental melodramas, but they also inscribed, in the new medium of film, the political and social images which lay behind the tango: the displacement of love and longing; the cultural identity of the Latin nation; urban life located in that emblem of the modern city—the streetcar. By 1915 *Nobleza Gaucha* would dramatize the passing of worlds, including a visit to the famous dance-hall "El Armenoville" where the tango in Argentina grew to fashion. By 1917, the melancholy and violent themes of the tango—and the war—shaped the familiar imprint of films with titles like *El Tango de la Muerte* (The Tango of Death).

In Paris, the world of the tango was the *bal,* the café-concert, the night-club, the sites where the dance of two bodies—and there had to be two—moved in space. Writer C. de Néronde collected early tango history in anecdotes, interviews, and visits to nightclubs and dance instructors in his slim volume *Les Danses nouvelles* (1920). Looking for the origins of the tango in Paris after Guiraldes, he found disagreement among partisans of theater and nightclubs. The aficionados of the stage were concise ("The first Parisian tango? It was danced at the Comédie Royale, directed by Max Viterbo . . .") while the *vieux boulevardiers* maintained, "the movement would have been born at Maxime's . . . the regulars at that after-hours establishment, saturated to nausea by the dislocated joints of the galloping suburban waltz, aspired to get an eyeful from some exotic dance, demanding something new at any price."[16] What the "regulars" found and created was a new form, a "poem of grace and the voluptu-ous":

> Enveloped by a cradling charm, two couples let themselves be taken slowly by a langourous music. . . . SHE takes a few steps with HE, who seizes her by the waist, allowing herself to be conducted and giving herself, delighted, in a charming movement of seduction.[17]

The introduction of the tango in Paris transformed the dance. In cultures with rich oral traditions, memories can be maintained and trans-mitted through the telling of stories and tales. So also can memories of dance be preserved in steps and styles passed down and taught from gen-eration to generation, teacher to student, dancer to dancer. Spoken mem-ories are shaped by tellers and listeners, bodily memories of dance by teachers—and dancers themselves. As the tango became Parisian, the memory of the dance was altered to accommodate French tastes, stan-dards, and expectations.

As with any salon dance, learning the tango was bodily memoriza-tion, training the feet, the back, the hands and shoulders to move cor-rectly to music. In Paris, the steps were taught in studios whose prices depended upon the notoriety of the instructor and the neighborhood, and lessons were given in rented theaters, cafés, café-concerts, and halls d'hotel. "Professeurs," according to Néronde, were "South Amer-icans, Argentines, Brazilians, Peruvians, and blacks from who knows where. . . ."[18] Néronde was not alone in this perplexity of many nation-alities, and his descriptions offer a portrait of what the tango represented to the Parisians. Some of the boundaries of the tango were explicit and codified by the French legal system. One particular regulation prohibited "foreign musicians" from performances unless attired in their "national costume," thus transforming the early tango players into stage gauchos, and confirming the Parisian image of the Argentine.[19]

This image was permeable, for the majority of Argentines in Paris were, for clear economic reasons, not musical ranch-hands, but members of wealthy families come to Europe to trade grain and beef, diverting themselves in Montmartre and Montparnasse. In the bals, cafés, and cab-arets of Montmartre, journalist and critic André Warnod wrote in 1913, "It's full of Argentines. They're at all the tables, they drink champagne sold to them at a dear price and they make a racket. They interrupt at every table, they make wild gestures, and they throw themselves about."[20] The French were astounded by the immigrants and visitors, and as

2e Temps. — Portez le pied droit à droite, puis réunissez le pied gauche au droit en comptant « Deux ».

3e, 4e, 5e et 6e Temps. — Sur chacun de ces temps, répétez identi-

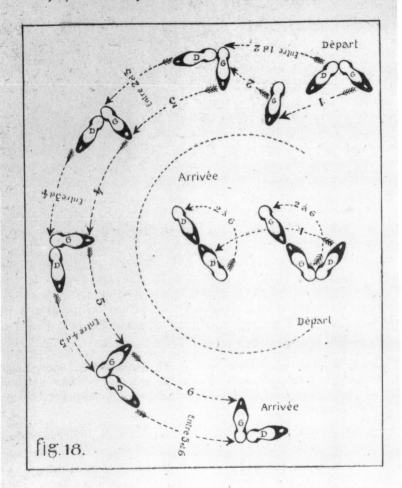

Figure 21 The memory of the dance: positions and steps for the Parisian tango. (*Source:* Dance Collection, New York Public Library for the Performing Arts. Astor, Lenox and Tilden Foundations)

Georges-Michel reported, all Hispanic and Latin communities in Paris were easily associated with the tango. The influx was a flood of unfamiliar faces, "freshly disembarked from the pampas, Spaniards, from Brazil, Portugese, from Argentina, creoles from Peru and from Ecuador," all (apparently) come to Europe because of "a dance which has succeeded." A certain alarming judgment accompanied this observation: "Yes, in opening itself up Paris has become larger: it's become Spanish!"[21]

For the small world centered on the specifics of teaching and learning the dance itself, "becoming Spanish" was a delicate balancing act between the South American and European worlds. The instructors certainly knew this. The most fashionable incarnated a familiarity with cultural difference, self-consciously playing on the vision of a transplanted Europe returning from its exotic roots. Thus in Néronde's interviews, "Le Professeur Duque" talks much of his "Brazilian origins" (close enough to Argentina) and weaves the Porteño mythology of voyaging to Paris as a young man to study medicine and remaining to dance. He incarnates both a passionate Latin origin and a European image of culture and grace. Says Néronde about Duque, "He carries in appearance the type of gentleman who is last off the boat."[22] Such double images helped move the tango from the café-concert to the ballroom, department store, and elegant soirée.

The authority of the change may have been in the hands of the artists and tastemakers at Maxime's or the Comédie Royale, but those hands were complemented by the disciplined feet of the dance instructors and their spaces—the studios and rented cafés, far from the glamour of the major halls. Here in these less dramatic settings the creation of a fashion altered the transmission of the dance. In a striking metaphor, dance instructor Duque described his craft and commented on the process by which the dance was reimagined as it moved across the Atlantic to Europe—and up another culture's social ladder:

> It's the stinking hide of beasts arriving from deepest Siberia, filthy and infected with miasmas, transformed by the magical hands of furriers until it becomes precious sable, a warm and perfumed caress on the fragile shoulders of the Parisians.

The change, as Duque suggests, depended not upon evolution, but craftsmen. As he commented about his own dance classes, "I have tried to eliminate what is excessive in these brutal and violent dances, and to idealize the beauties in order to adapt to the aesthetic of Paris." Each softening of gesture, each suppression of the "brutal" or "violent" was the teacher's knowledge of the dance, and his impression of what would attract and flatter his students, creating a form all at once "savage, wild, acrobatic, moderated, correct, elegant."[23]

Such transformation was not so much opportunistic as outrageous to some Argentine commentators who, noting the fuss in Paris, began to

regard the tango as part of an "authentic" cultural heritage. Eric Hobsbawm has noted the mass proliferation of "invented traditions" in the
late nineteenth century as nation-states and bourgeois elites sought to
legitimate their political authority with historical memory.[24] In Argentina,
the relatively recent origin of the tango did not prevent critics and publicists from expressing a certain offense with the Paris version of the
dance. In September 1913 the oft-ironic Buenos Aires review *P.B.T.* intoned, "The tango which we have exported and which in France is called
'le tango' has nothing traditional in it. Some dancers, among them the
most conscientious, have found in the Argentinian dance a *je ne sais quoi*
which makes it undignified for the high society which frequents 'tea-
tangos,' 'soup-tangos,' and 'lunch-tangos.'"[25]

This change and aestheticization of a new tradition was doubly
transcultural, for though the Paris version of the dance was ridiculed by
Buenos Aires Porteños who asserted something of a cultural patriotism
by supporting "our low dance-halls, with their gallop and atmosphere,"
these latter were the same who refused to dance their original, looking
longingly to Paris fashion. Paris shaped the tango for the fashionable
society of Argentina, giving back to Buenos Aires a European dance appropriate to Porteño society, distinct from the popular origins of the form
and the "anonymous troubadors" who had founded it with their oral
transmission and songs. In his *Recuerdos del 900*, writer Felipe Amadero
Lastra made an honest complaint, "If the truth be told, it must be re-
grettably admitted that the Argentines of the high Porteño society discovered the tango in Paris after the turn of the century and it is then, at
their return, that it was introduced into the salons of *la crème*."[26]

The aesthetic of Paris played deep in the Porteño imagination. Writer
Yvonne Sarcey commented, "The Argentines began by being infatuated
with our fashions; now they love the mind and spirit of our writers." Of
the Argentine women she wrote, "They speak French of a rare purity . . .
and their appetite to teach themselves, to read our poets and authors is
a remarkable thing."[27] The "remarkable" quality of another culture instructing itself in "our" culture was a theme also expressed by journalist
François Crastre: "There is always a domain in which we maintain an
indisputable superiority: that is the domain of the intellectual, literary,
dramatic, and artistic." Commenting on the theatrical works of Argentine
actors and writers, Crastre was not loath to comment, "One realizes easily
that the Argentine has more of a disposition for business than for dramatic literature."[28]

Importantly, such evaluations were not limited to French commentators. Argentine literary critic Juan-Pablo Echague, writing in the *Paris-
Journal* (May 1911), readily linked the cultural destinies of the two lands:
"France is for us the great nation of instruction; it is from her that we
borrow our ideas, our tastes, our civilization; it is thanks to her that we
hope one day to be worthy inheritors of the Latin tradition."[29] If, finally,
Argentina introduced Paris to the tango, it was already within the long

cultural shadow which Paris cast across the wealthy families of Buenos Aires. In 1911, the Argentine journal *El Hogar* could comment, with a bit of irony, that the dance which represented Argentina to the world was in the hands of French high society: "Paris, who imposes everything, will you end up making us accept the Argentine tango here at home? Truly, to see the tango accepted in its land of origin would not lack a certain piquancy."[30]

What Paris imposed back on Argentina was a dance shaped by a Latin American experience profoundly reminiscent of the recent French past. Upheavals of populations, remapped and overcrowded urban centers, and "lost illusions" were not unfamiliar to the history of nineteenth-century France. In addition to poverty, dislocations, and movements off the land, the neighborhoods of Buenos Aires were transformed in the 1890s the way Haussmann had shattered the Parisian *quartiers* a generation before.

Paris danced the transformation of Buenos Aires as Buenos Aires was transformed in the 1880s and '90s the way Paris had been at midcentury. In both cities demolitions, relocations, crowding and iron rails transformed urban life into a shifting, spectral landscape. Journalist Crastre reported from the Argentine capital, "As the intensive improvements to Buenos Aires date back so few years, it has not been possible to transform the original shape of the city all at once, in the manner of magicians in Arabian tales." Commerce and the built environment raised up streets and carved out boulevards, unreal and insubstantial. The neighborhoods were broken up, confused, the houses of the wealthy holding place with stables, sheds, workyards. Sometimes the two were the same; as in the Paris after Haussmann, the constant change and building rendered a false urban landscape. "Some Argentine landlords will mask these hovels behind magnificent façades. As at the theater, the palace is only a set, a glittering ornament hiding wattle and daub huts."[31]

Landscapes of change, struggle, and loss were the cradle of the tango, and the dance steps would capture the halting and propulsive rhythms of an accelerated memory of urban life. Journalist Henri Cordier captured the Porteño world for a Parisian audience with not gauchos, but economics and demographics. Standing at the great seaport of the Plata where sailors, traders, and immigrants had danced early tangos, he reported on the "movement" and "intense life" along the waterfront of La Boca and Barras. Astounded by the relentless growth of the city and its aggressive inhabitants, he wrote that "the man is enslaved to labor and speculation, chasing relentlessly after the bold stroke which will make him richer and more powerful." What finally gave Buenos Aires its "specific character, so special and impressive," was a dynamic, whirling vision of commercial urban life, "that perpetual agitation, that furious pursuit of wealth, that burning passion for business as business." Buenos Aires was a vision and a warning to Paris readers of the future and past of history: "In olden days civilizations, strong and fortified as our own, have disappeared or been transformed by contact with more numerous or robust elements; these are the steps in the history of civilization too often forgotten."[32]

The struggle for "civilization" being played out in Argentina was a competition of not only economics, but race. Cordier was attentive to this in the Porteño capital, writing back that Argentina was seeing a "formidable" explosion in immigration. He wondered, "With this enormous influx of immigrants, what is the future of the nation?" The unsettling demographics spun in a cauldron of racialist competition and biology. "Certainly the Argentines are proud of their race and country, and we wouldn't blame them for not wanting to be confused with the other South Americans to whom they consider themselves superior."[33] Official Argentine publications did not dispute this judgment. One Argentine government souvenir program from a commercial exposition in Roubaix, France, in 1911 forthrightly proclaimed the Argentine population as "essentially European," and argued that in Argentina, "we don't face problems with Indians, blacks, or yellow people." As the program proudly noted, the Indians had been converted to Catholicism, decimated by "various illnesses," or incorporated into society "as excellent elements of labor." The "yellow people" had been excluded by immigration policy. As for the blacks, "they've practically disappeared, eliminated by an inflexible biological law which condemns inferior organisms to give way to the superior races."[34]

In earlier chapters I described the evolutionary assumptions behind the memories created by clinical anthropologists in Paris and colonial administrators in the South Pacific. The tango, both Argentine and Parisian, also incorporated and defined a dynamic, accelerated memory of organisms, a point which can be read out of dance manuals such as Max Rivera's *Le Tango et les Danses Nouvelles* (1913). A slim volume of instruction which names the tango as the key to a European Renaissance, Rivera's work calls the tango "truly modern," the "representative dance of our era, the only one capable of bringing into favor an art too long discredited. With the tango, the love of dance returns to the old world." Throughout the text, Rivera refers to Europe as the "old world" in which Paris is nonetheless a "modern society." The Argentines, by contrast, descend from "a Spanish colony," and are "a race with primitive eastern origins by way of Arabs who occupied Spain for many centuries."[35]

Such characterizations of a "primitive" race irked Argentine writers like José Maria Salavencia, who maintained that "for the public of Paris or London, the tango is nothing but an exotic dance . . . which is danced for what it has of the sensual, perverted, and something barbaric."[36] Salavencia abhorred the idea of his culture falling under the sign of "exoticism," perhaps of the sort described by one Yvonne Sacrey, who published memoirs recounting her childhood visions of the American republic, "the very far away America, very problematic" country of "monsters and fairies; of lions and naked blacks; of monkeys scratching their behinds, and the cave of Ali-Baba."[37] These visions circumscribed the non-European world within an obviously confused (and rather African and Asiatic) series of stock images.

Yet the exoticism which Salavencia criticized was more complex for the French than the mere reduction of his homeland to a series of decorative folkloric pictures. The rhythms of the tango were not danced merely as a fantastic, picturesque homage to primitive ancestors, but as the revival of primeval "force" in a modern world ruled by accelerations of biology and economics. Oriental, Arab, and Latin, the Argentines, in Rivera's view, were a race apart from the Europeans, yet "race" and "primitive" spelled dynamism and energy. In establishing its exhibits for a 1910 International Exposition at Buenos Aires, the French Minister of Commerce and Industry declared Argentina "this new country where the evolution of wealth has developed so rapidly," and exhorted all of the other great states of Europe to take part as a duty—and an "economic necessity."[38] François Crastre looked out over Buenos Aires and wrote, "Inside this vast perimeter lives a businesslike, industrious population, engaged in a desperate 'struggle for life.' " A concern about the passing of old worlds for new lay deep in these words. Crastre wrote to his Parisian readers, "In any case, Argentina triumphantly refutes the theory of Latin inferiority; in the economic battle she deploys a vigor, a clearness of vision, and a prodigious tenacity."[39]

Literary critic Juan-Pablo Echague, cited above as so laudatory of the French cultural past, was skeptical of its future in another domain, which was becoming more important: the economic competition of nations. "It is a shame still that you satisfy yourself with this intellectual regime," Echague chided his French audience. "France, which held first place economically for us, has slipped to fifth."[40] In Max Rivera's dance manual France is modern, but desperately needs revival of its old order; Argentina is never regarded modern, but it belongs to the new world. Argentina is new not because of its modernity, but because of its youth—it stands at the beginning of time. Marguerite Moreno in her *Une Française en Argentine* (1914) wrote memoirs of a country she adored, and left a record little concerned with gauchos, pampas, or predictable folkloric tales. The society she knew was characterized by "an impression of haste, of the unachieved, of rapid and haphazard organization." Moreno's Argentine companion proudly agreed:

> Your impression is very fair Madame, Pio Valdez told me, we live too fast. Children are precocious, adolescents are men, men have a very short period of activity, and there are very few old people. Our land is too young and too rich . . . it will take quite a few years for us to reach the point of slowing down our race and walking at the same pace as the other nations.

Comparing "this young nation," with "old Europe," Pio Valdez concludes, "We have, in effect, given the world an example of what the love of freedom can do, and Europe, astonished, has seen a nation rise where she scarcely knew there were men."[41] Young, primitive, perhaps, but Argentina had a few things to teach the old world. What made the appeal of the tango so staggeringly modern was its apparent primitivism, understood as the incarnation of evolution and explosive growth. Commented Max Rivera, "in the South American music of Brazil or the Argentine Republic there are truly rhythmic themes of a singular force."[42]

The tango developed as a dance of stunning physicality, propelled by violence and change, separation, insecurity, and fragility, a straining for order and togetherness. Its many versions balanced both the sensuality and belligerence of two bodies, suspicious yet longing for annihilation, dancing union and also the impossibility of that union. In its early years, the tango was a frustrated nostalgia for the physical body, the displacement of immigrants and hopefuls, the Buenos Aires of men without women.

I emphasize the role of the man, for the tango was and is a male-dominated form. M. Antonio, one of the fashionable Parisian instructors, explained that "we are speaking about men naturally, because it's much simpler for the women, they need only allow themselves to be guided and it's useless to get into too much detail."[43] Yet this reactive role of the woman in the tango is doubly complex, for it was a role often originally danced by men. In a Buenos Aires of many immigrant males and few brides, a woman might be wooed on the dance floor—if the man already knew how to dance. Yet men could not permit themselves to be seen learning to dance in front of the feminine gaze. Though the men did practice their steps with female prostitutes, the tango evolved as a dance which men danced with each other in bars and on the waterfront, trading leader and follower, playing both male and female roles.

If each pass of the dance was about an urban modernity of confusion and separation, it was also about constantly redefining the limits of physical embrace and resistance. Men danced with, yet also against each other, realizing a dance of both seduction and conquest, of being both man and woman. The movements of tango developed as a fine play between passionate attraction and a matching of strength against strength. In its aggressive forms it was a dance of who had "the biggest balls." This sentiment was captured in the sad pride and menacing exhilaration of Guiraldes's poetry:

> Tango, in which each note falls heavily and as if
> spitefully, lowers a hand better suited
> to embrace the handle of a knife
> Tragic tango, whose melody plays a
> battle tune
> Slow rhythm, complicated harmony of hostile
> counterpoints

> Dance which puts vertigos of virile exaltation
> into spirits troubled by drink.

In Guiraldes's lines the musical notes fall upon the hand which reaches to clutch the knife. The strategy and the dance move together warily to "hostile counterpoints," and the promise of "vertigos of virile exaltation." Jorge Luis Borges, in his "Evaristo Carriego," has written, "many have underlined the sexual character of the tango, but few have remarked on its brawling character." His truth about the tango rests in the pressing together of the sensual and the moral with the crude and the violent: the violence of a masculine sensuality, frustrated, threatening, possessive, yet defensive. Juan-Pablo Echague commented in 1906: "The tango is an extension of the provocative modes of the *compadrito*, of his airs and insolent arrogance." This sentiment was echoed by Borges for his countrymen: "This is perhaps the mission of the tango: to give the Argentines the certainty of having been valorous, of having satisfied once and for all the demands of courage and honor."[44]

For the Parisians also, to talk of tango, or to dance tango, was to re-member male imperatives shaken since the Franco-Prussian War. The years before 1914 magnified the links between what might have been considered personal and national honor. The turn of the century was a period in which the "degeneration" fears which had haunted the fin de siècle were matched by a "national revival" movement centered on sport and exercise. Attention to physical culture expressed "moral nobility," in the words of one school instructor, and bore "the double authority of the most reliable science and the most vigilant patrotism."[45] Max Rivera, in his writings on the tango, spoke of the dance as a form of "rhythmic gymnastics," valuable from the point of view of "sport and health." M. Debrenne, director of one of the "most select" establishments of Mont-martre, explained the French moral politics which attended his instruc-tion of tango. To tango was to express the particular form of "French gallantry which has always been the honor of our country."[46] The se-duction of the tango guarded an art of revival, a patriotic celebration of honor defended in the struggle of two bodies meeting as one to music.

To cite again Borges, "I would go as far as to say that the tango and the milongas directly express something which poets have often tried to say with words: the conviction that battle can be a festival."[47] For France, the "festival" which Borges described was celebrated in violence in 1914. The dishonored memory of a nation, smoldering with vengeance for Se-dan and the Alsace-Lorraine, fueled a nationalist furor in the same years of the tango's greatest prewar popularity. Tango, the dance of modernity, loss, and nostalgia, was also the dance of nationalism, and the seductive, belligerent violence of settling an old account—Guiraldes's dance of "love and death."

If the link between the fashionable dance and the aggrieved memory of the nation appears ideologically strained, consider the preface to Néronde's book of dance steps by poet and playwright Jean Richepin, who would go on to write a play around the theme of the tango, which enjoyed success and the stardom of Eve de Lavallière. As part of his conclusion, Richepin draws together the tango with the finest classical image of masculine physicality and martial spirit: the Spartans at Thermopalaye. These are the brave warriors, who, "the morning of their final day, combed back their hair, rubbing oil upon their bodies and limbering their muscles. . . ." Richepin's remarks would be familiar to any close student of either popular or official culture, for they are a slightly edited version of a discourse he originally pronounced in October 1913—not in a café-concert, but before that bastion of French cultural identity, a meeting of the five Academies.[48]

A veritable history of dance from antiquity to the twentieth century, Richepin's speech could have served as the basis for the false Bergsonian lecture reported by *Le Sourire,* for in it he captures—in serious fashion—the essential themes of memory, body, movement, and finally, of the nation which betray the politics, ideology, and historical struggle behind the dance. His is a complicated and subtle argument, which says little actually about the tango itself; in its outlines it is a statement not about dance, but about the powerful historical reach of the Western tradition.

Richepin plays with warriors and classical culture in presenting the tango, and in his vision of dance, the particular historical roots of the tango, the "popular origins" are acknowledged, but disappear under an astounding transmutation of the dance into a form of Greek ceremony and celebration. Greeks for gauchos? The temple of reason for the pampas and the city streets of Buenos Aires? In truth, not the tango at all, but the traditions of classical culture are at the center of the discussion, masked by the image of a Latin America which is in fact being forgotten.

Richepin begins his tale by opening the memory palace. "I catch a glimpse inside the fabulous palaces which open up their marvels to us. There I contemplate, born again, the whole past life of Dance since its sacred origins." Richepin's vision of dance becomes a history reaching back to a pagan mythology, the presumed origin of all things, "since the time when it was religious, invented and practiced by the gods to symbolize the creation of the world and the rising and setting of the stars in the sky to the eyes of mortals." The innocence of "ancient Greece" is the ideal and model of a world being born, "this youth of humanity." It was there, says Richepin, that the teaching of beauty was learned, and "the eurythmy of the soul flowering to the eurythmy of the body." The artists of the tango are notably missing, but Richepin compensates by invoking other great dancers—Zeus, Demeter, and Apollo—calling their art "the tango known by the Ancients!"[49] These mythical images are the beautiful things which "dance still in my memory."

Richepin calls upon his colleagues, not just other poets, but also the

"savants" with their documents, to multiply the examples of this historical memory. As inspiration, he invites them to a repository of the past,
the British Museum, where "one can see, coming from deep beneath
Thebes, the dancers which dance it"—the tango—having as their only
garment belts plaited from golden strands. Who can say, after all—perhaps the tango is "the last survival of one of these sacred dances in which
Egyptian and Chaldean priests figured out the evolution of Being, writing
out the mathematical formula for the eyes of their initiates."[50] With
astonishing ease, the memory of historical experience, the nineteenth-
century upheavals of Europe and South America, vanish into the ancient
mysteries of archaelogical speculation.

Still, Richepin is no reactionary: he does not disavow or denigrate
the social, economic, and cultural strains which shaped the tango. He is
bold enough to chide his colleagues for any reluctance in accepting the
dance, pointing out the succession of foreign fashions adopted by France:
the Austrian waltz, the Polish mazurka, the Hungarian polka, and the
Boston from the United States. "As far as the foreign origin of the tango,
it is strange for it to be so accused in hospitable Paris."

> Think about it! A dance which had for its cradle the lowest brothels of Amer-
> ica! A dance of cattlemen, pallid woodsmen, gauchos, half-savages, blacks!
> Fi! The Horror! [51]

He goes further, mocking the snobbery of tastes in official culture,
extolling the dance's "popular origins." This stirring derision of the "ferocious moralists" explodes into a history lesson on the exquisite delicacy
and grace of French aristocratic dances: "All, yes all, were born rustic; all
are former peasant bustles and brawls."

The insufferable prejudices of aristocratic taste are a broad target for
Richepin, yet he hardly seems prepared to invite cattlemen, gauchos, half-
savages, or blacks into his company, for the company he keeps is a transcendent historical identity. The tango bears not the content of another
tradition for him, but the content of his own. The tango is dance, and
all dance must be championed. Not because of Argentina, but because
of Greece. "Because France is, like ancient Greece, and alone with her,
a country where dance is necessary to life." This extraordinary (and one
would say, obviously incorrect) statement not only enfolds ancient Greece
within modern France, but completely effaces the complexity of other
dance traditions which exist only as variations on an exercise produced
for the glory of French dance halls.

Richepin's discourse betrays a recurring concern of France before the
war: a nationalism manifested in physical vigor and an identity drawn
from an unbroken historical memory stretching from the ancient world
to French civilization. The defense of that tradition in 1913–14 is a martial spirit. Glorifying Austerlitz, Richepin exclaims, "They knew how to
dance, all these heros!" "That is why, from the time I was a child, it has
been right for us to teach dancing along with fencing." The tango sud-

denly appears all too appropriate as "the dance" which Richepin invokes. Perhaps this is why he chose it, the tango of physical spirit, its legacy of the "couteau," the blade, a dance to fence, to outdo the foe, the dance with the sword.

The strength of physical culture in dance defines a moral imperative to avoid the catastrophe of its desolate opposite, which Richepin renders in classical allusion. As Odysseus arrives at the island of Polyphemus and the Cyclopses, he asks old Silene the place where they are, "this land of horrors." The reply is devastatingly simple: "a land with no dancing." The lesson is clear, "France must never become that land!"

> Let us thank everything which prevents it, everything which brings back the old tradition which breathes life back into ancient Greece; to remain a land where one dances, where one does everything dancing, where one knows how to die dancing.

Finally, from this devolves a chronology, as Richepin explains: "By the tango I hear the Dance." Richepin's tango is a figure without its own history or antecedents, yet in this, his championing of the tango is equal to the mockery of the aristocrats. He has a more powerful tool of exclusion than scorn; he has a nationalist history, which collapses the world between France and the ancients, uniting them in a powerful story of human creation. The tango is "dance"; the rough folklore of the *arrabales*, the agitated memory of the modernizing Buenos Aires, the nostalgia for the lost woman, the sad night, the gaucho lament, come to this: the young men of Athens—and their unspoken corollary, the young men of France. The young men from lands where one knows what it is to die dancing. The young men, turning back to ancient Greece, dancing "like madmen all the night," after the presentation of Aeschylus' *Perseus*. Exalted by symbols, dancing, and as they dance also crying out "éperdument"—that is, desperately, wildly, madly: "Patrie!" "Patrie!" "Patrie!"

Figure 22 Obligations to the past: procession at the Place de l'Opéra. (*Source:* Bibliothèque Historique de la Ville de Paris)

Afterword

Memories: The History of the Present

Let us be rather of our own time. We have today something better than history to guide us.

—Fustel de Coulanges, Reply to Theodor Mommsen

On March 11, 1885, scholar Ernest Renan pronounced his famous *conférence* at the Sorbonne, "What Is a Nation?" In sweeping, yet densely detailed evocations of China, Egypt, Babylon, Israel, Rome, and Greece he traced the tribes, agglomerations, realms, confederations, dynasties, and empires by which peoples and cultures had associated themselves throughout the centuries. To these, he added investigations of race, tracing lines of descent through Etruscans, Saxons, and Gauls, employing a vocabulary drawn from anthropology, ethnology, and zoology. He considered languages or religions possibilities to be pondered while weighing the twisted roots of the Slavic, Arabic, Semitic, and Latin tongues, or while studying the meaning of mythologies, rites, and practices. Geography was also invoked, with its defining elemental challenges of rivers and mountains, barriers and frontiers.

Renan found no argument satisfying enough to answer his own question, and finally declared a nation "a soul, a spiritual principle." Yet, he noted, a nation was a soul with a past. "The nation, like the individual, is the end product of a long past of efforts, sacrifices, and devotions. Of all the cults, that of the ancestors is the most legitimate; the ancestors have made us what we are." The essential conditions of a people were "common glories in the past, and a common will in the present."[1]

Through the glories of the past manifested in the reverence of the ancestors, Renan tied the meaning of the nation not to its language, biology, or territories, but to its historical memory, that "rich legacy of remembrances." Notably, Renan's memory was defined not merely as

205

worship of the dead, but in the consciousness of memory as action, of a people "having done great things together, wanting to do them again." This will, activity, and *presence* of memory was what defined the nation and the people.

In associating memory and action, Renan's "grand solidarity" of the nation would always necessarily be a troubled figure. The memory of a "collective" was the memory of the forging of that collective—affirmation, yet also conflict and resistance. Renan was well aware of this, remarking, "Forgetting, and I would even say historical error, are essential factors in the creation of a nation; in this, the progress of historical studies is often a danger for *nationalité*. Historical investigation, in effect, brings to light facts of violence which took place at the origin of all political formations, even those whose consequences were the most beneficial. Unity is always brutally created."[2]

Renan saw a nation as a meeting of "convergent facts": wills, glories, ancestors. He also saw the violence at the heart of such a conception: the wealth and binding power of the past, but also its distresses, divisions, and dangers. I have tried, in my work here, to observe both these sides of the past by proposing a history of memory. In this I have pursued a broad "histoire générale," whose grand narrative is not a single story, but a constellation of memory places, a juxtaposition of detailed sites, each asking its own questions: Where are events embodied, celebrated, and forgotten? How are traditions invented and appropriated? How does knowledge of the past develop as scientfic theory, artistic expression, political power? Who controls what is remembered and who is believed?

Ranging from politics to neuroscience, imperialism to entertainment, what I have sought is to characterize the "memory" of an age not with a singular definition, but through multiple understandings of how it was evoked through nostalgia, commemoration, repetition, trace, ancestor, heritage, patrimony, and tradition in apparently dissimilar contexts and situations. I say "apparently" because the distinct "memory" challenges of Communards and stock-traders, Pacific Islanders and colonialists, children and doctors, dancers and soldiers, were nonetheless linked by a web of common references to acceleration and evolution, primitive and progressive, an historical consciousness shaped by political rivalry, scientific ideology, and global capitalism which I have called "modern" and used to define this "memory" of the fin de siècle.

Where has all this led? The answer, I would like to think, is to an understanding of the ways in which "modern" memory is, as Henri Bergson understood, concerned not with collecting fragments and elegiac images of the past, but with acting and making judgments in the present. I have argued for active, creative, contested memories, and tried to present each so that the reader will be reminded of the classical rhetorical role memory plays in bearing witness, informing judgment, and giving voice. In this work I have used such imperatives to address the historical moments and fates of ecstatic revolutionaries, criminal vagabonds, cinematic geniuses, defeated rebels, and passionate dancers; just a few among the many historical actors who implore us to *remember*.

Witness, judgment, and voice should have an even larger resonance for the historian. The European nineteenth century arguably ended in 1914 with the First World War. The century which followed has its own markers: in another war, in the legacies of imperialism and post-colonialism, in the institutions of a global financial system. Here is where the "witness," "judgment," and "voice" of memory will continue to weigh heavily and importantly, in trying to understand what obligations the history of the present bears—or does not bear—for the past.

In the preface to his *L'Avenir de la science* (1890), Renan praised the hope and progress of "l'esprit moderne," yet admitted frankly that his optimism for humanity was tempered by the uncertainties of his own age. He described that age as "a desert where one wanders by chance, to the north, to the south, because one must walk. No one knows, in the social order, which way is best. What consolation there is, comes from necessarily arriving somewhere . . . in short, though the knowledge of facts has been singularly increased by the incessant work of the nineteenth century, human destiny has become more obscure than ever."[3] Renan died in 1892. We must still necessarily arrive somewhere. The elements which compose and define our "memories" have kept the changing record of those arrivals, judging each, even while coming from and leading to the unimaginable.

Notes

Introduction: Histories

    1. Fernand Braudel, *The Identity of France*, Sian Reynolds, trans. (New York: Harper & Row, 1988), 17, 24.

    2. Natalie Zemon Davis and Randolph Starn make this point in the Introduction to *Representations 26: Memory and Counter-Memory* (Spring 1989): 2. The best elaboration is Richard Terdiman's discussion, "Historicizing Memory," which forms the first chapter of his *Present Past: Modernity and the Memory Crisis* (Ithaca: Cornell Univ. Press, 1993), 3–32. See also Paul Connerton, *How Societies Remember*, (Cambridge: Cambridge Univ. Press, 1989)and Jonathan Boyarin, ed., *Remapping Memory: The Politics of Time Space* (Minneapolis and London: Univ. of Minnesota Press, 1994).

    3. Frances Yates, *The Art of Memory* (Chicago: Univ. of Chicago Press, 1966), xi-xv.

    4. Pierre Nora, "Comment écrire l'histoire de France?," in *Les Lieux de mémoire*, tome III: *Les France*, vol. 3: *De l'archive à l'emblème* (Paris: Ed. Gallimard, 1993), 11. See also the essay by François Hartog, "Comment écrire l'histoire de France?," *Magazine littéraire*, no. 307 (Feb. 1993): 28–32. My thinking is much shaped by John Gillis, ed., *Commemorations: The Politics of National Identity* (Princeton: Princeton Univ. Press, 1994).

    5. Pierre Nora, in notes appended to "Between Memory and History: Les lieux de mémoire," in Marc Roudebush, trans., *Representations 26*, 25.

    6. Cited in Jacques Le Goff, *Histoire et mémoire* (Paris: Ed. Gallimard, 1988), 204.

    7. See Laura Otis, *Organic Memory: History and the Body in the Late Nineteenth and Early Twentieth Centuries* (Lincoln: Univ. of Nebraska Press, 1995),

and Philip Kuberski, *The Persistence of Memory: Organism, Myth, Text* (Berkeley and Los Angeles: Univ. of California Press, 1992).

8. Robert A. Nye, *Crime, Madness, and Politics in Modern France: The Medical Concept of National Decline* (Princeton: Princeton Univ. Press, 1984).

9. Henri Bergson, *Matter and Memory* Nancy Margaret Paul and W. Scott Palmer, (1896; New York: Zone Books, 1988), conclusion, esp. 239.

10. Ibid., 240.

11. See, especially, Stephen J. Gould, *Ontogeny and Phylogeny* (Cambridge, Mass.: Belknap, 1977), 96–97; Philip Kuberski, *The Persistence of Memory: Organism, Myth, Text* (Berkeley and Los Angeles: Univ. of California Press, 1992); Lucille Ritvo, *Darwin's Influence on Freud* (New Haven: Yale Univ. Press, 1991). For readers confused by the history of the psychological sciences, see Henri Ellenberger, *The Discovery of the Unconscious: The History and Evolution of Dynamic Psychiatry* (New York: Basic Books, 1981).

12. The principle of "universal acceleration" is discussed by E. D. Cope, Alpheus Hyatt, and Haeckel in Gould, *Ontogeny and Phylogeny*, 91–100.

13. E. B. Tylor, as cited in A. Posada, *Théories modernes sur les origines de la famille* (Paris: V. Girard and E. Brière, 1896). The professional context of Tylor's work discussed by Henrika Kuklick, *The Savage Within: The Social History of British Anthropology, 1885–1945* (Cambridge: Cambridge Univ. Press, 1991).

14. Mona Ozouf in *Magazine Littéraire*, no. 307 (Feb. 1993): 22–25. Eric L. Santner, *Stranded Objects: Mourning, Memory, and Film in Postwar Germany* (Ithaca: Cornell Univ. Press, 1990).

15. Matei Calinescu, *Five Faces of Modernity* (Durham: Duke Univ. Press, 1987), 5–13. See also Jürgen Habermas, *The Philosophical Discourse of Modernity*, Fredrick G. Lawrence, trans. (Cambridge, Mass.: MIT Press, 1987); Krzysztof Pomain, *L'Ordre du temps*, (Paris: Ed Gallimard, 1984); Reinhart Koselleck, *Futures Past: On the Semantics of Historical Time* (Cambridge, Mass.: MIT Press, 1985). See also John Bender and David Wellbery, eds., *Chronotypes: The Construction of Time* (Stanford: Stanford Univ. Press, 1991).

16. See Terdiman, *Present Past*, 14. Also David Krell, *On Memory, Reminiscence, and Writing: On the Verge* (Bloomington: Univ. of Indiana Press, 1990).

17. See Terdiman, *Present Past*, 12–13, for a discussion of the "mnemonic economy" based upon the principle of "reification as a memory disturbance." This citation from Jonathan Boyarin, *Storm from Paradise* (Minneapolis: Univ. of Minnesota Press, 1992), 49 for commentaries on awakening from "the nightmare culmination of commodity capitalism." Terdiman, Boyarin, and I all owe debts to the spectacular Benjaminian commentaries in Susan Buck-Morss, *The Dialectics of Seeing: Walter Benjamin and the Arcades Project* (Cambridge, Mass.: MIT Press, 1991), especially her discussions of natural history as "fossil" and historical nature as "ruin."

18. The title of Henrika Kuklick's social history of British anthropology, *The Savage Within*. Consider also John and Jean Comaroff, *Ethnography and the Historical Imagination* (Boulder and Oxford: Westview, 1992); Marianna Torgovnick, *Gone Primitive: Savage Intellects, Modern Lives* (Chicago: Univ. of Chicago Press, 1990); Adam Kuper, *The Invention of Primitive Society: Transformations of an Illusion* (London: Routledge, 1988).

19. Le Goff, *Histoire et mémoire*, 121.

20. Marc Augé, "Une histoire du présent," in *Magazine littéraire*, no. 307 (Feb. 1993): 38.

21. André Leroi-Gourhan, *Le Geste et la parole* (Paris: Albin Michel, 1964), ch. 9, "La Mémoire en expansion," 63–76. Also cited by Le Goff, *Histoire et mémoire*, 110. See also Marie-Noelle Bourguet, Lucette Valensi, and Nathan Wachtel, *Between History and Memory* (Chur, London, and Paris: Harwood, 1990).

22. Nora, "Between Memory and History," 7. See also the "time-space compression" thesis of David Harvey, *The Condition of Postmodernity* (Cambridge, Mass., and Oxford, Eng.: Blackwell, 1989), ch. 15, and questions of heritage and amnesia in David Lowenthal, *The Past Is a Foreign Country* (Cambridge: Cambridge Univ. Press), and Andreas Huyssens, *Twilight Memories: Marking Time in a Culture of Amnesia* (London and New York: Routledge, 1995).

23. Milan Kundera, *The Book of Laughter and Forgetting* (New York, Penguin, 1990), 7.

24. Le Goff, *Histoire et mémoire*, 14.

25. Yates, *The Art of Memory*, 20; also Patrick H. Hutton, *History as an Art of Memory* (Hanover and London: Univ. of Vermont, 1993).

26. See Alain Finkielkraut, *Remembering in Vain* (New York: Columbia Univ. Press, 1992). Memory as trauma or problem rather than as collective identity is also treated in Cathy Caruth, ed., *Trauma: Explorations in Memory* (Baltimore: Johns Hopkins Univ. Press, 1995); Henry Rousso, *The Vichy Syndrome: History and Memory in France since 1944* (Cambridge, Mass.: Harvard Univ. Press, 1991). See the discussion by Charles S. Maier, *The Unmasterable Past* (Cambridge, Mass.: Harvard Univ. Press, 1988), 44, concerning the question of World War II and memory in Germany, and James Knowlton and Truett Cates, eds., *Forever in the Shadow of Hitler* (New Jersey: Humanities Press, 1993). Around memory and warfare, Paul Fussell, *The Great War and Modern Memory* (Oxford and New York: Oxford Univ. Press, 1977); George Mosse, *Fallen Soldiers: Reshaping the Memory of the World Wars* (Oxford and New York: Oxford Univ. Press, 1991).

27. Nora, "Between Memory and History," 16; Yosef Hayim Yerushalmi, *Zakhor: Jewish History and Jewish Memory* (Seattle: Univ. of Washington Press), 1982; see also Pierre Vidal-Naquet, *Les Juifs, la mémoire et le présent* (Paris: Ed. La Découverte, 1991). Jewish memory and the Holocaust is a charged field. See Saul Friedlander, *When Memory Comes* (New York: Farrar, Strauss, Giroux, 1991), *Memory, History and the Extermination of the Jews in Europe* (Bloomington: Indiana Univ. Press, 1993), *Probing the Limits of Representation* (Cambridge, Mass.: Harvard Univ. Press, 1992), and the journal *History and Memory: Studies in Representation of the Past* (Tel Aviv and Indiana Univ. Press). Also Pierre Vidal-Naquet, *The Assassins of Memory* (New York: Columbia Univ. Press, 1993); Lawrence Langer, *Holocaust Testimonies: The Ruins of Memory* (New Haven: Yale Univ. Press, 1991); Yitzhak Zuckerman, *A Surplus of Memory: Chronicle of the Warsaw Ghetto Uprising* (Berkeley and Los Angeles: Univ. of California Press, 1993); *Politiques de l'oubli*, a special number of *Le Genre humain* (Oct. 1988).

28. See Margaret A. Lourie, Domna C. Stanton, and Martha Vicinus, eds., "Women and Memory," *Michigan Quarterly Review* 26, no. 1 (Winter 1987). See also Mark Freeman, *Rewriting the Self: History, Memory, Narrative* (London and New York: Routledge, 1993); Amritjit Singh, Joseph T. Skerrit, Jr., and Robert E. Hogan, eds., *Memory, Narrative, and Identity: New Essays in Ethnic American Literatures* (Boston: Northeastern Univ. Press, 1994).

29. For an overview of "degeneration," see Nye, *Crime, Madness, and Pol-*

itics, and Daniel Pick, *Faces of Degeneration: A European Disorder: c. 1848–c. 1918* (Cambridge: Cambridge Univ. Press, 1989).

30. Augé, "Une histoire du présent," 35.

31. On falling monuments, Alain Brossat, Sonia Combe, Jean-Yves Potel, and Jean-Charles Szurek, *A l'est: la mémoire retrouvé* (Paris: Ed. La Découverte, 1990); Rubie S. Watson, ed., *Memory, History, and Opposition under State Socialism* (Santa Fe: School of American Research Press, 1994); on historical time, Lutz Niethammer, *Posthistoire: Has History Come to Any End?*, (London and New York: Verso, 1992). Francis Fukuyama, *The End of History and the Last Man* (New York: Avon, 1993). See also Michael S. Roth, *Knowing and History: Appropriations of Hegel in Twentieth-Century France* (Ithaca: Cornell Univ. Press, 1988), and Henri Lefebvre, *La Fin de l'histoire* (Paris: Ed. de Minuit, 1970). On the erasure of history, Jean Baudrillard, *L'Illusion de la fin: ou la grève des événements* (Paris: Ed. Galilée, 1992).

32. See, for example, Roger Ganne and Brigitte Salomon, *La Carte à mémoire* (Paris: Eyrolles, 1990), a study of the microchip card which stores thousands of bits of information: "the *carte à mémoire* has become the symbolic instrument permitting us to see, understand, and act more effectively in the 'informational' landscape which surrounds us. Such transformations cannot be decreed; they are lived." Also, George P. Landow, *Hypertext: The Convergence of Contemporary Critical Theory and Technology* (Baltimore: Johns Hopkins Univ. Press, 1992).

Chapter 1: Monuments

1. Based on eyewitness accounts, *La Commune*, May 17, 1874.

2. See Alfred Normand, "Architectural Plans" of the Column and the Place Vendôme, collections of the Bibliothèque Historique de la Ville de Paris.

3. Maxime Vuillaume, *Mes cahiers rouges* (Paris, 1909), 125.

4. For reproductions of the essential images of the fallen column, see Michel Auray, "La Commune demolit la colonne Vendôme," *Gavroche*, no. 44 (March/April 1989). Also the many gravure reproductions from Georges Soria, *Grande histoire de la Commune* (Paris: Robert Laffont, 1971). The final whereabouts of the "Victoire" are disputed; some researchers argue it found its way to England or the United States: Albert Mousset, "Les trois Napoleon de la colonne," piece 7, in the archives of the Bureau des Batiments civils et des Palais Nationaux, Paris.

5. Paul Brandat and Frédéric Passy, *La Colonne* (Brest, 1871), 14.

6. Jean Bourguignon (Académie des Beaux-Arts), letter, archives of the Bureau des Batiments Civils, piece no. 9. See also "Monuments et oeuvres d'art a la gloire d'Austerlitz," *La Revue: seance annuelle des cinq académies* (Nov. 15, 1951): 338–39. The design and engineering of the column are discussed in Alfred and Charles Normand, "La Colonne Vendôme," *Bulletin de la société des amis des monuments parisiens* XI (1897); a journalistic history is recounted by Jules Dementhe in "Histoire de la colonne Vendôme," *L'Illustration* 2 (1873): the piece appears as a series, 115–18, 134–35, 150–51, 163–67, 178.

7. French history commemorates the battle as Napoléon's strategic victory over the Austro-Russian army commanded by the monarchs Alexander I and François II on Dec. 2, 1805. Also called the "Battle of the Three Emperors."

8. Cited by Achille Murat, *La Colonne Vendôme* (Paris: Palais Royale, 1970), 211. On the political and sacred qualities of memory and monuments in other contexts, Alain Brossat, Sonia Combe, Jean-Yves Potel, and Jean-Charles Szurek,

A l'est: la mémoire retrouvé (Paris: Ed. La Découverte, 1990); James E. Young, *The Texture of Memory: Holocaust Memorials and Meaning* (New Haven: Yale Univ. Press, 1993); *Representations 35: Monumental Histories* (Summer 1991).

9. Cited by Louis Reau, *Les Monuments détruits de l'art français* (Paris: Hachette, 1959), 197.

10. Soria, *Grande histoire*, 156; see also Victor Hugo, *La Colonne*, piece 8–1431 at the BHVP.

11. On the "drapeau blanc," see the reproduction of the image in Murat, *La Colonne*, 62–63. Carnot's letter noted in a letter to the Ministre des Affaires Culturelles, archives of Bureau des Batiments Civils, piece 622.

12. *Le Moniteur universel,* April 11, 1831.

13. See esp. Jean Tulard, "Le Retour des Cendres," in Pierre Nora, ed., *Les Lieux de Mémoire*, tome II: *La Nation,* (Paris: Gallimard, 1986), 81–110.

14. The Comte d'Argout, *Ordonnance Royale*, Ministre des Travaux Publics, archives Bureau des Batiments Civils, dossier Vendôme Column.

15. Anon., *Description de la colonne* (Paris: Gauthier, 1833), 20.

16. Jules Claretie, *Histoire de la révolution* (Paris, 1872), 125.

17. Georges Riat, *Gustave Courbet, peintre* (1906), 292–93. Based on notes by Castagnary (Cabinet des Estampes, papiers Courbet), Bibliothèque Nationale, Paris.

18. Communication to the Fédération des artistes, Sept. 4, 1870, cited in Louis Reau, *Les Monuments détruits de l'art français*, tome II *XIX et XX Siecles* (Paris: Hachette, 1959), 193.

19. Decree, April 13, 1871, from *Procés-Verbaux de la Commune*, Georges Bourgin and Gabriel Henriot, eds. (1924).

20. Jules Castagnary, *Courbet et la Colonne Vendôme* (Paris: Dentu, 1883). See also Roger Bonniot, "Le Deboulonner: Courbet et la reedification de la colonne Vendôme—interventions de ses amis santais en faveur de Gustave Courbet en exil 1875," *Gazette des beaux-arts,* no. 1185 (Oct. 1967): 221–24. Courbet's remark cited Reau, *Les Monuments*, 196.

21. Reau, *Les Monuments*, 193.

22. Cited in J. B. Clement, *La Commune et les artistes* (Paris: Nouvelles Editions Latines, 1980), 74.

23. For the scholarship on Courbet's role in the incident, see: Bernard Gagenbin, *Courbet et la colonne Vendôme* (Geneva: Faculte des Lettres, 1963); Pierre Borel, *Gustave Courbet et la colonne Vendôme* Oeuvres Libres (letters and correspondance) (1921); Georges Muller, "De la responsabilité de Courbet dans la destruction de la colonne," *Procés-verbaux et mémoires de l'académie des sciences, Belles-lettres et Arts de Besancon,* vol. 173, (1958–59); Jacques Levron, "Courbet et la colonne," *Mercure de France,* no. 1175 (July 1961): 535–37.

24. Karl Marx, *The Eighteenth Brumaire of Louis Napoleon, and the Civil War in France* (London: International Publishing, 1988).

25. Jules Vallès in *Le Cri du peuple,* May 17, 1871; Gustave Maroteau in *Le Salut public,* May 18, 1871.

26. Reported in *Le Bulletin du jour,* May 17, 1871, and "La Chute," from *La Constitution politique et sociale,* May 18, 1871.

27. See the collections of the Bibliothèque Historique de la Ville de Paris (BHVP), Photographs: Place Vendôme, G.P. IV, 12–14, 29–33, 33–52, 1871.

28. Vuillaume, *Mes cahiers rouges*, 249–50. See Claude Lefort's discussion of

the guillotine and its role in political symbolism. Prescient analyses in *Les Formes de l'histoire: essais d'anthropologie politique* (Paris: Ed. Gallimard, 1978). Equally indispensable is Ernst Kantorowicz's classic *The King's Two Bodies* (Princeton: Princeton Univ. Press, 1957), and Marc Bloch's *Les Rois Thaumaturges* (Paris: Ed. Gallimard, new edition, 1983).

29. Reported by Albert Mousset, "Les Trois Napoleon de la colonne," archives of the Bureau des Batiments Civils, Paris, dossier: Vendôme Column, piece no. 7. My evocation of multiple Napoleonic bodies should recall the discussion of the *colossos* by J. P. Vernant, *Mythe et penseé chez les grecs* (Paris: Maspero, 1971), 252–53: "It is not the image of the deceased which is incarnated and fixed in stone, it is his life in the beyond, this life which is opposed to that of the living like the night is to day. The colossus is not an image; it is a 'double,' as the deceased himself is the double of the living." See also Florence Dupont, "The Emperor God's Other Body," in Michel Feher, Ramona Addaff, and Nadia Tazi, eds., *Fragments for a History of the Human Body, Part Three* (New York: Zone), 397–419.

30. Festrine's remarks cited by Henri Lefebvre in *La Proclamation de la Commune* (Paris: Ed. Gallimard, 1969); Vuillaume's words from *Mes cahiers rouges*, 249–50.

31. *Le Père Duchêne*, no. 64, 29 Floreal, An. 79, pp. 3–4.

32. Vallès's editorials in *Le Cri du peuple*, nos. 77 and 78, (May 17–18, 1871); remarks from *Le Père Duchêne*, no. 64.

33. Eugene Léveque, *A propos de la colonne vendôme restaurée moins le couronnement* (1874), part I, "La Chute," 8.

34. Edouard D'Anglemont, *La Resurrection de la colonne* (Paris: E. Dentu, 1872), 5–10.

35. François Loyer, "Le Sacré-Coeur de Montmartre," in Pierre Nora, ed., *Les Lieux de mémoire*, tome III: *Les France*, vol. 3: *De l'archive à l'emblème* (Paris: Ed. Gallimard, 1993), 450–73.

36. Léveque, *A propos de la colonne Vendôme*, 8

37. For a detailed look at the bas-reliefs and the narrative they relate, Murat, *La Colonne Vendôme*, 186–206.

38. Alexandre Goujon, *Pensée d'un soldat sur la sépulture de Napoleon* (1821), 5–7.

39. For this interpretation, see Alain Malissart, "La Colonne Vendôme: une colonne Trajane à Paris," *Les Dossiers de l'archeologie*, no. 17 (July-Aug. 1976): 116–21. Also, H. Bressler, "La Colonne Vendôme: un monument sans histoire," *Techniques et architecture*, no. 331 (June-July 1980): 38–39. Discussion of the Vendôme Column and its correspondence with "la triomphale Romaine Trajane à Roma," also in documentation at the Bureau des Batiments civils, Paris dossier Vendôme Column, piece 622.

40. Paul Brandat and Frédéric Passy, *La Colonne* (1871), 1–2.

41. Ibid., 1–2.

42. Ibid., 11.

43. Ibid.

44. *Projet de loi* (April 25, 1871), National Archives, Series F17, carton 2685, dossier 1, piece no. 182.

45. Ibid.

46. M. Bertrand, *Rapport* (1871), National Archives.

47. Maurice Aghulon, *Histoire vagabonde* (Paris: Ed. Gallimard, 1988), 304–7.

48. Brandat and Passy, *La Colonne*, 12. "Patrimony" has become an essential concept (and practice) in the history of memory. See, especially, Françoise Choay, *L'Allegorie du patrimoine* (Paris: Ed. du Sevil, 1992); J.-P. Babelon and A. Chastel, "La Notion de patrimoine," *Revue de l'art*, no. 49 (1980): 5–30; Chastel's article in Pierre Nora, ed., *Les Lieux de mémoire*, tome II: *La Nation* (Paris: Ed. Gallimard, 1987); Jean-Michel Leniaud, *L'Utopie française: essai sur le patrimoine* (Paris: Menges, 1992); Edouard Pommier, *L'Art de la liberté: doctrines et débats de la révolution française* (Paris: Ed. Gallimard, 1991).

49. *Le Moniteur universel*, April 11, 1831.

50. *Procés-Verbaux de la Commune*, Seance of May 12, 1871, collected by G. Bourgin and G. Henriot (1924).

51. Reported in the daily accounts of the *Journal officiel de la commune*, May 17, 1871. See also the accounts dated September 17, 1870, on the reappropriation of Paris landmarks to their former revolutionary names.

52. Léveque, *A propos de la Colonne Vendôme*, 13.

53. Brandat and Passy, *La Colonne*, 12.

54. Ibid., 14–16.

55. Ibid., 2.

56. Henri Lefebvre, *La Proclamation de la Commune* (Paris: Ed. Gallimard, 1969), 125. Read also the reexamination of Lefebvre's thesis in Stewart Edwards, *The Paris Commune, 1871* (London: Quadrangle, 1971), 364–66, and Greil Marcus's *Lipstick Traces: A Secret History of the Twentieth Century* (Cambridge, Mass.: Harvard, Univ. Press, 1989), 138–47. Consider also Lefebvre's own arguments in *Espace et politique: le droit à la ville* (1968; Paris: Anthropos, 1973) and *La Pensée Marxiste et la ville* (Paris: Casterman, 1972), esp. 109–14, "Engels and Utopia."

57. *Journal officiel*, May 17, 1871.

58. See Patrick H. Hutton, *The Cult of the Revolutionary Tradition* (Berkeley and Los Angeles: Univ. of California Press, 1981), introduction and Ch. 1, esp. 8–12.

59. Felix Pyat in *Le Vengeur*, May 17, 1871.

60. Ibid.

61. Ibid.

62. Jules Vallès in *Le Cri du peuple*, no. 78 (May 18, 1871).

63. Murat, *La Colonne Vendôme*, 208–11.

64. *Journal officiel de la Commune*, April 20, 1871.

65. *Le Père Duchêne*, no. 64, p. 2.

66. P. O. Lissagaray, *L'Histoire de la Commune* (1876; Paris: Maspero, 1972), 291.

67. Murat, *La Colonne Vendôme*, 211.

68. Lissagaray, *L'Histoire de la Commune*, 287.

69. Ibid., 291. On the rebuilding of the monument, see the chronology detailed by architect Paul Domenec in a letter to the Ministry of Cultural Affairs, archives of the Bureau des Batiments Civils, dated May 5, 1966.

70. On the commemorations of the Mur des Fédérés, see the piece by Madeleine Réberioux, "Le Mur des Fédérés," in Nora, ed., *Les Lieux de mémoire*, tome I, vol. 1: *La République* (Paris: Ed. Gallimard, 1984), 619–49. For images of the column on national holidays and for military commemorations, see Murat, *La Colonne Vendôme*.

71. Article, source unknown, dossier Vendôme Column, Bureau des Batiments Civils et des Palais Nationaux, Paris.

Chapter 2: Numbers

1. Karl Marx, letter to César de Paepe (September 14, 1870), see citation by Jacques Le Goff and the "paralyzing weight of the past," in Le Goff, *Historie et mémoire* (Paris: Ed. Gallimard 1988) 52.

2. Karl Marx, "The Eighteenth Brumaire of Louis Bonaparte," all citations in Robert Tucker, ed., *The Marx-Engels Reader* (New York: Norton, 1978), 594–96.

3. Emile Zola, *Le Ventre de Paris* (Paris: Ed. Gallimard, 1979).

4. Gabriel Mourey et al., "La Bourse," in *Les Minutes parisiennes* (Paris: Paul Ollendorf, 1899), 1.

5. Georg Simmel, *The Philosophy of Money*, Tom Bottomore and David Frisby, trans. (Boston and London: Routledge & Kegan Paul, 1978), 506.

6. H. Cozic, *La Bourse mise à la portée de tous: présent, futur* (Paris, 1885), 27.

7. Karl Marx, "The Civil War in France," in Tucker, *Marx-Engels Reader*, 652.

8. Auguste Chirac, *L'Agiotage sous la troisième république,* (Paris: Albert Savine, 1877), 22, 80. See also Jules Bertaut, *La Bourse anecdotique et pittoresque* (Paris: Les Editions de France, 1933), 317: "It seems that nothing has changed since June 1870"; also Alfred Collig, *La Prodigeuse histoire de la bourse* (Paris: Editions SEF, 1949), 299, "1871–1900, a too beautiful season of capitalism at its apogee."

9. Georges Manchez, *Réorganization de la bourse de Paris* (1897), 14.

10. Felix Fauré, discourse of February 1893, reported in ibid., 38.

11. Cozic, *La Bourse*, 27.

12. Ibid., 28.

13. Gabriel Désert, *Apogée et crise de la civilisation paysanne 1789–1914,* tome 3 of Georges Duby et al., *Histoire de la France Rurale* (Paris: Ed. du Seuil, 1975–76), 403. For an overview of the economic and social implications and consequences of financial markets on France, see Maurice Lévy-Leboyen, "Le crédit et la monnaie: l'apprentissage du marché," in F. Braudel and E. Labrousse, eds., *Histoire economique et sociale de la France* (Paris: Presses Universitaires de France, 1973), tome 3, pp. 405–21. For movements off the land, Jacques Dupaquier, *Histoire de la population francçaise* (Paris: Presses Universitaires de France, 1988), vol. 3.

14. Raoul de la Grasserie, "De l'indisponibilité et de l'indivisibilité totales et partielles du patrimoine," in *La Réforme sociale*, (1899), 2.

15. Jean Perruche de Vecna, *Politique ouvrière du mouvement coopératif* (Jules Rousset, 1910), 5. For more on memory from a rural or non-urban perspective, see Pierre Nora, ed., *Les Lieux de mémoire*, tome III: Les France, vol. 2: "Traditions" (Paris: Ed. Gallimard, 1992), especially Armand Frémont's "La terre," and Thierry Gasnier's "Le local." Also the ethnological dissection of time by Françoise Zonabend, *The Enduring Memory: Time and History in a French Village*, A. Forster, trans. (Manchester: Univ. of Manchester Press, 1984).

16. Raoul de la Grassiere, *De la nostalgie et des instincts contraires comme facteurs psychologiques et sociaux* (Paris: M. Girard & E. Brière, 1911), 6, 14, 24.

Also, Michael S. Roth, "Dying of the Past: Medical Studies of Nostalgia in Nineteenth-Century France," in *History and Memory* 3, no. 1 (1991): 5–29; Christopher Shaw and Malcolm Chase, eds., *The Imagined Past: History and Nostalgia* (Manchester: Manchester Univ. Press, 1989).

17. De la Grasserie, *La Réforme sociale*, 1–2.

18. A. Joffroy and R. Dupoy, *Fuges et vagabondages* (Paris: Félix Alcan, 1909), 10.

19. Georges Plastra, *La Notion juridique du patrimoine* (Paris: Arthur Rousseau, 1903), 6; see also the discussion of goods, debts, and the "continuation of the person" in Henri Gazin, *Essai critique sur la notion de patrimoine* (Paris: Arthur Rousseau, 1910), 13, 247.

20. Alfred Comat, *La Dépopulation des campagnes: projet de loi 1910* (8F.4515) 21–23; see also M. J. Challamel, *Conservation des petits patrimoines* (8R.7705), (1898), document, Bibliothèque Nationale, Paris.

21. Cozic, *La Bourse*, 27.

22. Citations from L. Pagé, *La Bourse classique modernisée* (1911), 119–20.

23. Condette, *Causerie hebdomadaire sur la bourse: année 1884* (Roussel, 1884), 11; on the question of the meaning of "work" in the nineteenth century, see William Sewell, *Work and Revolution in France* (Cambridge: Cambridge Univ. Press, 1980).

24. L'Abbé Deville, *Les operations de bourse devant la conscience* (8V.6309), (1884), 89, document, Bibliothèque Nationale, Paris.

25. Alexandre Assier, *Le Portefeuille des pères de famille* (André Guede, 1887), in preface.

26. L'Abbé Deville, *Les operations de bourse*, 16.

27. Condette, *Causerie hebdomadaire*, 5–7; citation on "disordered movements" from anon., *Petit traité des opérations de bourse par un vieux boursier* (1873), 39.

28. Assier, *Le Portefeuille*, 68; for general histories of capital and savings in French society, see Charles A. Michalet, *Les Placements des épargnants français de 1815 à nos jours* (Paris: Presses Universitaires de France, 1968).

29. *L'Illustration journal universel* (1893); see Georges Montorgueil, *La Vie des boulevards* (Paris, 1896), 180, discussion of the history of the boulevards, notably "the royal road" of the Boulevard Sebastapol in 1858. Note also the overview of the projects provided by Henri Mallet, *Le Baron Haussmann et la rénaissance de Paris* (Paris: Ed. Municipales, 1973).

30. Montorgueil, *La Vie des boulevards*, x.

31. Victorien Sardou, cited in T. J. Clark, *The Painting of Modern Life* (New York: Knopf, 1985), 43. Clark's is an excellent and elaborate thesis on captialism and the reimagination of Parisian urban space in the second half of the nineteenth century, relying upon Guy Debord's concept of the "spectacle," that is, "capital accumulated until it becomes an image."

32. All citations from Montorgueil, *La Vie des boulevards*: "Champs-Elyseés," 61; "Le Marais-Rue d'Hauteville," 180, 199; "Les boutiques," iii; "La biére," x.

33. Ibid., iii.

34. Susan Buck-Morss, *The Dialectics of Seeing: Walter Benjamin and the Arcades Project* (Cambridge, Mass.: MIT Press, 1991), 64–67.

35. Mourey, *Les Minutes parisiennes*, 2, 10; Georges d'Avenel, *Le Mécanisme de la vie moderne* (1905), 65.

36. All citations, Mourey, *Les Minutes parisiennes,* "Intense effort," 19; "Au milieu d'une foule," 31; "Animalités, physionomies," 31.

37. Condette, *Causerie hebdomadaire sur la bourse: année 1884* (Paris: Roussel, 1884), 23, 11.

38. Emile André, *L'Art de n'etre pas volé, escroqué, estampé, etc.* (Paris: Garnier Frères, 1909), 21, 46. On capitalist space, see Marc Augé, *Non-lieux: introduction à une anthropologie de la surmodernité* (Paris: Le Seuil, 1992); Marshall Berman, *All That Is Solid Melts into Air: The Experience of Modernity* (New York: Penguin, 1982); Clark, *The Painting of Modern Life,* 23–78; Edward W. Soja, *Postmodern Geographies: The Reassertion of Space in Critical Theory* (London and New York: Verso, 1989), chs. 1–2.

39. D'Avenel, *Le Mécanisme de la vie moderne,* 66; consider also Anatole Leroy-Beaulieu, "Le Règne de l'argent," *Revue des deux mondes* (Dec. 15, 1897): 831.

40. Georg Simmel, *The Philosophy of Money,* Tom Bottomore and David Frisby, trans. (Boston and London: Routledge & Kegan Paul, 1978), 506.

41. André, *L'Art de n'être pas volé,* 72.

42. Gabriel Tarde, "Les Causes et les remèdes," *Etudes pénales et sociales* (Paris: G. Masson, 1892), 77.

43. Eugen Weber, *Peasants into Frenchmen* (Stanford: Stanford Univ. Press, 1976), 414–15, 419.

44. On the press in this period see Edward Berenson, *The Trial of Madame Caillaux* (Berkeley and Los Angeles: Univ. of California Press, 1992), ch. 6. On memory and typographic culture, Patrick H. Hutton, *History as an Art of Memory* (Hanover: Univ. of Vermont Univ. Press of New England, 1993); Walter J. Ong, *Orality and Literacy: The Technologizing of the Word* (London: Methuen, 1982); Friedrich A. Kittler, *Discourse Networks 1800/1900* (Stanford: Stanford Univ. Press, 1990).

45. *Les Annales de la bourse,* Jan. 15, 1893, p. 64.

46. Lucien Revon, *La Grammaire de la bourse* (1889), 5.

47. Tarde, "Les Causes et les remèdes," 77. Historical discussion of Tarde's work by Patrick Champgne in *Faire l'opinion: le nouveau jeu politique* (Paris: Ed. Minuit, 1990), 67–69; see of course also Tarde's major work on *L'Opinion et la foule* (1901); rpt., Paris: Presses Universitaires de France, 1989); see also Pierre Bourdieu, "Remarques à propos de la valeur scientifique et des effets politiques des enquêtes d'opinion," in *Pouvoirs 33, les sondages* (Paris: Presses Universitaires de France, 1985), 131–39, and "L'opinion publique: apologie pour les sondages," in *Faire de l'histoire,* collaborative work under the direction of Jacques Le Goff and Pierre Nora, tome 3: *Nouveaux objets* (Paris: Ed. Gallimard, 1974), 220–35.

48. *Les Annales de la bourse,* Jan. 15, 1893, p. 64.

49. Gabriel Tarde, "Les causes et les remedes," *Etudes pénales et sociales* (G. Masson, 1892), 76.

50. A Rallovich, *Le Marche financier en 1891* (Paris: Guillaumin, 1891), 1; the moment of the present and the promise of the future—in this case financial— yet based on an instant appreciation of the historical situation. Consider Henri Bergson (borrowing from Pierre Janet) and the notion of "l'attention du réel," or the implications of Walter Benjamin's idea of the "jetzeit," thesis XIV from "Theses on the Philosophy of History, in *Illuminations: Essays and Reflections,* Hannah Arendt, ed., Harry Zohn, trans. (New York: Schocken, 1968), 261.

51. Emile André, *L'Art de n'être pas volé*, 72; for a general record of the behavoir of the Bourse at the turn of the century (particularly its problems), see Louis Deville, *Crises de la bourse 1870–1910* (8F.22333), document, Bibliothèque Nationale.

52. Reported in Assier, *Le Portefeuille*, 22, and Revon, *La Grammaire de la bourse*, 5.

53. Assier, *Le Portefeville*, 7; for generalities, see R. Poidevin, *Les relations économiques et financières entre la France et l'Allemagne de 1898 à 1914* (Paris: Colin, 1969); *Finances et relations internationales 1887–1914* (Paris: Colin, 1970).

54. Jacques Plocque, *Les Sociétés par actions* (Paris: Arthur Rousseau, 1906), 9.

55. Ibid.

56. Assier, *Le Portefeville*, 27.

57. André, *L'Art de n'être pas volé*, 51.

Chapter 3: Words

1. *La Commune: Journal du soir*, May 17, 1871.

2. Krzysztof Pomian, "Les Archives," in Pierre Nora, ed., *Les Lieux de mémoire*, tome III: *Les France*, vol. 3: *De l'archive à l'emblème* (Paris: Ed. Gallimard, 1992), 168–69.

3. The classic text remains Frances Yates, *The Art of Memory* (Chicago: Univ. of Chicago Press, 1966). See also Mary Carruthers, *The Book of Memory: A Study of Memory in Medieval Culture* (Cambridge: Cambridge Univ. Press, 1990).

4. Edouard Manteaux, *La Mnémotechnie appliquée au sciences élémentaires* (Clermont-Ferrard, 1894), 19.

5. See Alain Lieury, *Des méthodes pour la mémoire* (Paris: Dunod, 1992); Aimé Paris, *Souvenirs du cours de mnémotechnie* (1830).

6. Ferdinand de Saussure, *Cours de linguistique générale* (Paris: Payot, 1916). For an introduction in Englis, see Roland A. Champagne, *French Structuralism* (Boston, Twayne Publishers, 1990).

7. See the discussion of Michel Foucault, Max Weber, and Jurgen Habermas in Scott Lash and Jonathan Friedman, *Modernity and Identity* (Oxford: Blackwell, 1992), 4–5.

8. Cited here, anon., *La Mnémonique universel-manuel* (1885); I. and M. De Bonit, *Aide-Memoire: quatre cent soixante-dix formules mnémotechniques pour la chronologie des principaux faits de l'histoire de France* (1891); Abbé Courdavault, *La Mnémotechnie* (Lille, 1905); L. Denis, *Calendrier de mémoire* (Epinal, 1891); Manteaux, *Mnemotechnie appliquée*.

9. P. Dugers and Felix Bernard, *Mnémonie classique formulaire methode* (1874), 1–2.

10. *Revue mensuelle de mnémotechnie ancienne et moderne et de l'art d'apprendre*, vol. I (1886), 2.

11. Abbé Chavauty, *Mnémotechnie, art d'apprendre et de se souvenir* (Tarbes, 1886), iv.

12. Dugers and Bernard, *Mnémonie classique*, 18–21.

13. Ibid. 23–24. The passion for inventions and machines as indicators of progress recalls the Universal Expositions, and the dominance of science and industry as the keys to human development. A century after Dugers and Bernard,

see also the same project of memory and history drawn together through technology in Michel Rival, *La Mémoire de l'humanité: les grandes inventions* (Paris: Larousse, 1991). Notably, Rival has abandoned mnemonic formulas and relies on more traditional images and text to constitute his version of "memory."

14. Dugers and Bernard, *Mnémonie classique*, 32–35.

15. Ibid., section on "Electricité," passim.

16. Ibid., 28–30.

17. Ibid., 9.

18. Ibid., 10–11.

19. A. Delapierre and A. Delamarche, *Exercises de mémoire* (1887). Hugo's declaration, 14; Regnard's injunction, 17; Rousseau's maxim, 20.

20. Ibid., preface. On French education, particularly the instruction of history, see Claude Bernard, "L'Enseignement de l'histoire en France au XIXe siècle selon les ministres de l'instruction publique" (Thèse, L'Université de Paris VIII, 1978); Jacques Ozouf and Mona Ozouf, *La République des instituteurs* (Paris: Gallimard/Le Seuil, 1992), esp. 28–32.

21. M. Delapierre, *Lycée Michelet: discours prononcé à la distribution des prix* (July 29, 1891), citations from introductory remarks, 2–4.

22. Ibid., 7.

23. Delapierre and Delamarche, *Exercises de mémoire*, 4, emphasis in original. On the question of reading and pedagogy and policy, see, for example, Mona Ozouf, *L'Ecole de la France: essais sur la révolution, l'utopie, et l'enseignement* (Paris: Ed. Gallimard, 1984), and *L'Ecole, l'eglise, et la république 1871–1914* (Paris: Ed. Cana, 1982). On memory, see the entire section (five essays) on "Pédagogie" in Pierre Nora, ed., *Les Lieux de mémoire*, vol. 1: *La République* (Paris: Ed. Gallimard, 1984).

24. Delapierre, *Lycée Michelet: discours*, 12.

25. Delapierre and Delamarche, *Exercises de mémoire*, 5.

26. Ibid., 7. The links between memory and the spoken word can be traced classically through Harry Caplan's essays *On Eloquence: Studies in Ancient and Medieval Rhetoric* (Ithaca: Cornell Univ. Press, 1970).

27. Manteaux, *La Mnémotechnie appliquée* citations from section one, "Physiques," 5.

28. Ibid., 7.

29. Ibid., 19. See also Mary Carruthers's *The Book of Memory* on the different types of symbols and references in memory systems, esp. ch. 2 and 5, "Descriptions of the Neuropsychology of Memory" and "Memory and the Ethics of Reading."

30. Manteaux, *La Mnémotechnie appliquée*, 9–10.

31. Ibid., 38, conclusion. On the role of Cicero in memory, see again Yates, Carruthers, and Caplan's essays, *On Eloquence*. For the role of Mnemosyne and the muses in the Greek classical tradition, Michel Simondon, *La Mémoire et l'oubli* (Paris: Belles Lettres, 1982).

32. Alfred Robichon, *La Syllabaire mnémonique* (1905), introductory remarks, vii-viii. See Jacques Derrida, *Of Grammatology*, Gayatri Chakravorty Spivak, trans. (Baltimore and London: Johns Hopkins Univ. Press, 1976), ch. 2, discussion of structural linguistics.

33. Robichon, *La Syllabaire mnémonique*, 3rd ed., *La Mémoire literaire: l'art de la cultiver* (1909), introduction, 2. On the distinction of syllables, consider Saussure's *Cours de linguistique générale* for its analysis of language as a system

of distinctions. The "structural" organization of antiquarian studies and their links to language and knowledge are explored in Arnaldo Momigliano, *The Classical Foundations of Modern Historiography* (Berkeley and Los Angeles: Univ. of California Press, 1990). On words and classics, Emile Littré's *Histoire de la langue française*, with its study of "origins, etymology, grammar, dialects, versification, and letters . . . ," and of course his *Dictionnaire de la langue française* (Paris, 1863).

34. Robichon, *La Mémoire literaire* (1909), 3.

35. Ibid., 139–40.

36. Ibid., 5.

37. Theodule Ribot, *Les Maladies de la mémoire/les maladies de la volonté* (Paris, 1881). Ribot was one of the founders of experimental psychology in France. He formulated the law of regression for memory loss, and was the founder of *La Revue philosophique* in 1866. See Michael S. Roth's piece on Ribot in *Representations 26* (Spring 1989): 49–68. On degeneration, see Robert Nye's *Crime, Madness, and Politics in Modern France* (Princeton: Princeton Univ. Press, 1984), as well as Max Nordau's splendidly titled classic, *Degeneration of Our Contemporary Civilization* (Lincoln and London; Univ. of Nebraska Press/Bison Books, 1993).

38. Robichon, *La Syllabaire mnémonique*, 140. For the impression of language on the body, see Michel Foucault, "Nietzsche, Genealogy, History," in *Language, Counter-Memory, Practice*, Donald F. Bouchard, ed. (Ithaca: Cornell Univ. Press, 1977), 139–64. Consider also the commentary by Lucien Lévy-Bruhl in *La Morale et la science des moeurs* (rpt., Paris: Presses Universitaires de France, 1953): "As sounds emitted by the vocal organs, words belong to the domain of movement, and they can be the object of laboratory studies. By their sense and syntax, by the evolution of their forms, they reveal psychological and social life . . . these phenomenona thus constitute the most natural transition between what used to be called the 'physical' and the 'moral,' " (p. 175).

39. Robichon, *La Syllabaire mnémonique* (1905), 58. In 1881 philosopher Victor Egger published *La Parole interieur*, a grand history of western thinking "à travers la Grèce classique et Rome." Eggers was primarily concerned with defining the "individual" which he saw in terms of "the internal continuity of his enunciation." His father was the noted philologist Emile Egger, author of *Grammaire comparée des langues classiques* (1852). See the commentary by Gabriel Bergounioux, "La Pathologie du langage entre les lettres et la medicine (1880–1900)," *Communications*, no. 54 (Paris: Ecole des Hautes Etudes en Sciences Sociales, 1992).

40. Jean-Marie Mayeur and Madeleine Rebérioux, *The Third Republic from Its Origins to the Great War 1871–1914* (Cambridge, Cambridge Univ. Press, 1987), 110.

41. Robichon, *La Syllabaire mnémonique*, viii. Battle of the books, Ancients and Moderns, by whatever title, controversy over the role of education has been an undying theme. The classical ideal of the citizen as the superior member of a ruling elite was challenged as undemocratic and unsuited to the needs of the modern world, a struggle which pitted liberal and left politicians against Catholics and led to reorganizations of the Ecole Normale and the Sorbonne. See Gustave Lanson, *L'Université et la société moderne* (Paris: Armand Colin, 1902), and the commentaries in Robert C. Grogin, *The Bergsonian Controversy in France* (Calgary: Univ. of Calgary Press, 1988).

42. Simon Schama, *Citizens: A Chronicle of the French Revolution* (New York: Alfred Knopf 1989), 162–74. Jean Starobinski, "La Chaire, la Tribune, le Barreau," in Pierre Nora, ed., *Les Lieux de mémoire*, tome II: *La Nation* (Paris, Ed. Gallimard, 1986), pp. 425–85.

43. P. Gachon, *Les Méthodes historiques et les historiens en France au XIXe siècle* (Montpellier, 1891), 12. Note James E. Young's commentary on monuments and memory from "The Biography of a Memorial Icon," *Representations 26* (Spring 1989): 71: "Unlike words on a page, always gesturing at something beyond the ink and paper and giving them form, memorial icons seem to embody ideas, inviting viewers to mistake material presence and weight for immutable permanence."

44. Delapierre and Delamarche, *Exercises de mémoire*, 23.

Chapter 4: Bodies

1. Dr. Rousseau, "Observation et autopsie d'une aphasique," *Bulletin de la société médicale de l'Yonne* (1882): 1–2.

2. Dr. A. Pitres, *L'Aphasie amnésique et ses variétés cliniques: leçons faites à l'hopital St. Andre de Bordeaux* (Paris: Félix Alcan, 1898), 45.

3. For a clear treatment of Broca's work and the history of aphasia studies in general, see Francis Schiller, *Paul Broca: Founder of French Anthropology, Explorer of the Brain* (New York: Oxford Univ. Press, 1992), 165–211.

4. Rousseau, "Observation et autopsie d'une aphasique," 4. Note Robert M. Young, *Mind, Brain, and Adaptation in the Nineteenth Century: Cerebral Localization and Its Biological Context from Gall to Ferrier* (Oxford and New York: Oxford Univ. Press, 1970), on the period between Gall and Ferrier: "In about 50 years, cerebral localization had moved from a conception of physiology dominated by psychological faculties with no precise designation of the related material processes, to a physiology of sensory motor processes which dominated the psychological functions." How and why did this happen? What were the implications for the study of "memory"?

5. Pitres, *L'Aphasie amnésique*, 38.

6. Dr. Legroux, *De l'aphasie* (1875).

7. As recounted by P. A. Lop, *Aphasie avec amnésie urémiques* (1895).

8. Dr. Georges Surbled, *La Mémoire* (Téquil, 1899), 107.

9. Paul Broca, translated and commented by Young, *Mind, Brain, and Adaptation*, 142–43.

10. Mathias Duval, *L'Aphasie depuis Broca* (1888), 20.

11. Dr. Favuelle, "Volonté, conscience, idées, mémoire," *Extrait du Bulletin de la Société d'Anthropologie* (Paris: A. Henneyer, 1885), 40; the memory of "recitation" has been given an excellent modern treatment by Israel Rosenfield, *The Invention of Memory: A New View of the Brain* (New York: Basic Books, 1988).

12. J. B. Bouchard, *Le Langage intérieur et les diverses formes de l'aphasie* (Bibliothèque Nationale, Td87.730), 2; see also the citation of this term in Gilbert Ballet, *Le Langage intérieur* (1886), 4: "the brain is a virtual organ . . . the brain is not a tabula rasa."

13. Pitres, *L'Aphasie amnésique*, 38.

14. Ibid., 49.

15. Dr. Paul Garnier, "Aphasie et folie," *Extrait des archives générale de medicine* (Paris: Librarie Faculté de Medicine, Feb./March 1889), 15–25.

16. M. J. Lefort, in *Annales d'hygiène publique et le médicine légale*, tome 38 July 1872, pp. 418–19.

17. Dr. Georges Surbled, *La Mémoire* (Téquil, 1899), 107; on the practice of actually producing written signs and training them as a form of expression with attention to exercises, posture, lighting, see Emile Javal, *Physiologie de la lecture et de l'écriture* (Félix Alcan, 1905; rpt., Paris: RETZ, 1978).

18. Lefort, 420; see also Lucien Lagrille, "Abcès du lobe temporal droit du cerveau d'origine inconnue," *Archives de neurologie* (1901), which records the growing recognition of a "new phenomenon" in aphasia of written language, "the forgetting of certain letters."

19. See the discussion by Dr. Ch. Mills in the *Review of Insanity and Nervous Diseases* (Sept./Dec. 1891), based on lectures by Legrand du Saulle, "Aphasia and Aphasiacs," *Lectures at la Salpêtriére, Gazette des hopitaux*, vol. LV (Paris, 1882); Briand's comments in Charles Briand, *L'Institution du notaire en second et des témoins instrumentaires* (Paris: Henri Jouve, 1904), 115.

20. Transcripts collected and commented in Georges de Lantigny, *Le Redan de M. Bertillon* (1904), a fascinating analysis examining the role of criminologist Alphonse Bertillon in interpreting the writing of Dreyfus for signs of forgery.

21. Henri Pieron, *L'Evolution de la mémoire* (Paris: Flammarion, 1910), 353. André Leroi-Gourhan has commented on the memory and its rhythms in terms of "the engagement of gestures and tools in the external organs of man" as the "most elaborated external memory." See his *La Geste et la parole*, 63–76.

22. Pieron's perspective was neither unique nor strictly national. Consider H. H. Donaldson, *The Growth of the Brain* (London: Walter Scott, 1895), 340: "We are told this age is one of nervous strain. From the beginning, the outer world has modified all animals possessed of a nervous system."

23. See, for example, the discussion by Le Goff on the process by which "printing revolutionized—slowly—western memory." Jacques Le Goff, *Histoire et mémoire* (Paris: Ed. Gallimard, 1988), 149. Also Elisabeth Eisenstein, *The Printing Press as an Agent of Change*, 2 vols. (Cambridge: Cambridge Univ. Press, 1979); Jack Goody, *The Interface between the Written and the Oral* (Cambridge: Cambridge Univ. Press, 1987); Marshall McLuhan, *The Gutenberg Galaxy: The Making of Typographic Man* (Toronto: Univ. of Toronto Press, 1962).

24. Reports from *Bulletin de la Société de Médicine Légale de France*, session of Feb. 11, 1901, p. 26, with commentaries by Dr. Gilles de la Tourette. Consider also Michel Foucault's conceptualization of autopsy in *The Birth of the Clinic: An Archaeology of Medical Perception* (New York: Random House, 1974), chs. 7–8, as well as Gilles Deleuze and Félix Guattari's "Body Without Organs," in *A Thousand Plateaus: Volume II of Capitalism and Schizophrenia* (Minneapolis: Univ. of Minnesota Press, 1980).

25. Henri Pieron, *L'Evolution de la mémoire* (Paris: Flammarion, 1910), 353. Consider Walter Benjamin's discussion of Henri Bergson's memory philosophy as arising in reaction to "the inhospitable, blinding age of big-scale industrialism," and his note on Freud that "consciousness as such receives no memory traces whatever, but has another important function: protection against stimuli." Walter Benjamin, *Illuminations: Essays and Reflections* (New York: Schocken, 1968), 157, 161.

26. Favuelle, "Volonté, conscience, idées, mémoire," 21.

27. Georges Hervé, *La Circonvolution de Broca: étude de morphologie cérébrale* (Paris: A. Delahaye & E. Lecrosiner, 1888), 6.

28. Ferrand, *Le Langage, la parole et les aphasies* (Paris: Rieff et Cie, 1894), 190.

29. Pieron's comments in Pieron, *L'Evolution de la mémoire*, 332–33.

30. Favuelle, "Volonté, conscience, idées, mémoire," 52. Notes Jacques Derrida's commentary on nerve endings, paths, and the neurological scheme of memory in Freud from "Freud and the Scene of Writing," in *Writing and Difference* (Chicago: Univ. of Chicago Press, 1978), 201: "The equality of resistances to the *breaching (frayage)* . . . would reduce all preference in the choice of itineraries. Memory would be paralyzed. The differences between the *breaches* are the true origin of memory and thus of psychic consciousness . . ."

31. Favuelle, "Volonté, conscience, idées, mémoire," 52.

32. For excellent overviews of the social politics of mind and body in the nineteenth century see Jan Goldstein, *Console and Classify: The French Psychiatric Profession in the Nineteenth Century* (Cambridge: Cambridge Univ. Press, 1987), and Roger Cooter, *The Cultural Meaning of Popular Science: Phrenology and the Organization of Consent in Nineteenth-Century Britain* (Cambridge, 1984); Robert A. Nye, *Crime, Madness, and Politics in Modern France* (Princeton: Princeton Univ. Press, 1984).

33. Schiller, *Paul Broca, 134.*

34. Dr. François Moutier, *L'Aphasie de Broca: travail du laboratoire, Bicêtre* (Paris: G. Steinheil, 1908), 3, 9.

35. Recounted in Dr. Paul Topinard, *A la mémoire de Broca: l'école, le laboratoire et le musée Broca.* Observations on the "materialists," 21; on the "commemorations," 16. Reports on the conflict with Fauvelle collected from *Le Matin,* Dec. 20, 1889.

36. Henri Bergson, *Matière et mémoire* (Paris: Presses Universitaires de France, 1896), translated by Nancy Margaret Paul and W. Scott Palmer, *Matter and Memory* (New York: Macmillan, 1919; rpt., Zone Books, 1988), 240.

37. Henri Bergson, *Oeuvres* (Paris: Presses Universitaires de France, 1959), 853.

38. Bergson, *Matter and Memory,* 242.

39. For Ribot's original formulation, see Théodule Ribot, *Les Maladies de la mémoire* (Paris: G. Balière et Cie, 1881), 136–38, with additional discussion on 164–65. For Bergson's commentary, see his *Oeuvres,* 855. See also the fine discussion of Ribot's work situated in the context of other nineteenth-century memory debates in Michael S. Roth, "Remembering Forgetting: *Maladies de la mémoire* in Nineteenth-Century France," *Representations* 26 (Spring 1989), 49–68.

40. Henri Bergson, *Mélanges* (Paris: Presses Universitaires France, 1972), 365; see also the commentaries in Rose-Marie Mossé-Bastide, *Bergson Educateur* (Paris: Presses Universitaires de France, 1955), 180–99, chapter on "Le But de l'enseignement: la formation du bon sens." Bergson's goal in teaching is read by Mossé-Bastide as "before anything else, discernment, the capacity to judge in a personal fashion."

41. As recounted by Moutier, *L'Aphasie de Broca,* 260.

Chapter 5: Testimonies

1. "L'Affaire Cayotte" (1908), dossier from archives of the Ministère de la Justice, Paris, BB 18 2374 137 A08, prosecutor's and investigator's reports.

2. News clippings collected in ibid., *La République*, Sept. 19, 1908; report from the prosecutor (April 22, 1908), collected in ibid.

3. Report from prosecutor (April 22, 1908).

4. For an elaboration of the many problems surrounding this theme, see notably the issue "Questions à la littérature," of *Le Débat*, no. 54 (March-April 1989), particularly the following articles: Hans Robert Jauss, "L'usage de la fiction en histoire," 89–113; Krzystof Pomian, "Histoire et fiction," 114–37; Natalie Zemon Davis, "Du conte et de l'histoire," 138–43; and David S. Landes, Jean Levi, and Hubert Monteilhet, "Quand l'historien se fait romancier," 144–65. See also N. Z. Davis's own study of pardoner's tales, *Fiction in the Archives* (Stanford: Stanford Univ. Press, 1987).

5. Henri Bergson, *Oeuvres* (Paris: Presses Universitaires de France, 1959), 863. Note also the importance of this idea to Walter Benjamin regarding works of art: "Even the most perfect reproduction of a work of art is lacking in one element: its presence in time and space, its unique existence at the place where it happens to be. This unique existence of the work of art determined the history to which it was subject throughout the time of its existence." *Illuminations: Essays and Reflections* (New York: Schocken, 1968), 220.

6. J. Maxwell, *L'Amnésie au point de vue de la médicine judiciaire* (Bordeaux, 1902), 1–2.

7. Emile Fourquet, *Les Faux-témoins* (Chalon-sur-Salone, 1901), 9.

8. Ernest Dupré, *Le Témoignage: étude psychologique et médico-légale* (1905), 345–47.

9. E. Paulus, *Du témoignage suspect* (Paris: A. Rousseau, 1912), 10; the science of testimony "a réuni un très grand nombre d'observations et en a tiré un ensemble de règles qu'il est indispensable de connaitre lorsqu'on étudie les sciences juridiques."

10. Paul Ricoeur, *De l'interpretation: essai sur Freud* (Paris: Ed. du Seuil, 1965), 36–44. Also Ricoeur's *History and Truth* (Evanston: Northwestern Univ. Press, 1965). Henri Ellenberger, *The Discovery of the Unconscious: The History and Evolution of Dynamic Psychiatry* (New York: Basic Books, 1970); Debora Silverman, *Art Nouveau in Fin-de-Siècle France: Politics, Psychology, and Style* (Berkeley and Los Angeles: Univ. of California Press, 1989), chs. 5, 15.

11. Jeffrey M. Masson, *The Assault on Truth* (New York: 1992); Paul Robinson, *Freud and His Critics* (Berkeley and Los Angeles: Univ. of California Press, 1993); Fredrick Crews, "The Myth of Repressed Memory," *New York Review of Books* XLI, nos. 19–20 (Nov. 17–Dec. 1, 1994); Donald P. Spence, *Narrative Truth and Historical Truth: Meaning and Interpretation in Psychoanalysis* (New York and London: W. W. Norton, 1992).

12. See Edward Berenson, *The Trial of Madame Caillaux* (Los Angeles and Berkeley: Univ. of California Press, 1992); Judith Walkowitz, *City of Dreadful Delight: Narratives of Sexual Danger in Late Victorian London* (Chicago: Univ. of Chicago Press, 1992), on the "multiple representations" of sexual danger; Shoshana Felman and Dori Laub, *Testimony: Crises of Witnessing in Literature, Psychoanalysis, and History* (New York and London: Routledge, 1992).

13. Dossier, "L'Affaire Cayotte," note of the *Chef du Bureau*, July 18, 1908.

14. Dupré, *Le Témoignage*, 345–47.

15. Fourquet, *Les Faux-témoins*, viii, intro.

16. Dupré, *Le Témoignage*, 345.

17. Ernest Naville, *L'Importance logique du témoignage* (1887), 3–5; the orders of truth summarized on 3.

18. Duverger's comment cited by E. Paulus, *Du témoignage suspect* (Paris: A. Rousseau, 1912), 2.

19. Georges Gagnèbe, *Du faux-témoignage* (Périgeux, 1900), 27. Exceptions to the oath: religious motives, discretionary power of the judge, individuals not exercising certain civil rights, minors of less than fifteen years old.

20. Ibid., 48; the historical background and the law of Moses also discussed on 6.

21. Alfred Niceforo, *La Police et l'enquete judiciaire scientifique* (Paris: Librarie Universelle, 1907), 399.

22. Dupré, *Le Témoignage*, 368.

23. Pierre Farcet, *Du faux-témoignage* (Poitiers, 1902), 5; for the parliamentary records, see the *Journel officiel* (Paris), sessions of Dec. 4 and June 22, 1882, references to debates over the oath on 997, 1110, 1533.

24. Dupré, *Le Témoignage*, 367.

25. Dossier, "L'Affaire Cayotte," prosecutor's and investigator's reports.

26. Dossier from archives of the Ministère de la Justice, BB 18 2374 139 A08, news clippings collected from *L'Action*, March 6, 1908.

27. Ibid.; news clippings collected from *La Petite républicaine*, Jan. 6, 1909; *Le Radical*, Jan. 6, 1909; *La Lanterne*, Jan. 6, 1909.

28. Dupré, *Le Témoignage*, 345. See Jan Goldstein, *Console and Classify: The French Psychiatric Profession in the Nineteenth Century* (Cambridge: Cambridge Univ. Press, 1987), ch. 6.

29. Dupré, *Le Témoignage*, 348.

30. Dr André Fribourg, "Nouvelles expériences sur le témoignage," in *Révue de Synthèse Historique* 14, no. 40 (1907): 405. In this literature see also Fribourg, "La Psychologie du témoignage en histoire," *Revue de synthèse historique* 12, no. 36 (1905): 265; Dr. Edouard Claparède, "Expériences collectives sur le témoignage," *Archives de Psychologie* 5, no. 20 (May 1906); article on testimony by Dr. Claparède, "La psychologie judiciaire," *Année psychologique* (1906).

31. Fribourg, "Nouvelles expériences," 4–5, 7.

32. Dupré, *Le Témorignage*, 353.

33. Reported in Fribourg, "Nouvelles expériences," 6, 9, 12.

34. Ibid., 12. See Shosana Felman and Dori Laub, *Testimony: Crises of Witnessing in Literature, Psychoanalysis, and History* (New York: Routledge, 1992).

35. In Fribourg, "Nouvelles expériences," 9–12; see also Niceforo, *La police et l'enquete judiciare scientifiques*, 399.

36. Fourquet, *Les Faux-témoins*, 9.

37. Dr. Ernest Dupré, *La Mythomanie: ouverture du course de psychiatrie mético légale: étude psychologique et médico-légale du mensonge et de la fabulation morbides* (1905), 28.

38. Ibid., 29–30.

39. Janice Haaken, "Sexual Abuse, Recovered Memory, and Therapeutic Practice: A Feminist Psychoanalytic Perspective," *Social Text* 40, 12, no. 3 (Fall 1994): 126. On the "category of Woman," see Judith Butler, "Gender Trouble: Feminist Theory, and Psychoanalytic Discourse," in Linda J. Nicholson, ed., *Feminism/Postmodernism* (New York: Routledge, 1990), 324–40.

40. Dupré, *Le Témoignage*, 357–58.

41. Fourquet, *Les Faux-témoins*, 9, and Dupré, *Le Témoignage*, 355.

42. See Joan B. Landes, *Women and the Public Sphere in the Age of the French Revolution* (Ithaca: Cornell Univ. Press, 1988); Craig Calhoun, ed., *Habermas and the Public Sphere* (Cambridge, Mass.: MIT Press, 1993); Janice Doane and Devon Hodges, *Nostalgia and Sexual Difference* (New York and London: Methuen, 1987); Karen Dubinsky, *Improper Advances: Rape and Heterosexual Conflict in Ontario, 1880–1924* (Chicago: Univ. of Chicago Press, 1993), 35–63.

43. Dupré, *La Mythomanie*, 20.

44. Ibid., 50.

45. Haaken, "Sexual Abuse," 116.

46. Karen Offen, "Depopulation, Nationalism, and Feminism in Fin-de-Siècle France," *American Historical Review* 89 (1984): 648–76. Ruth Harris, "The 'Child of the Barbarian': Rape, Race and Nationalism in France during the First World War," *Past and Present*, no. 141 (Nov. 1993): 170–206. Edward Berenson, *The Trial of Madame Caillaux* (Berkeley and Los Angeles: Univ. of California Press, 1992), 110–21. Silverman, *Art Nouveau in Fin-de-Siècle France*, 63–74.

47. Dupré, *Le Témoignage*, 357.

48. Dupré, *La Mythomanie*, 48.

49. This version as recounted by Fourquet, *Les Faux-témoins*, 118–29.

50. Ibid., 129.

51. Ibid., 118–29; Brouardel's comment cited by Fourquet, from Brouardel, "L'Hysterie et le mariage," *Revue de l'hypnotisme*, as cited in Fourquet, *Les Faux-témoins*, 285; for a modern and equally skeptical reading of the case against de la Roncière, see the thesis on the "impossible crime" by Pierre Maurice-Garçon, *L'Affaire la Roncière* (Tours: A. Mame, 1971); see also Robert A. Nye, *Masculinity and Male Codes of Honor in Modern France* (New York: Oxford Univ. Press, 1993), for insights on the duel.

52. Dr. Laennec, *Rapport médico-legal sur une enquete judiciare motivée par une fausse accusation de viol* (report dated July 20, 1888), 2–5.

53. See Geoffrey Hartman, "The Voice of the Shuttle: Language from the Point of View of Literature," in *Beyond Formalism: Literary Essays 1958–1970* (New Haven: Yale Univ. Press, 1970), as cited by Patricia Klindienst Joplin, "The Voice of the Shuttle Is Ours," in Lynn A. Higgins and Brenda R. Silver, eds., *Rape and Representation* (New York: Columbia Univ. Press, 1991), 35–36.

54. Laennec, *Rapport médico-legal*, 5. See also Jean-Marc Belier, *La police des moeurs sous la IIIe République* (Paris: Le Seuil, 1992); Mary Jacobus, Evelyn Fox-Keller, and Sally Shuttleworth, *Body/Politics: Women and the Discourses of Science* (New York and London: Routledge, 1989); Ann Dally, *Women Under the Knife: A History of Surgery* (New York and London: Routledge, 1992); on narratives, see Felman and Laub, *Testimony: Crises of Witnessing*, Katherine Cummings, *Telling Tales: The Hysteric's Seduction in Fiction and Theory* (Stanford: Stanford Univ. Press, 1992).

55. Laennec, *Rapport médico-legal*, 5. Questions of medical "seeing": Michel Foucault, *The Birth of the Clinic: An Archaeology of Medical Perception* (New York: Random House, 1974) chap. 7, "Voir/Savoir." Foucault argues that observation and experience are reconcilable, "but on the condition that questions are put only in the vocabulary and inside the language which has been suggested to it by the things observed" (p. 108).

56. Dupré, *Le Témoignage*, 353.

57. P. Brouardel, *Des causes d'erreur dans les expertises relatives aux attentats à la pudeur* (1884).

58. Dr. Ducor, *Rapport sur la réforme des expertises médico-légales* (Clermont: Daix frères, 1898), 8.

59. Brouardel, *Des causes d'erreur,* 3–4.

60. Ibid., 6.

61. See Luce Irigaray, "Any Theory of the Subject Has Already Been Appropriated by the Masculine," *Speculum of the Other Woman,* Gillian Gill, trans. (Ithaca: Cornell Univ. Press, 1985); Julia Kristeva, "Woman Can Never Be Defined," in Elaine Marks and Isabelle de Coutivron, eds., *New French Feminisms* (New York: Schocken, 1984).

62. Alexandre Lacassagne, *Précis de médicine légale* (Paris: Masson et Cie, 1906), 92.

63. Ducor, *Rapport sur la réforme,* 13. Though I do not treat the subject here, a serious understanding of the production of testimony would have to consider not only the assumptions and institutions behind the witnesses and experts, but also the "performative" aspect of testimony—its "material act." See the thesis of Katherine Fischer Taylor on the links between authority, evidence, and performance in *In the Theater of Criminal Justice: The Palais de Justice in Second Empire Paris* (Princeton: Princeton Univ. Press, 1993).

64. In the twentieth century, experts are both male and female, and as with Dupré's critique of Charcot's hysteria, debates rage over whether professional psychotherapists elicit or actually invent their patient's "memories." See Ellen Bass and Laura Davis, *The Courage to Heal: A Guide for Women Survivors of Child Sexual Abuse* (New York: Harper, 1994); Elizabeth Loftus and Katherine Ketcham, *The Myth of Repressed Memory: False Memories and Allegations of Sexual Abuse* (New York: St. Martin's, 1994), also Crews' "The Myth of Repressed Memory."

65. Dr. A. Motet, *Bulletin de la Société de Médicine Légale de France* (Clermont-Ferrand, 1899), 16.

Chapter 6: Identities

1. "Fin de siècle," from Max Nordau, *Degeneration of Our Contemporary Civilization* (Lincoln and London: Univ. of Nebraska Press/Bison Books, 1993); Joris-Karl Huysmans, *Against Nature* (New York: Penguin, 1982); Eugen Weber, *France: Fin de siècle* (Cambridge, Mass.: Belknap/Harvard Univ. Press, 1986); Hillel Schwartz, *Century's End* (New York: Doubleday, 1990); Daniel Milo, *Trahir le temps* (Paris: Belles Lettres, 1991).

2. Emile Fourquet, "Les Vagabonds criminels," *Revue des deux mondes* (Dec. 15, 1889): 418.

3. On memory and the state, see the essays collected under "L'Etat," from Pierre Nora, ed., *Les Lieux de mémoire,* vol. II: *La Nation* (Paris: Ed. Gallimard, 1986); Thomas Richards, *The Imperial Archive: Knowledge and the Fantasy of Empire* (London and New York: Verso, 1993); Christopher Dandeker, *Surveillance, Power and Modernity: Bureaucracy and Discipline from 1700 to the Present Day* (Cambridge: Polity, 1990); Mary Douglas, *How Institutions Think* (London: Routledge, 1986).

4. Gabriel Tarde, *La Philosophie pénale* (Paris: Maloine, 1905), 333; see also Marie and R. Meunier, *Les Vagabonds* (Paris: V. Girard & E. Brière, 1908), 45.

5. Report, *Prefecture de police to the President du conseil ministre de l'interieur* Paris (May 1902), Archives of the Prefecture de police, Series DB 284, doc.
3–4.

6. Emile Garçon, ed., *Le Code pénale* (annotated), Article 270, with history
(Paris: Dalloz, 1956).

7. Fourquet, "Les Vagabonds criminels," 418.

8. Vacher's testimony in Marie and R. Meunier, *Les Vagabonds*, 232. See
also detailed transcripts of trial arguments in Alexandre Lacassagne, *Vacher l'éventreur et les crimes sadiques* (Paris and Lyon: A. Storck & Cie., 1899).

9. Alfred Lagresille, *Du vagabondage et de la transportation* (Nancy, 1881),
6–7.

10. Ibid., 78.

11. Commentaries on proposed legislation by Maurice-Fauré to establish
shelters and work houses for disabled or unemployed workers (Session of the
Chamber of Deputies, May 9, 1891), in G. Mabille du Chêne, *Les Invalides du
travail* (Samur, 1892), 16. See also Alfred Comat, *La Dépopulation des campagnes: projet de loi 1910* (8F.4515), document, Bibliothéque Nationale, Paris, on
the establishment of the *caisse agricole* to provide financial support for farmers as
a remedy to rural migration and statistical increases in crime and vagabondage,
esp. 12, 21–24.

12. Eugen Weber, *Peasants into Frenchmen* (Stanford: Stanford Univ. Press,
1976).

13. Fourquet, "Les Vagabonds criminels," 400.

14. Ibid., 401–2.

15. André's comment, *Criminalité et civilisation* (1896), 34; Arsene
Dumont, *Dépopulation et civilisation* (1890; rpt., Paris: Economica, 1990),
179.

16. Statistical materials collected from Le Roy, *Vagabonds nomades et gens
sans aveu* (1899), 196; Mabille du Chêne, *Les Invalides du travail*, 2–3; Lagresille,
Du vagabondage et de la transportation 102–3.

17. Dumont, *Dépopulation et civilisation*, 180.

18. Fourquet, "Les Vagabonds Criminels," 402–3.

19. Alexandre Bérard, "Le Vagabondage en France," *Archives de anthropologie criminelle* 13 (1898): 601–14.

20. Adrien Sée, *Le Passeport en France* (Chartes: Garnier, 1907), 14; Fourquet, "Les Vagabonds criminels," 430.

21. Marie and R. Meunier, *Les Vagabonds*, 20–21.

22. Ibid., 24.

23. See Jean-Marie Charcot, *Leçons du mardi à la Salpêtrière 1887–1888*
(Paris: RETZ, 1974), 76–77 on somnambulism; literary discussion of wandering
and psychological disorder with reference to Lady Macbeth, 117–18; Commentaries on Charcot's work in Marie and R. Meunier, *Les Vagabonds*, 142.

24. See Pierre Janet, "Interprétation de l'oubli au réveil après la somnabul-
ism," *L'Automatisme psychanalytique* (Paris: Félix Alcan, 1899). Also A. Joffroy
and R. Dupoy, *Fuges et vagabondages* (Paris: Felix Alcan, 1909), 153–55.

25. Ibid., 3–5.

26. Emanuelle Regis, *La Dromomanie de Jean-Jacques Rousseau* (1910), on
Geneva, 6; on nature, 1–2.

27. Ibid., 6.

28. Jean Richepin—writer, poet, playwright (1849–1926), elected to the

Académie Française in 1908. This selection from Jean Richepin's *Le Cheminau* (1897), cited by Regis in ibid., 8. Richepin also exalted the inhabitants of the margins of society in *La Chanson des gueux* (1876).

29. Regis, *La Dromonanie,* 8.

30. Marie and R. Meunier, *Les Vagabonds,* 25.

31. Ibid., 38–40. Pagnier cited by Joffroy and Dupoy, *Fuges et vagabondages,* 155. Consider Gilles Deleuze's and Felix Guattari's "nomad philosophy," *A Thousand Plateaus: Capitalism and Schizophrenia,* vol. II, Brian Massumi, trans. (Minneapolis: Univ. of Minnesota Press, 1980).

32. Alexandre Lacassagne, *Précis de médicine legale* (Paris: Masson & Cie, 1906), 189.

33. Ibid.

34. Fourquet, "Les Vagabonds Criminels," 425.

35. "Le Vagabond," collected in Guy de Maupassant, *Le Horla* (Paris: Albin Michel, 1980), 231–32.

36. Le Roy, *Vagabonds nomades et gens sans aveu* 207.

37. Sée, *Le Passeport en France,* 136.

38. Ibid., 107. This question of identity was considered historically by La-cassagne, who cited the case of Martin Guerre in his work. See Natalie Davis, *The Return of Martin Guerre* (Cambridge, Mass.: Harvard Univ. Press, 1983).

39. See Rogers Brubaker, *Citizenship and Nationhood in France and Germany* (Cambridge, Mass.: Harvard Univ. Press, 1992), 27–29. Also, Claudine Dardy, *Identités de papiers* (Paris: Lieu Commun, 1990); Dieter Hoffmann-Axthelm, "Identity and Reality: The End of the Philosophical Immigration Officer," in Scott Lash and Jonathan Friedman, eds., *Modernity and Identity* (Cambridge: Blackwell, 1992), 196–218.

40. Sée, *Le Passeport en France,* 14.

41. Ibid., 137–38. Also, Marechal La Fontaine, *L'Invasion pacifique de la France par les étrangers* (1886). One hundred years later, the question of immigration and identity control continues: "Reinforced identity controls" and "New conditions for obtaining the French nationality," articles in *Le Monde,* (June 11, 1993), 11.

42. Le Roy, *Vagabonds nomades et gens sans aveu,* 207.

43. Reports from the Ministry of the Interior (Nov. 18, 1885), Archives of the Prefecture of Police, DB 284. See also the article from *Le Petit journal,* Aug. 26, 1881, offering a balance sheet of the nineteenth century: "the increase of transactions, extension of person to person exchanges, movement and circulation, rapid travel. . . ."

44. Gravures from *L'Illustration* (Nov. 10, 1887). See the collections of instruments and partial reconstitution of the "salle de mensuration" in the Museum of the Historical Collections of the Prefecture of Police, Hotel de Police du Ve arrondisement, Paris. On Bertillon, see his own Alphonse Bertillon, *Notice sur le fonctionnement du service d'identification de la prefecture de police* (Paris: G. Masson, 1889). In the prefecture's collections, cartons DB 47 and DB 48 contain a wide variety of documents pertaining to the Bertillon's "Service d'identité judiciaire."

45. Commentaries on Bertillon's system by Alfred Niceforo, *La Police et l'enquete judiciaire scientifique* (Paris: Librarie Universelle, 1907): 379. See also the placement of figures and backgrounds in Louis Tomellini, *Photographique metrique système Bertillon* (Lyon: A. Rey, 1908).

46. Reported in *Le Matin* (Dec. 17, 1903), collected by the Prefecture de Police, DB 47.

47. Niceforo, *La Police*, 394.

48. Motlet cited by R. A. Reiss, *Un code télégraphique du portrait parlé* (A. Maloine, 1907), 1.

49. Dr. S. Icard, "Code signaletique international," *Archives d'anthropologie criminelle et de médecine legale* (Lyon, August-Sept. 1912): 565. The following code description, p. 571.

50. Ibid., 561.

51. *La Republique française*, Dec. 7, 1876, "Une serie d'experiences extrement interessantes d'un system de photographie télégraphique," and *Les Droits de l'homme*, Feb. 1, 1877.

52. See Gabriel Tarde, *La Philosophie pénale* (Paris: Maloine, 1905), 333; also Fourquet's citations of Tarde in Fourquet, "Les vagabonds criminels," 427–28.

53. Niceforo, *La Police*, 65. This part of the chapter on the science of the trace owes much to Carlo Ginzburg, "Clues: Roots of an Evidential Paradigm," in *Clues, Myths, and Historical Method*, John and Anne C. Tedeschi, trans. (Baltimore: Johns Hopkins, Univ. Press, 1989).

54. Dr. Fouveau de Courmelles, *Identité par les os et les dents* (Vannes, 1919), 9. A devastating fire at a charity bazaar raised the eternal question of identification to the Prefecture of Police, which sent a proposal to the Conseil Municipal of Paris regarding the possible creation of an "identity medallion" which could not be altered by fire. (The proposal was refused.) Collections of the Prefecture de police, DB 109, April 29, 1899.

55. Fouveau de Courmelles, *Identité parles os et les dents*, 13.

56. Cited in Lacassagne, *Vacher l'éventreur*, 309.

57. Ibid., 1–70 passim for Lacassagne's report and legal-medical commentaries. See also Marie and R. Meunier, *Les Vagabonds*, 241 for Lacassagne's conclusions.

58. Lacassagne, *Vacher l'eventreur*, collected documents and reports: the doctor's conclusions on Vacher's method, 17; impulsive rage, 29; strangulation and Eugenie Delhomme, 43; blood, 44; Destot's report on the x-ray of Vacher's ear, 309.

59. "Histologie du myelencephale de Vacher," *Revue de psychiatrie* (Clermont: Daix Frères, 1900). The brain was examined primarily by Dr. Edouard Toulouse, who also sent parts of it to the Salpêtrière and to the Asile Saint-Anne. Toulouse reported, "one notes certain pyramidal cells which do not appear normal." Lombroso reported, "we have found in Vacher anomalies which one especially finds in born-criminals."

59. Marie and R. Meunier, *Les Vagabonds*, 242.

Chapter 7: Distances

1. *Note sur la collection ethnographique du musée de Caen* (M. E. Eudes-Deslongchamps, 1889), 37 and 42.

2. Le Père Lambert, *Moeurs et superstitions des Néo-Calédoniennes* (Noumea, 1900), 67.

3. Marguerite and Georges Lobsiger-Dellenbach, "Les gravures sur bambou, transcription authentique de la langue et de la pensée des

Néo-Calédoniennes," *Geographica Helvetica*, no. 4 (1966): 1. Also, Lobsinger-Dellenbach, *Trois bambous gravés* (1957) and *Bambous gravés de la Nouvelle Calédonie* (1936). See also Eliane Metais-Daudre, *Les Bandes dessinées des Néo-Calédoniennes* (1973).

4. Edmond Bruyant, *Etude sur la transportation* (Paris: Arthur Rousseau, 1889), 1.

5. Larousse, *Grand dictionnaire universel du XIX siècle*, tome XVI (1877). 442.

6. Alexandre Bérard, *La Transportation des recidivistes et les colonies françaises* (Lyon, 1885), 15; M. Michaux in Edouard Teisseire, *La Transportation pénale et la relegation* (Paris, 1893), 422.

7. G. Pierret, *Transportation et colonisation pénale* (La Tribune des colonies et des protectorates, 1892), 2. See also C. Forster, "French Penal Policy and the Origins of the French Presence in New Caledonia," *Journal of Pacific History* 26 (Dec. 1991): 135–50.

8. L. Manouvrier, "Les Cranes des supplicies," *Archives de anthropologie criminelle*, no. 1 (1886): 125.

9. Alfred Lagresille, *Du vagabondage et de la transportation* (Nancy, 1881), 80–81.

10. Speech of March 31, 1854, cited by James-Nathan, *Essais sur la réforme penitentiaire* (Paris: Société générale des prisons 1886), 40.

11. Robert Badinter, *La Prison républicaine* (Paris: Fayard, 1992); M. d'Haussonville, "Rapport à l'Assemblée Nationale," *Journal officiel* (Aug. 21–27, 1874). See Gaile McGregor, *The Noble Savage in the New World Garden: Notes Toward a Syntactics of Place* (Toronto: Univ. of Toronto Press, 1988).

12. Alphonse Bertillon, *L'Identité des récidivistes et la loi de rélegation* (Paris: G. Masson, 1883), 1, 8–10.

13. Dr. A. Bordier, "Les Récidivistes," *Le National*, Sept. 13, 1881.

14. Ibid.

15. Louise Michel, *Légendes et chantes de gestes canaques* (Keva, 1885). Letter dated June 26, 1875.

16. Dr. M. A. Legrand, *Au pays des canaques: la Nouvelle Calédonie et ses inhabitants en 1890* (Librarie militaire de L. Baudon, 1893), 188. See Anthony Pagden, *European Encounters with the New World: From Renaissance to Romanticism* (New Haven: Yale Univ. Press, 1993).

17. Larousse, *Grand dictionnaire universel du XIX siècle*, tome XVI (1877), 442.

18. Leon Moncelon, *Les Canaques de la Nouvelle-Calédonie* (Paris: Henri Jouve, 1886), 5–6.

19. Jules Garnier, "La Nouvelle Calédonie a l'exposition de 1878," *Bulletin de la société de géographie* (Feb. 1879): 9–10.

20. Missionary notes from *La Tribu de Wagrap, d'après les notes d'un missionaire mairiste* (Chadenet, 1890), 8.

21. M. Ben-Mill, *La Nouvelle Calédonie devoilée: considerations sur la révolte des naturels et de l'avenir de la colonie* (no date), 7.

22. Moncelon, *Les Canaques*, 32.

23. Press reaction from *Le Voltaire*, Aug. 25, 1881. Reports from the Prefecture of Police cited in a report to the Ministry of the Interior, Archives of the Prefecture of Police, Paris, Series DB 284, documents 3–4.

24. Robert Nye, *Crime, Madness, and Politics in Modern France* (Princeton: Princeton Univ. Press, 1984), 83.

25. Edmond Bruyant, *Etude sur la transportation* (Paris: Arthur Rousseau, 1889), 58, and G. Pierret, *Transportation et colonisation pénale* (Paris: La Tribune des colonies et des protectorates 1892), preface.

26. James-Nathan, *Essais sur la réforme penitentiaire,* 37–38.

27. Lagresille, *Du vagabondage et de la transportation,* 80.

28. Mirail, speech of March 31, 1854, cited by James-Nathan, *Essais sur la réforme penitentiaire,* 40.

29. Bruyant, *Etude sur la transportation,* 58.

30. Charles Ploix, Discourse at meeting of July 6, 1871, collected in *Bulletins de la Société d'Anthropologie de Paris,* tome 6 (Paris: G. Masson, 1877), 23.

31. These commentaries from ibid., 25; Edmond Plauchut, "La Révolte des canaques," *Revue des deux mondes* (Dec. 1, 1878): 688; Michaux in Edouard Teissière, *La Transportation pénale et la relegation* (L. Lapose & Forel, 1893), 423; Legrand, *Au pays de canaques,* 111.

32. Henri Rivière, *Souvenirs de la Nouvelle Calédonie: l'insurrection Canaque* (Paris: Calman-Levy, 1881), 11–12.

33. Bruyant, *Etude sur la transportation,* 58.

34. See *Lettres de la Nouvelle Calédonie,* no date, collections of the Bibliothèque Nationale. On ministerial telegrams, see Ministère de la Marine et des colonies, *Notice sur la transportation à la Guyane française et à la Nouvelle Calédonie pour l'année 1885* (1889), 550, Oct. 24, 1885.

35. Mirail, speech of March 31, 1854, cited by James-Nathan, *Essais sur la réforme penitentiaire,* 27; *Du vagabondage et de la transportation,* 80.

36. Ministère de la marine et des colonies, *Lois, décrets, et regelements relatifs à la transportation* (1886), article 4, p. 65.

37. Bruyant, *Etude sur la transportation,* 43.

38. Ministère de la Marine et des colonies (1889), 550, July 30, 1885.

39. Charles Bertheau, *De la transportation des recidivistes incorrigibles* (A. Marescq, 1882), 63.

40. James-Nathan, *Essais sur la réforme penetentiaire,* 27–28.

41. Bruyant, *Etude sur la transportation,* 44–45.

42. P. Oregas's *Le non-cosmopolitisme de l'homme* (1885), for the Ministère de la Marine.

43. Bruyant, *Etude sur la transportation,* 2.

44. Commentaries by Ben-Mill, *La Nouvelle-Calédonie devoilée,* 14; Legrand, *Au pays des canaques,* 119; Bruyant, Etude, *sur la transportation,* 55.

45. Garnier, "La Nouvelle Calédonie a l'exposition de 1878," 10.

46. Plauchut, "La Révolte des canaques," 676. For commentaries on this event and other political and social unrest in the islands, see Apollonaire Anova Ataba, *D'Atai à l'independence* (Nouméa: Edipop, 1984); Alex Philcat, *La Révolte des poyes en Nouvelle-Calédonie* (Nanterre: Académie Européene du Livre, 1989). On historical confrontation see Joel Dauphiné, Pouebo: *Histoire d'une tribu Canaque sous le second empire* (Paris: L'Harmattan, 1992).

47. Leon Moncelon, "Lettre à l'Amiral Peyron, Ministre de la Marine," in *Les canaques,* 28–29. On colonial tropes, David Spurr, *The Rhetoric of Empire: Colonial Discourse in Journalism, Travel Writing, and Imperial Administration* (Durham: Duke Univ. Press, 1993); on revolt, E. J. Hobsbawm, *Primitive Rebels*

(New York: Norton, 1959); Michael Adas, *Prophets of Rebellion: Millenarian Protest Movements against the European Colonial Order* (Cambridge: Cambridge Univ. Press, 1979).

48. Comments cited by Jean Baronnet and Jean Chalou in *Communards en Nouvelle Calédonie* (Paris: Mercure de France, 1987), 323 and 327. Also, "Les Deportés de la Commune à Nouvelle-Calédonie il y a un siècle," special issue of *La Commune,* nos. 9–10 (Amis de la Commune de Paris, March 1978). For details on the conditions of the Communards in the islands, see also Georges Pisier, *Les Déportés de la commune à l'Ile des Pins* (Société des Océanistes, 1971), and *Kounié ou l'ile des Pins* (Noumea: Société des Etudes Historiques de la Nouvelle-Calédonie, 1971). See also testimonies from Jean Allemane, *Mémoires d'un communard: des barricades au bagne* (Librarie socialiste, n.d.); Henri Messager, *Lettres de déportation 1871–6* (Le Sycomore, 1979); Joannes Caton, *Journal d'un déporté: 1871–79 de la commune à l'Ile des pins* (France-Empire, 1986); *Déportés et Forçats de la Commune: de Belleville à Noumea* (Ouest éd., 1991). The best new work on the deportation and Communard memory is Alice Bullard, "Self-Representation in the Arms of Defeat: Fatal Nostalgia and Surviving Comrades in French New Caledonia, 1871–1880," in "Primitivism and the Paris Commune, the Making of French National Identity" (Ph.D. dissertation, Univ. of California, Berkeley, 1994).

49. Amoroux and Henri Place, *L'Administration et les maristes en Nouvelle Calédonie: insurrection des kanaks en 1878–9* (Perinet, 1887), 6.

50. Le Père Lambert, *Moeurs et superstitions,* 47.

51. See Tzvetan Todorov, *On Human Diversity: Nationalism, Racism, Exoticism in French Thought* (Cambridge, Mass.: Harvard Univ. Press, 1993), 111–13, 133–35.

52. Ploix, Discourse at meeting of July 6, 1871, 20–21.

53. Dr. Victor de Rochas, *La Nouvelle Calédonie et ses inhabitants* (Ferdinand Sartorius, 1862), 157.

54. Ben-Mill, *La Nouvelle-Calédonie devoilée,* 19.

55. Eliane Métais, *Au commencement était la terre: réflexions sur un mythe canaque d'origine* (Bordeaux: Presses Universitaires de Bordeaux, 1988), 14–15. Also, Nathan Wachtel, *La vision des vaincus: les indiens du Pérou devant la conquete espagnole* (Paris: Ed. Gallimard, 1971); Clifford Geertz, "From the Native's Point of View: On the Nature of Anthropological Understanding," in *Local Knowledge: Further Essays in Interpretive Anthropology* (New York: Basic Books, 1983), 55–70.

56. Lagresille, *Du vagabondage et de la transportation,* 81. On colliding narrative frameworks, Marshall Sahlins, *Islands of History* (Chicago: Univ. of Chicago Press, 1985); and *Historical Metaphor and Mythical Realities* (Ann Arbor: Univ. of Michigan Press, 1981); Gananath Obeyesekere, *The Apotheosis of Captain Cook: European Mythmaking in the Pacific* (Princeton and Honolulu: Princeton Univ. Press and Bishop Museum Press, 1992).

57. Ibid., 81; also Moncelon, *Les Canaques,* 32.

58. Legrand, *Au pays des canaques,* 39. On developing the islands see the timetable of Joel Dauphiné, *Chronologie foncière et agricole de la Nouvelle-Calédonie 1853–1903* (Paris: L'Harmattan, 1987). Also, Fredrick Cooper, "Colonizing Time: Work Rhythms and Labor Conflict in Colonial Mombasa," in Nicholas B. Dirks, ed., *Colonialism and Culture* (Ann Arbor: Univ. of Michigan Press, 1992), 209–246.

59. Place and Place, *L'Administration*, 25, 32; Garnier, "La Nouvelle Calédonie," 20; Rivière, *Souvenirs*, 281–82.

60. Place and Place, *L'Administration*, 7; Louise Michel, *Légendes et chantes*, 144. See the important thesis of Johannes Fabian, *Time and the Other: How Anthropology Makes Its Object* (New York: Columbia Univ. Press, 1983), esp. "Our Time, Their Time, No Time: Coevalness Denied," 37–70.

61. Legrand, *Au pays des canaques*, 119; Rivière, *Souvenirs*, 282; Place and Place, *L'Administration*, 8. On the European logic of the other becoming the self through a totalizing dialectic, see Robert Young, *White Mythologies: Writing History and the West* (London and New York: Routledge, 1990), 1–68, and Michel de Certeau, *The Writing of History*, Tom Conley, trans. (New York: Columbia Univ. Press, 1988).

62. Eliane Métais, *Au commencement était la terre*, 149–50.

63. Comment by Jean Allemane, cited by Baronnet and Chalou in *Communards en Nouvelle Calédonie*, 328. For the further history of Atai's head, see Roselène Dousset-Leenhardt, *Terre natale, terre d'exil* (Paris: G. P. Maisonneuve & Larouse, 1976), 17; also, Dousset-Leenhardt's *Colonialisme et contradictions, la Nouvelle-Calédonie 1878–1978: les causes de l'insurrection de 1878* (Paris: L'Harmattan, 1978).

Chapter 8: Spectacles

1. Michel Georges-Michel, *En Jardinant avec Bergson* (Paris: Albin Michel, 1926), 14–16; interviews with the famous and celebrated; the specific date of the Bergson encounter not cited. On Bergsonian memory and cinema, Gilles Deleuze, *Cinema I/Cinema II*, H. Tomlinson, B. Habberjam, and R. Gareta, trans., 2 vols. (Minneapolis: Univ. of Minnesota Press, 1986/1989), esp. vol. 1, "The Movement-Image."

2. Méliès's mémoirs, Malthéte Méliès, ed., *Centennaire de Georges Méliès* (1861–1961), BN 8LN27.73389, Bibliothèque Nationale, Paris, 62; for an excellent survey, Georges Sadoul, *Histoire générale du cinéma*, vol. I: *L'Invention du cinéma*, and vol. II: *Les Pionniers du cinéma 1897–1909* (Paris: Denoel, 1948)

3. See Maurice Bessy and Lo Duca, *Méliès, mage* (J. J. Pauvert, 1961); Georges Sadoul, *Georges Méliès* (Paris: Hachette, 1973); Paul Hammond, *Marvelous Méliès* (New York, 1974).

4. Andreas Huyssens, "Monument and Memory in a Postmodern Age," *Yale Journal of Criticism* 6, no. 2 (1993): 249–61. On cinema, memory, technology, and perception, see Paul Virilio, *La Machine de vision* (Paris: Ed. Galilée, 1988), esp. 13–27; Maureen Turim, *Flashbacks in Film: Memory and History* (London and New York: Routledge, 1989); Robert A. Rosenston, ed., *Revisioning History: Film and the Construction of a New Past* (Princeton: Princeton Univ. Press, 1995).

5. The "Hegelian dialectic" between the brothers Lumière and Méliès is the thesis of Sigfried Kracauer, *Theory of Film: Redemption of Physical Reality* (Oxford: Oxford Univ. Press, 1960).

6. Boleslas Matuszewski, *Une nouvelle source de l'histoire* (March 1898), BN 8V 12363, Bibliothèque Nationale, Paris, p. 9.

7. On modern vision, see Jonathan Crary, *Techniques of the Observer* (Cambridge, Mass.: MIT Press, 1990); Martin Jay, *Downcast Eyes: The Denigration of Vision in Twentieth-Century French Thought* (Berkeley and Los Angeles: Univ. of

California Press, 1993); David Michael Levin, ed., *Modernity and the Hegemony of Vision* (Berkeley and Los Angeles: Univ of California Press, 1993); Tony Bennett, "The Exhibitionary Complex," in Nicholas B. Dirks, Geoff Eley, and Sherry B. Ortner, eds., *Culture/Power/History* (Princeton: Princeton Univ. Press, 1994), 123–154.

8. Matuszewski, *Une nouvelle source*, 10.

9. Ibid., 10.

10. In Méliès, *Centennaire de Georges Méliès*, 16; see also Léo Savage, *L'Affaire Lumière: du mythe à l'histoire, enquête sur les origines du cinéma* (Paris: L'Herminier, 1985). On the Lumière's attachment to science, see Auguste et Louis Lumière, *Résumé des travaux scientifiques* (Lyon, 1914) and *Annales des laboratoires* (Société des brevets Lumière, 1921); see also Jacques Rittaud-Hutinet, *Le Cinéma des origines: les frères Lumière et leurs opérateurs* (Champ Vallon-Seyssel, 1985), 19–32.

11. Text reproduced in Georges Sadoul, *Lumière et Méliès* (Paris: L'Herminier, 1961), 19. For Méliès's appraisal of his colleagues and competitors Lumiére, Gaumont, and Pathé, see Savage, *L'Affaire Lumière*, 33. For a complete listing of Méliès's work, see the project undertaken by the Centre Nationale de la Cinématographie, *Essai de reconstitution du catalogue français de la Star-Film* (1987). Also of note, *158 Scénarios de films disparus de Georges Méliès* (Paris: Association des Amis de Georges Méliès, 1986).

12. See the photographs and plans of Méliès's studio and atélier in Sadoul, *Lumière et Méliès*, 207, 218. For excellent reproductions of Méliès's set pieces and examples of his technological imagination, see the images in Centre Nationale de Photographie and the Cinémathèque Française, *Méliès: un homme d'illusions* (1986).

13. Méliès's writings collected in Méliès, *Centennaire de Georges Méliès*, 55–56; see also Georges Méliès, "Les Vues cinématographiques" (1907) cited in Sadoul, *Lumière et Méliès*, 90. On phantasmagoria, Susan Buck-Morss, *The Dialectics of Seeing: Walter Benjamin and the Arcades Project* (Cambridge, Mass.: MIT Press, 1991).

14. See comments on Méliès's *Le Couronnement du roi d'Angleterre Edouard VII* (1902) by Fernand Nozière in *L'Intransigeant*, Sept. 1913; also the report by *Le Petit bleu*, "denouncing the inauthenticity of the film" *Le Couronnement du roi d'Angleterre* cited by René Jeanne et Charles Ford, *Le Cinéma et la presse 1895–1960* (Paris: Armand Colin, 1961).

15. Edouard Poulain, *Contre le cinéma/pour le cinéma* (Strasbourg: Imp. de l'Est, 1917), 143.

16. Ibid., 136.

17. Ibid., 24; see Jean Baudrillard's commentary on the crash of the Tupelov at the Paris air show as the pilots watched themselves die on television, "L'Hyperréalisme de la simulation," in *L'Echange symbolique et la mort* (Paris: Galilée, 1976), 115–16. Note his description of "a hyperspace of representation in which everyone is already technically in possession of the instantaneous reproduction of his own life."

18. Poulain, *Contre le cinéma*, 24, 26.

19. Matuszweski, *Une nouvelle source*, 7.

20. René Doumic, *La Revue des deux mondes* (Aug. 15, 1913).

21. *La Poste*, Dec. 30, 1895; *Le Radical*, Dec. 30, 1895; see also the commentaries in Jeanne and Ford, *Le Cinéma et la presse;* articles published by *Le*

Radical, La Poste, Le Monde illustré, and *Le Magasin pittoresque* also collected by Sadoul, *Lumière et Méliès,* 102–3. On popular reaction to early motion pictures, see René Jeanne, *Cinéma 1900* (Paris: Flammarion, 1965), esp. 231–43.

22. Pierre Bourdieu, *Un art moyen: essai sur les usages sociaux de la photographie* (Paris, 1965), 53–54; see commentary by Jacques Le Goff, *Histoire et mémoire* (Paris: Gallimard, 1988), 161.

23. *Le Monde Illustré,* Jan. 25, 1896. Note also Sadoul's observation on the terminology used to designate early cinematic apparatuses—all coined from roots referring either to "life" or to "movement": vitascope, vitagraph, bioscope, biograph, kinetoscope, kinetograph, cinematograph. Sadoul, *L'Invention du cinéma,* 298.

24. *Le Monde illustré,* Jan. 25, 1896; on the question of the new urban landscape, Jacques Delandes, *Le Boulevard du cinéma à l'epoque du Georges Méliès* (Paris: Ed. du Cerf, 1963). A commanding theoretical attempt to understand the meaning of the motion picture image in Kracauer, *Theory of Film:* "Since any medium is partial to the things it is uniquely equipped to render, the cinema is conceivably animated by a desire to picture transient, material life, life at its most ephemeral" (p. ix).

25. *La Poste,* Dec. 30, 1895.

26. J. Rosen, "Ciné Journal," reproduced in Poulain, *Contre le cinéma,* 26.

27. *Le Progrès,* June 12–14, 1895, reports from the 14th.

28. *Les Annales,* April 28, 1896. On the effect of doubling, see Edgar Morin, *Le Cinéma ou l'homme imaginaire: essai d'anthropologie* (Paris: Ed. Minuit, 1956), chs. 2, 5, 8.

29. Maksim Gorky, in Nijegorodskilistok, July 4, 1896, collected in Emanuelle Toulet, *Cinématographe, invention du siècle* (Paris: Ed. Gallimard, 1988), 137.

30. Méliès, *Centennaire de Georges Méliès,* 62.

31. Ibid., 60.

32. Fernand Nozière in *L'Intransigeant.* On Méliès's directing style see Pierre Jenn, *Georges Méliès cinéaste* (Paris: Albatross, 1984).

33. E. Maugras and M. Guégan, *Le Cinématographe devant le droit* (Paris: V. Girard & E. Brière, 1908), 3–4.

34. Ibid., 15.

35. Ibid., 101–2.

36. Jean Marchais, *Du cinématographe dans ses rapports avec le droit de l'auteur* (Paris: V. Girard & E. Brière, 1912), 92. Note the commentaries on "partisans and detractors" of silent films in Roger Icart, *La Révolution du parlant vue par la presse française* (Perpignan: Institut Jean Vigo, 1988), ch. 4. Speaking films did not become commercialized in France until 1928–31.

37. Marchais, *Du cinématographe,* 92. See Christian Metz, *Langage et cinéma* (Paris: Albatross, 1977), esp. "Cinema and Writing," 191–97.

38. Maugras and Guégan, *Le Cinématographe,* 104–5.

39. Marchais, *Du cinématographe,* 35–36.

40. Maugras and Guégan, *Le Cinématographe,* 16–17.

41. Ibid., 18.

42. Marchais, *Du cinématographe,* 92.

43. Robert Dorgeval, "Le Cinéma contre le théâtre," from *Excelsior* Nov. 18, 1913.

44. Méliès, *Centennaire de Georges Méliès,* 65.

45. René Doumic, *La Revue des deux mondes,* Aug. 15, 1913. See Anne Friedberg, *Window Shopping: Cinema and the Postmodern* (Berkeley and Los Angeles: Univ. of California Press, 1993), and the concept of the "virtual mobilized gaze"; William C. Wees, *Light Moving in Time: Studies in the Visual Aesthetics of Avant-garde Film* (Berkeley and Los Angeles: Univ. of California Press, 1992).

46. Poulain, *Contre le cinéma,* 107.

47. Nozière, *L'Intransigeant.*

48. Maugras and Guégan, *Le Cinématographe,* 18; see also "Le cinématographe et l'art," *Excelsior,* Sept. 18, 1913, noting a competition to encourage writers and poets "of value" to find original formulas for stories to be made into films.

49. Gorky, in Toulet, *Cinématographe,* 138.

50. These images widely reproduced; see collections of the Cinémathèque Française in Paris. Of easier access, reproductions in Nicole Schmitt, *Affiches françaises du cinéma muet* (Institut Lumière, n.d.), part of an exhibition at Lyon, the birthplace of the cinema camera.

51. Méliès, *Centennaire de Georges Méliès,* 66.

Chapter 9: Desires

1. *Le Sourire,* xvi, no. 27 (July 1914). Also cited by R. C. Grogin, *The Bergsonian Controversy in France* (Calgary: Univ. of Calgary Press, 1988).

2. "Tangoville," from *L'Illustration journal universel* (1909–13): 282–83. See also caricatures by SEM (Georges Goursat) in a folio, *Tangoville sur mer* (Aug. 1913) at the Bibliothèque de l'Arsenal, Paris. For an overview of the subject, see Irene Frain, "Les premières tangos a Paris," *L'Histoire,* no. 79 (June 1985): 94–96.

3. For these commentaries, see *Londoners—The English Newspaper of Buenos Aires,* cited in Claude Fléouter, *Le Tango de Buenos Aires* (Paris: J. C. Lattès, 1979), 46.

4. Maria Susana Azzi, *Anthropologia del Tango* (Buenos Aires: Ed. de Olavarria, 1991); Pedro Figar, *Tango y condombre en el Rio de la Plata, 1861–1979* (Buenos Aires: Libreria Colonial, 1979); *La Historia del tango* (Buenos Aires: Corregidor, 1976); Simon Collier, "The Popular Roots of the Argentine Tango," *History Workshop Journal* 34 (1992); Donald S. Castro, *The Argentine Tango as Social History. 1880–1955: The Soul of the People* (Lewiston: Edward Mellen Press, 1991).

5. Juan Alvarez, *Origenes de la música Argentina* (Rosario, 1908), 21.

6. Documents collected in *Le Tango de Carlos Gardel* (Bibliothèque municipale de Toulouse, Nov. 1984). See also the thesis on tango and the insecurity of urban life in Buenos Aires in Horacio Salas, *Le Tango* (Paris: Actes Sud, 1989); Alice Dubronje-Ortiz, *Buenos Aires* (Paris: Presses Universitaires de France, 1984); Domingo F. Casadevall, *Buenos Aires: arrabal, sainete, tango* (Buenos Aires: Los Libros del Mirasol, 1968); Francisco Garcia Jimenez, *El Tango: historia de medio siglo, 1880–1930* (Buenos Aires: Editorial Universitaria de Buenos Aires, 1965). Also Christopher Shaw and Malcolm Chase, eds., *The Imagined Past: History and Nostalgia* (Manchester: Manchester Univ. Press, 1989); Noemi Ulla, *Tango: rebellion y nostalgia* (Buenos Aires: Centro Ed. de America Latina, 1982). See also the impressive thesis of Marta E. Savigliano, *Tango and the Political Economy of Passion* (Boulder, Colo.: Westview Press, 1995).

7. Fléouter, *Le Tango*, 50.

8. See *Le Tango: hommage a Carlos Gardel* (Univ. of Toulouse-Le Miral Eché, 1985), a collection of essays; Pedro Orgambide, *Gardel y la patria del mito* (Buenos Aires: Legasa, 1985). Consult collections of the Association Carlos Gardel, Centre de Documentation, 14, rue Alfred de Vigny, 31400 Toulouse, and the Centre Culturel Argentin at 27 avenue Pierre 1er de Serbie, 75016, Paris.

9. In Fernando O. Assunçao, *El Tango y sus circunstancias* (Buenos Aires: El Ateneo), 240. See also Paulette Patout and Alberto Blasi, *Guiraldes y Larbaud, una amistad creadora* (Buenos Aires: Nova, 1970). For fun reading, see Enrique Cadicamo, *La Historia del tango en Paris* (Buenos Aires: Corregidor, 1975).

10. Ricardo Guiraldes, "Tango," in *Obras Completas* (Buenos Aires, Emecé Ed., 1962), 63.

11. *Le Tango: hommage à Carlos Gardel*, 26. Also cited in C. de Néronde, *Les Danses nouvelles, le tango, la maxixe bresilienne, la forlane* (1920), 8V.40534, Bibliothèque Nationale, Paris, p. 28.

12. Michel Georges-Michel, *L'Epoque tango, cahiers d'une comedienne: la vie mondaine avant la guerre* (1920), 1–2.

13. Ibid., 2. Later in the text, the heroine runs into philosopher Henri Bergson in the street, watching the crowd go by. She asks him his opinion of the war which is coming: "Ah! It is a great contingency." On dance and war, Modris Eksteins, *Rites of Spring: The Great War and the Birth of the Modern Age* (New York: Anchor/Doubleday, 1989).

14. Catalogue, "Cartes postales de l'époque 1910–1914," from exhibition, *Le Tango de Carlos Gardel* (Bibliothèque municipale de Toulouse, Nov. 1984); Francisco Jiménez, *Estampas de tango* (Buenos Aires: Ed. Rodolfo Alfonso, 1968); also reproductions in Gilberte Cournand, "Apologie du tango," in P. Reinoso, O. Araiz, and A. Stampone, *Tango* (Lausanne: Pierre-Marcel Favre, 1982).

15. Fléouter, *Le Tango*, 44.

16. De Néronde, *Les Danses nouvelles*, 14.

17. Ibid., 26. Consider Jan Kott, *The Memory of the Body*, (Evanston: Northwestern Univ. Press, 1992), 113–22.

18. Ibid., 35.

19. Fléouter, *Le Tango*, 47.

20. André Warnod, *Bals, cafés, et cabarets* (Paris: E. Figuière, 1913), 15. See also Concetta Condemi, *Les Café-concerts: historie d'un divertissement 1849–1914* (Paris: Quai Voltaire, 1992); Marie-Véronique Gauthier, *Chanson, sociabilité et grivoiserie aux XIXe siècle* (Paris: Aubier, 1992).

21. Georges-Michel, *L'Epoque tango*, 54. For a general historical view, see "La Colonie-américaine de Paris en 1913," in Paulette Patout, *Alfonso Reyes et la France* (Paris: Klincksieck, 1978), 81.

22. De Neronde, *Les Danses nouvelles*, 35.

23. Ibid., 35.

24. Eric Hobsbawm and Terence Ranger, *The Invention of Tradition* (Cambridge: Canto, 1983); Jane K. Cowan, *Dance and the Body Politic in Northern Greece* (Princeton: Princeton Univ. Press, 1990).

25. *La Revue P.B.T.*, Sept. 22, 1913, cited also by *Le Tango*, 124.

26. Felipe Amadero Lastra, *Recuerdos del 900*, cited in Ulla, *Tango*, 27. See also the remarks by the Argentine minister in Paris as reported to *The Dancing Times: A Social Review of Dancing and Music*, no. 39 (Dec. 1913): 207: "To Argentine ears, tango music evokes ideas which are really unpleasant."

27. Yvonne Sarcey in her preface to Marguerite Moreno, *Une française en Argentine* (Georges Cres, 1914), 8–9. See Mary Louis Pratt, *Imperial Eyes: Travel Writing and Transculturation* (London and New York: Rutledge, 1992), 1–15; David Spurr, *The Rhetoric of Empire: Colonial Discourse in Journalism, Travel Writing, and Imperial Administration* (Durham: Duke Univ. Press, 1993), 43–75.

28. François Crastre, *A travers l'Argentine moderne* (Paris: Hachette, 1910), 33–36.

29. Juan-Pable Echague, *Paris-Journal*, May 12, 1911.

30. *El Hogar*, Dec. 20, 1911.

31. Crastre, *A travers l'Argentine moderne*, 8. See the thesis of Assunçao, *El Tango y sus circunstancias*, on the Buenos Aires of the 1870s: "each time more accelerated, in the process of economic and, one could say, technological change: streetcars, railway lines, running water, gas, electricity, telegraph . . . " (p. 46.)

32. Henri Cordier, *Buenos Aires en 1910, extrait du correspondant* (1910), 28–31.

33. Ibid., 30.

34. *Souvenir de la réepublique Argentine: exposition internationale du nord de la France à Roubaix* (1911), 1.

35. Max Rivera, *Le Tango et les danses nouvelles* (Paris: Les Petits Bouqins, 1913), 10.

36. Assunçao, *El Tango y sus circumstances*, 242.

37. Yvonne Sarcey in Moreno, *Une française en Argentine*, 7.

38. *Expositions internationales de Buenos Aires: rapport du commissaire générale du gouvernement de la république* (1910), 194. The report is also a catalogue of four major categories of exposition: agriculture, railways and land-based transport, health, and fine arts.

39. Crastre, *A travers l'Argentine moderne*, 13–14. Note gendered language: "If the woman in Buenos Aires is a pretty decoration, precious and delicate, having need of wealth and support, the man is a slave to work" (p. 13).

40. Juan-Pablo Echague, *Paris-Journal*, May 12, 1911.

41. Moreno, *Une française en Argentine*, 92–94.

42. Rivera, *Le Tango*, 12.

43. De Néronde, *Les Danses norvelles*, 35.

44. Jorge Luis Borges, *Evaristo Carriego: A Book About Old-Time Buenos Aires*, Norman di Giovanni and Susan Ashe, trans., (New York: Dutton, 1984), 145-35. Juan Pablo Echague as cited in Carlos Vega, *Danzas y canciones Argentinas* (Buenos Aires, 1936).

45. M. Lintilhac, "Noblesse morale des exercises physiques," Discours prononcé à la distribution des prix du Lycée Michelet (Aug. 5, 1890), 15. See also Eugen Weber, "Faster, Higher, Stronger," in *France: Fin de siècle* (Cambridge, Mass.: Belknap/Harvard Univ. Press, 1986), 213–33.

46. Rivera, *Le Tango*, 13–15; Debrenne cited in de Neronde, *Le Danses nouvelles*, 19–20.

47. Borges, *Evaristo Carriego*, 134–5.

48. Jean Richepin, "A propos du tango," *Seance publique annuelle des cinq académies*, (Paris: Firmin-Didot, Oct. 25, 1913). See also Gladys Beattie Crozier, *The Tango and How to Dance It* (London: Andrew Melrose, 1913), 9–10, for her report that M. Richepin's lecture at the Académie "created quite a stir."

49. Richepin, "A propos du tango," 81.

50. Ibid., 83.
51. Ibid., 86, and all citations to end.

Afterword: Memories

1. Ernest Renan, *Qu'est-ce qu'une nation?* (1885; Paris: Presses Pocket, 1992), 54. See also a translation and annotated version by Martin Thom in Homi K. Bhaba, ed., *Nation and Narration* (New York and London: Routledge, 1990), 8–22.
2. Renan, *Qu'est-ce qu'une nation?*, 41.
3. Ernest Renan, "Préface de l'avenir de la science" (1890), in ibid., 62.

Index

Accelerated memory: and drawing together of past and present, 15; and evolution, 9; and film, 166, 167, 180; and identity, 138; and language/brain, 81, 90, 98; Marx's views about, 11; and movement, 13; and stock exchange, 54–56, 59; and tango, 196, 197; and "universal acceleration," 9
Aghulon, Maurice, 33
Aide-mémoire, 65
Alsace-Lorraine, 8
Alvarez, Juan, 187
Amnesia, 97–98, 129–30
André, Emile, 53–54, 58, 59
André, Paul, 127
Anglemont, Edouard d', 29
Anthropology, 9, 146–48. *See also* Broca, Paul
Aphasia: and amnesia, 97–98; definition of, 81; and the Jules G. case, 85; and the Madame H. case, 79, 80; Marie's work on, 93–94; and philosophers, 95–98; and politics, 93; as rupture in connections, 81, 85, 86; and the

"Tan" case, 81, 83, 98–99; vocabulary about, 97. *See also* Brain; Language
Argentina: tango of, 186, 187–88, 191–92, 194–97, 203
Aristotle, 80
L'Arosseur arossé (film), 182
Ars memoria systems, 62
The Art of Memory (Yates), 4–5
Art, works of, 24–25, 33–34
Assier, Alexandre, 50, 58, 59
Atai (New Caledonia chief), 156, 162
"Atavique" criminals, 10, 145, 147, 152
Augé, Marc, 13, 16
Austerlitz, battle of, 21, 29, 37, 45, 202
Avenel, Georges d', 52, 54
L'Avenir de la science (Renan), 207

Badinter, Robert, 146
Bamboo stick, 13, 143, 159
Barbey d'Aurevilly, Jules Amédée, 21, 37, 38
Bataille, Frédéric, 69
Baudelaire, Charles, 11

Ben-Mill, M., 155, 158

Benjamin, Walter, 12, 52, 166

Bérard, Alexandre, 128

Bergson, Henri: on film, 165–66, 167, 172, 179; on historical practice, 102; on language, 95–98; and memory as action, 8, 9, 14, 95–98, 206; mentioned, 71; on mind-body relationships, 80; and mnemonics, 74

Bernard, Felix, 65–68, 73

Bertheau, Charles, 154

Bertillon, Alphonse, 88, 135–39, 140, 147

Bertrand, M., 32

Big business, 48–49

Binet, Alfred, 71

Blanqui, Auguste, 36

Body/physical culture: Bergson's views about, 95–98; as evidence in crimes, 116–17; as image, 95–98; and location of memory, 9; and mnemonics, 65, 71–72; and rejuvenation of France, 8; and tango, 199, 200, 201, 202–3

Bordier, A., 147–48, 154

Borges, Jorge Luis, 16, 200

Born criminals, 12, 136, 145

Bossaut, Louis, 151

Bouchaud, J. B., 84

Bourdieu, Pierre, 172

Bourgeoisie, 32, 35, 38, 42–43, 75

Bourse: and "acceleration of history," 54–56, 59; "amnesia" of, 43–45; and big business, 48–49; and capitalists-Communards polemics, 43–45; and commercialism, 51–52; as commodities exchange, 43; cosmopolitanism of, 54; as engine of modernity, 45; as heart of modern Paris, 42; impact of, 54–56, 58–59; and international markets, 44, 58–59; military analogy about, 59; and morality of money, 49–50; and nostalgia, 43–45, 46–48, 50–52, 59; Paris as image of, 51; and patrimony, 46–48, 50, 55; and politics, 56–58; power of, 42–43; and print culture, 54–56; and reimagined space, 53–

54; rites and rituals of, 52–54; and rural areas, 45–46; and stock quotations as predictions of future, 56–58; as temple of atavistic savagery, 52–53; as temple of time, 52–53, 59; and types of investments, 50–51; and volatility of information, 56–58; as weapon of capitalism, 42

Brain: and acceleration of memory, 81, 90, 98; autopsy of, 12, 80, 81–82, 97–98; as center of language, 80, 81–83, 90; and evolution, 81, 90, 93; faculties of, 81–82, 92, 98, 122; and judgment, 92–93, 98; mapping of, 83, 84, 98; and recapitulation, 90–91; ruptures in, 81, 85, 86, 97, 166; scientific reconceptualization of, 95; as switching power, 85; of Vacher, 141; as virtual organ, 84. *See also* Aphasia; Language

Brandat, Paul, 31, 33, 35

Braudel, Fernand, 4

Briand, Charles, 87

Broca, Paul: Bertillon's use of techniques developed by, 135; brain/language studies of, 12, 80, 81–84, 85, 90, 91, 93, 94, 95, 97, 98–99; mentioned, 147; and racial inferiority/superiority, 135, 157

Brotherhood, 44

Brouardel, P., 114, 116–17

Bruno, Giordano, 61, 62

Bruyant, Edmond, 144, 150, 155, 156

Buenos Aires. *See* Argentina: tango of

Le Bulletin du jour (newspaper), 25–26

Calendrier de mémoire, 65

Calinescu, Matei, 11

Canaques. *See* New Caledonia: natives of

Capitalism/capitalists, 11, 42, 43–45, 52, 54

Carnot, Lazare, 22

Catholicism, 45–46, 189

Cayotte affair, 101–3, 104, 106–7, 117

Charcot, Jean-Martin, 80, 103, 113, 114, 116, 129
Children, 107–8, 110–12, 116–18, 155–56, 179. *See also* Cayotte affair
Chirac, Auguste, 44
Cicero, 14
Cinema. *See* Film
Du Cinematographe dans ses rapports avec le droit de l'auteur (Marchais), 176, 177–78, 179
Le Cinematographe devant le droit (Maugras and Guegan), 176, 178, 179, 181
The Civil War in France (Marx), 43–44
Civilization: advancement of, 158–61; definition of, 158; and evolution, 12, 161; goal of, 158; on New Caledonia, 157–62; and race, 157–61; and savages, 152; and transportation policy, 161–63; trophies of, 162
Claparède, Edouard, 109–10
Class issues: and education, 75; and film, 179, 182–83; and mnemonics, 75, 76; and tango, 186, 202, 203; and transportation policy, 157
Classical education, 75
Classical world: and French Revolution, 76; memory in, 13–14; and mnemonics, 64–65, 70–71, 73–75; and moral education, 70–71; and rejuvenation of France, 8; and statue of Napoleon, 30; and tango, 201–2, 203
Clergy, 101, 107
Collective memory, 12
Comat, Alfred, 48
Commemoration, 7, 14, 21–22, 24, 38–39, 62
Commercialism, 37–38, 51–52, 191
Commodities, 43
Communards: beliefs of, 36–38; and capitalism, 43–45; deportation of, 149–50, 157; execution of, 38; internationalism of, 24, 34; and negation of history, 34–35; and new world order, 35–38; and patrimony, 33–34, 35. *See also* Paris Commune; *specific person*

La Commune (newspaper), 61–62, 76–77
Community, sense of, 125–26
Condette, 49, 53
Condorcet, Antonie Nicolas Caritat, Marquis de, 76
La Constitution (newspaper), 26
Contre le cinema (Poulain), 179
Convicts. *See* Criminals; New Caledonia; Transportation policy
Cordier, Henri, 196, 197
Cosmopolitanism, 54. *See also* Internationalism
Cosse, Victor, 157
Courbet, Gustave, 23–25, 26, 33, 37, 38
Courmelles, Foveau de, 140
Courbevoie, France: statue of Napoleon at, 27
Cozic, H., 43, 44–45, 48
Crastre, François, 195, 196, 198
Le Cri du peuple (newspaper), 25, 28
Criminal investigations, 13, 132, 135–40, 144–45. *See also* Vacher (Joseph) case
Criminals: "atavique," 10, 145, 147, 152; "born," 12, 136, 145; and film, 179; and heredity versus environment, 145–46, 147–48; identity of, 132, 135–40, 144–45; instinct of, 151; and recidivism, 150; redemption of, 146, 150, 151, 153, 160; as savages, 10, 145, 148; study of skulls of, 147–48; and vagabondage, 121–24, 126; views about transportation policy by, 150–51; women as, 154–55

Daily events: film of, 171–73
Les Danses nouvelles (Néronde), 191–92, 194, 201
Darwin, Charles, 93
De Inventione (Cicero), 14
Debrenne, M., 200
Delamarche, A. P., 65–66, 68–71, 77
Delapierre, A., 65–66, 68–71, 74, 77
Democratization: of print culture, 55–56
Desert, Gabriel, 45

Deville, Abbé, 49–50
Diderot, Denis, 65, 94
Dignes de foi, 105–6, 118
Doctors: as experts, 117, 119, 141
Documentary papers, 132–34. *See also*
    Passports
Documentum, 62, 65–66
Doumic, Rénée, 180
Dramatic skills. *See* Rhetoric/speech
Dreyfus affair, 87–88, 170
Les Droits de l'homme (newspaper),
    139
Ducor, Dr., 117, 119
Dugers, P., 65–68, 73
Dumont, Arsene, 127
Dumont d'Urville, 131, 133
Dumont (artist), 24
Dupoy, Dr., 47
Dupré, Ernest, 103, 104, 105, 106,
    108, 109, 110, 111, 112–14, 115,
    117
Duval, Mathias, 84
Duverger, M., 105

Echague, Juan-Pablo, 195, 198, 200
Ecole d'Anthropologie, 90, 94–95,
    135, 147, 157
Economic issues, 5, 37–38, 134, 198.
    See also Bourse; Capitalism
Edison, Thomas, 166
Education, 10, 13, 55, 64–65, 75,
    91–92, 126, 127. *See also* Moral
    education
18th Brumaire (Marx), 25, 41, 53
Encyclopédie (Diderot), 65
Environment, 130–31, 144–46, 147–
    48
"Ethics of responsibility," 65
Etymology, 73–74, 131, 172, 186
"Evaristo Carriego" (Borges), 200
Evolution: and brain, 81, 90, 93;
    and capitalism, 11, 52; and
    civilization, 13, 160; and language,
    90–91; and memory, 8–9, 10–11;
    and tango, 10, 199; and
    transportation policy, 148, 160. *See
    also* Recapitulation
Exercises de mémoire (Delapierre and
    Delamarche), 65–66, 68–71, 74, 77
Experts, 108, 117–19, 141

Faculties, of brain, 81–82, 92, 97,
    122
Family: pictures of, 172, 182–83; and
    transportation policy, 151–55, 156–
    57, 160–62; and vagabondage,
    125–26
Farcet, Pierre, 106
Fauré, Felix, 44
Fauvelle, Dr., 84, 90, 92, 94
Feminism, 15, 112
Ferry, Jules, 10, 12, 55, 64, 126
Ferry laws. *See* Education
Festrine, Henri, 27
Fiche anthropometriques, 137, 138,
    139–40, 147
Fiche signaletique, 135–39
Film: as accelerated memory, 166,
    167, 180; and "auteur," 177–79;
    and children, 179; and class issues,
    179, 182–83; as creator of
    reproductions, 178–79; and crime,
    179; of daily events, 171–73;
    development of, 167–70; as
    falsification of historical record,
    170–71; of family, 172, 182–83; as
    fantastic, 166, 169, 170, 174, 183;
    fictional–documentary, 170; first
    posters about, 181–83; first public
    cinema for, 169; as gravure, 176,
    179; and identity, 12; as illusion,
    167, 169, 170, 174; immediacy of,
    171, 173–74, 179–80; as invasive,
    173–74; and language, 174–79; and
    legal issues, 176–79; mass appeal of,
    179–81; and moral issues, 167, 179,
    180–81; movement in, 167, 171–
    73, 174, 175, 177, 178, 179–80,
    181, 183; and newspapers, 171; and
    oral tradition, 173; as producer of
    originals, 178–79; and reality, 166–
    67, 168, 170, 174; and Roubaiz
    incident, 170; as science, 169, 170;
    and tango, 191; theatre versus, 175–
    76, 179, 181; and vision, 176–77,
    179; and *vues cinematographiques*,
    169–70; as witness, 168, 175, 176–
    79
Financial markets, 50. *See also* Bourse;
    Stock exchange
Fléouter, Claude, 191

Fludd, Robert, 62
la Foi du serment, 105
Footprints, 139
Foreign investments, 58–59
Foreigners, 134, 192, 194
Fourquet, Emile: on centralization of
  criminal files, 132; and vagabonds,
  121, 124–25, 126–27, 128, 132,
  135, 140, 141; and witnesses, 103,
  104, 110, 111, 114
France: cultural superiority of, 195–
  97; degeneration of, 5, 7–8, 30,
  200; German influence on culture
  of, 5; Germany as threat to, 5; and
  ideal of French society, 151;
  patrimony of, 49; resurrection of,
  29; rural areas as part of glory of,
  48. *See also* Paris, France
Franco-Prussian War, 5, 7, 20
Free will, 74, 97, 130
French Revolution, 21, 33, 39, 76,
  94
Freud, Sigmund, 12, 71, 80, 103–4
Fribourg, André, 108, 109

Gachon, P., 76
Gagnebe, Georges, 105–6
Gall, Franz Joseph, 82–83
Gardel, Carlos, 188–89, 191
Garnier, Jules, 149, 158, 160
Garnier, Paul, 85, 97
Gauchos, 187, 188, 191, 203
Gautier, Th., 69
Gender issues, 14, 104, 110–18, 170,
  199–200
Generational issues, 189, 198–99
Genetics. *See* Evolution; Heredity
Georges-Michel, Michel, 165–66,
  189–90, 192, 194
Germany, 5, 8, 24, 25, 68. *See also*
  Franco-Prussian War
Gorky, Maksim, 175, 181
Goujon, Alexandre, 30
Gould, Stephen Jay, 8–9
Grasserie, Raoul de la, 46
Gravure: film as, 176, 179
Great individuals, 68, 69–70
Guegan, M., 176, 178, 179, 181
Guiraldes, Ricardo, 189, 199–200
Guyana, 144, 155

Les Halles (Paris), 42
Hamy, Ernest, 143
Haussmann, Georges Eugène, 12, 50,
  183, 196
Haussonville, Baron d', 146
Health/hygiene, 71–72, 75
Hegel, George Wilhelm Friedrich, 11
Heredity, 130–31, 144–46, 147–48.
  See also Evolution
L'Histoire du consulas et de l'empire
  (Thiers), 61–62, 76–77
Histoire et mémoire (Le Goff), 7
Historie de la commune (Lissagaray),
  26
History: categories of, 4, 11; end of,
  37–38; as endlessly recomposed, 10;
  erasing/negation of, 34–35, 144–
  45, 146, 153; as everchanging
  present, 12; of memory, 4–5;
  memory as general, 3–4, 7, 10; and
  memory as history of the present,
  15–16; retelling of, 14–15; selection
  of moments of, 7, 10. *See also*
  Accelerated memory; Memory;
  specific person for views
History (discipline), 65, 66–68, 72
Hobsbawm, Eric, 195
Hugo, Victor, 21
Huysmans, Joris Karl, 15, 121
Huyssen, Andreas, 166

Icard, Severin, 138
L'Identité de la France (Braudel), 4
Identity: and centralization/
  standardization of records, 133,
  135–39; and criminal investigations,
  13, 132, 135–40, 144–45; and
  documentary papers, 132–34; and
  economic issues, 134; and experts,
  141; and *fiche anthropometriques,*
  137, 138, 139–40, 147; and *fiche
  signaletique,* 135–39; and film, 12;
  of foreigners, 134; and gender
  issues, 15; of Jews, 12; and
  memory, 14; and memory of the
  state, 121–24, 140–41, 144; and
  mnemonics, 68–71, 139; national
  versus local, 126–28; and race/
  ethnicity, 15; and tango, 191, 201,
  202–3; and technology, 125, 132,

Identity (*continued*)
    138–40, 141; and trace studies,
    141. *See also* Vagabondage
L'Illustration (journal), 50–51, 185
Immigration, 134, 187, 188, 197
L'Importance logique du temoinage
    (Naville), 104–5
Industrial/commercial ventures:
    investments in, 50–51
Information, 54–58. *See also* Criminal
    investigations
Instincts, 8–9, 151
Intermarriage, 155–57, 160–61
International markets, 44, 58–59
Internationalism, 24, 34
L'Intransigeant (newspaper), 179
Inventions, 66–68. *See also*
    Technology
Investments, 50–51, 58–59. *See also*
    Bourse

James-Natan, M., 151, 155
Janet, Pierre, 71, 129–30
Joffroy, Dr., 47
Le Journal Officiel de la Commune,
    34, 36, 37
Judgments: and brain, 92–93, 98; of
    experts, 119; and memory, 14; and
    mnemonics, 65, 69–70, 72, 73, 76;
    and "modern" memory, 206, 207;
    and speech/rhetoric, 14; and
    writing, 87–88
Jules-Marey, Etienne, 166

Kundera, Milan, 14

La Fontaine, Jean de, 69
La Rochefoucauld, François, 14
Lacassagne, Alexandre: and
    transportation policy, 145; and
    vagabondage, 121, 131, 132, 135,
    139, 140, 141; on witnesses, 118
Laennec, Dr., 114–16
Lagresille, Alfred: on civilization, 160;
    and transportation policy, 145, 150,
    151, 153; and vagabondage, 125,
    126, 128
Lambert, Pére, 143, 157, 159
Language: and accelerated memory,
    81, 90, 98; brain as center of, 80,

81–83, 90; definition of, 90; and
    education, 91–92; and evolution,
    90–91; and film, 174–79; and
    localization theories, 81–86, 91, 97;
    memory as essential to, 63, 80, 83;
    memory of, 9; of modern memory,
    7; and moral issues, 92, 97; as
    movement, 80–81, 83–98; and
    nervous system, 80, 91–92, 95, 98,
    99; and philosophy, 95–98; as
    system of signs, 63; and technology,
    88–89; and vagabondage, 131. *See
    also* Aphasia; Mnemonics; Words;
    Writing
Lannois, Dr., 141
Le Lanterne (newspaper), 107
Lastra, Felipe Amadero, 195
Le Goff, Jacques, 7, 12, 13, 14
Le Play, Frédéric, 45–46
Le Roy, P., 127–28, 133, 134
Lefebvre, Henri, 35
Lefort, M. J., 86
Legal issues: and film, 176–79; and
    tango, 192; and transportation
    policy, 153–54; and vagabonds,
    124–25; and writing, 86–88. *See
    also* Testimonies; Witnesses
Legrand, M. A., 148, 155, 161
Legroux, Dr., 85
Leroi-Gouhran, André, 13
Léveque, Eugene, 28–29, 34
Levillier, Roberto, 189
Lieu method, 62–63
Les Lieux de mémoire (Nora), 5–6, 7,
    13
Lissagaray, Prosper, 26, 27, 38
Littré, Emile, 73
Localization theories, 81–86, 91, 97
Lombroso, Cesare, 12, 136, 141, 145
Louis XIV, 27, 39
Louis XVI, 27
Louis-Napoleon, 5, 22–23, 27, 41
Lumière, Auguste and Louis, 165–66,
    167, 169, 174, 181–82

Mabille du Chêne, G., 126, 128
Machines. *See* Technology
Madame H. (case study), 79, 80
*Maladies de la Mémoire/Maladies de
    la volonté* (Ribot), 74

Manchez, Georges, 44

Manouvrier, L., 145

Manteaux, Edouard, 65–66, 71–73, 74

Marchais, Jean, 176, 177–78, 179

Marchand affair, 107, 118

Marie, Pierre, 93–94

Maroteau, Gustave, 25

Marriage: and race issues, 155–57. *See also* Intermarriage

Marx, Karl, 11, 25, 36, 41–42, 43–44, 52, 53, 103

Matière et mémoire (Bergson), 8, 95

Le Matin (newspaper), 136

Matuszweski, Boleslas, 167–69, 171, 175

Maugras, E., 176, 178, 179, 181

Maupassant, Guy de, 132

Maurras, Charles, 8

Maxwell, J., 102–3

Mayer, Simon, 157

Medical-legal Report on a Judicial Inquiry Motivated by a False Accusation of Rape (Laennec), 114–16

Méliès, Georges, 166, 167, 169–70, 180, 183

Mémoire en expansion, 13

Mémoire et evolution (Pieron), 88–89

La Mémoire littéraire (Robichon), 65–66, 73–75

Memorization, 63, 102–3

Memory: accuracy of, 168; collective, 12; definition of, 8, 9, 12, 13; erasing/negation of, 144–45, 146, 153; evidence of, 6–7; externalization of, 56; as general history, 3–4, 7, 10; as generic or specialized term, 6; as history of the present, 15–16; location of, 9; and mémoire en expansion, 12; multiple understandings of, 206; as organism, 7, 8–9; periods of, 4–5, 11; as presence, 9–10; revolution as struggle over, 36–38; of species, 9; as taxonomy/categorization, 109–10; words as part of, 7. *See also* History; *type of memory*

Memory of the state: and identity, 121–24, 140–41; and transportation policy, 146, 151, 153, 159

Memory training, 63–65, 72. *See also* Mnemonics

Métais, Eliane, 159

Meunier, Marie and Raymond, 124, 128–29, 130–31, 141

Michaux, M., 152

Michel, Louise, 148, 157, 159, 160

Michelet, Jules, 4

Military: and Bourse analogy, 59; and statue of Napoleon, 23–24, 25, 38; and vagabondage, 126, 127

Mills, Charles, 86

Miral, M. de, 146, 151, 153

Mnemonics: aides for learning, 65–77; and class issues, 75, 76; and classical world, 64–65, 70–71, 73–75; Delapierre and Delamarche's studies about, 65–66, 68–71, 74, 77; development of, 4–5; and documentum, 62, 65–66; Dugers and Bernard's studies about, 65–68, 73; and education/moral education, 64–65, 68–71, 74–76; and free will, 74; and health/hygiene, 71–72, 75; and history (discipline), 66–68, 72; and identity, 139; and "judgments," 65, 69–70, 72, 73, 76; and the *lieu* method, 62–63; Manteaux's studies about, 65–66, 71–73, 74; and memory training aids, 63–65; Paris's system of, 62–63; and patriotism, 69, 75–76; and physiology of memory, 65, 71–72; and print culture, 55; and reading, 70; and republicanism, 64, 65, 76; and rhetoric/speech, 70–71, 74, 75, 76; Robichon's studies about, 65–66, 73–75; teacher's role in teaching, 69; and words, 73–75, 76–77; and writing, 75

Mnémonie classique (Dugers and Bernard), 65–68, 73

La Mnémotechnie appliquée aux sciences elementaires (Manteaux), 65–66, 71–73, 74

Modern memory: and capitalism, 11; characteristics of, 5, 7–8, 10, 43; elements of, 12; and evolution, 10–

Modern memory (*continued*)
11; as general history, 3–4;
language of, 7; material of, 5–7;
and movement, 13; prehistoric/
primitive aspects of, 11–12; and
technology, 12–13; and
vagabondage, 126. *See also*
Accelerated memory
Moncelon, Leon, 148–49, 156, 160
Le Monde illustré (newspaper), 172
Money, 49–50, 59
Montorgueil, Georges, 51
Moral education, 68–71, 74–76
Moral issues: and film, 167, 179,
180–81; and intermarriage, 155;
and language, 92, 98; and memory,
14; and money, 49–50; and statue
of Napoleon, 30; and tango, 203;
and testimonies, 106, 112; and
transportation policy, 152, 153,
155; and vagabondage, 126, 128;
and women, 153. *See also* Sex
crimes
Moreno, Marguerite, 198
Le Mot d'ordre (newspaper), 61–62,
76–77
Motet, A., 138
Mourey, Gabriel, 42, 52–53
Moutier, François, 93
Movement: in film, 167, 171–73,
174, 175, 177, 178, 179–80, 181,
183; language as, 80–81, 83–98;
and memory as action, 8, 9, 13,
95–98, 206; and tango, 190, 196,
201; and writing, 88–89
Muybridge, Edward, 166

Napoleon, statue of: and classical
world, 30; as commemoration, 21–
22, 24; and commercialism, 37–38;
at Courbevoie, 27; debate about,
30–33; and decline of France, 30;
defenders of, 28–30; design of, 21–
22; destruction of, 19–20, 23, 25–
28, 30–33, 35–36; and end of
history, 37–38; and military, 23–24,
25, 38; and moral issues, 30; and
new world order, 35–38; and
patrimony, 33–34; and patriotism,
30; poetry about, 22, 28–29, 30;

press views about, 25–28; as
property, 31–33; reinstallation/
rebuilding of, 22–23, 38; as
representative of nation, 31–33; and
resurrection of nation, 29; and
savagery, 31; souvenirs of, 20, 37–
38; as symbol, 20–21, 22–23, 27–
28, 30–33; testimony about, 38–39;
and unfolding of history, 29–30; as
work of art, 24–25, 33
Napoleon III, 5, 22–23, 27, 41
Nation: definition of, 205–6;
resurrection of, 29; statue of
Napoleon as representative of, 31–
33
La Nationale (newspaper), 149–50
"Natural men," 149
Naville, Ernest, 104–5
Néronde, C. de, 191–92, 194, 201
Nervous system, 9, 80, 91–92, 95,
97, 98
New Caledonia: civilization on, 157–
62; description of, 144; Hamy's
collection from, 143; insurrection of
natives in, 156–57, 160, 162;
natives of, 149, 155–62; as
paradise, 148–49; as prison
experiment, 144, 146, 148–49;
trophies from, 162. *See also*
Transportation policy
New world order, 35–36
Newspapers, 55–56, 171. *See also*
Press; *specific newspaper*
Niceforo, Alfred, 106, 139
Nietzsche, Friedrich Wilhelm, 11, 46
Nora, Pierre, 5–6, 7, 14, 54
Nordau, Max, 15, 121
Nostalgia: and Bourse, 43–45, 46–48,
50–52, 59; and capitalists-
Communards polemics, 43–45;
and commercialism, 51–52;
definition/characteristics of, 46;
and information, 55; and money,
59; and Paris city plan, 50–51;
and patrimony, 46–48; about
rural areas, 46, 127; and tango,
186, 188, 191, 199, 200, 203;
and transportation policy, 144–
45, 151, 153; and vagabondage,
127

De la Nostalgie (Grasserie), 46
Nozière, Fernand, 180
Nye, Robert, 8

Observations et autopsie d'une aphsique (Rousseau), 79, 80
On the Causes of Error in Expertise Relative to Indecent Assault (Brouardel), 116–18
"Open Letter to the German Army" (Courbet), 24, 25
Les Operations de bourse devant la conscience (Deville), 49–50
Oral traditions, 12, 55–56, 143, 159, 161–62, 173, 192
Oregas, P., 155
Origines de la musica argentina (Alvarez), 187
Ozouf, Mona, 10

Page, L., 48–49
Pagnier, (psychologist), 131
Paris, Aimé, 62–63, 66, 68, 73
Paris Commune, 7, 20, 24, 38. *See also* Communards; Napoleon, statue of
Paris, France: boulevards of, 50–51, 183; as image of Bourse, 51; nostalgia for "old," 50–51; physical setting of, 11, 50–51, 183, 196–97. *See also specific structure or section of Paris*
Passports, 133–34, 136
Passy, Frédéric, 31–32, 33, 34–35
Pathe Journal (film), 171
Patrimony: and Bourse, 46–48, 50, 55; and Communards, 33–34, 35; and statue of Napoleon, 33–34; and transportation policy, 144–45, 152, 153, 156–57; as vocabulary of memory, 7; and writing, 87
Patriotism: and mnemonics, 69, 75–76; revival of, 8; and statue of Napoleon, 30; and tango, 186, 200–201, 202–3; and transportation policy, 157
Pau case, 177–79
Paulus, E., 103, 110
Pedagogy. *See* Education
Péguy, Charles Pierre, 15

Le Père Duchêne (newspaper), 28, 37, 39
Perier, Casimer, 22, 33
Le Petit Journal (newspaper), 56
Le Petit Parisien (newspaper), 56
Petit patrons, 48–49
La Petite Républicaine (newspaper), 107
Peyeron, 156
Philosophy, 95–97
Philosophy of Money (Simmel), 43
Photography, 12, 26, 27, 139–40. *See also* Film
Phrenology, 82–83
Phylogenetics. *See* Evolution; Recapitulation
Physical evidence: in testimonies, 116–18
Pictures, 131, 178. *See also* Film; Photography
Pieron, Henri, 81, 88–90, 91–92
Pierret, G., 145, 150
Pitres, A., 80–81, 84–85, 96
Pius X (pope), 189
Place, Amoroux and Henri, 157, 160, 162
Place Vendôme, 38–39. *See also* Napoleon, statue of
Plauchut, Edmond, 156
Ploix, Charles, 152, 158
Ploque, M., 59
Pomian, Krzysztof, 61–62
Le Poste (newspaper), 172, 173
Poulain, Edouard, 179
Press: and Cayotte affair, 101–3; and destruction of statue of Napoleon, 25–28; and Dreyfus Affair, 87; rise of popular, 12. *See also* Newspapers; *specific newspaper*
Primitives. *See* Savages
Print culture, 12, 55–56. *See also* Newspapers
Printing press, 88–89, 98
Prisons, 146. *See also* New Caledonia; Transportation policy
Le Progrés (newspaper), 174
Property: Communards destruction of, 31–34, 35; investments in, 50–51; and patrimony, 47; and transportation policy, 151–52, 153–54, 156–57

Prostitution, 187
Prudence, 14
Public opinion: emergence of
    quantification of, 57–58
Public works: investments in, 50–51
Pyat, Félix, 36, 44

Quatrefages, Armand de Bréau, 157

Race: and civilization, 157–60;
    definition of, 157; and identity, 14;
    inferiority/superiority of, 135; and
    marriage, 155–57, 161–62; and
    tango, 197–99; and transportation
    policy, 157–61
Le Radical (newspaper), 107, 167,
    172
Railway projects, 49
Rallovich, (financial writer), 58
Rape, 112–16, 118. *See also* Sex
    crimes
Reading: and mnemonics, 70
Reality: and film, 166–67, 168, 170,
    174
Recapitulation, 9, 53, 90–91, 131,
    146, 152
Recuerdos del 900 (Lastra), 195
Redemption: of criminals, 146, 150,
    151, 153, 159
La Reforme sociale (journal), 45–46,
    47–48
Regis, Emmanuelle, 130
Reimagined space, 53–54
Religion, 45–46, 91, 105–7, 154,
    189. *See also* Clergy
Renan, Ernest, 16, 158, 205–6, 207
Republicanism, 64, 65, 76, 101, 106,
    107, 146
Le Republique Française (newspaper),
    106, 138–39
Reputations, 56
Reské, Jean, 189
Responsibility, 14, 65
La Resurrection de la colonne
    (d'Anglemont), 29
Le Reveil du people (newspaper), 26
Revolution/revolutionaries:
    bourgeoisie as, 42–43; goals of
    French, 41–42; Marx's views about,
    41–42, 43–44; as struggle over

memory, 36–38. *See also* French
    Revolution
Revon, Lucien, 54, 56
La Revue de deux mondes
    (newspaper), 156
*Revue mensuelle de mnémotechnie
    ancienne et moderne et de l'art
    d'apprendre*, 65
Rhetoric/speech, 14, 44, 70–71, 74,
    75, 76
Ribot, Théodule, 74, 97
Ribot (Théodule) Commission, 75
Richepin, Jean, 130, 201–3
Ricoeur, Paul, 103
Rivera, Max, 197, 198, 199, 200
Rivière, Henri, 152, 160–61, 162
Robichon, Alfred, 65–66, 73–75
Rochas, Victor de, 158
Roncière, Emile de la, 113–14
Rosen, J., 171
Roubaix incident, 170
Rousseau, Dr., 79, 80
Rousseau, Jean-Jacques, 61, 69, 130,
    149
Rural areas: and Bourse, 45–46, 47–
    48; depopulation of, 48, 55, 124,
    127; nostalgia about, 46, 47–48,
    127; and oral versus print culture,
    55; as part of glory of France, 48;
    and patrimony, 47–48, 55; and
    transportation policy, 144–45, 146,
    151–52; and vagabondage, 127

Sacrey, Yvonne, 197–98
Sager, Xavier, 190–91
Salavencia, José Maria, 197, 198
Le Salut public (newspaper), 25
Santner, Eric, 10
Sarcey, Yvonne, 195
Sardou, Victorien, 50–51
Saussure, Ferdinand de, 63
Savages: and civilization, 12, 152; and
    collective memory, 12; criminals as,
    9, 145, 148; New Caledonia natives
    as, 160; and the savage within, 12;
    and statue of Napoleon, 31;
    vagabonds as noble, 130, 131–32
Science: and civilization, 160; film as,
    169, 170; of memory, 91–95; and
    religion, 91; of testimony, 103,

104–5, 108–9, 110, 118; and
transportation policy, 146–48
Seduction: Freud's theory of, 103–4;
of tango, 200
Sée, Adrien, 128, 133, 134
Sex: and tango, 200
Sex crimes: and clergy, 107; physical
evidence in, 116–18; polemics of,
107; testimonies about, 101–3,
104, 112–18; and victimization,
112
Simmel, Georg, 43, 54
Simon, Jules, 20–21
Société d'Anthropologie, 81, 84, 90,
93, 97, 98, 152, 158
Le Sourire (newspaper), 201
Space, 53–54
Species memory, 9
Speech. *See* Rhetoric/speech
State: memory of the. *See* Memory of
the state
Statue of Napoleon. *See* Napoleon,
statue of
Stenography, 62–63
Stock exchange, 43. *See also* Bourse
Stock quotations, 56–58
Structuralism, French, 63
Surbled, Georges, 83, 89
Le Syllabaire mnémonique (Robichon),
65–66, 73–76

Taine, Hippolyte, 7, 16
"Tan" (case study), 81, 83, 97–98
Tango: and accelerated memory, 196,
197; of Argentina, 186, 187–88,
191–92, 194–97, 203; Argentinians
as teachers of, 192, 194; Catholics
forbidden the, 189; as civilization
issue, 191–92, 194–97; and class
issues, 186, 202, 203; and classical
world, 201–2, 203; and
commercialism, 191; as dance of
love and death, 189, 200; and
economic issues, 198; etymology of,
186; and evolution, 10, 199; and
film, 191; of France, 186, 188–89,
191–92, 194–97, 201–3; and
gauchos, 187, 188, 191, 203; and
generational issues, 189, 198–99;
and identity, 191, 201, 202–3; and

immigrants, 187, 188, 197;
instruments for playing the, 186;
lecture about, 185; and legal issues,
192; as male-dominated, 199–200;
and moral issues, 203; and
movement, 190, 196, 201; and
nostalgia, 186, 188, 191, 199, 200,
203; and oral tradition, 192; and
patriotism, 186, 200–201, 202–3;
and physical culture/body, 199,
200, 201, 202–3; poetry about,
189, 199–200; popularity of, 185–
86; "primitive" nature of, 197–99;
and race, 197–99; as representative
of epoch, 189–91, 197; seduction
of, 200; sexual nature of, 200;
sources of music for, 186–88;
teaching of, 192, 194; and theatre,
192; and urbanization, 186, 187,
188, 191, 196–97
"Tango" (Guiraldes), 189
Tarde, Gabriel, 55, 56–58, 124, 139,
145
Tattoos, 12, 131
Technology: and criminal
investigations, 12, 132, 139–40;
and identity, 125, 132, 138–39,
141; and language, 88–89; and
modern memory, 12–13; and print
versus oral culture, 56. *See also* Film
Terdiman, Richard, 11, 43
Testimonies: of children, 107–8, 110–
12, 116–18; and *dignes de foi*, 105–
6, 118; and experts, 108, 117–19;
and gender issues, 104, 110–18,
170; historical writing as different
from, 104–5; and integrity, 102–3;
and memorization, 102–3; and
moral issues, 106, 112; oaths
concerning, 105–6, 110; and orders
of truth, 105; physical evidence in,
116–18; and religion, 105–7; and
republicanism, 101–3, 106, 107;
science of, 103, 104–5, 108–9,
110, 118; about sex crimes, 101–3,
104, 107, 112–18; about statue of
Napoleon, 38–39. *See also* Witnesses
Theatre: film versus, 175–76, 179,
181; and tango, 192
Théatre Robert Houdin, 169, 183

Thiers, Louis Adolphe, 20, 31, 32, 33–34, 61–62, 76–77
Third Republic, 5
Topinard, Paul, 94–95
Tourette, Gilles de la, 89
Trace studies, 139–40, 141
The Train's Arrival in the Station (film), 181
Trajan's column, 30
Transportation policy: characteristics of, 144–45; and children, 155–56; and civilization, 161–63; and class issues, 157; and Communards, 149–50, 157; criminals views about, 150–51; diversity of expectations about, 150–51; and erasing of memory, 144–45, 146, 153; and evolution, 148, 160; and family, 151–55, 156–57, 160–63; and intermarriage, 155–57, 161–62; and legal issues, 153–54; and memory of the state, 146, 151, 153, 160; and moral issues, 152, 153, 155; and nostalgia, 151, 153; and *patrie*, 157; and patrimony, 152, 153, 156–57; and property, 151–52, 153–54, 156–57; purpose of, 144–45; and race, 157–61; and recapitulation, 146; and redemption, 146, 150, 151, 153, 159; and religion, 154; and republicanism, 146; and rural areas, 146, 151–52; and science, 146–48; and women, 153, 154–55; and work, 151–52, 153, 156–57. *See also* New Caledonia
Truth, 105–6, 118. *See also* Testimonies
Tylor, E. B., 10

Une Française en Argentine (Moreno), 198
Universal Expositions, 36, 94, 143–44, 149, 158, 162
Urbanization, 186, 187, 188, 191, 196–97. *See also* Rural areas: depopulation of

Vacher (Joseph) case, 121, 123–24, 125, 126–27, 132, 135, 140–41

Vagabondage: as disease, 128–30; and documentary papers, 132–35; factors contributing to, 126–27, 128; and free will, 130; and heredity versus environment, 130–31; and language, 131; and legal issues, 124–25; and memory of the state, 121–24; and "migratory impulse," 130–31; and moral issues, 126, 128; New Caledonia natives compared with, 159; and nostalgia, 127; numbers on, 127–28; poetic aspects of, 124; and progress, 126–27; and recapitulation, 131; and rural areas, 124, 127; as social danger, 125–26, 128; and vagabonds as noble savages, 130, 131–32. *See also* Vacher (Joseph) case
Valdez, Pio, 198–99
Vallés, Jules, 25, 26–27, 28, 37
Vanini, Lucilio, 61
Vecna, Jean Perruche de, 46
La Ventre de Paris (Zola), 42
Victims, 103–4, 112, 118, 141
Violence, 31, 206
Vision, 168, 176–77, 179
Vocabulary, 70, 98. *See also* Words
Voltaire, François Marie Arouet de, 61, 94
Vucetich, J., 138
Vuillaume, Maxime, 20, 27–28, 44

Warnod, André, 192
Waterloo, battle of, 45
Weber, Eugen, 55
Weber, Max, 121
Wernicke, Carl, 80
Wilde, Oscar, 15
Witnesses: children as, 107–8, 110–11, 116–18; credibility of, 110–11, 118; experts compared with, 118–19; fantasizing of victimization by, 103–4; and film as witness, 168, 175, 176–79; and Freud's seduction theory, 103–4; and gender issues, 104, 110–18; intentions of, 106, 117; and "modern" memory, 206, 207; reliability of, 109–10, 114–16, 118;

sincerity of, 106, 110–11, 112–14; women as, 104, 110–18. *See also* Testimonies

Women: as criminals, 154–55; and moral issues, 153; testimonies of, 104, 110–18, 170; and transportation policy, 153, 154–55; as victims, 118

Words: etymology of, 73–74; and language, 83, 94; and mnemonics, 61–77; as part of memory, 7; and pictures, 178

Work: of New Caledonia natives, 159; and transportation policy, 151–52, 153, 156–57; and vagabondage, 125–26

Works of art, 24–25, 33–34

Writing, 75, 86–89, 98, 104–5

X-rays, 139–40

Yates, Frances, 4–5, 12, 14

Yerushalmi, Yosef, 15

Zola, Emile, 42, 87